SOVEREIGNTY, PROPERTY AND EMPIRE, 1500–2000

This book analyses the laws that shaped modern European empires from medieval times to the twentieth century. Its geographical scope is global, including the Americas, Europe, Africa, Asia, Australia and the Poles. Andrew Fitzmaurice focuses upon the use of the law of occupation to justify and critique the appropriation of territory. He examines both discussions of occupation by theologians, philosophers and jurists, as well as its application by colonial publicists and settlers themselves. Beginning with the medieval revival of Roman law, this study reveals the evolution of arguments concerning the right to occupy through the School of Salamanca, the foundation of American colonies, seventeenth-century natural law theories, Enlightenment philosophers, eighteenth-century American colonies and the new American republic, writings of nineteenth-century jurists, debates over the carve-up of Africa, twentieth-century discussions of the status of polar territories, and the period of decolonisation.

ANDREW FITZMAURICE is Professor of History at the University of Sydney.

IDEAS IN CONTEXT

The books in this series will discuss the emergence of intellectual traditions and of related new disciplines. The procedures, aims and vocabularies that were generated will be set in the context of the alternatives available within the contemporary frameworks of ideas and institutions. Through detailed studies of the evolution of such traditions, and their modification by different audiences, it is hoped that a new picture will form of the development of ideas in their concrete contexts. By this means, artificial distinctions between the history of philosophy, of the various sciences, of society and politics, and of literature may be seen to dissolve.

The series is published with the support of the Exxon Foundation.

A list of books in the series will be found at the end of the volume.

SOVEREIGNTY, PROPERTY AND EMPIRE, 1500–2000

ANDREW FITZMAURICE

CAMBRIDGE
UNIVERSITY PRESS

CAMBRIDGE
UNIVERSITY PRESS

University Printing House, Cambridge CB2 8BS, United Kingdom

Cambridge University Press is part of the University of Cambridge.

It furthers the University's mission by disseminating knowledge in the pursuit of education, learning and research at the highest international levels of excellence.

www.cambridge.org
Information on this title: www.cambridge.org/9781107076495

First published 2014

A catalogue record for this publication is available from the British Library

Library of Congress Cataloguing in Publication data
Fitzmaurice, Andrew, author.
Sovereignty, property and empire, 1500–2000 / Andrew Fitzmaurice.
pages cm. – (Ideas in context)
Includes bibliographical references and index.
1. International law–History. 2. Indigenous peoples–Legal status, laws, etc.–History.
3. Colonization–History. 4. Sovereignty–History. 5. Conquest, Right of–History. I. Title.
KZ1242.F58 2014
341.4′2–dc23 2014022411

ISBN 978-1-107-07649-5 Hardback

For Ismaïl and Yamin

Contents

Acknowledgements

I first conceived of this book in 1996. It has undergone many reconceptions since then. It has also been put to one side a number of times while other projects and responsibilities took priority. Researching and writing a book over so many years, I have incurred more debts than I can possibly recall and I apologise to those whom I neglect.

Importantly, the research for this book would not have been possible without the generous support of more than one grant from the Australian Research Council. I have also had invaluable support from my university and, in particular, from my wonderful colleagues in the vibrant Department of History at the University of Sydney, and from my students. Indeed, this book has little to say about the colonisation of Australia, but it is unquestionably a product of an Australian perspective on the intellectual history of empire. It is invidious to name particular colleagues, but I cannot ignore the faith that Shane White has maintained (or appeared to maintain!) in this project over many years, nor the countless emails sent by Dirk Moses, the methodological insights of Chris Hilliard and Glenda Sluga, and the boundless enthusiasm of Alison Bashford. Duncan Ivison helped to form the argument at a crucial time. Kit Morrell has not only been an excellent research assistant but also an insightful critic.

I have benefited greatly from conversations and correspondence with Bain Attwood, Kate Beattie, Duncan Bell, Lauren Benton, Alastair Blanshard, Richard Bourke, Annabel Brett, Barbara Caine, Michel Collet, Fred Cooper, Ann Curthoys, Moira Gatens, Ian Hunter, Sue James, Martti Koskenniemi, Sankar Muthu, Paul Patton, Dean Pavlakis, Jennifer Pitts, Henry Reynolds, Tim Rowse, Phil Stern, Jan Vandersmissen, Kathryn Welch and Phil Withington. Benjamin Straumann and Chris Tomlins made many helpful suggestions. Conal Condren discussed the project with me over many years. Quentin Skinner has always been a wonderful support – a source of encouragement, inspiration and subtle advice.

I am particularly grateful to the anonymous readers for Cambridge University Press. They provided challenging reports which enabled me to make significant improvements to the manuscript. They were generous with their time, making close readings of the text with numerous suggestions and references. I am also greatly indebted to the editors at the Press, and particularly Elizabeth Friend-Smith, for their grace and efficiency. My warmest thanks also to Jon Lloyd for his meticulous copy-editing and Maria denBoer for her extraordinary index.

My two greatest debts are to David Armitage and Saliha Belmessous. David has discussed this book with me ceaselessly since the outset sixteen years ago – a long conversation. I am deeply indebted to his encyclopaedic knowledge, acuity and sense of intellectual adventure. Saliha has graciously suffered this project since 1997. Her wit and criticism have sustained my research and led me to rethink numerous questions. She continued to believe in the importance of the project on the occasions when I had doubts. She read and provided detailed commentary upon various forms of the manuscript more times than I can count.

Elements of this manuscript have appeared in previous publications. For permission to revise previously published material, I am grateful to the editors of the *American Historical Review*, *Australian Historical Studies*, the University of North Carolina Press and Palgrave.

what is SOVEREIGNTY?
what is 'WESTERN'?

a bit like Ashcroft

CHAPTER I

Introduction

This book concerns one of the most common explanations in Western political thought for the origin of property and, for that matter, the beginning of political society. That explanation for property and sovereignty is the law of occupation: namely, the notion that something which belongs to nobody becomes the property of the first person to take it. This book examines the history of the ways in which the idea of occupation was used by theologians, philosophers, publicists, jurists and colonisers over the course of several hundred years from medieval law through to the Space Race. My focus will be upon instances in which these people used the idea of occupation to debate the justice of European overseas empires. I focus upon empire in part because arguments of occupation held a central role for Europeans in their understanding of what they were doing in establishing empires. Moreover, the concept of occupation was equally important, as I shall show, to a sustained critique of and opposition to empire from the sixteenth century to the twentieth century. Whether as a justification or critique of empire, the law of occupation was a common denominator in European understandings of property, sovereignty and empire, tying these concepts into a complex and evolving interrelationship for the duration of modern European history.

For a generation now, historians and other scholars in the humanities and social sciences have shown that Western political thought was deeply implicated in the creation of modern European empires and the abuses associated with those empires. Canonical political theorists, such as Hugo Grotius, John Locke, Emer de Vattel, John Stuart Mill and Alexis de Tocqueville, developed their understandings of freedom, rights, free trade, sovereignty and the law of nations in the context of rationalising European states' overseas empires. My purpose in this book is to show that Western political thought was more fractured and divided than these accounts allow for. While there is no question about the complicity of Western political thought in empire, many writers on political thought over the past

500 years expressed grave doubts about the justice of empire. One of their principal tools in expressing those concerns was the idea of occupation.

While occupation remained central to understandings of property and sovereignty over the several hundred years covered by this book, my concern is above all with changes in those understandings over time. Two transformations, in particular, are salient. In medieval Europe, the idea of occupation, or *occupatio*, was used to explain how people came to have rights in things. Indeed, *occupatio* was one of the most important medieval explanations for the origin of rights, and discussions of occupation were amongst the earliest discussions of how a person could have a right in something. At the same time, it justified the idea of property. Thus, the earliest analyses of rights were also discussions of rights in property.[1] In these medieval texts we may therefore find the beginnings of a possessive rights discourse that came to dominate Western political thought.[2] As occupation assumed a great role in debates over European overseas empires, those discussions largely turned around a discourse of possessive rights. If we seek the ideological underpinnings of the possessiveness of modern European empires, a good place to start is with the medieval idea of occupation, but in these medieval analyses, occupation remained primarily a tool of legal and political discourse. The medieval theory of occupation as a theory of rights lacked an element that would drive the massive appropriations of territory that were characteristic of European expansion: namely, the link between the idea of occupation and economic progress. That economic element was established by the first transformation of the idea of occupation.

Prior to the seventeenth century, political discourse had little to say about economics and commerce other than to be sceptical of the corrupting effects of wealth upon the political process. With the growing

[1] Brian Tierney, *The idea of natural rights* (Grand Rapids, 1997): Richard Tuck, *Natural rights theories: their origins and development* (Cambridge, 1979).

[2] There are long-standing debates over the modern history of possessive discourse. One conclusion that can be drawn from these debates is that theories of possessive rights pre-dated the rise of liberalism in the nineteenth century. For some scholars, identifying 'possessive individualism' means pushing back the origins of liberalism to a time when the term did not exist. C. B. Macpherson, *The political theory of possessive individualism* (Oxford, 1962) is the most celebrated contribution to this interpretation. For others, such as Brian Tierney and Richard Tuck, the presence of possessive rights theories in medieval jurists' writings indicates that there is more to liberalism than possessive rights. See also Jeremy Waldron, *The right to private property* (Oxford, 1988), p. 93, who argues that individualistic political theory is not exclusively the product of capitalism. This is not to diminish competing and also complementary traditions within Western political thought, such as those which concern duties: see Quentin Skinner, *The foundations of modern political thought*, 2 vols. (Cambridge, 1978).

commercial wealth of European nations in the seventeenth and eighteenth centuries, writers on politics increasingly sought ways to reconcile theories of politics with commercial life. The greatness and even the survival of modern states were now understood to be based upon wealth. This meant that European states sought political self-preservation not in military power, as had been the case for the Romans and Renaissance Italians, but in commercial power.[3] Modern history, according to David Hume, began in the seventeenth century when economics began to be perceived as an 'affair of state'.[4] Scarcely any ancient writer, he observed, had anything to say about the relation between politics and economics, and 'even the Italians have kept a profound silence with regard to it'.

The understanding of occupation was taken up in the new concern with political economy. In the sixteenth century, in the lectures and writings of Spanish theologians and jurists, particularly the so-called School of Salamanca, occupation was used to examine economic as well as political and legal questions. Between the seventeenth and eighteenth centuries, the idea of occupation was increasingly used – for example, by John Locke and Adam Smith – to explain the historical progress of human societies from a hypothetical state of nature to an agricultural state. These philosophers and historians would argue that it was through the occupation of land and goods that humans were able to preserve themselves and, in so doing, create civil societies. Indeed, the idea of occupation was pivotal to the development of an understanding of human history in terms of economic progress. Moreover, these early modern authors stressed that occupation could not simply be a taking of something 'with the hands', as it had been for medieval authors. Rather, they argued that occupation was only achieved by *use* or, in Locke's terms, improvement. Thus, occupation introduced an understanding of property in terms of the exploitation of nature. This process of exploitation is what drove society from one step in history to the next.

Occupation was a key idea, therefore, for both the medieval understanding of rights and the early modern understanding of history as progress. The notion of a stage in human society that possessed superior rights to preceding stages was created by the combination of the two discourses of

3 Istvan Hont, *Jealousy of trade: international competition and the nation-state in historical perspective* (Cambridge, MA, 2005); Andrew Fitzmaurice, 'The commercial ideology of colonisation in Jacobean England: Robert Johnson, Giovanni Botero and the pursuit of greatness', *William and Mary Quarterly*, 64(4) (2007), 791–820; Andrew Fitzmaurice, 'Neither neo-Roman nor liberal empire', *Renaissance Studies*, 26(4) (2012), 479–90.

4 Hont, *Jealousy of trade*, p. 8.

rights and progress, in each of which occupation was a common element. And it was this concept of occupation, combining rights and progress, that provided an immensely powerful justification for modern empires. The most persistent idea driving European expansion was not religious righteousness, nor was it simply the superiority of European civilisation. Rather, it was the notion that states, and indeed humanity itself, could only preserve themselves through the exploitation of the earth's resources to which all people had a common right, but to which particular people gained superior and particular rights through their acts of exploitation or occupation. Therefore, the first great transformation of the idea of occupation was from being a term of legal and political discourse to also being central to economic discourse. It hardly needs to be pointed out that the current environmental predicament of the planet is the consequence of the development of an understanding of property in terms of the exploitation of nature, combined with the globalisation of the consequences of that understanding through its link to European expansion.

While early modern agents of empire pursued the occupation of territories outside Europe, they feared the wealth and commerce that occupation could produce or, defensively, they sought to portray their activities as being consistent with the politics of virtue. The use of *occupatio*, and Roman law more generally, to think about the justice of empire reflected, at least until the eighteenth century, Europeans' disposition to analyse what they believed to be the greatest ever empire, the Roman Empire, in order to understand the new empires they were creating.[5] Roman historians and moral philosophers taught that the means of establishing empire was through the exercise of martial virtues, but, as Sallust in particular pointed out, that conquest created riches and luxury which effeminised the same martial culture and led to decline.[6] As commercial society developed in the seventeenth and eighteenth centuries, philosophers and historians sought ways to overcome the neo-Roman fears that wealth was a cause of corruption. David Hume and Charles-Louis de Secondat, Baron de Montesquieu, inverted the Sallustian account of empire by arguing that the

[5] Anthony Pagden, *Lords of all the world: ideologies of empire in Spain, Britain and France* (New Haven, 1995); David Armitage, *The ideological origins of the British Empire* (Cambridge, 2000); J. G. A. Pocock, *Barbarism and religion: the first decline and fall*, vol. 3 (Cambridge, 2003); Andrew Fitzmaurice, *Humanism and America: an intellectual history of early English colonisation, 1500–1625* (Cambridge, 2003); Benedict Kingsbury and Benjamin Straumann (eds.), *The Roman foundations of the law of nations: Alberico Gentili and the justice of empire* (Oxford, 2010); David A. Lupher, *Romans in a new world: classical models in sixteenth century Spanish America* (Ann Arbor, 2003).

[6] Pagden, *Lords of all the world*; Armitage, *Ideological origins of the British Empire*; Pocock, *Barbarism and religion*; Fitzmaurice, *Humanism and America*.

danger to civil society was not commerce, but the martial cultures that were needed to maintain the large landed empires.[7] Those empires generated conflicts such as the Seven Years' War (1756–63) that imposed burdensome taxes upon the metropolis. The critics opposed the occupation, or settlement, of large landmasses, as had been the case in the Americas, and proposed instead that European influence could be extended through commerce, or an empire of trade – the *douceur* of commerce, attributed to Montesquieu – without conquest.[8] Their hopes were realised, to some degree, in the ideologies and practices of the so-called 'second' empires of the nineteenth century that sought control over sovereignty rather than the large-scale settlement of land.[9]

The second transformation of the understanding of occupation was in a greater refinement of its application to the progressive idea of history and, in particular, the development of a concept that was appropriate to commercial empire rather than the continental empires of the Spanish, Portuguese, French and English in the Americas. While occupation was used in medieval discourse and in the sixteenth century to examine rights of property, and in the seventeenth and eighteenth century to explain the development of agricultural society, by the nineteenth century it was used

7 Albert O. Hirschman, *The passions and the interests: political arguments for capitalism before its triumph* (Princeton, 1997), p. 60; Pagden, *Lords of all the world*, p. 115. See also Céline Spector, 'Was Montesquieu liberal?', in Raf Geenans and Helena Rosenblatt (eds.), *French liberalism from Montesquieu to the present day* (Cambridge, 2012), p. 68 on Montesquieu's portrayal of the harmful aspects of commerce.

8 Spector points out that although Montesquieu establishes a 'correlation' between softness and commerce, he does not actually use the terms 'doux commerce' or 'la douceur du commerce' – these being attributed to him in the work of Albert Hirschman and Pierre Rosanvallon. See Spector, 'Was Montesquieu liberal?'.

9 On the decline of continental empires and the rise of commercial empires, see: John Gallagher and Ronald Robinson, 'The imperialism of free trade', *Economic History Review*, 6(1) (1953), 1–15; Pagden, *Lords of all the world*; Anthony Pagden, 'Empire and its anxieties', *American Historical Review*, 117(1) (2012), 141–8; Anthony Pagden, 'Fellow citizens and imperial subjects: conquest and sovereignty in Europe's overseas empires', *History and Theory*, 44(4) (2005), 28–46; Jörg Fisch, 'Law as a means and an end: some remarks on the function of European and non-European law in the process of European expansion', in W. J. Mommsen and J. A. De Moor (eds.), *European expansion and law: the encounter of European and Indigenous law in 19th and 20th-century Africa and Asia* (Oxford, 1992), p. 28; George Steinmetz, 'Imperialism or colonialism? From Windhoek to Washington, by way of Basra', in Craig Calhoun, Frederick Cooper and Kevin W. Moore (eds.), *Lessons of empire: imperial histories and American power* (New York, 2005), p. 140, who distinguishes modern territorial empires from 'imperial*ism*'; Charles Maier, *Among empires: American ascendancy and its predecessors* (Cambridge, MA, 2006). Carl Schmitt, *The nomos of the earth in the international law of the jus publicum Europaeum*, trans. G. L. Ulmen (New York, 2003 [1950]) argues that European continental empires gave way to American informal empire, although, due to his focus upon land, he has little to say about European informal empires other than to acknowledge the doctrine of extraterritoriality and to observe: 'In the nineteenth century, special forms of European extraterritoriality and consular jurisdiction were developed for half-civilized and exotic countries' (p. 172).

to understand rights of sovereignty when European empires turned increasingly to political rather than material appropriations: that is, to controlling other peoples' land, labour and capital rather than supplanting or exterminating them through colonisation.

This is not to argue for a clear break between early modern continental empires and post-Enlightenment commercial empire. The foundations of commercial empires were in the Dutch and English East India Companies established in the early seventeenth century.[10] In the seventeenth century, Samuel Pufendorf rejected the idea that sovereignty could be occupied and restricted the possibility only to property, but when Enlightenment philosophers such as Jean-Jacques Rousseau embraced the idea of the occupation of sovereignty, they reached back to Hugo Grotius, who had developed the concept partly in relation to his work for the Dutch East India Company. Moreover, while the nineteenth century saw a growing emphasis upon 'free trade imperialism', to use John Gallagher and Ronald Robinson's term, it also witnessed the establishment or consolidation of new settler societies, for example, in Australia and New Zealand. By the end of the nineteenth century and the beginning of the twentieth century, a number of commercial protectorates, such as in Africa, were increasingly brought under direct forms of rule. Thus, the focus for occupation was constantly shifting between property and sovereignty.

It is possible, however, to identify a particular nineteenth-century preoccupation with the occupation of sovereignty in legal discourse – an attempt to develop a legal framework for commercial empires. The idea of occupation was used by nineteenth-century jurists to extend the progressive theory of history through the development of a hierarchical understanding of sovereignty. In light of the complex shifts between territorial and commercial empires, the notion of the occupation of sovereignty reflected these jurists' ideals as much as it articulated imperial realities. While many were prepared to concede that non-European peoples possessed forms of sovereign civil society, they claimed that those sovereignties were 'personal' and thus comparable with the feudal societies of medieval Europe. Territorial sovereignty, they argued, was only to be found in modern states. Such states were to be placed higher in the progress of

[10] This is not to argue that these companies were purely commercial enterprises. See Philip J. Stern, *The company-state: corporate sovereignty and the early modern foundations of the British Empire in India* (Oxford, 2011) on the sovereign political ambitions of the seventeenth-century English East India Company. On the links between corporations and political sovereignty more generally, see F. W. Maitland, *State, trust and corporation*, eds. David Runciman and Magnus Ryan (Cambridge, 2003); and Joshua Barkan, *Corporate Sovereignty* (Minneapolis, 2013).

history and therefore possessed superior rights, just as seventeenth-century Europeans had argued that agricultural society possessed superior rights to people living in a supposed state of nature. Having thus extended the progressive theory of history, these jurists argued that it would be possible to occupy the territorial sovereignty of lands where such sovereignty had not already been 'taken', including over the 'personal' sovereignties of Africa and Asia. This understanding of occupation was closely tied to and extended by the unequal treaties employed in the nineteenth century. Contrary to the Westphalian myth, the possibility that one form of sovereignty could be contained within another, in this case personal sovereigns subsumed within territorial sovereigns, like Chinese boxes, was no more alien to the nineteenth century than it was to the Italian jurist Bartolus of Saxoferrato (1313–57) in the fourteenth century.[11] The idea of occupation did not merely reflect these changes, but was also used to drive and shape them. It was in part the critique of the occupation of property in the first European overseas empires, which reached its peak during the Enlightenment, that inspired the development of a theory of imperial occupation restricted to sovereignty, and that idea in turn served to legitimise the commercial empires of the nineteenth and twentieth centuries.

We may well ask why European states felt it necessary to legitimise their expansion overseas. There were moments, as we shall see, for example, in the first year in which the Virginia Company established a colony in the Chesapeake in 1607, in which colonisers discussed whether justification was desirable or necessary, and concluded that silence on such questions was prudent. More frequently, modern European empires went to great lengths to justify their existence. The language of justice defined and extended what it was possible to do. Although empires are almost always autocratic to a degree, they nevertheless find it necessary to provide some form of self-rationalisation. Power may come from the barrel of a gun, but force cannot be successfully sustained, even in the more Machiavellian understandings of politics, as an everyday means of establishing political compliance (as Machiavelli himself stressed). Indeed, autocratic regimes need to work harder at establishing their legitimacy than do popular forms of government in which legitimacy is a premise of the political system. For

[11] Edward Keene, *Beyond the anarchical society: Grotius, colonialism and order in world politics* (Cambridge, 2002) argues that the Westphalian ideal of non-intervention and sovereign equality was reserved for relations between European states, while the notion of divisible sovereignty was employed for empire.

global empires, force is further limited by the need to stretch resources over distance, so the cohering power of ideology assumes even greater importance. Moreover, justifications of empire were more likely to be aimed at metropolitan rather than subject audiences. The need to justify European empires reflected metropolitan concerns about the dangers of expansion, and a concern, with deep roots in Roman and Greek thought, that civil society should embrace a group of people in close communication with each other, without recourse to long journeys.[12] Opponents of empire, as we shall see, were quick to point to such dangers and to injustices.

Between the fifteenth and the seventeenth centuries, the Spanish justified their conquests in the Americas *as* conquests.[13] From the seventeenth century, the English, French and Dutch were more disingenuous than the Spanish in their understanding of what constituted legitimate expansion. They represented what would appear to any neutral observer as conquests – that is, the taking of something that belongs to somebody else – to be something altogether different. They claimed that they were taking things that belonged to nobody, albeit that the lands they took were inhabited by other peoples. They called this the 'occupation' of territory and they distinguished it from conquest. It is hard to legitimise taking things that belong to other people, but much easier to justify taking things that belong to nobody.

The disingenuous claim to occupy became the dominant justification of European empires between the sixteenth and twentieth centuries, albeit that imperial powers also used other important kinds of justifications for taking territory. With diminishing conviction, the Portuguese and the Spanish appealed to the Papal Bull *inter caetera* of 1493 and the 1494 Treaty of Tordesillas, which together partitioned the newly discovered lands of the world between the two powers – the West for Spain and the East for Portugal. While the Spanish also claimed the right of conquest, the French in seventeenth- and eighteenth-century New France made numerous agreements and alliances with various North American nations, although they made only one formal treaty.[14] English colonisers in North America, and subsequently the United States, made extensive use of

[12] Pagden, *Lords of all the world*, p. 61. [13] *Ibid.*, pp. 64–6.

[14] On the Spanish claim to the right of conquest, see Pagden, *Lords of all the world*. On French claims, see Alain Beaulieu, 'The acquisition of aboriginal land in Canada: the genealogy of an ambivalent system (1600–1867)', in Saliha Belmessous (ed.), *Empire by treaty: negotiating European expansion, 1600–1900* (Oxford, 2014); and Brian Slattery, *French claims in North America 1500–1559* (Saskatchewan, 1980).

treaties or land purchases (with varying degrees of integrity).[15] The Dutch relied upon treaties in the East Indies in the seventeenth century.[16] And in the nineteenth century, European states and companies made numerous treaties throughout Africa and the Pacific.[17] While explorers and politicians persisted with claims of discovery, jurists insisted that original title came from occupation and that derivative title came from conquest and cession. Their arguments increasingly had an impact upon practice. Even when claiming rights from cession, discovery and conquest, European powers often complemented these claims with the sometimes contradictory argument that they were taking something that, in any case, belonged to nobody. Moreover, increasingly from the eighteenth century, a distinction was made between the occupation of sovereignty, by which European empires claimed their titles, and the purchase of property through treaties, often employed by settlers themselves. This linking of occupation and treaty was common in North America in the eighteenth century and in Africa in the nineteenth century.

While all empires seek justification, the terms upon which they do so are contingent: that is, they are determined by the particular context and circumstances of each. The use of occupation to justify modern European empires was shaped by the Reformation. The concern with behaving justly to other peoples – or, rather, with being seen to behave justly – was not based upon a common sense of humanity, albeit that such notions were often employed in the justifications. Although the concern with justice contained a commitment to universal values, that commitment was motivated by narrow self-interest rather than universality for its own sake.

[15] Stuart Banner, *How the Indians lost their land: law and power on the frontier* (Cambridge, MA, 2005), pp. 49–95; Cynthia van Zandt, *Brothers among nations: the pursuit of intercultural alliances in early America, 1580–1660* (New York, 2008); Colin G. Calloway, *Pen and ink witchcraft: treaties and treaty making in American Indian history* (New York, 2013). For the Native American perspective on treaties, see Robert Williams, *Linking arms together: American Indian treaty visions of law and peace, 1600–1800* (New York, 1999).

[16] Peter Borschberg, 'Hugo Grotius, East India trade and the King of Johor', *Journal of Southeast Asian Studies*, 30(2) (1999), 225–48; Peter Borschberg, 'The seizure of the Sta. Catarina revisited: the Portuguese Empire in Asia, VOC politics and the origins of the Dutch-Johor alliance (1602–c.1616)', *Journal of Southeast Asian Studies*, 33(1) (2002), 31–62; Martine van Ittersum, *Profit and principle: Hugo Grotius, natural rights theories and the rise of Dutch power in the East Indies (1595–1615)* (Leiden, 2006).

[17] Many of these treaties were documented in E. Hertslet, *The map of Africa by treaty*, 3 vols. (London, 1967, first printed in 1909); and M. F. Lindley, *The acquisition and government of backward territory in international law* (London, 1926). See also C. H. Alexandrowicz, *The European-African confrontation: a study in treaty making* (Leiden, 1973); Mamadou Hebié, 'Les accords conclus entre les puissances coloniales et les entités politiques locales comme moyens d'acquisition de la souveraineté territoriale' (PhD dissertation, Graduate Institute for International Studies and Development, Geneva, 2012); and Belmessous (ed.), *Empire by treaty*.

The concern with justice arose from the desire of European states, both Protestant and Catholic, to derive their legitimacy from sources other than the Church.[18] This desire gained even greater impetus following the wars of religion and the Thirty Years' War (1618–48). These wars revealed that, when the legitimacy of states rested upon religious piety, they paid the price of fractured sovereign power, chaos and a massive waste of life. Out of their own desire for self-preservation, these states established a system of rules, the law of nations, which demanded that wars, and relations between peoples more generally, have some basis in law and justice.[19] These rules applied between European states, but their principles necessarily had to have some claim to universality or they risked falling back into the communal ideas that had fed more than a century of war.

In the pursuit of a secular basis to political justice, the idea of occupation was lifted from Roman private law and introduced into the nascent law of nations, or *ius gentium*, to address the legitimacy of *both* states and empires.[20] At the very start of the Reformation, and in response to the Protestant claim that the only just society is a godly society, the Spanish theologian Francisco de Vitoria argued that a just society is one that has shown an ability to exploit nature, one that has taken things and made them into property, and thus one that has occupied both physical and political space. It was on this basis that Vitoria condemned the arguments of the Spanish Conquistadors, who had claimed that their possession of true religion justified their conquests. While he may have been at risk of arguing his monarch out of an empire in the Americas, Vitoria was mindful that, as Holy Roman Emperor, Charles V was at risk of losing much of his European empire to Protestant rulers who based their legitimacy upon their godliness and who, upon the same claim, fought endless wars.[21]

Indeed, for many political leaders, jurists and philosophers, the security, stability and peace of their own state or intra-European empire was more important than the justification of extra-European empire. This did not mean that they always ignored overseas empires, although some did.

18 Skinner, *The foundations of modern political thought*, vol. 2. For the implications of these concerns for early modern empires, see Pagden, *Lords of all the world*, pp. 47–9.

19 Richard Tuck, *The rights of war and peace: political thought and the international order from Grotius to Kant* (Oxford, 1999).

20 On private law sources for the law of nations, see: Hersch Lauterpacht, *Private law sources and analogies in international law: with special reference to international arbitration* (London, 1927); and Randall Lesaffer, 'Argument from Roman Law in current international law: occupation and acquisitive prescription', *European Journal of International Law*, 16(1) (2005), 25–58.

21 Anthony Pagden and Jeremy Lawrence (ed.), *Vitoria: Political writings* (Cambridge, 1991).

Often, it meant that they engaged with the question of the justice of empire only to conclude that it was in conflict with principles upon which peace, self-preservation, sovereignty and sometimes liberty were established within their own states. Across four centuries, justifications of empire were often opposed with the claim that non-European peoples were the rightful occupiers of their own lands or occupiers of their sovereignty, again bringing the question of occupation to the foreground of thinking about imperial justice. Political leaders, theologians, philosophers and jurists, often in dialogue with each other, established a sustained and powerful critique of empire. That critique was developed in opposition to the role that many Western political thinkers played in driving European expansion. Writers on politics, philosophy and law, including Hugo Grotius, John Locke and John Stuart Mill, were directly involved in colonising or overseas trading enterprises.[22] Moreover, these figures often developed their ideas through reflecting on the experience of empire. Some historians are now prepared to argue that the architecture of Western political thought – including the theories of sovereignty, rights, property and international law, as well as the understanding of reason itself – is inherently disposed towards empire or inherently disposed towards Western interests and values.[23] They have thus attacked what they regard as a

?

[22] For Grotius, see Ittersum, *Profit and principle*. For Locke, see: Barbara Arneil, *John Locke and America: the defence of English colonialism* (Oxford, 1996); James Tully, *An approach to political philosophy: Locke in contexts* (Cambridge, 1993); David Armitage, 'John Locke, Carolina, and the two treatises of government', *Political Theory*, 32(5) (2004), 602–27. For Mill, see Uday Singh Mehta, *Liberalism and empire: a study in nineteenth-century British liberal thought* (Chicago, 1999); Jennifer Pitts, *A turn to empire: the rise of imperial liberalism in Britain and France* (Princeton, 2005), pp. 123–62.

[23] Robert A. Williams, *The American Indian in Western legal thought* (Oxford, 1990); Dipesh Chakrabarty, *Provincializing Europe: postcolonial thought and historical difference* (Princeton, 2000); Tuck, *Rights of war and peace*, pp. 14–15 and 234; Antony Anghie, *Imperialism, sovereignty and the making of international law* (Cambridge, 2005); Martti Koskenniemi, *The gentle civilizer of nations: the rise and fall of international law 1870–1960* (Cambridge, 2001); Martti Koskenniemi, 'Empire and international law: the real Spanish contribution', *University of Toronto Law Journal*, 61(1) (2011), 1–36. For Emmanuel Jouannet, the ethnocentric European origin of international law and its universal aspirations is a 'paradox' that can 'be overcome, but only in a temporary and provisional manner': Emmanuel Jouannet, 'Universalism and imperialism: the true-false paradox of international law', *European Journal of International Law*, 18(7) (2003), 379–407, at 407. See also Emmanuel Jouannet, *The liberal-welfarist law of nations* (Cambridge, 2012). For scepticism of these post-colonial interpretations, see: George Cavallar, *The rights of strangers: theories of international hospitality, the global community, and political justice since Vitoria* (Aldershot, 2002); Georg Cavallar, 'Vitoria, Grotius, Pufendorf, Wolff and Vattel: accomplices of European colonialism and exploitation or true cosmopolitans?', *Journal of the History of International Law*, 10 (2008), 181–209; Pablo Zapatero, 'Legal imagination in Vitoria: the power of ideas', *Journal of the History of International Law*, 11 (2009), 221–71; Paul Corcoran, 'John Locke on the possession of land: native title vs. the "principle" of vacuum domicilium', *Proceedings, Australasian Political Studies Association Annual Conference* (2007); Andrew Fitzmaurice, 'A genealogy of *terra nullius*', *Australian Historical Studies*, 129(1) (2007), 1–15; Andrew Fitzmaurice, 'Moral uncertainty in the dispossession of Native

liberal myth: namely, that the instruments of political thought are objective or neutral standards.

Ironically perhaps, Carl Schmitt, the conservative German jurist and political theorist, is a common authority for many critics of the interdependence of empire, international law and political thought.[24] The wars of the twenty-first century have provoked a resurgence in the topicality of empire, leading scholars to seize upon Schmitt's perceptive analyses of conflict and empire in order to understand American hegemony.[25] These analyses have led to deeper reflection on the broader history of empire and political thought, beyond the events of the past generation. As Antony Anghie observes: 'Many of Schmitt's arguments bear a striking resemblance to the arguments made by post-colonial and Third World scholars regarding the character and geopolitics of international law.'[26]

For Schmitt, international law, and to a large degree modern political thought, was the creation of modern European, and subsequently American, empire and hegemony. In words that have been echoed by many recent historians of empire, he argued that the European 'discovery of a new world . . . did not occur by chance'. It was 'an achievement of newly awakened Occidental rationalism, the product of an intellectual and scientific culture'.[27] The justification for European hegemony following the conquest of the Americas, he argued, was that it was 'made only by

Americans', in Peter Mancall (ed.), *The Atlantic world and Virginia* (Chapel Hill, 2007); Andrew Fitzmaurice, 'Anti-colonialism in Western political thought: the colonial origins of the concept of genocide', in A. Dirk Moses (ed.), *Empire, Colony, Genocide: Conquest, Occupation, and Subaltern Resistance in World History* (New York, 2008); Andrew Fitzmaurice, 'Liberalism and empire in nineteenth-century international law', *American Historical Review*, 117(1) (2012), 122–40.

24 For the use of Schmitt to explore the links between empire and legal and political thought, see, for example, China Miéville, *Between equal rights: a Marxist theory of international law* (Leiden, 2005), pp. 27–31, although Miéville, like many authors employing Schmitt, is also strongly opposed to the 'radical right'; Koskenniemi, *The gentle civilizer of nations*, pp. 413–40; Martti Koskenniemi, 'International law as political theology: how to read Nomos der Erde?', *Constellations*, 11(4) (2004), 492–511; see Steinmetz, 'Imperialism or colonialism?'; Lauren Benton, *A search for sovereignty: law and geography in European empires, 1400–1900* (Cambridge, 2010). pp. 282–4 for a critical view. For a short biography, see Bardo Fassbender, 'Carl Schmitt (1888–1985)', in Bardo Fassbender, Anne Peters, Simone Peter and Danuel Hogger (eds.), *The Oxford handbook of the history of international law* (Oxford, 2012), pp. 1073–178. For the argument that Schmitt's value lies in his historical critique rather than his conceptual innovation, see William Hooker, *Carl Schmitt's international thought: order and orientation* (Cambridge, 2009).

25 Koskenniemi, 'International law as political theology'; Louiza Odysseos and Fabio Petito, *The international political thought of Carl Schmitt: terror, liberal war and the crisis of global order* (London, 2007); David Chandler, 'The revival of Carl Schmitt in international relations: the last refuge of critical theorists?', *Millennium: Journal of International Studies*, 37(1) (2008), 27–48.

26 Antony Anghie, 'Identifying regions in the history of international law', in Fassbender *et al.* (eds.), *The Oxford handbook of the history of international law*, p. 1074.

27 Schmitt, *Nomos of the earth*, p.132.

peoples intellectually and historically advanced enough to apprehend the discovered by superior knowledge and consciousness'.[28] 'The intellectual advantage', he declared, 'was entirely on the European side, so much so that the New World could simply be "taken"'. Schmitt observed that *occupatio*, as he put it, had been the title that jurists claimed in the New World. 'The New World', he argued, 'was open for occupation.' For him, occupation was an idea that was used to legitimise empire, not to oppose it, and in this understanding he is followed by many more recent commentators. The idea of occupation, he argued, was fitted to the new order of a competition between states for territory because, rather than awarding new territories to Europeans as a whole, it entitled only those who appropriated land. The taking of land and the division of space, he argued, was the beginning of political society. 'This original act is nomos' and it is 'the fundamental act of apportioning space'.[29] Few writers on occupation over the centuries would have disagreed with him. At the same time, he acknowledged that occupation was rhetoric, dressing up the brutal reality of discovery and conquest that he saw as the true basis to title: 'a discoverer knows his prey better than the prey knows himself, and is able to subjugate him by means of superior education and knowledge'.[30]

The disposition of Western political thought to empire raises the question of whether Western societies can escape the logic of expansionism given the political architecture they have inherited.[31] A paradox of the post-colonial critique of liberalism, and of its critique of Western political thought more broadly, is that it argues for a relatively coherent European political and legal understanding of international society and the non-European world, and in so doing slips into precisely the kind of rationalist universalism that it decries. Western political thought is a fractured and incoherent body with porous boundaries. The focus on the complicity of important political thinkers in empire has obscured the anti-imperial currents in Western political thought. It has concealed the debates that were conducted within the so-called Western political tradition over whether colonisation and empire were just and on what terms they could or could not be just.[32] Those debates were part of a broader history of political

[28] *Ibid.* [29] *Ibid.*, p. 78. [30] *Ibid.*, p. 132.

[31] A point Tuck makes strongly in *Rights of war and peace.*

[32] Another challenge to the notion of an inherent European disposition to empire comes from scholarship examining the ways in which non-Europeans were engaged in the development of modern political thought. This scholarship de-centres Europe and challenges the idea of its coherence. The point is made in different ways, for example, by: Lauren Benton, *Law and colonial cultures: legal regimes in world history* (Cambridge, 2002): Sanjay Subramanyam, *Courtly*

thought that was marked by disagreement rather than a set of coherent principles.[33] When a self-conscious liberal tradition was established in the nineteenth century, that tradition too was defined by a multitude of perspectives rather than by doctrine. Schmitt argued that when Europeans spoke of international law, they meant *European* international law, when they spoke of humanity, they meant *European* humanity, civilisation meant *European* civilisation, and progress was *European* progress.[34] In Dipesh Chakrabarty's words, Europe thus becomes the 'silent referent in historical knowledge', the 'subject of all histories'.[35] But these claims diminish a history of scepticism about precisely such terms of political discourse.

The emphasis upon the complicity of Western political thought in empire has marginalised the very great degree to which many writers on politics and law opposed empire for a variety of reasons. For one of the strongest arguments of opposition to empire, we again need to turn to the concept of occupation. The argument of occupation was used as much to oppose as to justify expansion, and the grounds of opposition were that non-European peoples had established property rights and political rights through their occupation of physical and political space. Thus, opposition to imperial appropriations was driven as much by a discourse of possession as was support for expansion. In threatening the possessions of others, empires were often perceived to be a threat to property at home and, more broadly, to threaten domestic political space, to pose the threat of tyranny.

It is true that political ideas were interpreted in ways that consistently favoured the interests of European empires. But the interests of states or, rather, the perceived interests of the subjects and citizens of those states were not always consistent with the interests of empire. The instruments of political thought were tools and as such they could be, and were, used to different ends. Similarly, guns or the knowledge of how to ride horses could be used both to further the ends of empire and to oppose it. Indigenous knowledge of the land was used to resist empire and also to reveal new territories for conquest. This book looks at ways in which political ideas were used both to support and to critique European empires.

encounters: translating courtliness and violence in early modern Eurasia (Cambridge, MA, 2012); Sebastian Conrad, 'Enlightenment in global history: a historiographical critique', *American Historical Review*, 117(4) (2012), 999–1027.

33 See Isaiah Berlin, 'Two concepts of liberty', in *Four essays on liberty* (Oxford, 1969), pp. 118–72; Quentin Skinner, *Liberty before liberalism* (Cambridge, 1998); John Gray, *Two faces of liberalism* (New York, 2000), pp. 31–3; Jürgen Habermas, *Between facts and norms* (Cambridge, MA, 1998), Chapter 3.

34 Schmitt, *Nomos of the earth*, p. 228.

35 Chakrabarty, *Provincializing Europe*, pp. 28–9.

Some historians have argued that anti-imperial sentiment reached a peak in the Enlightenment, only to be buried by nineteenth-century nationalism and scientific racism, which, combined, drove a new era of empire.[36] This claim may be true, but it requires two important qualifications. First, the cosmopolitan ideals of the Enlightenment were used to justify empires, particularly the informal empires that followed in the nineteenth century. Second, the Enlightenment-inspired critique of empire endured throughout the nineteenth century and was employed not only to oppose continental empires but also commercial empire and the pretensions of the civilising mission.

Because this book examines these debates over hundreds of years concerning the status of empires extending over the entire globe, including the Poles, it is 'global' in scope. From at least the sixteenth century, occupation was understood to be a law which regulated the division of the globe. This is therefore a global history insofar as it examines ways in which the idea of occupation was imposed upon territories on every continent of the globe, as well as upon the oceans (as a negative argument). It is also a transnational history, as intellectual history has always been, because it examines ideas which were shared across national boundaries. But it is a European history insofar as it is concerned with the transmission of a self-conscious Roman law tradition, passed between generations of Europeans law-makers and philosophers.[37] Occupation was a law that was employed widely in works of moral philosophy and politics, but it was also a principle of a legal code and a part of the law of nations. Scholars as diverse as Schmitt and Jörg Fisch have argued that, prior to decolonisation, the law of nations was always the *European* law of nations.[38] This is only partly true. The law of nations was not a coherent body. Prior to the nineteenth century, it belonged to a broader literature on the government of states, and specifically to aspects of that literature that dealt with the external relations of those states.[39] A common topic of debate was whether

[36] See, for example, Sankar Muthu, *Enlightenment against empire* (Princeton, 2003); Pitts, *A turn to empire*; Anthony Pagden, *The Enlightenment and why it still matters* (New York, 2013).

[37] This study is not global in the sense of concerning ideas that developed through the meeting of cultures. On these various understandings of global intellectual history, see Samuel Moyn and Andrew Sartori, 'Approaches to global intellectual history', in Samuel Moyn and Andrew Sartori (eds.), *Global intellectual history* (New York, 2013), pp. 2–20. For global history forged through the commensurability of cultures, see Subramanyam, *Courtly encounters*.

[38] Schmitt, *Nomos of the earth*; Jörg Fisch, *Die europäische Expansion und das Völkerrecht* (Stuttgart, 1984).

[39] Annabel S. Brett, *Liberty, right and nature: individual rights in later scholastic thought* (Cambridge, 1997), p. 165; Martti Koskenniemi, 'International law and *raison d'état*: rethinking the prehistory of international law', in Kingsbury and Straumann (eds.), *The Roman foundations of the law of nations*, p. 298.

the rules of the law of nations applied exclusively to relations between European nations or whether other peoples were also subject to them.[40] But up until the nineteenth century, the law of nations was certainly European insofar as it was largely a product of European discourses, and even when it was imagined to be universal, it was generalised from European moral philosophy.[41]

When occupation was employed to justify colonisation, it was not employed in the context of equal relations between sovereign states, but as part of relations between dominant and dependent parts of the globe. Occupation functioned as part of a law of nations that was both a tool of empire as well as a critique of empire.[42] Therefore, this is not simply a history of the law of nations, or international law, although both are relevant – it is also a history of the law of empire understood as the projection of European understandings of property and sovereignty: that is, their projection over the state and beyond. There are aspects of the imperial law of nations that can only be fully understood in the context of exchanges with non-European peoples.[43] The most important example of this kind of legal exchange is found in the history of treaties. To the degree that a global history of the law of nations has been written for the period of European expansion prior to the twentieth century, it has focused upon treaties.[44] One of the remarkable features of the doctrine of occupation was that when it was used to justify colonisation, it assumed that, by definition, the people of the territory concerned were without any legal standing, or none above that which prevails in nature. In other words, occupation was a unilateral doctrine of appropriation and it is therefore resistant to a genuinely global approach to history. It required no negotiation with peoples who inhabited the territory concerned and left no historical trace

40 Jennifer Pitts, 'Empire and legal universalisms in the eighteenth century', *American Historical Review*, 117(1) (2012), 92–121.

41 Martti Koskenniemi, 'International law in Europe: between tradition and renewal', *European Journal of International Law*, 16(1) (2005), 113–24. For the development of a non-European law of nations from the nineteenth century, see Arnulf Becker Lorca, *Mestizo international law: a global intellectual history 1850–1950* (Cambridge, 2012).

42 On the law of nations as a tool of subordination rather than reciprocity, see Jörg Fisch, 'Power or weakness? On the causes of the worldwide expansion of European international law', *Journal of the History of International Law*, 6 (2004), 21–6.

43 On the problem of Eurocentrism in the history of international law, see Arnulf Becker Lorca, 'Eurocentrism in the history of international law', in Fassbender *et al.* (ed.), *The Oxford handbook of the history of international law*, pp. 1034–57; Martti Koskenniemi, 'Histories of international law: dealing with Eurocentrism', *Rechtsgeschichte*, 19 (2011), 152–76.

44 A pioneer in this field was C. H. Alexandrowicz, *An introduction to the history of the law of nations in the East Indies (16th, 17th and 18th centuries)* (Oxford, 1967). See also Belmessous (ed.), *Empire by treaty*.

of exchange.[45] It is hardly surprising, in these circumstances, that it is associated with instances of the worst destructions of indigenous societies in the history of colonisation (as, for example, in North America and Australia), as the premises of the doctrine gave no recognition to those societies. Even when a theory of the occupation of sovereignty was developed in the nineteenth century which conceded that a particular people may possess property or even 'personal' sovereignty, this new doctrine assumed a void of territorial sovereignty that, in order to be seized, required no permission from the inhabitants of the territories, although it was complemented with treaties ceding the rights of those personal sovereignties.

While historians increasingly recognise that the law of nations has a European origin, they are divided on the origin of empire. For some historians, the concept of empire is a subject for linguistic contextualism, a genealogy to be constructed from the Roman idea of *imperium*.[46] For others, empire is a form of political organisation, of 'large political units' that govern 'multiple populations', which has been experienced by diverse human communities over thousands of years.[47] I will adopt the former approach. In Roman law, *imperium* referred to the possession of unlimited authority over a territory.[48] This included authority over the city of Rome itself and the territories it ruled. Medieval European rulers revived this concept in order simultaneously to assert authority over the territory they claimed in competition with both internal feudal rivals and external powers, including the Church and the Holy Roman Empire. A further signification of *imperium* from the late Roman Empire was of rule over a number of distinct territories (this idea became clear by the seventh century, when the Empire was no longer integrative but still possessed a ruler who claimed authority over distinct provinces).[49] This understanding

[45] The question of how non-European peoples engaged with this unilateral European discourse is important, but is largely outside the scope of this study, which attempts to demonstrate the continuities and differences within this self-consciously European tradition over hundreds of years. I have begun to explore the engagement between Europeans and non-Europeans over the question of occupation in Andrew Fitzmaurice, 'Powhatan legal claims', in Saliha Belmessous (ed.), *Native claims: indigenous law against empire* (Oxford, 2012).

[46] For this approach, see: Pagden, *Lords of all the world*, pp. 12–16; Armitage, *Ideological origins of the British Empire*, especially pp. 29–36.

[47] For this approach, see Jane Burbank and Fred Cooper, *Empires in world history: power and the politics of difference* (Princeton, 2010), p. 8.

[48] Armitage, *Ideological origins of the British Empire*, p. 29.

[49] *Ibid.*, p. 33. For the uses of federal and unitary understandings of *imperium* in medieval Spain, see Hélène Sirantoine, *Imperator Hispaniæ. Les idéologies impériales dans le royaume de León (IXe–XIIe siècles)* (Madrid, 2012).

of empire was important both for the creation of the composite monarchies of early modern Europe and even for the diverse territory claimed by the French Crown. Thus, the first modern European empires were forged in the creation of the first European states.[50] The sense of rule over diverse provinces was maintained when, in the sixteenth century, these states began to extend their power overseas, so that the term 'empire' was used to refer to the possession of territories beyond the state. In the sixteenth and seventeenth centuries, 'empire' was a term as likely to be used to describe particular European powers as it was for their growing overseas possessions. My own focus is upon the overseas conquests of European states, although my discussion begins in the medieval period, when claims to *imperium* were being used to carve out European states and this was a process, as we shall see, that included claims to occupation. By the sixteenth century, 'empire' was a term used to describe Spanish conquests in the Americas and it was similarly employed by the English from the early seventeenth century to include their American possessions.[51] These early modern uses of 'empire' often spoke of the *imperium* of the state, or sovereign, and the expansion of that *imperium* through the creation of overseas colonies as one and the same thing. In 1623, James I's Charter of Avalon in Newfoundland declared that the colony would 'enlarge the extents of the Christian World, & there withal of our Empire and Dominion'. Similarly, George Calvert, Lord Baltimore, wrote to Charles I in 1629 that his colonising ventures in America were pursued for the purpose of 'enlarging your Maiesties empire in this part of the world'.[52] In both cases, empire was still understood as the sovereign's authority, but it included the sense of projection of power beyond the boundaries of the state which would later dominate the understanding of the term.

The contexts in which occupation was employed – textual contexts and contexts of imperial practice – changed dramatically over the course of 500 years. While this study of occupation traverses a great span of time, I nevertheless seek to reconstruct the understanding of that idea through careful attention to a series of contexts. These changing contexts generated different theories of occupation, so that the concept itself, and not just the ways in which it was used, also underwent great changes. Its Roman law

[50] Elizabeth Mancke, 'Empire and state', in David Armitage and Michael Braddick (eds.), *The British Atlantic world, 1500–1800* (New York, 2002).

[51] On Spain's conquests as empire, see Pagden, *Lords of all the world*.

[52] *The Charter of Avalon* (7 April 1623), in Gillian T. Cell (ed.), *Newfoundland discovered: English attempts at colonisation, 1610–1630* (London, 1982), p. 258; Calvert to Charles I, 19 August 1629, in Cell (ed.), *Newfoundland discovered*, p. 296.

articulation was as different from twentieth-century understandings of occupation as a Roman trireme was from an aircraft carrier, albeit that both are ships. Importantly, this history of occupation is not conceived in the manner of A. O. Lovejoy as the history of a 'unit-idea'.[53] In other words, it is not a history that examines what successive generations had to say about a relatively stable concept. It is 'transtemporal' but not transhistorical.[54] Intellectual history now treats ideas as arguments and, as arguments, ideas are used by particular people addressing particular circumstances.[55] This study will ask *who* was arguing about occupation and what their circumstances were.

As much as the continuities, it is the differences that reward a *longue durée* perspective upon the question of occupation. A pattern of change emerges from those differences. The core of this change is that discussions of occupation moved from being predominantly concerned in medieval times with rights – that is, with legal and political questions – to a theory of economic stages in the seventeenth century, while in the nineteenth century it was extended to include a theory of the territorial sovereignty appropriate to commercial expansion. The different contexts in which occupation was used produced not only different answers to questions about property, sovereignty and empire but also different questions. One might conclude that the differences in these understandings are so divergent as to leave us without a meaningful history of a whole to be written. There are, however, continuities in the history of occupation from its Roman law origins through to twentieth-century debates over property and sovereignty in space. To ignore these continuities would be to risk approaching history as a 'mail-train hauling self-synchronised periods in series like boxcars'.[56] Since the so-called 'linguistic turn' in the 1960s, intellectual historians have focused upon synchronic contexts more than conversations over time (although, as David Armitage has observed, a number of classic works of intellectual history in the past thirty years have had broader scope).[57] This study is both synchronic and diachronic.

53 See the critique of such an approach in Quentin Skinner, *Visions of politics: regarding method* (Cambridge, 2002), pp. 84–6.

54 For this understanding of *longue durée* intellectual history, see David Armitage, 'What's the big idea? Intellectual history and the longue durée', *History of European Ideas*, 38(4) (2012), 493–507.

55 Skinner, *Visions of politics*, pp. 87–8.

56 Herbert F. Tucker, 'Introduction' to *Context*, a special edition of *New Literary History*, 42(4) (2011), ix.

57 Armitage, 'What's the big idea?', 499. Armitage's examples are J. G. A. Pocock, *The Machiavellian moment: Florentine political thought and the Atlantic republican tradition*, 2nd edn (Princeton, 2003); Tuck, *Rights of war and peace*; Quentin Skinner, 'A genealogy of the modern state', *Proceedings of the British Academy*, 162 (2009), 325–70.

Historical contingency must not be taken so far as to deprive the subjects we discuss of an historical consciousness, trapped in an everlasting present. Discourses are tools that are used to different ends, are defined by those ends and are changed each time they change contexts. But, at the same time, tools are passed between peoples and across generations. To treat contexts as entirely generative of their own particular and unique tools guided by supposedly general and universal motivations, such as interests, is to abandon history.

The historical investigation of ideas that endured long periods of time raises the question of why certain ideas, or certain arguments, persist longer than others. Concepts such as empire, property, occupation, citizenship, the republic and liberty have been reformulated over thousands of years, while others such as seisin, serfdom, mercantilism, Whiggism, phrenology, liberalism and the state were or are of relatively short duration. Whether certain concepts, such as 'human rights', belong to the former or the latter category is a question that provokes passionate debate.[58] An obvious explanation for the endurance and adaption of certain concepts is that, as tools, they remain useful, although this response merely begs the question why they remain useful. An empirical answer to this question (although by no means a complete answer) is that many Roman law concepts have endured thousands of years in European political thought. In this category we find empire, property, citizenship, liberty and the republic. These Roman law terms remain central to modern political discourse and occupation belongs in this group.

It is sometimes argued that the only people who had knowledge of political and legal ideas in pre-democratic times were so-called 'elites' who had access to texts. Such a claim assumes that historically most people had no access to the processes by which knowledge is transmitted – it denies historical consciousness to those people. In this book, I try to show ways in which ideas employed by 'elites' or 'theorists' were also employed by people engaged in the business of empire or by relatively undistinguished lawyers, merchants, religious figures and politicians in Europe. Sometimes these middling figures were putting the ideas of philosophers to work, while at other times we see them developing ideas which would later be given more systematic and coherent treatment by philosophers. Because of the great scope of the book, I cannot show the depth of these discourses to the degree that is possible, but I do attempt to reconstruct contexts

[58] See the debate triggered by Samuel Moyn, *The last utopia: human rights in history* (Cambridge, MA, 2010).

through the examination of what Emma Rothschild has called 'medium' ideas, or thought by 'not very estimable characters' in the history of ideas.[59] I also follow recent scholarship, which has shown that many of the so-called elite theorists were themselves agents of empire.[60]

In Chapter 2, I begin the analysis with a discussion of Roman law and medieval civil and canon law. In Roman law, property was said to have had its origins in people taking things and calling them their own. According to this theory, the first person to take something which belonged to nobody would become its owner.[61] This was known as the law of occupation, or *occupatio*. According to the Roman digests of law, occupation was a principle of the law of nature, so it was an example of the way in which civil, or positive, law followed natural law. This dual status of occupation as both natural and positive law was sustained in discussions of the idea from medieval times through to the twentieth century.

Medieval civil lawyers revived Roman law in the eleventh and twelfth centuries when they sought to establish rules to govern the emerging city-states of Europe. At the same time, lawyers of the medieval Church employed Roman law to examine the claims upon property that could be made by the poor.[62] As part of this revival, these lawyers elaborated the Roman theory of the origin of property, or *occupation*, which they began to describe as *res nullius*. Those jurists and medieval philosophers also revived the natural law theories that justified their Roman theory of property. Underlying the idea that a person becomes the owner of something if she or he is the first to take it was an Aristotelian assumption that nature exists in potential and that it is the duty of humankind to release the potential in nature by exploiting it.

For medieval jurists and philosophers, occupation helped explain the origin of political society as well as individual rights. In pre-modern European political thought, political society was conceived as a *res publica*, a 'commonwealth' or 'city', that is, as a form of relations between a particular people, with a weak, fluid and partly metonymical link to place, such as the walled city, or *urbs*, or any particular territory.[63] However, the

[59] Emma Rothschild, 'Language and empire, c.1800', *Historical Research*, 78(200) (2005), 209–10.

[60] John Locke has been a focus of these studies, but they include many other canonical figures in the history of political thought, such as Hugo Grotius, John Stuart Mill and Henry Sumner Maine. See note 22.

[61] See, for example, J. A. C. Thomas (ed.), *The institutes of Justinian* (Amsterdam, 1975), bk. II, i, 11–12.

[62] Tuck, *Natural rights theories*, p. 15; Tierney, *The idea of natural rights*, pp. 54–5.

[63] Annabel Brett, *Changes of state: nature and the limits of the city in early modern natural law* (Princeton, 2011).

relation between political society and the place in which people lived was made tangible through the law of occupation. It was through the taking of things that had previously been common that particular political societies made claim to particular places.

Pursuing the notion of how particular political societies made claim to particular places, the theologian Francisco de Vitoria introduced occupation to discuss the justice of empire in the sixteenth century. He did so in order to raise doubts about the justice of the Spanish conquests.[64] He argued that the 'Indians', as he called the inhabitants of the Americas, already occupied their lands and so possessed rights of property over their territories and goods. A number of theologians agreed with and extended Vitoria's arguments, but colonisers seized on the potential to use the idea of occupation to describe the newly discovered lands as unowned. The question of how property was established in something that belonged to nobody was believed to have particular relevance to the vast territories of the newfound lands. Of course, these lands were inhabited and the peoples who lived in them believed themselves to be the owners. While Europeans acknowledged the existence of native peoples, they questioned whether these peoples had taken the lands and exploited their resources for themselves or whether they remained in unrealised potential, open to the first taker.

It appears that Europeans adapted the law of *occupatio* to their perception that the New World was relatively void of ownership. But there is evidence, as I discuss in Chapter 3, that they did something more profound than that. As conquerors, English colonisers in North America in the seventeenth century used the law of occupation to invent the perception that the lands they were appropriating were void of exploitation and ownership. The claim that the new lands belonged to nobody because they had not been taken was not simply a description of a belief but a redescription of experience. This redescription evaded the laws of conquest which would have demanded the recognition of the property rights of the conquered. It enabled the conquerors to ignore the claims of indigenous peoples and to portray themselves as 'settlers': that is, as people who occupy land that previously belonged to nobody. In making this redescription, these colonisers also began to use the idea of occupation as part of an argument that would have been foreign to Vitoria in another way: that is, not merely as a question of legal right but as a description of a stage in economic and historical development. Vitoria lacked such a stadial

[64] Anthony Pagden, *The fall of natural man*, revised edn (Cambridge, 1986).

understanding of history. The stadial theory of history began to be elaborated in José de Acosta's history of the Americas in the late sixteenth century and Acosta's distinctions between levels of society were employed by early seventeenth-century promoters of English colonies.

While the Spanish had grappled with the question of occupation in Central and South America, they also acknowledged themselves to be conquerors.[65] The English too used the language of conquest, but it was they who fully seized the opportunity of portraying themselves in North America as taking something that had previously been void of ownership.[66] The use of the idea of occupation to criticise empire created difficulties for English colonisers when they started to establish permanent plantations in America in the early seventeenth century. They responded by changing their descriptions of Native American peoples and by using occupation to describe a stage in history as much as a legal right. While initially they had often commented upon the civility of those people and remarked upon signs of their exploitation of nature, they now argued that they resembled beasts in a state of nature. Only in this way could the land be said to have been taken by no one. John Locke built this progressive theory of history into his understanding of property, observing that labour made the difference to the value of property. What has been described as a Lockean or agriculturalist argument was a powerful justification for colonisation in America in the eighteenth century.

It was the seventeenth-century writers on natural law (discussed in Chapter 4), notably Hugo Grotius, Thomas Hobbes, Samuel Pufendorf and John Locke, who seized upon the concept of a state of nature to distinguish levels of historical progress, and in the process refined many of the assumptions that had been used by colonial promoters early in the century (Grotius had worked for a trading company, Hobbes attended numerous meetings of the Virginia Company, and Locke held the early colonial tracts on his bookshelves while at the same time being deeply involved in the colonisation of Carolina). Grotius and Hobbes were both trained in the Renaissance humanist tradition, but they sought to develop

65 Pagden, *Lords of all the world*, pp. 64–6.

66 On English appeals to conquest, see Fitzmaurice, *Humanism and America*, pp. 146–8; Ken MacMillan, *Sovereignty and possession in the English New World: the legal foundations of empire, 1570–1640* (Cambridge, 2006); Ken MacMillan, *The Atlantic imperial constitution: center and periphery in the English Atlantic world* (New York, 2011), pp. 15–16; Anthony Pagden, 'Law, colonization, legitimation, and the European background', in Michael Grossberg and Christopher Tomlins (eds.), *The Cambridge history of law in America. Volume 1 Early America (1580–1815)* (Cambridge, 2008), pp. 5–14.

a theory of natural rights that would avoid (or, for Grotius, extend) medieval assumptions of sociability which, during the wars of religion, no longer provided a persuasive account of human action. They took the late-humanist concern with self-preservation, which was more in tune with the violence of the times, and presented it as the foundation of rights. Seventeenth-century natural law theorists built their arguments from these assumptions, and when they came to account for property, with the exception of Hobbes, they turned to the theory of occupation, not only as a stage in history but also as an act of survival.

These philosophers and historians argued that property was first created in nature through occupation. Many of the seventeenth-century natural law writers were sceptical of the metaphysical assumptions that underpinned Roman and medieval writings on natural law. When Grotius, Hobbes and Pufendorf came to the question of the origin of property, they challenged the notion that merely because somebody takes something it becomes hers or his. Such acts could be described as theft from what is common to all people. The origin of property, they argued, was not in nature but in agreements. According to this theory, property first came into existence because groups of people, seeking self-preservation, agreed between themselves upon rules that would determine its nature. Thus, property was created by the consent of a group of people. In order to protect that property, and their lives, these peoples then moved up another step through history by creating civil societies. The form of these societies was something that they also would agree upon. Civil society created its own rules governing property, but, again with the exception of Hobbes, these authors agreed that one of the laws that all civil societies adopted was *occupatio* – civil society recognised the importance of occupation to survival. By contrast, for Locke, occupation and property preceded the agreements which for Grotius and Pufendorf led to civil society.

Many historians have represented Locke's understanding of property and labour as the dominant justification for colonisation in America, as well as the foundation for the ideology that drove the American Revolution.[67] In Chris Tomlins' recent account, the value placed upon work and labour led the English, ironically, to elevate 'land over people as the

[67] For Locke and American colonisation, see: Arneil, *John Locke and America*; Tully, *An approach to political philosophy*; and most recently Christopher Tomlins, *Freedom bound: law, labor and civic identity in colonizing English America, 1580–1865* (Cambridge, 2010). For the liberal and Lockean interpretation of the American Revolution, see: Joyce Appleby, *Liberalism and republicanism in the historical imagination* (Cambridge, MA, 1992); Thomas Pangle, *The spirit of modern republicanism: the moral vision of the American founders and the philosophy of Locke* (Chicago, 1988); Steven

primary objective of the colonizers' attention', which in turn meant that, unlike the Spanish, they sought to exterminate or ignore the indigenous population rather than to exploit them.[68] This understanding of colonisation, which placed so much emphasis upon land and labour, was a 'peculiarity of the English'. As I argue in Chapters 5 and 6, there are a number of problems with these accounts which emphasise the exceptional, and Lockean, nature of English and later British North American colonisation. First, occupation was certainly the dominant justification for English colonisation in the seventeenth and eighteenth centuries, but occupation was not understood only in terms of labour. In many accounts, occupation was achieved through compacts, conventions or contracts. The compact theory of property found numerous English adherents, including Thomas Hobbes amongst philosophers (although he ignored the question of occupation). Similarly, for example, amongst American colonists, John Bulkley has been represented to be a Lockean, but on closer examination he proves more complex, drawing upon both Lockean and compact theories of occupation. Second, many non-English authors used the idea of occupation to explain property and gave similar emphasis to labour and land. The French Huguenot Jean Barbeyrac and the German Gottlieb Gerhard Titius, for example, were both enthusiasts for Locke's understanding of property, which they represented in terms of the law of occupation. Finally, these accounts of the Lockean nature of English colonisation do not give space to the use of occupation, and even Lockean arguments, to oppose colonisation or, if not to oppose, to acknowledge native rights. As we shall see, one such example, albeit disingenuous, was the claims made by the Suffering Traders.

Occupation was therefore represented as the means by which people first moved away from a state of nature and it was argued to be the foundation of property in all civil societies. Because occupation was also understood to be a means of self-preservation for both individuals and states, it provided a powerful rationalisation for the outward expansion of early modern states. But the contract-based understanding of what constituted a legitimate society and property could pose problems for the justification of European empires because, according to these terms, it

Dworetz, *The unvarnished doctrine: Locke, liberalism and the American Revolution* (Durham, NC, 1990). For scepticism of the influence of Locke, see: Bernard Bailyn, *The ideological origins of the American Revolution* (Cambridge, MA, 1967); John Dunn, 'The politics of John Locke in England and America in the eighteenth century', in John Yolton (ed.), *John Locke: Problems and perspectives* (Cambridge, 1969).

[68] Tomlins, *Freedom bound*, p. 133.

would be very difficult to represent the property and the political relations of any non-European peoples as illegitimate, or non-existent, if these people were able to determine their own terms of legitimacy. This relativism would be important in nineteenth-century scepticism of empire and the civilising mission.

Throughout the eighteenth century, philosophers such as Jean Barbeyrac and Gershom Carmichael remained attached to the idea that the right of property arises directly from the occupation, or exploitation, of nature, commonly expressed through the Lockean theory of labour. The rival theory that property arises from compacts also found numerous adherents. In both these accounts of property, however, occupation was understood not only to give rise to a right but also to distinguish a stage of historical evolution driven by the need for self-preservation. This notion of history as progress from a pre-civil state to hunter-gatherers and then to agricultural society found its greatest refinement in the writers of the Scottish historical school, particularly in the work of David Hume and Adam Smith. The Scottish philosophers turned away from the natural law explanation of rights, but nevertheless maintained the idea of occupation as part of an historical explanation of the evolution of property. At the same time, these authors added another stage to historical progress: namely, commercial society. They argued against the expansion of trade through war and condemned the extension of territorial empires through the occupation of property.

From 1763, following the Seven Years' War, there was a further change in the use of occupation to understand colonisation. At this time, European philosophers began to distance themselves from the justifications of the appropriation of other nations' property through the idea of occupation, which they saw as a barely concealed form of conquest. But American colonists remained strongly attached to the argument of occupation, both for the rights in nature they believed it conferred and for the superiority of agricultural society that they believed it underpinned. Complementing scepticism of landed empire, the British Crown claimed to exercise sovereignty west of the Appalachian Mountains, but forbade further settlement there and even withdrew from a number of western forts. The colonists employed the theory of occupation not only to defend their dispossession of Native Americans but also to resist the claims of the Crown. The law of occupation thus facilitated the development of a new political claim which would ultimately underpin the revolutionary struggle. Previously, occupation had been used both to defend and to attack the idea that indigenous Americans held rights. It had been used either to justify the colonising power or to critique it. For the first time, it was now being used *simultaneously* to deny that indigenous people possessed rights and to critique the imperial state, and was thus able to prise open a new political space.

Central to this new political claim was an issue that runs through the history of occupation and, indeed, through the history of Western political thought: namely, the question of whether property rights, and other rights, can be established outside the state or only as a creation of the state.[69] In the writing of the seventeenth-century natural lawyers, the colonists found the justification for their claim that property could be established outside sovereignty and, indeed, that sovereignty was created to protect those rights. This debate was conducted through the course of the eighteenth century and nowhere more dramatically than in North America. While the British Crown insisted that all rights came from the state, the American revolutionaries argued that they had established property rights independent of the Crown. Here was the purest kind of unfettered possessive individualism that political theorists have both lauded and derided: namely, an occupation-based theory of property that requires no mediation by the state. But such an understanding of possession was only a small part of a much more complex whole (and, as we shall see, not all eighteenth-century American land speculators held such views).

In the aftermath of the American Revolution, sovereignty increasingly dominated the discussion of occupation and property. Ironically, albeit unsurprisingly, the newly established American republic was quick to claim that rights of occupation could only be established by sovereign powers. In this instance, the debate was over the contested north Pacific coast of the continent, otherwise known as the Oregon Territory. The obverse of the question of whether the property of individuals could exist without sovereignty was whether individuals acting without the support of any nation could establish sovereignty. Jeffersonians appealed to the right of occupation for westward-moving citizens of the United States who, with that right, could establish their own property on the west coast and establish new republics, which might or might not join the United States. But the Jeffersonians were defeated in Congress by proponents of the Monroe Doctrine, who rejected the Lockean arguments that the revolutionaries had employed. In rejecting Locke, they agreed with Emer de Vattel, the Swiss authority on the law of nations, that only nations have

[69] Habermas, *Between facts and norms*, Chapter 3.

rights of occupation and that the United States and not independent citizens had the strongest claim to the new territories.

In Chapters 7, 8 and 9, I show that the notion that sovereignty could be the object of occupation reached its peak in the second half of the nineteenth century. At this time, politicians, diplomats and jurists were attempting to establish conventions of occupation in the law of nations that would remove disputes and confusions. These attempts surrounded the Berlin Conference, a meeting (illustrated on the cover of this book) of the major powers in 1884/5 addressing tensions arising from the carve-up of Africa. According to the conventions agreed at the Berlin Conference, occupation could only be pursued by sovereign powers and must be 'effective'. Jurists celebrated the Berlin agreement for having established occupation in the positive law of nations after centuries as a code of normative natural law.[70] The Conference and the subsequent meetings of jurists also established a new understanding of occupation: namely, one which could take territorial sovereignty rather than property as its object. The powers agreed that a people who exercised sovereign rights could nevertheless be occupied if the sovereignty they possessed was personal rather than territorial, although they stipulated that the property and other rights of these peoples must at the same time be respected. Thus, the Conference accommodated Enlightenment critiques of the early modern continental empires while establishing the rules for commercial empires. Such an understanding of occupation was indispensable to the extension of empire in a densely populated continent such as Africa. These conventions gave birth to a new concept regarding the occupation of territory in international law: namely, the concept of *territorium nullius* (the subject of Chapter 9).[71]

The great irony, indeed the hypocrisy, of the agreements made at the Berlin Conference is that they were accompanied by the granting of rights to a private association to establish a state. This was the *Association Internationale du Congo*, a single-shareholder company, a private individual in the eyes of international law, not a sovereign power. The granting to the

70 By contrast, Wilhelm Grewe regarded the conference as a failure because of the weakness of its resolutions: Wilhelm G. Grewe, *The epochs of international law*, trans. Michael Byers (Berlin, 2000), pp. 547–8.

71 While Carl Schmitt lamented that the Berlin Conference inaugurated the decline of the European international legal and spatial order and the beginning of American informal empire, it would be more accurate to say that it recognised practices of extraterritoriality and informal empire that Europeans and Americans had employed in China, Africa and the Levant since at least the 1830s: Schmitt, *Nomos of the earth*, pp. 219–27.

Association Internationale du Congo of sovereignty over the Congo directly contradicted, as a number of critics protested, the simultaneous attempt to define individuals out of the international system. This irony was all the greater when some of those people who had worked to establish principles restricting international law to the club of sovereign powers joined the campaign for recognition of the Congo Free State.

Even as Enlightenment critiques of empire were worked into a new understanding of 'informal' or commercial expansion, late nineteenth-century jurists developed new critiques of empires based upon an attack on the rhetoric of civilisation. These critiques also drew upon Enlightenment discourses, particularly philosophers such as Immanuel Kant. Underlying the critiques was not humanitarian sentiment (which had a long history as an imperial conscience and thus as a form of apology for empire), but a fear of the possible disastrous consequences that cultural chauvinism could have for conflict amongst the diverse nations of Europe.

In Chapter 10, I show that in the late nineteenth and early twentieth centuries, imperial powers turned their attention to the Poles, the only remaining parts of the globe untouched by European empires. In these harsh climates, however, the theory of occupation faced new challenges. How could sovereignty or property be established through occupation in regions where habitation was precarious or, as in the case of the Antarctic, impossible? Initially, it was agreed that such areas should be respected as a *terra nullius*: that is, as areas that were uninhabited, void of sovereignty and property, and would remain so, closed to occupation and open only to scientific exploration. In the 1920s and 1930s, the discussion of *terra nullius* continued to focus on the Poles, although nationalist competition between Scandinavian powers over Spitsbergen and Greenland led to a new understanding of the concept: namely, as land void of sovereignty and property but *open* to sovereign claims, albeit with diminished expectations of effective occupation.

In the 1930s, members of the Joint Seminar in International Law at Columbia University, who had been following the East Greenland debate, picked up the concept of *terra nullius* and considered whether it could be used as shorthand for occupation, and sometimes even for conquest. This broadened meaning of the term was subsequently adopted in treatises of international law after the Second World War during the period of decolonisation. Over centuries, European empires had provoked debate over the rights of non-Europeans that encouraged the development of complex and nuanced understandings of the occupation of territory, reaching their peak in the nineteenth century. With the decline of these empires, the debates over the appropriation of territory also diminished. The new hegemonic powers, the United States and the Soviet Union, did not care to describe themselves as empires, particularly given that defeat of empire was central to their foundation stories.[72] They accordingly shunned the language, the legal and political taxonomy, of empire, including the complex understandings of the acquisition of sovereignty and property developed over previous centuries. If, as John Seeley famously stated, the British Empire had been acquired in a fit of absence of mind, the new informal empires, if they were empires, were acquired in a state of complete denial.[73] The two cases may be closer than it seems. Seeley was referring to an inability to adapt the imagination to a new reality, and the same could be said of the so-called American empire.[74] There was, however, at least one important exception to the silence on such questions: namely, in the debate over property and sovereignty in outer space in the context of the Space Race between the Soviets and the United States from the 1950s. Apart from this exception, the great complexity of the justifications for European empire that were evident in the late nineteenth century were often reduced in the second half of the twentieth century to a generalised historical claim that non-European lands that had not achieved self-determination had simply been *terra nullius*. Moreover, the history of the occupation of those lands was read retrospectively with that concept. In the 1970s and 1980s, the term *terra nullius* was taken up by scholars internationally and used to describe both the law of occupation and its history.

While use of the concept of *terra nullius* to discuss European expansion is relatively recent, the history of the idea of occupation is far richer and played a more significant role in empire than discussions of *terra nullius* have allowed.[75] Indeed, the notion of a coherent and enduring doctrine of *terra nullius* has disguised the complex history of occupation and its constantly changing significance. Just as the concept *terra nullius* (a kind of Lovejoyian unit-idea in the hands of many historians and political scientists) collapsed the great diversity of arguments concerning occupation into one doctrine, it also gave that doctrine one polemical direction: namely, as a justification of colonisation and empire. This understanding of *terra nullius* ignored the long history whereby occupation was employed

72 Maier, *Among empires*; and on the Soviet Union as an anti-imperial empire, see Burbank and Cooper, *Empires in world history*, pp. 393–5.

73 John Robert Seeley, *The expansion of England* (London, 1883), p. 8.

74 On Seeley and the imagination, see Armitage, *Ideological origins of the British Empire*, p. 16.

75 For a survey of the literature on *terra nullius*, see Chapter 10.

to oppose or to critique empire. It also elided the evolution of occupation from a legal to an economic concept used to explain the development of agricultural society, and subsequently its use to justify commercial empire. Even instances of serious doubts about the justice of empire could be reinterpreted as elaborate apologies for empire. Indeed, *terra nullius* became proof of the disposition of Western political thought to empire. Historically, no such doctrine known as '*terra nullius*' was employed to discuss empire prior to the late nineteenth century and even '*res nullius*' was a creation of medieval and early modern civil law. The concept of *terra nullius* reflects a particular chapter in the history of European occupation: namely, the 'post-colonial' period, a period in which debate over the rights of colonised peoples came to a virtual halt either because their domination was complete or because they had achieved self-determination. *Terra nullius* was the antithesis of self-determination and may in some ways be seen as the price of self-determination. While the legal status of non-European societies had been a matter of debate in Europe for centuries, by the mid-twentieth century, the debate was largely over. Those societies that had gained self-determination no longer endured serious debate over the legitimacy of their sovereign claims (even if they were subject to continuing forms of economic and political hegemony). And those societies that were swallowed up by the settler societies also had their claims to property and sovereignty almost entirely buried by the doctrine of *terra nullius*.

Over the past ten years, social scientists and historians have demanded greater sensitivity to the history of ideological justifications of empire. Their motives have been twofold. First, they recognise that the rights of indigenous peoples in settler societies have not been extinguished, despite sustained efforts to that end. Second, many commentators have argued that we live in a time of a new imperialism.[76] For both of these reasons, occupation – whether as settlement or as 'informal empire' through the control of sovereignty – is an argument of imperial and colonial justification that remains very much alive. It is central to the history of empire, but

[76] Calhoun, Cooper and Moore (eds.), *Lessons of empire*. For the claim that empire is a necessity of power, see Niall Ferguson, *Empire: the rise and demise of the British world order and the lesssons for global power* (New York, 2003); Michael Ignatieff, *Empire lite: nation building in Bosnia, Kosovo, Afghanistan* (London, 2003). Not all historians are convinced that 'empire' is the appropriate term for the twentieth-century projection of power beyond the state; see, for example, Frederick Cooper, 'Empire multiplied: a review essay', *Comparative Studies in Society and History*, 46(2) (2004), 247–72. For a contrasting view, see Jennifer Pitts, 'Political theory of empire and imperialism', *Annual Review of Political Science*, 13 (2010), 211–35.

this history continues to be played in the present, for example, in the rights claims of indigenous peoples and in continuing instances of settlement, such as in the Palestinian West Bank and Indonesian West Papua. Even the current 'Occupy' movement could be understood in this context. The movement presents the idea of re-taking what it claims are public goods, things that belong to everybody, as a response to the excesses of global capitalism. This also means occupying space within public debate, particularly through the use of social media in the virtual world of the internet. The 'Occupy' movement may not seem to be a response to empire, but it is consistent with the history of the idea of occupation as critique: namely, the use of the idea of something being already taken as a rejection of the claims of a hegemonic power.[77]

Understanding the history of occupation is therefore central to the politics of empire and hegemony in the present. Rather than continuing in a state of imperial denial, the politics of empire today can be illuminated by paying closer attention to the legal and political vocabularies of the past. This book attempts to bring back to our consciousness some of the concepts that animated past empires and, through their distinctions and debates, attempts to better understand the present. However, it is essential to learn from this history that, as much as justifying empire, the history of occupation offers a complex tradition whereby we might be sceptical of occupying other peoples' property or sovereignty. This book describes those alternatives.

[77] See Jo Guldi, 'What is being occupied?', http://landscape.blogspot.com.au/2011/10/what-is-being-occupied.html.

CHAPTER 2

Occupation from Roman law to Salamanca

Occupation in Roman law

In Roman law what belonged to nobody became the property of the first person to take it. Most discussions of *occupatio* in Roman law claimed that this rule was founded on the law of nature and would apply even where no positive law prevailed. When Roman law was revived in Europe in the eleventh and twelfth centuries, *occupatio* was recovered as a principle of positive law, but a tension remained over whether it was only a human convention or whether it would hold in nature in any case. The salient view by the late medieval period was not only that *occupatio* was a law of nature but that it also explained the origin of property. It was frequently, although not unanimously, accepted that occupation could lead to the creation of property outside the bounds of sovereignty and law. One consequence of such an argument was that occupation could give rise to rights which lay outside the *imperium* of the Holy Roman Empire. Accordingly, the first medieval discussions of occupation can be placed in the context of critiques of *imperium* rather than apologies for it.

It is a matter of continuing debate whether the Romans had a concept of natural right as well as natural law.[1] For the Romans, a *ius* was a law or what was just. Whether they believed a *ius* gave a person a right in something is unclear. For medieval jurists and theologians, *ius* could

[1] The question of whether Romans had a concept of subjective, or individual, right is controversial. In a highly influential account, the French neo-Thomist Michel Villey attacked the idea and argued that William of Ockham first developed the theory of subjective rights in the fourteenth century. See: Michel Villey, *Leçon d'histoire de la philosophie du droit* (Paris, 1957); Michel Villey, *Seize essais de philosophie du droit* (Paris, 1969); Michel Villey, *Critique de la pensée juridique moderne* (Paris, 1969). In a critique of Villey's arguments, Tierney, *The idea of natural rights*, pp. 13–42 shows that canon lawyers of the late twelfth century employed the idea of individual rights. For the argument that the Romans did have a notion of subjective right, see: G Pugliese, '"Res corporals", "res incorporales" e il problema del diritto soggetivo', in *Studi in onore di Vincenzo Arangio-Ruiz* (Naples, 1954), vol. 3, 223–60; Charles Donahue, '*Ius* in the subjective sense', in D. Maffei (ed.), *A Ennio Cortese* (Rome, 2001), vol. 1, pp. 506–35; Benjamin Straumann, *Hugo Grotius und die Antike* (Baden-Baden, 2007).

signify either what was just or a right in something, what we call a subjective or individual right. When medieval authors spoke of a *ius* of occupation, they were speaking of a right to property that arose from occupation. This sense of *ius* would have a crucial impact on discussions of occupation for the next 800 years. In particular, it disposed discussions of occupation as much to a defence of the rights of those who held property – that is, to a right *in* property – as it did to an argument that a particular person or state could have a right *to* occupy. In other words, occupation could be used to make two different kinds of claim, one of which was that it was possible to do something and the other of which was a claim to a property right. The distinction is important. Occupation as a right to *do* something was central to justifications of European expansion while occupation as a right *in* something was central to the defence of peoples subject to European expansion. We shall see that both Innocent IV and Francisco de Vitoria were amongst the first of many Europeans to use the second kind of claim, to a right in property, in relation to non-European peoples.

The *Digest of Justinian* and the *Institutes* provided the most influential Roman law discussions of occupation. Both the *Digest* and the *Institutes* were compiled between the years 530 and 533, during the reign of the Emperor Justinian. The *Digest* was a codification of the writings of eminent jurists from Imperial and Republican Rome, while the *Institutes*, based upon the writings of the mysterious second-century jurist Gaius, was intended as a first book for students of the law.[2] According to the *Institutes*:

> things become the property of individuals in many ways: for of some things ownership arises by natural law which, as we have said is called the law of nations [*ius gentium*], and of others at civil law. It is more convenient to start with the older law and, obviously, the older law is natural law which the nature of things introduced with humankind itself ... Hence, wild animals, birds and fish, i.e. all animals born on land or in the sea or air, as soon as they are caught by anyone, forthwith fall into his ownership by the law of nations [*ius gentium*]: for what previously belonged to no one is, by natural reason, accorded to its captor [*quod enim ante nullius est id naturali ratione occupanti conceditur*].[3]

Similarly, in the *Digest* we read that 'what presently belongs to no one becomes by natural reason the property of the first taker [*Quod enim*

[2] William Warwick Buckland, *A text-book of Roman law from Augustus to Justinian* (Cambridge, 1921), pp. 41–6.

[3] Thomas (ed.), *The institutes of Justinian*, bk. II, i, 11–12.

nullius est, id ratione naturali occupanti conceditur]'.[4] There were a number of instances in Roman law in which the absence of ownership was discussed in terms of the principle of occupation, including the division of things in law, sacred things, islands that arise in the sea, an inheritance without an heir and treasure troves.[5] Some of these things had no owner because they had not been occupied, for example, treasure troves and islands that arise in the sea. Others, such as sacred things, had no owner because they could not be occupied. This distinction between what could and what could not be occupied endured in discussions of property through to the present day.

In his classic account of Roman law, William Buckland observed that *occupatio* was 'not in practice of great significance' in Rome and that its chief application was to wild animals.[6] This law, which was drawn from the *ius gentium*, was not often used to discuss land, as would be the case in the sixteenth century, and it was restricted to private law and not to matters of state, as would also later be the case.[7] Having said that, the distinction between land and movable goods was not as important in Roman law as it would be in modern European law.[8] Nevertheless, the legal principles upon which *occupatio* was based were reflected more broadly in Roman culture and are well known, for example, from the writings of Cicero, the late Republican Roman orator and statesman. Cicero's discussions of property were partly influenced by Stoic philosophers, whom he acknowledged, but they also expressed, as Peter Garnsey has argued, a Roman aristocratic defence of private property.[9] In his principal work of moral philosophy, *On duties*, Cicero argued that in nature, property was common and that it became private only 'by long occupation (as when men moved into some empty property in the past), or by victory (when they acquired it by war), or by law, settlement, by

[4] Theodor Mommsen (ed.), *Digest of Justinian* (Philadelphia, 1985), vol. 4, 487a. See also: *Gai Institutiones or Institutes of Roman Law by Gaius*, with a translation and commentary by Edward Poste, 4th edn, revised and enlarged by E. A. Whittuck, with an historical introduction by A. H. J. Greenidge (Oxford, 1904), 2.66: 'things that we get by first taking and which become ours because previously they belonged to no one' (*quia antea nullius essent*).

[5] For the division of things, see: Dig. 1.8.2; Inst. 2.1; Dig. 1.8.1; Gai. 2.9; Gai. 2.11; Dig. 41.1.14. For sacred things, see: Dig. 1.8.1; Dig. 1.8.6.2; Inst. 2.1.7; Gai. 2.9. For islands that arise in the sea, see: Inst. 2.1.22; Dig. 41.1.30.4. For an inheritance without an heir, see: Dig. 1.8.1; Gai. 2.9; Gai. 2.200; Dig. 43.24.13.5; Dig. 47.19.6. For treasure troves, see: Dig. 41.1.31.1.

[6] Buckland, *A text-book of Roman law*, p. 207.

[7] On Roman law as a source for the law of nations, see Lauterpacht, *Private law sources and analogies in international law*; and Lesaffer, 'Argument from Roman law in current international law'.

[8] Buckland, *A text-book of Roman law*, p. 188.

[9] Peter Garnsey, *Thinking about property* (Cambridge, 2007), p. 113.

agreement, or by lot'.[10] Whereas the Roman law discussions of *occupatio* were mainly concerned with examples such as wild animals and treasures, Cicero showed that Romans also thought of these principles in relation to land or a place into which one could move. He did not specify whether occupation could only create property within a civil state, although his statement that law was a separate means with which to create property suggests that he at least thought of *occupatio* as a natural law. In *On ends*, Cicero cited the Stoic Chrysippus to argue that sociability was natural, but this principle did not mean that all property must be socialised. In what would later be a widely quoted passage, he argued that property was something removed from the common, as for example: 'though a theatre (for instance) is a shared amenity, it can still be right to say that a seat in it belongs to the man who takes it: by the same token, the system is not against a man having things of his own within the community of a state, or of the world at large'.[11] Again, the fact that these principles were held in the world at large indicated that they were true in natural law as well as civil law.

Occupation in medieval civil and canon law

After centuries of decline, Roman law was vigorously revived in the eleventh and twelfth centuries by medieval civil lawyers who sought a legal system to govern the increasingly complex relations, including property relations, of medieval society. The canon lawyers of the medieval Church also revived Roman law. The Church was a new kind of institution in that it was 'designed (at least in part) for charitable purposes'.[12] Accordingly, the Church's canon lawyers used Roman law to explore the kinds and extent of claims, including claims upon property, that could be made by people in need, particularly the poor. Moreover, medieval society, as Brian Tierney has argued, was 'saturated with a concern for rights': 'Medieval people first struggled for survival; then they struggled for rights.'[13] These rights-claims included the claims of emperors against popes, popes against emperors, and bishops and barons against kings, right down to peasants against feudal lords, including peasants who were emigrating to lands in the 'still vast' wastelands of medieval Europe beyond, as they argued, the claims of the feudal lords.[14] They understood these claims not only as

[10] Cicero, *On duties*, ed. M. T. Griffin and E. M. Atkins (Cambridge, 1991), 1.21.
[11] Cicero, *On ends*, trans. H. Rackham (Cambridge, MA, 1914), 3.67. See also Garnsey, *Thinking about property*, p. 116.
[12] Tuck, *Natural rights theories*, p. 15. [13] Tierney, *The idea of natural rights*, pp. 54–5. [14] *Ibid.*

matters of what is just or right but as rights in things, *ius in rem*, both corporeal (such as land) and incorporeal, such as the right of communication. Following these concerns, the civil lawyers, known as Glossators, and canon lawyers, known as Decretists, turned to occupation as an explanation for the origin of property. The Roman law discussions of occupation provided them with one of the most common examples of a subjective right.[15]

The Glossators of the eleventh and twelfth centuries who revived civil law accepted the sovereignty of the Holy Roman Empire as a given.[16] They believed there to be only one undivided sovereign order descended from the Romans for which they were recovering the system of law. Their principal task was to use their commentaries, or glosses, to remove contradictions in the various texts of Roman law that they inherited. Amongst the Glossators, Azo of Bologna (*c.* 1150–*c.* 1230) provided an influential discussion of occupation that summarised the main topics treated in the *Institutes*. In his chapter 'Concerning the division of things and acquisition' in Book 2 of his *Summa Perutilis*, Azo observed:

> it is said that thing which belongs to no one goes to the one occupying. To which I respond that things are said to belong to no one in very many ways: by nature, for example wild animals, birds and fishes, in these cases the law has a place. By opinion things can belong to nobody, for instance, sacred and religious and sanctified things, which are not in the goods of a private individual. Similarly things that belong to everyone or public things, and those things that are amongst the goods of God. And in some cases . . . things are even said to belong to no one by accident: as for instance things inherited from a dead man before the inheritance has been submitted to a referee.[17]

In the fourteenth century, the post-Glossators, including Bartolus of Saxoferrato, questioned the sovereignty of the Holy Roman Empire over the city-states of Italy and thus challenged the unquestioning acceptance of the Glossators. The post-Glossators seized upon a distinction that some of their predecessors had used between *dominium directum* and *dominium utile*.[18] *Dominium directum* was 'true property'. *Dominium utile* was the right that comes from the use of property that belongs to another, or

[15] *Ibid.*, pp. 142–3. [16] See Skinner, *The foundations of modern political thought*, vol. 1, pp. 8–9.

[17] Azo, *Summa super Codice et Institutis* (Speyer, 1482), leaf 12; This wording agrees with Azo, *Summa Azonis* (Lyon, 1530), bk. 2, fol. cclxxiii, verso.

[18] There is a continuing debate amongst historians about when the distinction between *dominium directum* and *dominium utile* was made. See Tuck, *Natural rights theories*, pp. 13–17; Garnsey, *Thinking about property*, p. 200; Brett, *Liberty, right and nature*, pp. 20–2.

usufruct. For the post-Glossators such as Bartolus, this distinction allowed them to point out that the city-states had *de facto* independence even if, *de jure*, the emperor was sole ruler of the world.[19] They questioned law that was not consistent with facts, but they nevertheless held to the view of Roman law as the basis of law – they only rejected those principles that were not consistent with the multiplication of sovereignty, and occupation was not one of these. On the contrary, the law of occupation furthered their argument that rights could arise from outside the legitimate *de jure* basis of sovereignty. There is some debate about whether the Glossators and post-Glossators perceived the holder of *dominium directum* or *dominium utile* as possessing the stronger *dominium* in the case of a dispute, but the outcome of that debate does not affect the question here: namely, that occupation was used to split the sense of undivided *dominium.*[20] In its very first revival in medieval civil law, therefore, the idea of occupation was employed not in order to extend *imperium* – the *imperium* of the Holy Roman Empire – but to question it. This is not to argue that the post-Glossators used occupation to conceive of sovereign status as something like the modern state system – a system of discrete sovereigns side by side in an international community. Rather, their sense that sovereignty could be divided referred to a cascading of *dominium* or of different persons being able to claim rights of *dominium* over the same thing. They articulated a fundamentally feudal conception of *dominium* and their idea of occupation arose from that context.

The tensions between customary and natural law explanations for the origin of property were evident in the medieval canonists' attempts to harmonise the numerous and contradictory principles of law they inherited from previous generations of the Church. Gratian, a twelfth-century Bolognese canon lawyer, led this effort. The title for his *Decretum* (*c.* 1140), *A concord of discordant canons*, revealed the nature of the enterprise.[21] Gratian argued that the origin of property was in human law, but he added that any human law that was inconsistent with the laws of nature was invalid. For Rufinus, writing in around 1160, property was created through human agreement, but prior to a political state.[22] Late in the twelfth century, Huggucio, or Hugh of Pisa, who studied in Bologna, wrote a commentary on Gratian's *Decretum* and resolved the tensions

[19] Skinner, *Foundations of modern political thought*, vol. 1, p. 9.
[20] For this debate, see Brett, *Liberty, right and nature*, pp. 20–2.
[21] Tierney, *The idea of natural rights*, p. 138. [22] *Ibid.*, p. 139 and, on Rufinus, p. 62.

using what Brian Tierney describes as the most commonly recurring argument.[23] Huggucio argued that property could exist only by virtue of natural law, and therefore outside human law, but pointed out that human law gave the natural law principles of property their full expression and that it explained the different modes of possession.[24] Similarly, the 'great jurist-pope', Innocent IV, argued that property was a 'right by the natural law of reason' and that civil law only provided the means by which property claims were pursued in court.[25] In a discussion that would later be influential in the sixteenth century, he argued that this right could be exercised by all peoples, including infidels. Innocent thus helped establish occupation as a claim not only to do something, to take something that belonged to nobody, but also a claim in something, a right in property already held.

The views of the Decretists and Glossators on property were supplemented by medieval theologians, notably Thomas Aquinas (1225–74). Aquinas did not cite the Roman law of occupation to speculate on the origin of property, although he did when discussing treasure troves.[26] He presented property as the creation of the exercise of natural reason.[27] Humans had a natural domain and created property by employing their reason in releasing the potential in nature: 'man has a natural dominion over external things because, by means of his reason and will, he is able to make use of external things to his own advantage'.[28] Crucially for the discussions of property in the School of Salamanca to which we are about to turn, Aquinas' discussion of purposeful action that led to the creation of property was a justification of the creation of individual rather than common property. He argued that 'human affairs are conducted in a more orderly manner if each man is responsible for the care of something which is his own' and he agreed with Aristotle that we are more diligent in our labours when we work to our own individual benefit rather than the common good.[29]

[23] *Ibid.*, p. 141. [24] *Ibid.*, p. 143. [25] *Ibid.*

[26] *Ibid.*, p. 146. For Aquinas on treasure troves in the *Summa theologiae*, see Thomas Aquinas, *Political writings* ed. and trans. R. W. Dyson (Cambridge, 2002), p. 213: 'With regard to things found, there is a distinction to be made. For some things were never anyone's property, such as the stones and gems found on the seashore; and one who finds such things may keep them. The same applies to treasure buried in the ground long ago, of which no one is the owner; except that, if he finds it on the land of another, the finder is bound by civil law to give half of it to the owner of the land.'

[27] Aquinas, *Political writings*, pp. 205–6: 'Whether it is natural for man to possess external things'; and pp. 207–9: 'Whether it is lawful for anyone to possess something as his own.'

[28] *Ibid.*, p. 206. [29] *Ibid.*, p. 208; Koskenniemi, 'Empire and international law', 17.

The School of Salamanca

While occupation had been a legal and political concern for medieval jurists and theologians, in the sixteenth century it also became simultaneously tied to economic questions and to the justice of overseas conquests. More than 200 years after Aquinas wrote the *Summa Theologiae*, the idea of private property was transforming Europe and its developing relations with the rest of the world. The gold and silver from the Spanish conquests in the Americas stimulated commerce in Europe and beyond, while also stimulating banking and the development of large trading corporations. For the first time, a world economy was being brought into existence. At the heart of this system was a state monopoly in Seville that controlled the flow of bullion across the Atlantic. This vast new wealth did not sit easily with Christian scepticism of riches or with the Renaissance humanist tradition, which saw wealth as a corroding influence upon civic virtue. In part due to such anxieties, a number of Spanish theologians and jurists, mainly associated with the university in Salamanca, began to debate the legitimacy of the new world order: notably, Francisco de Vitoria and his students Domingo de Soto, Melchior Cano and a later generation that included Diego de Covarrubias y Leyva and the humanist jurist Fernando Vázquez de Menchaca. The Salamanca theologians and jurists were concerned not merely with the conquests in the Americas, but with far broader questions touching the new world economy, including the legitimacy of usury, interest, property and war. They placed their discussions of occupation in the Americas in that context. Vitoria wrote a treatise on just war and he also accepted a partly market-based theory of a just price as something set by circumstances of time and place.[30] Soto, along with the Salamanca jurist Martín de Azpilcueta and, later, the Jesuit Luis de Molina, developed a theory of interest diminishing the idea that 'usury' is a bad thing by explaining that money has value over time and therefore justifying differentials between money lent and owed. The Salamanca theologians agreed with Aquinas that private property was created as a consequence of purposeful activity and, as Covarrubias argued, all people had a right not only to their property but also to benefit from their property.

At the same time, these theologians and jurists were deeply engaged in the debates arising from the Reformation – Soto, Covarrubias and Vázquez de Menchaca were representatives at the Council of Trent (Soto in 1545,

[30] On Vitoria and just-price, see Koskenniemi, 'Empire and international law', 20–1.

Covarrubias between 1562 and 1564, and Vázquez in 1561). The Council worked to establish the grounds of religious orthodoxy in the face of reform. In particular, it opposed the Protestant doctrine of justification by faith alone (known as 'external' justification and minimising the offices of a church) with the Thomist doctrine of faith *and* intrinsic justification whereby we are justified in the eyes of God when our sins are washed away (implying, amongst other things, confession, a priest and a church). The legal context for these issues was the ongoing Inquisition into religious orthodoxy. One concern of the Inquisition was the heretical, and Protestant, argument that the only just society is a godly society, a claim that was rumoured to have been used by some Conquistadors to justify possessions in the New World.[31] The rising concerns not only about the justice of the American conquests but also about the kinds of arguments used to justify those conquests led to the famous debate between Bartolomé de Las Casas and Juan Ginés de Sepúlveda, over which Soto sat as judge.[32] In this debate, in which the participants were never in the same room at the same time, Sepúlveda argued that Native Americans were natural slaves and as such possessed no rights, while Las Casas argued that they possessed both private and public dominion.

The Salamancans' understanding of dominion and right was central to the debate over the justice of the conquest of the New World, and Vitoria is key to that understanding. According to Vitoria, in his lectures on Aquinas' *Summa*, rights could both be objective, in the sense of something being just, or subjective in the sense of a person having a power over something.[33] A right, he argued, was distinguishable from dominion, albeit that some authors, such as the Tübingen theologian Conrad Summenhart writing shortly before Vitoria, treated them as equivalent.[34] For Vitoria, as for Soto, dominion held the two senses to be found in Roman law: that is, as a kind of superiority (or *dominium jurisdictionis*), as for a ruler over her or his subjects, and as the ownership of property (or *dominium rerum*).[35]

[31] Pagden, *The fall of natural man*, p. 67. [32] Lupher, *Romans in a new world*, pp. 103–49.

[33] In distinguishing objective and subjective rights, Vitoria departed from Aquinas. Daniel Deckers argues that Vitoria's theory of subjective rights is a mark of his 'modernity', while Annabel Brett and Brian Tierney have pointed out that it is continuous with medieval canonists' understandings of rights and is therefore a sign of his 'traditionalism'. See Daniel Deckers, *Gerechtigkeit und Recht: Eine historisch-kritische Untersuchung der Gerechtigkeitslehre des Francisco de Vitoria (1483–1546)* (Freiburg, 1991), pp. 160, 215; Brett, *Liberty, right and nature*, pp. 130–1; Tierney, *The idea of natural rights*, p. 257.

[34] Tierney, *The idea of natural rights*, p. 260. Compare Brett, *Liberty, right and nature*, p. 148 on Vitoria's 'equation of *dominium* and right' in contrast to Soto.

[35] Tierney, *The idea of natural rights*, p. 260; Pagden, *Lords of all the world*, pp. 50–1; Lupher, *Romans in a new world*, p.62.

Property came into existence, Vitoria argued, because all things had been created by God for the use of humankind. Following Aquinas, Soto agreed that *dominium rerum* was 'the power or capacity of taking up some object for our use'.[36] Initially, all people had natural dominion over all things, but they came to hold individual property rights by virtue of tacit agreements to divide the goods of the world amongst them. Here, therefore, was an understanding of property that helped justify the expanding public and private dominions of Europe.

For Soto and Vitoria, natural law dictated that all things should conserve themselves. Soto argued that self-preservation followed from the first of all natural goods, which is 'to be'.[37] Humans could not preserve themselves without using other creatures and things. The agreement to create public and private dominion helped them to achieve this end. Civil society was necessary in order to escape the perils of the natural state. Society was thus at least in part a consequence of the need for self-preservation. Vitoria declared that humans were born 'frail, weak, helpless, and vulnerable, destitute of all defence and lacking in all things'. To 'make up for these natural deficiencies', people were 'obliged to give up the solitary life of nomadic animals, and to live life in partnerships (*societates*)'.[38] The city, or civitas, was according to this reasoning 'the most natural community'.[39] For these reasons, Vitoria observed, 'Aristotle shows in his *Politics* that man is a social animal'.[40] Soto explained that while self-preservation is an impulse common to all animals, humans have on top of this an inclination to 'society and civility'.[41]

Vázquez de Menchaca responded to Vitoria's and Soto's analyses of dominion by further exploring the distinction between particular and common property in the second book of his *Controversarium illustrium* (1564, hereinafter referred to as '*Controversies*').[42] Vázquez's *Controversies* presented a radically different understanding of politics from that found in Soto and Vitoria. Whereas for the Dominicans, rights were founded upon nature, and the political was natural, Vázquez opposed politics to nature. For him, civil society was created in order to protect people from the dominating behaviour of others, whereas for the Dominicans, it was a creation of the same sociable motives that they held in nature.[43]

[36] Cited in Lupher, *Romans in a new world*, p. 62. [37] Brett, *Liberty, right and nature*, p. 143.
[38] Francisco de Vitoria, *On civil power*, in Pagden and Lawrence (eds.), *Vitoria: political writings*, p. 7.
[39] *Ibid.*, p. 9. [40] *Ibid.*, p. 7. [41] Brett, *Liberty, right and nature*, p. 144.
[42] For Vázquez, see *ibid.*, pp. 165–204. [43] *Ibid.*, p. 173.

According to Vázquez, all things were originally created in common for the use of all beings. Reflecting his Augustinian outlook, he argued that private property had come about as a result of the decline of humankind from innocence into wickedness. Movable goods, he agreed, come to be the property of somebody through their use, through artifice and exploitation, and such purposes were not inconsistent with virtue: 'the maker is accustomed to have control of his own object'.[44] He differed from Vitoria and the Dominicans, however, in that he regarded the use and exploitation of things as contingent and artificial rather than natural.[45] Property in land, moreover, was the consequence of the desire to dominate. The subject of the second book of Vázquez's *Controversies* was prescription, a variant of the Roman law of *occupatio* in which a thing becomes the property of a person by her or his long and continued possession of it. It was only by such continued possession, he argued, that a person could establish property in immovable things: 'he who adduces that a certain immovable thing is his own, must prove it, because he has against him the presumption of the law ... but that proof, if we took away the practice of prescription, would be almost impossible'.[46] The law of prescription established a link between occupation and custom, expressed in the notion of continued possession. Prescription therefore brought together two of the intellectual traditions with which Vázquez was deeply concerned: namely, Roman law, on the one hand, and, on the other, legal humanism with its emphasis upon custom and fact as the basis of right.[47] He preferred prescription for understanding property to *occupatio* more generally because he believed property to be mutable. The Roman law of prescription provided a better description than simple occupation for how property comes to exist and also how it is lost when abandoned.

For Vázquez, prescription not only offered an explanation for how private property came into existence and was lost, it also explained why some things remain common. The distinction he made in this regard was between different kinds of immovable goods: namely, the land and the sea. There was an extensive medieval debate, beginning with Bartolus, over whether the sea could be owned.[48] This debate was conducted partly in relation to whether Venice had a monopoly over the Adriatic and Genoa

44 Cited in *ibid.*, p. 188. 45 *Ibid.*, p. 204. 46 Cited in *ibid.*, p. 189.

47 On legal humanism and André Tiraqueau, an important model for Vázquez, see Donald Kelley, *Foundations of modern historical scholarship: language, law and history in the French renaissance* (New York, 1970).

48 Julius Goebel, *The struggle for the Falkland Islands: a study in legal and diplomatic history* (London, 1927), p. 61; Brett, *Liberty, right and nature*, p. 189.

over the Ligurian Sea, and many jurists concluded that those seas were the property of those cities. In a discussion to which Hugo Grotius would later turn, Vázquez disagreed.[49] Using the idea of prescription, he argued that property in things comes from exploitation, from continued possession, and also because it is expedient for all people that some things should not be shared. There was no expedience, he pointed out, in making the sea the property of particular people, nor could it be continually possessed in the same way as the land. Indeed, he added in a passage that Grotius conspicuously ignored that the seas were created in order to keep peoples apart and, for this reason, the creation of empires by traversing the seas was a transgression of nature.[50]

While Soto and Vitoria were developing a theory of property and sociability that justified the developing property relations of sixteenth-century Europe, their ideas, along with those of Vázquez, also weakened the claims of their sovereign over his American empire. It was difficult to develop a theory that commanded respect for dominion as a universal right without destabilising Spanish claims over the public and private dominions of the Americas. To recognise such claims, Soto observed, would be to acknowledge that France could enter Spain 'for the same purpose'.[51] Both the public and private dominion that Soto and Vitoria described was evident, they observed, in the Americas. In his lectures at the University of Salamanca between 1534 and 1539, Vitoria addressed the question of whether the peoples of the Americas had been justly dispossessed of their property, whether they had justly been enslaved and killed, and whether their societies had been justly destroyed. He systematically analysed, from the perspective of natural law, the claims by the Conquistadors and subsequently by the Spanish Crown to have justly conquered. At the heart of his discussion of the rights of the American peoples was the Aristotelian argument that all things exist in potential and that it is in the nature of humans to release that potential through the recognition and exploitation of the laws of nature.[52] To be just and therefore hold rights of possession, a society needs to have manifested the propensity to exploit nature in the creation of both physical and political structures. It was evident, Vitoria argued, that the peoples of the Americas had 'some order in their affairs'.

[49] For Grotius' use of Vázquez, see Peter Borschberg, *Hugo Grotius' 'Comenarius in Theses XI': an early treatise on sovereignty, just war, and the legitimacy of the Dutch Revolt* (Bern, 1994), pp. 73–101.

[50] Fernando Vázquez de Menchaca, *Controversarium illustrium* (Frankfurt, 1572), II.20. 11–20. See also David Armitage, 'Introduction', to Hugo Grotius, *The free sea*, trans. Richard Hakluyt, with William Welwod's *Critique* and Grotius' *Reply*, ed. David Armitage (Indianapolis, 2004), p. xvii.

[51] Pagden, *Lords of all the world*, p. 52.

[52] See Pagden, *The fall of natural man*.

They had sufficiently understood natural law to be able to create societies. 'They have', he declared, 'properly organised cities, proper magistrates, marriages and overlords, laws, industries, and commerce, all of which requires the use of reason'.[53] In this case the 'Indians' had also established their humanity.

Turning to the claim of discovery, Vitoria recalled 'that possession of these countries was by right of discovery'. 'The title by right of discovery', he argued, 'was the only title alleged in the beginning, and it was with this pretext alone that Columbus of Genoa first set sail.'[54] He proceeded to argue that this title seemed just because it could be supported by the Roman law of occupation, or what Vitoria described as the law *ferae bestiae*, the law of wild beasts, because wild beasts were the examples used for occupation in the *Digest of Justinian*: 'All things which are unoccupied or deserted become the property of the occupier by natural law and the law of nations' and the Spaniards 'were the first to discover and occupy these countries'. In his dialectical fashion, he concluded: 'But on the other hand, against this third title, we need not argue long', because 'the barbarians possessed true public and private dominion': that is, both civil society and private property. The law of nations, he argued, 'expressly states that goods which belong to no owner pass to the occupier', but that 'the goods in question here had an owner'.[55] Occupation was thus not only the title that the Spaniards might wish to claim, it was also the basis of the Indians' title and upon which Spanish title was precluded. Crucially, Roman law discussions of occupation had been concerned with private law and dominion over things or property. Vitoria and Soto, by contrast, extended the sense in which it was possible to occupy to the question of supremacy, the Roman law equivalent of *dominium jurisdictionis*. The distinction between the occupation of property, in private law, and of sovereignty, in the *ius gentium* (later the law of nations), would be vital to questions of the justice of empire through to the twentieth century.

As we shall see, subsequent jurists, such as Grotius and Pufendorf, opposed occupation to discovery. Vitoria, by contrast, virtually equated the two in the passage above. The title by discovery (*inventio*) appeared right, he argued, because occupation (*occupatio*) gives title. He was not opposing the argument of discovery as a justification of title, but rather was opposing the idea that the Americas remained undiscovered when there

[53] Francisco de Vitoria, *On the American Indians*, in Pagden and Lawrence (eds.), *Vitoria: political writings*, p. 250.

[54] *Ibid.*, p. 264. [55] *Ibid.*, p. 265.

were people living there clearly in possession of their goods and affairs. In Vitoria's understanding of the *ius gentium*, therefore, discovery was a legitimate basis to title, but one could not claim a right of discovery in a land that was already occupied by another people. According to him, *ferae bestiae* clearly did not apply to the American lands because the people who lived there had used natural reason to realise the potential in nature and to establish dominium in both corporeal and incorporeal things. Thus, he argued that if the Spanish conquest was just, justice must arise from one of a number of other legal bases, including: the claim that the Holy Roman Emperor, Charles V, was Lord of all the world; the Bulls of Donation made by Pope Alexander VI in 1493; because the Indians were sinners; or because they were madmen.

The claim that the Holy Roman Emperor was Lord of all the world had been sustained by the Glossators and was even nominally conceded by the post-Glossators. Soto, Covarrubias and the humanist jurist Vázquez de Menchaca poured scorn on the idea and warned against the dangers of over-extended empires. Human communities, they argued, are created for the good of their members, and when they become large, it is increasingly difficult for their laws to be harmonious with the customs of each of the peoples from which they are constituted.[56] According to Vitoria, it was precisely the post-Glossators' concept of overlapping dominium – the idea that it was 'possible for several parties to have dominion over the same thing' – that made it possible to argue that Indians could have dominion and yet still be under the jurisdiction of Charles V. He pointed to the 'jurists' well-worn distinctions between high and low (*dominium altum, bassum*), direct and usable (*directum, utile*), and mere and mixed (*merum, mixium*).[57] Vitoria argued that his monarch, Charles V, who was Holy Roman Emperor, was 'not master of the whole world' and that he only could be by virtue of natural law, divine law or human law.[58] Aquinas, he argued, had shown that all men are free according to natural law. Supremacy came from human law and, as such, there was no reason why 'imperial dominion' should belong to the Spaniards rather than the French.[59] Bartolus had been wrong to attribute rule of all the world to Nebuchadnezzar's empire because the Jews were not his subjects.[60] And, on the matter of spiritual law, Christ had not been master of all the world

[56] Domingo de Soto, *Releccion 'De Dominio'*, trans. and ed. Jaime Brufau Prats (Salamanca, 1964), pp. 135–59; Pagden, *Lords of all the world*, pp. 55–6.
[57] Vitoria, *On the American Indians*, p. 252. [58] *Ibid.*, p. 253. [59] *Ibid.*, p. 254. [60] *Ibid.*

in temporal matters.[61] Finally, it was easy to show that human law did not grant universal empire to any ruler because no such law had been enacted and, even if it had been, 'an enactment presupposes the necessary jurisdiction'.[62]

In this passage on the limited claims of the Holy Roman Emperor, Vitoria made it clear how different his understanding of sovereignty was from that employed by post-Glossators such as Bartolus. In common with Bartolus, Vitoria understood the idea of occupation as a tool with which to critique *imperium* rather than simply to endorse it. In contrast to Bartolus, however, Vitoria challenged the feudal order, and while he agreed that sovereignty could be multiple, he was more inclined to perceive sovereigns as neighbours than as Chinese boxes. Although he did not go so far as the French jurist Jean Bodin later in the century in terms of articulating sovereignty as absolute and indivisible, Vitoria nevertheless placed his concept of occupation within the context of an understanding of sovereignty as relatively discrete. For him, the Indians belonged to a separate sovereign system that arose from their occupation of territory and their use of reason.

Vitoria rejected title based upon the Donation of Alexander because he rejected the possibility that the Church could hold the temporal power with which to make such a donation. In response to the claim that the pope was 'empowered to constitute the kings of Spain as kings and lords of those lands', he argued that he had 'no temporal power over these barbarians, or any other unbelievers'.[63] He rejected the idea that the Indians were sinners as a justification of conquest because that argument invoked the dangerous Protestant heresy that the only just society was a godly society. He rejected the notion that the Indians were madmen because, as he had shown, they clearly 'have some order in their affairs'.[64] It was true, he observed, that some of their customs appeared obnoxious, but this was because of the Indians' barbarous education and not because they were not men and were incapable of the use of reason. At this point Vitoria raised the possibility that the Indians could be in the infancy of reason. If, and he emphasised 'if', this were the case, such a state could not justify conquest. In this case the relationship of the Spaniards in relation to the Indians could be like of that of a guardian to a child.[65] While a child requires protection, she or he maintains possession of property. Melchior Cano

[61] *Ibid.*, p. 255. [62] *Ibid.*, p. 256. [63] *Ibid.*, p. 262. [64] *Ibid.*, p. 250. [65] *Ibid.*, p. 264.

later responded that even this title was invalid because neither a person nor a nation could be forced to accept charity.[66]

Vitoria then turned to the question of whether the Spaniards had fought a just war against the Indians and therefore had the right to appropriate the property of the vanquished. He concluded that a just war could only have been fought on the grounds that there had been a violation of the Spaniards' natural law rights to 'natural partnership and communication', that is, travel, friendship, trade and the sending of ambassadors and missionaries.[67] Of this stage in Vitoria's analysis, James Tully observes: 'After advancing a number of objections to the standard justifications, Vitoria concluded his long discussion with a justification of conquest he believed to be invulnerable. Since both Spaniards and Amerindians are in the state of nature, if the Spaniards conduct themselves in accordance with the law of nature, then they have the right to defend themselves against any wrong committed by the Amerindians and "to avail themselves of the rights of war".'[68] Similarly, Robert A. Williams concludes: 'In Vitoria's discourse of New World conquest, reason as well as Rome were granted the right to initiate enforcement of Christian Europe's universally binding norms.' 'Francisco de Vitoria', he continues, 'was the first articulator of a European discourse of conquest founded on secularly rationalisable norms and values. His Law of Nations justified the extension of Western power over the American Indians as an imperative of the Europeans' vision of truth.'[69] For Antony Anghie, Vitoria did not theorise the imposition of Western sovereignty onto non-Western societies; rather, he developed a theory of sovereignty, a theory embodying inequality, that only acquired its character because of its colonial context.[70]

The problem with these interpretations is that Vitoria resisted the extension of Spanish power over the American Indians. For these historians, because Vitoria argued that a violation of 'the natural partnership of communication' would be a ground for just war against the Indians, he therefore justified the Spanish conquest. However, Vitoria never stated – neither in *On dietary laws*, nor in *On the American Indians*, nor in *On the law of war* – that the Indians had violated the 'natural partnership of communication' with the Spaniards. Indeed, it appears that the force of this natural law argument for Vitoria was to demonstrate once again that

[66] Lupher, *Romans in a new world*, p. 86. [67] Vitoria, *On the American Indians*, pp. 278–84.
[68] Tully, *An approach to political philosophy*, pp. 142–3.
[69] Williams, *The American Indian in Western legal thought*, pp. 105–7.
[70] Anghie, *Imperialism, sovereignty and the making of international law*, pp. 29–30.

there was no justification for the conquest and that perhaps it was the Spaniards who had violated natural law in this way. Cano agreed. It was unclear, he argued, 'that the Indians have done any injury... especially since the Spaniards [have entered] not as travellers but as invaders – unless one were to label Alexander [the Great] a traveler'.[71] Vitoria's sense that it was Spaniards who violated natural law was nowhere clearer than in his letter to Miguel de Arcos on 8 November 1534. He began: 'Very Reverend Father, As for the case of Peru, I must tell you, after a lifetime of studies and long experience, that no business shocks me or embarrasses me more than the corrupt profits and affairs of the Indies. Their very mention freezes the blood in my veins.' He alluded to the political dangers of holding an opinion on the subject and then continued: 'But if utterly forced to give a categorical reply, in the end I say what I think ... First, I do not understand the justice of the war ... as far as I understand from eyewitnesses who were personally present during the recent battle with Atahuallpa [in the conquest of Peru], neither he nor any of his people had ever done the slightest injury to the Christians, nor given them the least grounds for making war on them.' 'Other more recent conquests', he observed, 'have, I think, been even more vile.'[72]

Vitoria was more adamant in his lectures, *On civil power*, that a Christian king has no right to usurp non-Christians 'of their kingship or power'.[73] He concluded *On the American Indians* by declaring that it was possible that the Spanish had no just title in the New World at all.[74] As a consolation, he offered the idea that there were unoccupied areas of the New World which the Spanish could claim, although Soto disagreed, arguing that the Spanish should be barred from seizing unexploited things that American peoples held in common – such things fell within the Americans' domain as it was determined in the original division of the world.[75] Vitoria also suggested that if enough Indians were converted to Christianity, it would be neither 'just nor expedient' for Charles V to abandon the administration, or *dominium iurisdictionis*, over those territories.[76] Here Vitoria had not entirely abandoned Bartolus' categories: namely, in being able to conceptualise overlapping claims to the same lands. It would seem that for Vitoria, as for Bartolus, the claim of those

[71] Cited in Lupher, *Romans in a new world*, p. 87.
[72] Pagden and Lawrence (eds.), *Vitoria: political writings*, pp. 331–2.
[73] Vitoria, *On civil power*, p. 18. Nevertheless, this rejection still left the door ajar because it was based solely on the use of religion as a justification of conquest.
[74] Vitoria, *On the American Indians*, pp. 291–2. [75] Pagden, *Lords of all the world*, p. 52.
[76] Vitoria, *On the American Indians*, p. 292.

who held *directum utile*, in this case the Indians, may have been stronger than the titular claim of the Spanish emperor. Nevertheless, this conclusion introduced ambivalence into his discussion. This ambivalence may have arisen in part from a need to delicately balance the political implications of his argument. Certainly, the Emperor Charles V himself would not have agreed that Vitoria was merely sanitising Spanish conquests. On learning of Vitoria's lectures on the Indies, Charles wrote to the prior of San Estaban, the Dominican house where Vitoria and Soto lived, and rebuked him for allowing such 'prejudicial and scandalous' discussion.[77]

The School of Salamanca has been the focus of a number of other accounts exploring the ties between Western political thought, particularly the law of nations, and empire.[78] For these historians, Vitoria's and Soto's writings are foundational for understanding the disposition of Western political thought to empire, but this interpretation does not sit easily with the Salamanca theologians' tone. Acknowledging the ambivalence of the Salamanca authorities, Martti Koskenniemi suggests that their contribution to the imperial character of international law lies not in their discussion of the status of the American societies, but in their understanding of *dominium*, *ius gentium* and just war.[79] These are the ideas that justified the emergence of centralised states, a global economic system based upon private property, and continual warfare to uphold the principles of that system. Very similar principles, as we shall see, were advanced by Hugo Grotius in support of the claims of the Dutch East India Company and they remain salient, as Koskenniemi argues, in the understanding of informal empire that has prevailed in the post-colonial period from the mid-twentieth century, and arguably since the Enlightenment. While it is true that Vitoria, Soto, Covarrubias and Azpilcueta made universal claims for their understandings of dominion and the right to trade and commerce, it is doubtful whether they understood themselves to be theorising a system of global capitalism while they addressed the immediate problems

[77] Pagden, *The fall of natural man*, p. 106.

[78] See, for example, Miéville, *Between equal rights*; Brett Bowden, 'The colonial origins of international law: European expansion and the classical standard of civilisation', *Journal of History of International Law*, 7 (2005), 1–23; and earlier than Anghie and Williams, Henry Méchoulan, 'Vitoria, père du droit international?', in Antonio Truyol Serra (ed.), *Actualité de la pensée juridique de Francisco de Vitoria* (Brussels, 1988), pp. 11–26. For a reaction against these post-colonial readings, see: Georg Cavallar, 'Vitoria, Grotius, Pufendorf, Wolff and Vattel: accomplices of European colonialism and exploitation or true cosmopolitans?', *Journal of the History of International Law*, 10 (2008), 181–209; Pablo Zapatero, 'Legal imagination in Vitoria: the power of ideas', *Journal of the History of International Law*, 11 (2009), 221–71, at 221.

[79] Koskenniemi, 'Empire and international law', 11–12.

of the Reformation and the rapid expansion of the money economy. This is not to deny that such theories developed, or that the Salamanca authors were used in developing them, and it is to that process that the following chapters will turn. At the same time, uncertainty about the justice of European expansion remained salient through the following centuries, as did anxieties about over-extended empires, and the Salamanca authors would also be a reference point for these concerns.

A genealogy of *res nullius*

The concept of *res nullius* has achieved wide currency amongst historians, particularly historians of empire, over the past thirty years. *Res nullius* has been represented as having a central place in the *ius gentium*, the law of nations and international law from late antiquity to the present. According to this understanding, it was a doctrine of occupation whereby things (*res*) which belong to nobody (*nullius*) become the property of the first taker. In particular, this understanding of the right of occupation expressed by the term '*res nullius*' is believed to have been used to justify colonisation from the sixteenth century through to the twentieth century.[80] Anthony Pagden, for example, observes that 'the British, and to a somewhat lesser degree the French, were driven to legitimize their settlements in terms of one or another variant on the Roman Law argument known as *res nullius*'.[81]

There are, however, a number of problems with the scholarship on *res nullius* which are largely the consequence of a series of anachronisms: first, that scholars identify *res nullius* as a Roman law doctrine which remained largely continuous through to the twentieth century.[82] The term '*res nullius*' is absent, however, in the Roman law discussions of occupation, albeit that it is sometimes implicit. It was employed in medieval civil law, but it was not a widely used and reified tool in the law of nations before the eighteenth century. *Res nullius* was also used as much to describe things

80 Amongst numerous recent studies, see: Pagden, *Lords of all the world*; Nicholas P. Canny, *Making Ireland British 1580–1650* (Oxford, 2001), p. 133; Armitage, *Ideological origins of the British Empire*; Fitzmaurice, *Humanism and America*; J. H. Elliott, *Empires of the Atlantic World. Britain and Spain in America, 1492–1830* (New Haven, 2006), pp. 12, 30, 32; Ken MacMillan, *Sovereignty and possession in the English New World* (Cambridge, 2006), p. 12; Garnsey, *Thinking about property*, p. 115; Lauren Benton and Benjamin Straumann, 'Acquiring empire by law: from Roman doctrine to early modern European practice', *Law and History Review*, 28(1) (2010), 1–38. The term was influential in historical and political analysis (not to mention legal scholarship) throughout the twentieth century; see, for example, Schmitt, *Nomos of the earth*, p. 175.

81 Pagden, *Lords of all the world*, p. 76.

82 A classic discussion is Buckland, *A text-book of Roman law*, pp. 184–6.

that could not be occupied as it was to articulate the Roman law and natural law doctrine of the first taker.[83] As I shall show in a subsequent chapter, discussions of *res nullius* have also paid little or no attention to the different meanings of the term depending on whether it was employed by the writers who assumed that rights over property could exist outside a political community or by the natural law writers, beginning with Grotius and Pufendorf in the seventeenth century, who argued that all property rights were the creation of political societies or of a movement towards the creation of political society.

Each of these problems underlies a larger point: namely, that rather than being a transhistorical concept, *res nullius* was reified in medieval civil and canon law as part of the effort by the Glossators and Decretists to tidy up Roman law, to remove its contradictions and to create a body of doctrine. It is possible to find numerous statements in Roman law regarding occupation. As with other aspects of the law, these statements were not all consistent and were unwieldy. They were, however, captured by one concept, *res nullius*, which stated one relatively simple principle: namely, that which belonged to no one would become the property of the first taker. For medieval jurists, *res nullius* was the opposite of *ius in res*, or having a right in a thing, and it differed from the Roman law of occupation just as an *ius* as a right differed from *ius* as a sense of what is right in Roman law.

It is true that in recent years historians have begun to cast a more critical eye over the historical evidence for the use of *res nullius* and, more particularly, its cognate term *terra nullius*.[84] A number of historians have now accepted that the concept of *terra nullius* was a branch of the 'Roman law' discussion of *res nullius* rather than a term from Roman law itself. Even these historians, however, continue to accept that *res nullius* was a doctrine clearly articulated in Roman law, so while *terra nullius* has begun to be understood as an historical term, *res nullius* has maintained a transhistorical quality.[85] While these historians cannot point to the words '*res nullius*' in the Roman law of occupation, they find that the doctrine is nevertheless present. Where, however, the terms which describe a concept are absent from its articulation, the burden of historical proof to establish its presence is great. In this case that evidence is absent. As Quentin

[83] See Fitzmaurice, 'A genealogy of *terra nullius*'. This point is also made in Benton and Straumann, 'Acquiring empire by law'.

[84] For scepticism regarding the term *res nullius*, see: Fitzmaurice, 'A genealogy of *terra nullius*'; and Tomlins, *Freedom bound*, pp. 119 and 146. For the historiography of *terra nullius*, see Chapter 10.

[85] Benton and Straumann insist on this point; see 'Acquiring empire by law', p. 2: 'our analysis will show that *res nullius* was a concept with a firm foundation in Roman legal sources'.

Skinner has demonstrated, the emergence of the modern state was tied to the emergence of a specific meaning for the term 'state'.[86] An historical understanding of the terms of political discourse has been extended to much of the language that accompanied the emergence of the state, for example, the idea of a 'right' or '*ius*' or the idea of freedom, but some elements in that vocabulary have escaped attention. *Res nullius* is one such term and yet one which does much to shed light on the relationship between state and empire in early modern Europe.

Analyses of *res nullius* frequently begin with Roman law, identifying the discussions of occupation in the *Digest of Justinian* and the *Institutes* of Roman law as the origin of the doctrine. As we have seen, according to the *Institutes*: 'what previously belonged to no one is, by natural reason, accorded to its captor [*quod enim ante nullius est id naturali ratione occupanti conceditur*]'.[87] Similarly, in the *Digest of Justinian*, we read that 'what presently belongs to no one becomes by natural reason the property of the first taker [*Quod enim nullius est, id ratione naturali occupanti conceditur*]'.[88] While there is a clear statement of the origin of property in these passages, we do not find the term '*res nullius*'.

To some degree, this is a mere grammatical point. The grammar of classical Latin does not require that '*res*' accompanies '*nullius*' because it is already implied in the use of '*nullius*'. Moreover, '*quod . . . nullius*' conveys the meaning of 'that which is nobody's', which is barely different from *res nullius*, or 'nobody's thing'. In some instances '*res*' and '*in nullius bonis*' could be found in the same sentence.[89] In others, '*res*' was implied by the context or stated shortly beforehand.[90] For these reasons the various

[86] Quentin Skinner, 'From the state of princes to the person of the state', in Quentin Skinner, *Visions of politics: volume 2, Renaissance virtues* (Cambridge, 2002), pp. 368–413; and Skinner, 'A genealogy of the modern state'.

[87] *The institutes of Justinian*, bk. II, i, 11–12.

[88] *Digest of Justinian*, vol. 4, 487a. See also: Gai. 2.66: 'things which we get by first taking and which become ours because previously they belonged to no one' (*quia antea nullius essent*).

[89] Dig. 1.8.6.2: 'Things sacred or religious or sanctified are no one's property' (*Sacrae res et religiosae et sanctae in nullius bonis sunt*). Dig. 1.8.1.pr: 'things comprising a deceased person's estate are not in anyone's ownership until someone becomes heir' (*res hereditariae, antequam aliquis heres existat, nullius in bonis sunt*). In these instances there are also adjectives qualifying *res*.

[90] Inst. 2.1.pr: 'now let us consider things (*de rebus*). These are either capable of being owned or not capable of being owned. Some, again, are common to all by natural law, others are public, yet others the property of a community and some belong to no one (*quaedam nullius*): then there are many things which belong to individuals'. Dig. 1.8.1.pr: 'Summa rerum divisio in duos articulos deducitur: nam aliae sunt divini iuris, aliae humani. divini iuris sunt veluti res sacrae et religiosae. sanctae quoque res, veluti muri et portae, quodammodo divini iuris sunt. quod autem divini iuris est, id nullius in bonis est: id vero, quod humani iuris est, plerumque alicuius in bonis est, potest autem et nullius in bonis esse: nam res hereditariae, antequam aliquis heres existat, nullius in bonis sunt. hae autem res,

means of expressing the absence of ownership in Roman law were not attached to '*res*', whether when speaking of '*in nullius bonis*' (in nobody's ownership), *nemo dominus est* (no one is the owner), *sine domino* (without an owner) or *quadem nullius* (that which is nobody's). In addition to occupation, there are a number of instances in Roman law in which the absence of ownership is discussed, including the division of things in law, sacred things, islands that arise in the sea, an inheritance without an heir and treasure troves. In all the discussions for each of these cases, the term '*res nullius*' never appears.[91]

quae humani iuris sunt, aut publicae aut privatae. Quae publicae sunt, nullius in bonis esse creduntur, ipsius enim universitatis esse creduntur: privatae autem sunt, quae singulorum sunt.'

91 For the division of things, see: Dig. 1.8.2.pr: 'Some things belong in common to all men by *jus naturale*, some to a community corporately, some to no one, but most belong to individuals severally' (*quaedam nullius*); Inst. 2.1.pr: 'now let us consider things (*de rebus*). These are either capable of being owned or not capable of being owned. Some, again, are common to all by natural law, others are public, yet others the property of a community and some belong to no one (*quaedam nullius*): then there are many things which belong to individuals'; Dig. 1.8.1.pr: 'something which is subject to human right does in most cases belong within someone's property, though it can happen that it is not so' (*potest autem et nullius in bonis esse*); Gai. 2.9: 'what is under human law . . . is generally someone's property but may also be no one's' (*potest autem et nullius in bonis esse*); Gai. 2.11: 'Public things are regarded as no one's property; for they are thought of as belonging to the whole body of the people' (*Quae publicae sunt, nullius videntur in bonis esse*); Dig. 41.1.14.pr: 'shores are public, not in the sense that they belong to the community as such but that they are initially provided by nature and have hitherto become no one's property' (*in nullius adhuc dominium pervenerunt*).

For sacred things, see Dig. 1.8.1.pr: 'what is subject to divine right is not anyone's property' (*quod autem divini iuris est, id nullius in bonis est*); Dig. 1.8.6.2: 'Things sacred or religious or sanctified are no one's property' (*Sacrae res et religiosae et sanctae in nullius bonis sunt*); Inst. 2.1.7: 'what belongs to heaven is part of no man's estate' (*quod enim divini iuris est, id nullius in bonis est*); Gai. 2.9: 'what is under divine law cannot be private property' (*quod autem divini iuris est, id nullius in bonis est*).

For islands that arise in the sea, see Inst. 2.1.22: 'If an island arise in the sea, an uncommon event, it is open to occupation for it is regarded as belonging to no one' (*nullius enim esse creditur*); Dig. 41.1.30.4: 'if I build on an island arising in the sea, it is mine forthwith; for what belongs to no one is open to the first taker' (*quod nullius sit, occupantis fit*).

For an inheritance without an heir, see Dig. 1.8.1.pr: 'things comprising a deceased person's estate are not in anyone's ownership until someone becomes heir' (*res hereditariae, antequam aliquis heres existat, nullius in bonis sunt*); Gai. 2.9: 'Things in an inheritance are no one's property until someone emerges as heir' (*res hereditariae, antequam aliquis heres existat, nullius in bonis sunt*); Gai. 2.200: 'the authorities of the other school think that the thing belongs to no one in the meantime' (*sed diversae scholae auctores putant nullius interim eam rem esse*); Dig. 43.24.13.5: 'Nor is it an obstacle, Labeo says, that nobody was the owner at that time; for nobody is the owner of a tomb either, but if anything is done to it I may avail myself of the interdict against force or stealth' (*quod eo tempore nemo dominus fuerit: nam et sepulchri nemo dominus fuit*); Dig. 47.19.6.pr: 'There can be no theft of a thing part of an inheritance any more than of anything which has no owner' (*rei hereditariae furtum non fit sicut nec eius, quae sine domino est*).

For treasure troves, see Dig. 41.1.31.1: 'Treasure is an ancient deposit of money, memory of which no longer survives, so that it is without an owner; thus, what does not belong to another becomes the property of him who finds it' (*Thensaurus est vetus quaedam depositio pecuniae, cuius non exstat memoria, ut iam dominium non habeat: sic enim fit eius qui invenerit, quod non alterius sit*).

It may seem a largely semantic question whether the particular words were employed for what seems, on the face of it, recognisable as what would later be described as the concept of *res nullius*. But words do matter. The term became the concept. The absence of '*res*' attached to '*nullius*' in the Roman discussions is almost unnoticeable unless they are contrasted with the medieval analyses of *res nullius*, in which the term was reified and employed in the context of natural law assumptions about property and sovereignty that were different from those which prevailed in Roman law. By projecting *res nullius* back in time, the moment at which the term *was* coined becomes invisible, as do the motivations of the people who were engaged in developing the concept. We cannot see authors at work developing a new understanding of occupation in civil law or the law of nations when we believe that what they were doing in coining the term *res nullius* had already stood since at least late antiquity.

Some of the most prominent medieval civil lawyers, such as Bartolus of Saxoferrato, and theologians such as Thomas Aquinas, who are frequently cited as sources for modern discussions of *res nullius*, make no use of the term.[92] Aquinas did not employ *res nullius* in his discussions of property.[93] Bartolus provided one of the most extensive medieval commentaries on the Roman law of occupation, but he did not add '*res*' to '*nullius*'.[94] It was, however, medieval civil lawyers who began to employ the word '*res*' with '*nullius*' when describing the Roman law of occupation. In addition to putting order into an eclectic body of law, a further reason we might give for the appearance of *res nullius* in medieval commentaries on Roman law may be that the grammar of medieval Latin was influenced by the grammar of a number of European vernacular languages. In vernacular grammars, such as English, it was necessary to specify *what* did not belong to somebody when saying that something was 'nobody's'. Amongst the medieval Glossators, who revived and tidied up Roman law in the eleventh and twelfth centuries, Azo of Bologna felt it necessary to specify *res* when speaking of *nullius*. As we have seen, in his chapter 'Concerning the division of things and acquisition' in Book 2 of his *Summa Perutilis*, Azo

[92] For Bartolus as a source, see Goebel, *The struggle for the Falkland Islands*, pp. 74–9; Grewe, *The epochs of international law*, p. 124.

[93] A search of Aquinas' complete works (see www.corpusthomisticum.org/iopera.html) reveals that he did not use '*res nullius*' or '*in nullius bonis*'.

[94] Bartolus, *Tractatus de insula* in *Consilia quaestiones et tractatus Bartoli* (Lyon, 1535), ff. 222–3: 'Insula que in mari nascitur quod raro accidit occupantis fit quando nullius esse credit[ur?]' ('An island which arises in the sea, which rarely happens, becomes [the property of] the occupier, because it is thought to be nobody's').

observed, introducing things that were nobody's, that 'etiam dicuntur res nullius... [things are said to be *res nullius*...]'.[95]

In *De legibus et consuetudinibus Angliae* (*On the law and constitution of England*), Henry de Bracton (1210–68) began his discussion of the law with the Roman law division of things. Bracton was trying to bring order to the laws of England at the same time that, like Azo, he was trying to bring order to his Roman law tools. He borrowed heavily from Azo on many questions, including the adoption of *res* with *nullius*. In his '*De rerum divisione*', Bracton, like Azo, made distinctions, familiar from Roman law, between common and universal things, particular things, religious things and things which belong to nobody. This last category, '*quaedem nullius*', included 'wild beasts, birds, and fish', sacred things, things derelict and treasures. He described these things as '*Res quidem nullius...*', '*res in nullius*' and '*res natura nulli*'.[96] In this category of things belonging to nobody, he was mixing those things which are nobody's because they have not been appropriated (for example, wild beasts) and those things which are nobody's because they cannot be appropriated (such as sacred land). He thus distinguished categories found in later discussions of *res nullius*, although in a less systematic way.

In the fourteenth century, a number of prominent writers specified *res* when speaking of that which belonged to nobody. William of Ockham (*c.* 1288–*c.* 1348) wrote of 'res... quae in nullius bonis'.[97] Similarly, a number of fifteenth- and sixteenth-century civil lawyers continued to combine *res* with *nullius* in stating a doctrine of occupation that conformed largely to its Roman law contours even as the civil law felt the impact of Renaissance humanism. While Andrea Alciato (1492–1550) was one of the leading legal humanists of his generation, he was educated as a lawyer and had a thorough knowledge of the post-Glossators.[98]

95 Azo, *Summa Azonis*, Bk. 2, fol. cclxxiii, verso. This wording agrees with an incunabula edition of Azo: *Summa super Codice et Institutis*, leaf 12.

96 Henry Bracton, *De legibus et consuetudinibus Angliæ* (London, 1569), f. 8r–v agrees with Bracton, *De legibus et consuetudinibus Angliæ* (London, 1640), f. 8r–v. Bracton's modern editor, George Woodbine, changed 'res in nullius...' to 'res nullius' in his classic version of the Latin text. See Henry Bracton, *De legibus et consuetudinibus angliae* ed. George Woodbine with an English translation and notes by Samuel E. Thorne, 4 vols. (Cambridge, MA, 1968 and 1977) vol. 2, p. 41.

97 H. S. Offler, *Guillelmi de Ockham Opera politica*, 2 vols. (Manchester, 1963), vol. 2, p. 435: 'Ponatur igitur quod sit aliqua res, puta vestis, habita pro derelicta, quae in nullius bonis sit nec ad alicuius spectet dominium neque speciale neque commune.' See also vol. 2, p. 438: 'res, quae in nullius bonis sunt'.

98 See Skinner, *Foundations of modern political thought*, vol. 1, pp. 203–4.

Writing on occupation in his commentaries on Roman law, Alciato spoke of '*res in bonis nullius*'.

The Protestant citizen of Wittenberg, Melchior Kling (1504–71), one of the leading German civil jurists of the sixteenth century, provided a definition of *res nullius* that was consistent with Azo's and Bracton's discussion 300 years earlier and contained features of many later discussions. Under the subtitle 'Res nulli', Kling stated that 'Res nullius sunt duplices': that is, they consist of things such as wild beasts which become the property of the first taker and they also include things, such as sacred places, which because of their nature cannot become the property of someone. Common property was thus divided into what could and could not be transformed into things belonging to individuals, but in a somewhat more systematic way than had been the case in Bracton's writings. This division remained central to many subsequent discussions of *res nullius*.[99] It was also a division that would become increasingly important in the *ius gentium* and the law of nations, particularly in Hugo Grotius' discussion of the law of the sea.

Historians identify the writings of Francisco de Vitoria, in the first half of the sixteenth century, as an important step in which the doctrine of *res nullius* was adapted from Roman and civil law to a discussion of the justice of empire. This connection between *res nullius* and empire has been a focus of modern historiography on the doctrine. The problem with this historiography, once again, is that Vitoria did not use the term '*res nullius*' to describe the Roman law concept of occupation even though contemporary civil lawyers were familiar with the usage. Rather, he referred to the law of wild beasts, or *ferae bestiae*, taking its title from its subject.[100] The grip of *res nullius* on the minds of modern historians is such that the term has even found its way into the text of the Cambridge edition of Vitoria's writings: 'Secondly, in the law of nations (*ius gentium*) a thing which does not belong to anyone (*res nullius*) becomes the property of the first taker, according to the law *Ferae bestiae*.'[101] The Latin original of this sentence,

99 Melchior Kling, *In quatuor Institutionum Iuris libros Enarrationes* (Lyon, 1550), p. 92. On Kling, see Jan Schröder, 'The concept of (natural) law in the doctrine of law and natural law of the early modern era', in Lorraine Daston and Michael Stolleis (eds.), *Natural law and laws of nature in early modern Europe* (Farnham, 2008), p. 59; and Harold J. Berman, *Faith and order: the reconciliation of law and religion* (Cambridge, 2000), p. 164.

100 Vitoria, *On the American Indians*, p. 212: 'All things which are unoccupied or deserted become the property of the occupier by natural law and the law of nations, according to the law *Ferae bestiae* (Institutions II.1.12)'; see also p. 280.

101 *Ibid.*, p. 280. In this edition of Vitoria's writings, Pagden and Lawrence prefer the more accurate 'ferae bestiae'.

however, does not contain the term '*res nullius*': 'Secondo, quia, quae in nullius bonis sunt, iure gentium sunt occupantis (*Inst.*, De rerum divisione, §ferae bestiae).'[102] Similarly, it has been claimed that Vitoria argued 'explicitly from *res nullius*' when he declared that: 'The law of nations, on the other hand, expressly states that goods which belong to no owner pass to the occupier.'[103] But the Latin original of this passage merely repeated the *Institutes* almost word for word, stating: 'Ius autem gentium est, ut, quod in nullius bonis est, occupanti conceditur, ut habetur expresse in dicta§ *ferae bestiae*.'[104] In each case, Vitoria spoke of goods that belonged to nobody when discussing the division of things, but he conspicuously did not use the more reified legal term 'nobody's things' or '*res nullius*'. It might be thought that the use of '*res nullius*' in the Cambridge edition of Vitoria's writings has had a role to play in the subsequent identification of Vitoria as a modern source of the concept, although, as we shall see, the identification of his work with the doctrine of *res nullius* has its roots in nineteenth-century international law.

The absence of *res nullius* in Vitoria's discussion of these problems should prompt us to ask what subsequent writers were doing when they introduced the term into their discussions of empire. When *res nullius* was introduced into the law of nations, it was employed as a test not just of property and of individual rights, but also, and unambiguously, as a law established by compacts governing the actions of states. Roman law discussions of '*nullius in bonis*' were concerned with private law, as were medieval discussions of *res nullius*.[105] But from the sixteenth century onwards, *res nullius* was used to debate matters of private law and the public law of nations. In the nineteenth century, jurists alert to these distinctions portrayed *res nullius* as the private law principle of occupation, with public law equivalents termed *territorium nullius* and *terra nullius*. As we shall see, some writers were able to use the concept of *res nullius* not only to adopt Vitoria's sceptical tone but also to do so in a way that did not share his ambivalence about the usurpation of property and sovereignty.

[102] Francisco de Vitoria, *De indis et de jure belli relectiones*, ed. Ernest Nys, Carnegie Institution (Washington DC, 1917), p. 259.

[103] Benton and Straumann, 'Acquiring empire by law', p. 21 citing Vitoria, *On the American Indians*, p. 264.

[104] Vitoria, *De indis*, p. 244.

[105] Lesaffer, 'Argument from Roman law in current international law'.

CHAPTER 3

The Salamanca School in England

In the sixteenth century, Francisco de Vitoria, as we have seen, and his successors in the so-called School of Salamanca made the first use of occupation to consider the position of colonised peoples.[1] The Salamanca writers were widely read in Europe and (outside Spain) nowhere more so than in England. Yet we have only a very sketchy understanding of the reception of these Spanish theologians in England and, in particular, we know very little about how they were employed to consider the justice of English colonisation. The Salamanca theologians had used natural law to argue that rights reside in the subject or individual, and on this basis they employed the idea of rights to defend Native Americans against Spanish colonisation. The English, famously in the work of John Locke, used natural law to support the justice of colonisation and to deny the rights of indigenous peoples. They inverted the force of Vitoria's and Soto's arguments. As we remain largely unaware of the reception of the Salamanca theologians in England, so the dramatic nature of this turn has not been clear to historians, nor have we understood how it was made. It was at the moment that the English established the Virginia colony, I will argue, that the Salamanca understanding of rights was used to dispossess indigenous peoples.

Reading backwards from Locke, we might expect that the natural law justifications of Indian dispossession in the generations before he wrote would share, if not his philosophical clarity, at least his certainty that dispossession was justifiable. Indeed, 'dispossession' is the wrong term for Locke's understanding of the implications of colonisation for Native Americans. For Locke, there was no question of Indian dispossession because he did not believe Indians to be in possession of the lands upon which they lived. Locke's moral certainty was in no way typical of the discussion of the legal status of Indians in sixteenth- and seventeenth-

[1] The classic study is Pagden, *The fall of natural man*.

century England. Early modern English people often acknowledged the rights of Indians and only overcame their consciousness of those rights with considerable difficulty. Even as they reversed the force of the natural law discussion of Indian rights, they were unable fully to escape the polemical defence of indigenous rights for which that tradition had originally been employed.

The fact remains that the natural law arguments of trade and friendship and occupation were used by Europeans to dispossess indigenous Americans and other indigenous peoples. These arguments, while for Vitoria prohibiting invasion, provided a tool that could be and was turned against colonised peoples (and it is from that outcome that historians have anachronistically read the Salamanca theologians).

There was, then, a turn. The question we are left with is when it happened – the historiography provides little sense of that. I will argue that the turn occurred in the English reception of the Salamanca writers. The most important event for that reception was the first twenty years of the foundation of the English colony in the Chesapeake. This is not, however, to argue that many of the features of the early seventeenth-century English arguments about occupation and use of the land were not present in earlier discussions of the New World.[2] Thomas More declared in his *Utopia* of 1516, for example, that when the island of Utopia's cities became over-crowded, they would establish colonies on the adjacent mainland 'wherever the natives have plenty of unoccupied and uncultivated land'. The natives could join these colonies, if they chose to, and benefit from the Utopians' superior understanding of how to exploit resources. Land that had 'seemed too barren and paltry even to support the natives' was now able to provide an 'abundance for all'. If, however, the natives chose to resist, the Utopians could make war upon them and drive them out. Such a policy, as More pointed out, was consistent with the law of nature: 'The Utopians say it is perfectly justifiable to make war on people who leave their land idle and waste yet forbid the use and possession of it to others who, by the law of nature, ought to be supported from it.'[3] More thus introduced the Roman law of occupation, and the Roman law of war, to consider the status of the New World more than a decade before Vitoria delivered his lectures in Salamanca.

More

[2] Chris Tomlins rightly points out that many of the early seventeenth-century arguments deployed by the Virginia Company were evident in English discussions of colonisation a quarter of a century earlier: Tomlins, *Freedom bound*, p. 132, n. 141.

[3] Thomas More, *Utopia*, eds. George M. Logan and Robert M. Adams (Cambridge, 1989), p. 56. On More's discussion of colonisation, see Armitage, *Ideological origins of the British Empire*, pp. 49–50.

In 1532 and 1533, Francis I dismissed Spanish claims to the New World upon the basis that the Spaniards did not occupy all the territories they claimed.[4] Elizabethan promoters of English colonies also employed arguments about the exploitation of land as the justification for their claims in the New World. These claims were rarely coherent. Elizabethans were as likely to appeal to legal humanism or the rights of conquest, religion, cession or royal grant to justify their claims to new territories.[5] In contrast to Thomas More's view of the lands colonised by the Utopians, and as these alternative legal claims reflect, Elizabethans frequently perceived the native inhabitants of the Americas to inhabit civil societies. This incoherence persisted into the seventeenth century, as did uncertainty about the justice of the enterprises, but it was at that time that these uncertainties began to be overcome by a more systematic discussion of the idea of occupation and the description of the inhabitants of the northern continent of the Americas as uncivilised. One of the principal stimulants to these discussions was the reception of the Salamanca authors. Spanish discussions of the New World were familiar to Elizabethan audiences. Bartolomé de Las Casas' *Brevísima relación de la destrucción de las Indias* had been translated into English and published in London in 1583 under the title *The Spanish colonie.*[6] It was frequently cited by promoters of colonies, but it was employed in order to propagate the Black Legend of Spanish Empire rather than to develop legal arguments for occupation. Las Casas was not a Salamanca theologian and his arguments did not employ the same natural law reasoning. The texts of the Salamanca theologians did not attract significant attention in England prior to the reign of James I. This leads us to the question of why, from the rule of James, promoters of the Virginia Company colony troubled themselves with reading sixteenth-century Thomist theology. The Salamanca authors had provided the most extensive early modern consideration of the legality of colonisation. Their writings, as we shall presently see, were felt to be directly relevant to concerns about justifying the Chesapeake colony.

The Virginia Company promoters

There is, however, a prior question of how the promoters of the Virginia colony were able to read and obtain texts of the Salamanca theologians.

[4] Saliha Belmessous, 'Greatness and decadence in French America', *Renaissance Studies*, 26(4) (2012), 559–79, at 561.

[5] Fitzmaurice, *Humanism and America*, pp. 137–66.

[6] *Ibid.*, pp. 141–2.

Most of those people who wrote to promote the Virginia Company were university educated and many were read in theology, and so would have had access to the libraries of Oxford and Cambridge.[7] The Oxford University Library was, however, being created at this time by Thomas Bodley and the Cambridge University Library was weak. The college libraries were inferior to many private collections of books. It is instructive to consider the example of St John's College Library, Cambridge, particularly given that many members of the Virginia Company attended this college. Samuel Purchas, the great compiler of voyage narratives, said that it was at St John's College that he 'first conceived with this Travelling Genius'.[8]

Prior to 1626, St John's College Library did not hold the books of the Salamanca Thomists because this was the date upon which it received the first part of an endowment that included those works (the aim of the endowment was to provide books which were not already held at the library).[9] Could, therefore, the promoters of the Virginia Company have used private collections for their reading of the Salamanca authors? This appears undoubtedly to have been the case, particularly if we believe Purchas' claim to have consulted 700 authors in the composition of the first edition of *Purchas his pilgrimage* alone.[10] Members of the Virginia Company had access to a number of private libraries. Henry Percy, the 'wizard' Earl of Northumberland, created one of the largest libraries in Jacobean England. His brother, George Percy, was one the first Chesapeake colonists. Richard Hooker, the former tutor of Edwin Sandys, who was a leading figure in the Virginia Company, also collected a very large library.[11] The great early modern lawyer and philosopher John Selden, who was associated with the Virginia Company and its members, was also in the process of creating a large library.

There was, however, a library even closer to the circles of the Virginia Company. This was the library of William Crashaw, preacher at the Middle Temple and later at Whitechapel, and one of the many important

[7] On the education of these writers, see *ibid.*, pp. 62–7.

[8] Samuel Purchas, *Hakluytus posthumus or Purchas his pilgrimes*, 4 vols. (London, 1625), vol. 3, Epistle dedicatory. On members and supporters of the Virginia Company who attended St John's College, see Fitzmaurice, *Humanism and America*, pp. 66–7.

[9] See P. J. Wallis, 'The library of William Crashaw', *Transactions of the Cambridge Bibliographical Society*, 2(3) (1956), 213–28; R. M. Fisher, 'William Crashaw's library at the Temple', *The Library*, 30(2) (1975), 116–24.

[10] Samuel Purchas, *Purchas his pilgrimage* (London, 1613), Epistle dedicatory.

[11] Sandys also sponsored the publication of Richard Hooker's *Laws of ecclesiastical polity*. On Hooker and Sandys, see Theodore K. Rabb, *Jacobean gentleman: Sir Edwin Sandys, 1561–1629* (Princeton, 1998).

but unexplored figures involved in the Company.[12] Crashaw delivered a sermon promoting the Virginia colony (which was subsequently published), but more importantly he organised other promotional efforts on behalf of the Company, including tracts by William Symonds (another London preacher), an anonymous tract promoting the Bermudas and the tract of the Chesapeake colonist William Whitaker (the son of the former Master of St John's College), and he clearly had a part in commissioning *The proceedings of the English colonie in Virginia.*[13] He was closely associated with the Virginian plantation until his death in 1625 (he remained in London during the plague of that year in order to care for the sick, but is assumed himself to have become one of its victims).[14]

It was from Crashaw's library, via the patronage of the Earl of Southampton (a leader of the Virginia Company), that St John's College received its new library in 1626 (both Crashaw and Southampton were former students at the College).[15] By 1612, Crashaw had created the third-largest library in England, exceeding 4,000 books and manuscripts. At this time, only the library created by Bodley in Oxford and the library of Richard Bancroft, Archbishop of Canterbury, were larger.[16] Thus, at the

[12] Wallis, 'The library of William Crashaw'; Fisher, 'William Crashaw's library at the Temple'. See also P. J. Wallis, *William Crashaw. The Sheffield puritan* (Transactions of the Hunter Archaeological Society, 1963).

[13] William Symonds' letter concluding that tract begins: 'Captain Smith I return to you the print of my labours, as Mr Croshaw requested me', see T. Abbay and William Symonds (eds.), *The proceedings of the English colonie in Virginia* (Oxford, 1612), p. 110. Note that William Strachey also presented Crashaw with a copy of his *Articles, Lawes and Orders, dyvine politique and martiall for the Colonye of Virginia*; see Wallis, *William Crashaw*, p. 42. As late as 1620, Crashaw was active in promoting the colony's affairs. The Virginia Company Court Minutes for 23 June 1620 record: 'A writing being sent from Mr Crashaw intimatinge of one that will make Commodities in Virginia of good worth wch shalbe merchantable in all places of the world war referred to the said Mr Crashaw and Mr Deputy to confer wth him': S. M. Kingsbury (ed.), *The records of the Virginia Company of London*, 4 vols. (Washington DC, 1906–35), vol. 1, p. 370. In 1617, Crashaw published *Fiscus papalis* (London, 1617 and 1621) in which he declared 'let covetous Merchants goe to the Indies, and Gallants to Guiana, let silly Catholicks goe dwell in Ireland, and fooles into Virginia' (sig. A3v). This comment could be taken as an illustration of the early modern English ambivalence about colonisation, except that it was made in a thickly ironic text. The irony is apparent from the puritan Crashaw's declared purpose in 'Laying downe the spiritual riches and infinite treasure which (as sure as the Pope is holy & true) are to be found in the Catholike Roman Church' (title page). The irony is also apparent in the continuation of the passage above: '... fooles into Virginia. Let us take a wiser course and post to Rome'. My thanks to Karen Kupperman for alerting me to *Fiscus papalis.*

[14] For Crashaw's death, see Wallis, *William Crashaw*, p. 51, n. 108. In his will he employed the good offices of two leaders, of opposing factions, in the Virginia Company, Edwin Sandys and Robert Johnson; see Wallis, *William Crashaw*, p. 12.

[15] The endowment of Crashaw's books occasioned the construction of a new library building, which is the present-day rare books and manuscripts library.

[16] Fisher, 'William Crashaw's library at the Temple', p. 119.

heart of the dominant colonial venture of early modern England was one of the greatest libraries of Jacobean England, created, it should be added, by a man of relatively humble status. Moreover, it is clear from Crashaw's letters and those of his contemporaries that he allowed his collection to be used as a lending library.[17] The catalogue of that part of Crashaw's collection that reached St John's College lists the complete works of Vitoria and also books by Vitoria's followers, including Domingo de Soto, and the Jesuit Luis de Molina.[18]

Recognition of Native American society

If we appreciate that the early modern English were often sceptical of colonisation, it becomes easier to understand why they were enthusiastic readers of the Spanish theologians.[19] Their enthusiasm for the Salamanca authors has been conventionally, but weakly, attributed to the desire to propagate the 'Black Legend' of Spanish colonisation. By contrast, the Salamanca defence of indigenous rights supported English anxiety about colonial dispossession. Minutes from one of the meetings of the Virginia Council held between 1606 and 1609 provide powerful testimony to this anxiety. The minutes record a debate held by the Council – the colony's governing body – on whether 'some form of justification of our plantation might be conceived, and pass . . . into many handes'. After a long deliberation, it was decided against arguing for the justice of the colony for several reasons. First, it was noted that when the Spanish monarch subjected the Spanish conquests to the consideration of the 'Casuists, and Confesssors', the result was they 'declyn'd him from that severe and unjust course' and concluded that there can be 'gathered for him no title, of Dominion or property, but only a Magistracy, and Empire'. The casuists and confessors here are, of course, the Salamanca theologians. Clearly, therefore, it was not only the promoters of the Virginia Company who felt that it was necessary to grapple with the Spanish authors. The members of the Company and the governing council itself had found it necessary to read Vitoria and his followers, and to discuss amongst themselves the implications of their writings for their enterprise. Moreover, this concern pre-dates the promotion of the colony in print, so the subsequent published

[17] Fisher, 'William Crashaw's library at the Temple'.

[18] *Catalogus librorum bibliotecæ Johanensis*, St John's College Library, MS U.4.

[19] On early modern scepticism of colonisation, see Armitage, *Ideological origins of the British Empire*, pp. 125–45; and Fitzmaurice, *Humanism and America*, pp. 2–4.

discussion of the arguments of the Salamanca theologians would seem to arise from within the Council. The second reason the Council decided not to argue for the justice of the colony prior to 1609 was that it was felt that publicity would anger the Spaniards and put pressure on James I, who was equivocal about the question of colonies. And, finally, it was held that: 'Because therefore, we shal be putt to defend our title, not yet publiquely quarrelled, not only comparatively to be as good as the Spaniards . . . but absolutely to be good against the Naturall people: some thought it better to abstayne from this unnessisary way of provocation, and reserve ourselves to the defensive part.'[20] What the Council clearly acknowledged here, with the Salamanca writings in mind, was that it would be difficult to justify the colony against the rights of the native peoples of the Chesapeake.

This anxiety was expressed both negatively and positively. It was expressed negatively, for example, when John Smith, one of the first governors in the Chesapeake, and his supporters repeatedly complained about the Virginia Council being excessively concerned about native sensibilities. One of Smith's allies complained that 'the command from England was so straight not to offend them [the Chesapeake peoples] as our authority bearers (keeping their houses) would rather be anything than peace breakers'.[21] He continued: 'The patient council, that nothing would move to warre with the Salvages, would gladly have wrangled with captaine Smith for his cruelty.'[22] War in America, as members of the Council knew from their own reading of the Salamanca authors, would be extremely difficult to justify.

This anxiety about dispossession was also expressed positively in promotional pamphlets when in 1609 the Virginia Company changed its policy and began publishing in defence of its right to colonise. Many early modern English critics as well as promoters of colonies expressed the view that Native Americans lived in civil societies. On the first question put by Vitoria – namely, is the country of the barbarians unclaimed, does *ferae bestiae* apply? – promoters and critics of English colonisation alike often agreed that the colonisers could not be the 'first takers' in Virginia. Native Americans were frequently represented as living in civil society and in possession of their land and goods. In pre-modern European cultures, the health of political systems was believed to depend as much on the character

[20] 'A justification for planting in Virginia' in Kingsbury (ed.), *The records of the Virginia Company of London*, vol. 3, pp. 1–3, printed from Tanner Manuscripts, XCIII, folio 200, Bodleian Library, Oxford. See also Armitage, *Ideological origins of the British Empire*, p. 93.

[21] Abbay and Symonds (eds.), *Proceedings of the English colonie in Virginia*, pp. 23–4.

[22] *Ibid.*, pp. 24–5.

and spirit of a people – that is, upon the virtue of the citizens – as it did upon the strength of political institutions.[23] It is important in this context that English reports frequently praised Indian virtues, particularly martial virtues.[24] The artist John White, governor of the short-lived Roanoke colony in 1585, represented Indians living in towns, cultivating fields, catching fish and employing a number of familiar technologies. It was also clear to the English that the Indians possessed a political system for which many writers expressed admiration. As John Smith observed: 'Although the countrey people be very barbarous, yet they have amongst them such government, as that their Magistrates for good commanding, and their people for due subjection, and obeying, excel many places that would be counted very civil. The form of the Common wealth is a monarchical government.'[25] His observation of the nature of rule by the 'King' Wahunsonacock (often known as 'Powhatan' after his tribe) would have struck a familiar chord with readers in Jacobean England: 'the lawes whereby he ruleth is custome. Yet when he listeth his will is law'.[26] Of Wahunsonacock's seat, Smith observed: 'The great King hath foure or five houses, each containing four score or an hundred foote in length' overlooking a countrey in which lay 'an hundred houses and many large plaines . . . together inhabited'.[27] Indians were also acknowledged to practise a religion, which for the natural law theorists demonstrated civility. Similarly, Alexander Whitaker, one of the more negative writers on Indians, conceded that the Indians must be counted amongst those who exploit nature: 'There is civill governement amongst them which they strictly observe, and shew thereby that the law of Nature dwelleth in them: for they have a rude kinde of Commonwealth, and rough governement, wherein they both honour and obey their Kings, Parents, and Governours . . . they observe the limits of their owne possessions, and incroach not upon their neighbours dwellings.'[28]

From the perspective by which Indians were recognised to constitute a civil society, it was common that promoters of colonies would respond to the Spanish theologians by observing that they would not dispossess the Native Americans. Samuel Purchas was one of the most emphatic writers on the injustice of dispossessing Native Americans, albeit that he was

[23] See Quentin Skinner, 'Political philosophy', in Charles B. Schmitt and Quentin Skinner, *Cambridge history of Renaissance philosophy* (Cambridge, 1988), pp. 389–452.
[24] See Fitzmaurice, *Humanism and America*, pp. 162–3.
[25] John Smith, *A map of Virginia* (Oxford, 1612), p. 34. [26] *Ibid.*, p. 35.
[27] John Smith, *A true relation* (London, 1608), sig. B4v.
[28] Alexander Whitaker, *Good newes from Virginia* (London, 1613), pp. 26–7.

generally referring to the Spanish conquests. As for many English writers, criticism of the Spanish placed clear limits on what could be allowed to the English. Purchas' observations on the injustice of dispossession are particularly trenchant in his essay 'Of the propertie which Infidels have in their Lands and Goods' in *Hakluytus posthumus*.[29] Purchas has been described as 'the early modern British writer who showed the greatest familiarity with Vitoria's writings' (although Alberico Gentili might challenge for that place), and it is certainly clear that Vitoria was the main instrument he employed in the defence of indigenous rights.[30]

It is true that Purchas was at times untroubled by the Spanish dispossession of Native Americans. In a passage in which he cited Vitoria in the margin as his authority, he observed: 'innumerable are the compacts and contracts mentioned in Histories, whereby the rule of Countries and States have beene made over to new Masters'.[31] Accordingly, in the 'Animadversions on the said Bull of Pope Alexander', he acknowledged that howsoever unjust the Spanish conquest may have been, with the passage of time, their title became just:

> I question not the right of the Spanish Crowne in those parts ... The Castilian Industry I honour (as appears in the former relations) their Right may, for that which is actually in their Possession, without this Bull, plead Discoverie even before this [i.e., the Donation of Alexander] was written, the Sword, Prescription, subjection of the Inhabitants, long and quiet possession; which, howsoever the Case was at first (wherewith I meddle not) must now, after so long Succession, be acknowledged Just. I quarrel the Pope only.[32]

Purchas' quarrel with the Pope was over the Donation of Alexander, by which the Catholic Church granted possession of the New World to the Spanish. There was scarcely an English writer on colonisation who did not make the same complaint.[33] The legal basis of the objection concerned the temporal powers of the Roman Church: 'Christs Kingdome is not of this world, and properly neither gives nor takes away worldly properties, civill and political interests.'[34] This argument, as Purchas pointed out, is 'cited by Vitoria', 'largely proving these propositions, That the Pope is not

[29] Purchas, *Hakluytus posthumus*, vol. 1, pp. 14–16.
[30] Armitage, *Ideological origins of the British Empire*, p. 88.
[31] Purchas, *Hakluytus posthumus*, vol. 1, bk. 1, ch. 5, p. 15.
[32] Purchas, *Hakluytus posthumus*, vol. 1, bk. 2, ch. 1, p. 20.
[33] See Fitzmaurice, *Humanism and America*, pp. 148–57.
[34] Purchas, *Hakluytus posthumus*, vol. 1, bk. 1, ch. 5, p. 14.

Lord of the World, That the Temporall Power depends not of him, That it is not subject to his Temporall Power'.[35]

In his quarrel with the Pope, Purchas abandoned his claim that the Spanish conquests had become just. It is ungodly to 'rob Kings of their supremacy and preheminence, subjects of their land and state, as if to convert to Christ were to evert out of their possessions, and subvert states'. 'The rights of men', he insisted, 'by the royall or common lawes established (all derived from that of nature ... are in conscience of Gods commandment to be permitted them.' To deny those rights is a crime against nature of the same order as 'filthy Sodomites, sleepers, ignorant beasts, disciples of Cham, Balaam, and fore, rockes, clouds without water, corrupt trees twice dead, raging warres, wandering stares, to despise government ... spots and blots, wells without water, clouds carried about without a tempest, to whom the black darknesse is reserved for ever'.[36] Again citing Vitoria, he insists that infidels and, in this case, Native Americans cannot be deprived of their property: 'nor can Infidelitie which concerneth Divine Law, yea in matters supernaturall, take away that right which Positive or Naturall Law hath given; nor exclude from just title on Earth [in margin "Vict. de Ind", i.e., Vitoria, "On the American Indians"]'.[37] Indeed, he argued, it would be unjust not only to challenge Native American dominion but even to breach sovereignty:

> And for Ophir, long before inhabited (as appeareth Gen. 10) he [Solomon] did not for the discovery thereof, then new, challenge jurisdiction or sovereigntie, as Lord of that Sea or region by him discovered (no more than the Ophirians had been Lords of Israel, if they had then discovered it) but left things as he found them, the Countrey appropriate to the Inhabitants [Vitoria cited again in margin].[38]

Purchas was not exceptional in his agreement with Vitoria on this point. In *Mare liberum*, as we shall see, the Dutch philosopher and statesman Hugo Grotius had made the same argument, and had made it also on the authority of Vitoria: namely, that the Indians could no more be dispossessed of their land than the Europeans dispossessed by the Indians. According to Grotius: 'Victoria therefore rightly saith that the Spaniards got no more authority over the Indians for this cause than the Indians had over the Spaniards if any of them had come formerly into Spain.'[39] Grotius' *Mare liberum* had been translated into English by Richard

[35] Purchas, *Hakluytus posthumus*, vol. 1, bk. 2, ch. 1, p. 23.

[36] Purchas, *Hakluytus posthumus*, vol. 1, bk. 1, ch. 5, p. 14. [37] *Ibid.*, p. 16. [38] *Ibid.*

[39] Grotius, *The free sea*, p. 15.

Hakluyt. Given that Hakluyt had left Purchas all his papers (which Purchas employed in composing *Hakluytus posthumus*), we could also assume that Purchas was familiar with Grotius' work.

Citing Vitoria, Purchas argued that even the preaching of Christianity could not justify the dispossession of the Indians:

> And in his [Vitoria's] Relectiones of the Indians he sayeth, that it doth not appeare to him, that the Christian Faith hath so beene preached to them, that they are bound sub novo peccato to beleeve it, having had no probable perswasion, as Miracles and examples of Religious life, but contrarie; yea, had the faith beene never so probably propounded, and they rejected it, yet might they not be spoyled of their Goods, or pursued by Warre.[40]

Alberico Gentili, the professor of law in Elizabethan Oxford, had made the same argument in *De jure belli libri tres*. In the chapter 'Whether it is just to make war for the sake of religion', Gentili cited 'the learned Vitoria' for the argument that 'religion was not a just reason for the war of his Spanish countrymen against the Indians'.[41]

Many of the Virginia Company promoters also warned of the problems of dispossession. One of the Company's hired pens, Robert Gray, declared 'that there is no intendment to take away from them by force that rightful inheritance they have in that Countrey'.[42] And William Crashaw, who kept the works of the Salamanca theologians in a room above the chapel at the Middle Temple, concluded: 'A Christian may take nothing from a heathen against his will . . . We will take nothing from the Savages by power nor pillage, by craft nor violence, neither goods, lands nor libertie, much lesse life.'[43] The Virginia Company's anonymous *True declaration of the estate of the colonie in Virginia* paraphrased Vitoria in a further statement of these fears and explicitly acknowledged the debt to 'Salamanca'. According to the report, Christianity must be preached in Virginia in:

> one of these three waies: [1] Either meerly Apostolically, without the helpe of man, (without so much as staffe [2] (or meerly imperiallie, when a Prince hath conquered their bodies, that the Preachers may feede their soules; [3]

[40] Purchas, *Hakluytus posthumus*, vol. 1, bk. 2, ch. 1, p. 20.

[41] Alberico Gentili, *De jure belli libri tres*, translation of 1612 edn, first published 1598, ed. John C. Rolfe, 2 vols. (Oxford, 1933), vol. 1, p. 39.

[42] Robert Gray, *A good speed to Virginia* (London, 1610), sig. [C4]r.

[43] William Crashaw, *A sermon preached before right honourable the Lord Lawarre* (London, 1609), sig. [D3]v–D4v. William Symonds, another Company promoter, raised the same problem: 'the countrey, they say, is possessed by owners, that rule and governe it in their owne right: then with what conscience, and equitie can we offer to thrust them, by violence out of their inheritances?' William Symonds, *Virginia* (London, 1609), p. 10.

> Or mixtly, by discoverie, and trade of merchants; where all temporall meanes are used for defence, and security, but none for offence, or crueltie. For the first (to preach Apostolicallie) it is simplie impossible: except we had the gift of tongues, that every nation might heare the word of God in their owne language . . . For the second, to preach the Gospell to a nation conquered, and to set their soules at liberty when we have brought their bodies to slaverie; It may be a matter sacred in the Preachers, but I know not how justifiable in the rulers, who for their mere ambition to set upon the glosse of religion. Let the divines of Salamanca, discusse that question, how the possessor of the west Indies, first destroyed and then instructed.[44]

With this appeal to the authority of the Salamanca theologians, the author concluded that 'The third belongs to us' – namely, the third method of colonisation is 'by discoverie and trade of merchants, where all temporal means are pursued for defence and securitie but none for offence or crueltie'.

Vitoria and the right of communication

Here we see where English colonial promoters began to enter the door left open by Vitoria. They insisted that they would not conquer, but that they had a right to enter the lands of the Indians for trade and to defend themselves in that situation if necessary. The right to trade also included the right to trade for land, thus the prominent colonist John Rolfe concluded his *Relation of the state of Virginia* by observing that he had described the colonists' 'several places of . . . abode'. 'Which places, or seates', he noted, 'are all our owne ground, not so much by conquest . . . but purchased of the [Indians] freely, and they very willingly selling it.' Similarly, William Strachey insisted that in the 'Law of nations', the right of 'Community betwixt man and man' permitted the English to trade with the Indians.[45] It was but a short step to claim that the natural right of communication had been denied, and Strachey, along with many of his contemporaries, argued that in that case the Roman and natural law right to meet force with force would justify the use of violence against the Indians.[46]

44 *A true declaration of the estate of the colonie in Virginia* (London, 1610), pp. 6–9. Compare Francisco de Vitoria, *On the American Indians*, in Pagden and Lawrence (eds.), *Vitoria: political writings*, pp. 278–81.

45 William Strachey, *The historie of travell into Virginia Britannia* [1609–12], eds. Louis B. Wright and Virginia Freund (London, 1953), pp. 22–3.

46 Fitzmaurice, *Humanism and America*, pp. 144–7.

It was clear, however, that the right to communication and commerce was not a right of property, far less sovereignty. In other words, it did not provide secure tenure for a coloniser. At this point, the legal profile of English colonisation looked much more appropriate to Portuguese factories than to settler communities. Indeed, the argument of commerce implicitly assumes that rights reside in the persons with whom one is trading. The English insisted on the right to commerce with the Indians by using precisely the same arguments that they had used to insist on free trade (when they chose to insist on free trade) with other European nations, particularly the Spanish and the Dutch and their dependencies. It was no accident that Richard Hakluyt, the premier Elizabethan promoter of colonies, had chosen to translate Grotius' *Mare liberum*, of which the principal thesis was that 'it is lawful for any nation to go to any other and trade with it'.[47] Hakluyt's translation of Grotius (at some point between 1609 and 1616) may have been commissioned by the English East India Company to help it in its struggles with both the Portuguese and the Dutch for the right to trade in the East Indies. Grotius had written *Mare liberum* to support the claims of the Dutch East India Company. Hakluyt was at this time working for the English East India Company (which shared leaders and membership with the Virginia Company, notably Thomas Smith). But Hakluyt could not have completed this translation without being mindful that it supported contemporary justifications for the Virginia colony. The colonisation of America had, after all, been the principal concern of his life's work. He had always placed that concern within a global context. In common with many of his contemporaries, he understood the colonisation of America to be part of a political and religious struggle between European powers which was being conducted on an increasingly global scale. Grotius' *Mare liberum*, while specifically addressing the East, was also engaged with conflicts arising from that global competition.

Just as freedom of the sea was interesting Hakluyt, it was important that the title to Purchas' chapter on the rights of infidels was 'Of the proprietie which Infidels have in their Lands and Goods: Of proprietie in the sea, and of Solomon's proprietie of the sea and Shoare of Ezion Geber'.[48] The issue of property in the sea had been central to disputes about freedom of commerce. The two issues turned on the same principle. Freedom of the seas was based upon the Roman law notion of *res communis*: namely, that things which could not be taken would rest the property of all, and

[47] Grotius, *The free sea*, p. 6. [48] Purchas, *Hakluytus posthumus*, vol. 1, bk. 1, ch. 5, pp. 14–16.

therefore could be made the particular property of nobody. The existence of the sea as common property, or the property of nobody, was fundamental to the right of communication and free movement. Freedom of commerce was also understood to be an extension of the natural communication that should exist between man and man. To have the freedom of the sea was to have freedom of commerce. For many Europeans, such as Vitoria, to demand these rights of Native Americans was to ask no more than what was demanded from other Europeans (although, as we shall see, others such as Pufendorf would disagree). The demand recognised that Native Americans had a place at the legal table. The justification of colonies by commerce, therefore, was concerned much more with whether Native Americans would grant rights and less with the question of whether they possessed rights (taking for granted the fact that they did).

Alberico Gentili had emphasised this disjunction between arguments from commerce and the justification of dominion in a passage that does not fit his belligerent image. He argued:

> No one doubts today that what we call the New World is joined to our own and has always been known to the remote Indi. And that is one reason why the warfare of the Spaniards in that part of the world seems to be justified, because the inhabitants prohibited other men from commerce with them; and it would be an adequate defence, *if the statement were true*. For commerce is in accordance with the law of nations [*ius gentium*], and a law is not changed by opposition to it. But the Spaniards were aiming there, not at commerce, but at dominion. And they regarded it as beyond dispute that it was lawful to take possession of those lands which were not previously known to us; just as if to be known to none of us was the same thing as to be possessed by no one [*in nullius bonis*].[49]

Scepticism on the same question was repeated in Hakluyt's translation of Grotius' *Mare liberum*: 'For they who pursue the barbarians with war, as the Spaniards do the people of America, are wont to pretend two things: that they are hindered from trading with them, or because they will not acknowledge the doctrine of true religion.'[50] As they sought a colony rather

[49] Gentili, *De jure belli*, vol. I, p. 89, emphasis added. Anthony Pagden argues that Gentili here conflates the argument of communication and the argument of occupation. On the contrary, it would seem that Gentili, like Vitoria, was progressively considering each natural law claim to title before dismissing it. See Anthony Pagden, 'Gentili, Vitoria, and the fabrication of a "natural law of nations"', in Kingsbury and Straumann (eds.), *The Roman foundations of the law of nations*, pp. 358–9. See also Benjamin Straumann, 'The corpus iuris as a source of law between sovereigns', in Kingsbury and Straumann (eds.), *The Roman foundations of the law of nations*, pp. 113–14.

[50] Grotius, *The free sea*, p. 11.

than a factory, the English had to find a justification appropriate to a colony and one less vulnerable to the cynicism of their contemporaries.

Acosta and the redescription of Native Americans

The most important innovation by the promoters of Virginia was not in exploiting the gaps on communication opened by Vitoria; rather, it was completely to reverse the moral force of the argument of occupation which was the strongest pillar in the Salamanca defence of indigenous rights. Once reversed, occupation would become the principal weapon in the attack upon indigenous rights. The nature of this reversal was, of course, astoundingly simple – so simple that many historians, as we have seen, would like to conclude that it was Vitoria's intention all along. All that was required was a change in empirical description while adhering to the metaphysical assumptions regarding the exploitation of nature made by the Salamanca theologians. Rather than recognising that Indians lived in civil societies, as they had done, the English started describing Native Americans as devoid of society, closer in this respect to animals than humans, living off nature rather than exploiting it. William Strachey demanded:

> Who will think it is an unlawful act, to fortefye, and strengthen our selves (as Nature requires) . . . in the wast and vast, unhabited groundes of their amongst a world of which not one foot of a thousand, do they either use or know how to turne to any benefit, and therefore lyes so great a Circuit vayne and idle before them?[51]

The 'Natives' had failed to create political societies. Importantly, these claims were made by reference to the natural law theory developed by the Spanish theologians and again by direct reference to Salamanca and Salamanca-influenced writers. John Donne, glossing *ferae bestiae*, observed in his sermon before the Virginia Company: 'In the law of Nature and Nations, a land never inhabited, by any, or utterly derelicted and immemorially abandoned by the former Inhabitants, becomes theirs that will possesse it.'[52] Neither, he argued, does a man 'become proprietary of the Sea, because he hath two or three Boats, fishing on it'. Whereas freedom of the sea had been used to support arguments for commerce with the Indians, now the idea of free seas was used to compare sea and land, and

[51] Strachey, *Historie of travell into Virginia Britannia*, p. 25.

[52] John Donne, *A sermon preached to the honourable company of the Virginian plantation* (London, 1622), pp. 25–7.

to find that the land could also be void of ownership. The Native Americans had failed to turn trees into chairs. And, most damnably, they had failed to demonstrate their humanity. They were accordingly condemned as 'participating rather of the nature of beasts than men' and as people who 'doe but live like dear in heards'.[53]

Alberico Gentili's writings clearly provided part of the context for these descriptions of men as beasts.[54] In passages reminiscent of Juan Ginés de Sepúlveda, the Spanish apologist for conquest, Gentili had argued that it is just to wage war against those 'who wearing the human form, live the life of the most brutal of beasts', and citing Cicero's *De officiis*, he observed that 'some men differ very little from the brutes. They have the human form, but in reality they are beasts'.[55] In contrast to Sepúlveda, however, he was not specifically referring to the people of the New World in either case. In 'Of an honourable reason for waging war', Gentili did exclaim: 'why should Covarruvias [Vitoria's student, Diego de Covarrubias] reproach me and others for that other war, waged by the Spaniards against the violators of the law of nature and of common law, against cannibals, and monsters of lewdness'.[56] Here, and against claims he made to the contrary, Gentili accepted an account of the peoples of the New World as having committed crimes against nature and a justification of conquest on that basis. But this was not equivalent to the descriptions, made by Strachey, Donne, Symonds and Gray, of the people of the New World as brute beasts who do not possess dominion or sovereignty. On the contrary, people with no dominion or sovereignty cannot really be conquered; their territory is merely occupied.

Gentili rejected the notion that the Roman emperor could be lord of all the world and he likewise rejected the papal donations. Having turned away from these justifications of global order, he adopted private law principles from Roman law as the basis for a law of peoples.[57] One of these private law principles was *occupatio*. In clear reference to the Roman law *ferae bestiae*, Gentili declared that 'the seizure of vacant places is regarded as a law of nature'. 'The ruling of our jurists', he argued, 'with regard to unoccupied lands is, that those who take it have a right to it, since it is the property of no one. And even though such lands belong to the sovereign of that territory, as others maintain, yet because of that law of

53 Gray, *A good speed to Virginia*, sigs. Br–v; and Symonds, *Virginia*, p. 15.

54 See Williams, *The American Indian in Western legal thought*, p. 211 on parallels in Robert Gray and Gentili's descriptions of Indians.

55 Gentili, *De jure belli*, vol. 1, pp. 41 and 7.

56 *Ibid.*, pp. 122–3.

57 Straumann, 'The Corpus iuris as a source of law between sovereigns', pp. 101–23.

nature which abhors a vacuum, they will fall to the lot of those who take them.'[58] He included lands in the New World in this category, but he also included much of Italy, Spain and Greece:

> But are there today no unoccupied lands on the earth? Is it not, pray, being reduced more and more to the wilderness of primeval times, or in this decrepit old age is it more fruitful than ever before? What is Greece today, and the whole of Turkey? What is Africa? What of Spain? It is the most populous country of all; yet under the rule of Spain is not almost all of the New World unoccupied? Why should I name thee, Italy, in this connexion, and the country about Aquileia, Pisa, and Rome itself, unkempt and unwholesome because of the small number of its inhabitants?[59]

While Gentili brought Roman law, and occupation in particular, to the understanding of global order, he did not use these tools to provide a clear vindication of the dispossession of Native Americans. Rather, he reminded his audience that occupation was a double-edged sword and that Montezuma (or Wahunsonacock for that matter), had he conquered Europe, may have exercised dominion (even around Rome, the centre of Europe's greatest civilisation) with perhaps more justice than the Europeans had in America.

The employment of the works of José de Acosta was far more important than the writing of Gentili for the reversal of the force of *ferae bestiae* found in writers on Virginia. Born in 1540 and educated partly at Salamanca, Acosta died in 1600 as rector of the Jesuit College in Salamanca.[60] He was a Jesuit whose 'mind had been formed by Vitoria and his successors'.[61] In contrast, however, to the theologians of Salamanca, Acosta spent sixteen years in the Americas. He was a missionary whose thoughts on the justice of colonisation were shaped by long experience in Peru. He was, like Vitoria, disturbed by the violence of the Spanish conquests. 'Great harm', he argued, 'has been done to the Faith in this region from the first from the great liberty taken to participate in violence.'[62] In the second book of his *De procuranda Indorum* (1588) concerning just and unjust war (*De jure et iniuria belli*), he agreed with the Salamanca authors that 'in no way whatsoever' was infidelity a just cause to wage war: 'God alone is judge and avenger of that.'[63] He also refuted the doctrine that war can be waged against those who commit crimes against nature. He pointed out that only

58 Gentili, *De jure belli*, vol. 1, pp. 79–80. 59 *Ibid.*, pp. 80–1.

60 José de Acosta, *De procuranda Indorum salute*, trans. G. Stewart McIntosh, 2 vols. (Tayport, 1995–6), vol. 1, pp. i–v; Pagden, *The fall of natural man*, p. 147.

61 Pagden, *The fall of natural man*, p. 147. 62 Acosta, *De procuranda Indorum*, vol. 1, p. 41.

63 *Ibid.*, p. 58.

God has the authority to punish sin, concluding: 'The fact that a republic sins by making stupid and pernicious laws, or that its prince or its magistrates fall into bad habits, does not give the right to another neighbouring republic or its prince to promulgate better laws, nor the right to use force against them in order to apply such laws or make them be obeyed.'[64] At the same time, he agreed that commerce and preaching were just causes for 'incursions into the lands of the barbarians'.[65]

For Vitoria, however, the American Indian was an abstract and undifferentiated creation. Acosta's experience in the Americas led him to distinguish between Native Americans on the basis of cultural signs. He accordingly developed a progressive theory of barbarism (and civilisation). In the 'first class' he placed 'those who do not depart greatly from true reason and the common way of life', for which the best example were the Chinese. Such peoples 'have a stable form of government, legal system, fortified cities, magistrates' and prosperous commerce. Of most importance was that the barbarians of this first category have 'the use and knowledge of letters, for where there are books and engraved monuments there the people are more human and civilised'.[66] In the 'second class' he placed 'Barbarians who did not achieve the use of writing nor the knowledge of philosophy or civil rights'. Nevertheless, this second category of barbarians would have government, fixed settlements, leaders, law and order, military capability and some form of religion. In this class Acosta placed the Mexicans and Peruvians 'whose empires and republics, laws and institutions, are truly worthy of admiration'.[67] For these people to receive the Gospel, there was an argument, he claimed, that they should fall under the *imperium* of Christian princes, but that they should not be deprived of *dominium* – that is, 'they are not to be deprived of the free use of their riches and inheritance'.[68] This argument was consistent with Vitoria. The sovereignty, or *imperium*, of a Christian prince over the second class of barbarians might be justified, but not *dominium*, not the dispossession of land and goods or the destruction of social systems. As we have seen, this second class of barbarism fitted many of the descriptions of 'Virginian' natives from the 1580s through to the first years of the Chesapeake colony. Thus, such descriptions could support *imperium*, but not dispossession.

Where Acosta would prove particularly useful, however, was in his creation of the 'third class' of barbarians. 'There are', he argued, 'many groups and nations of them in the New World. Amongst them are savages similar to wild animals, who hardly have human feelings – without law,

64 *Ibid.*, p. 63. 65 *Ibid.*, pp. 84–5. 66 *Ibid.*, p. 4. 67 *Ibid.* 68 *Ibid.*, p. 5.

without agreements, without government, without nationhood, who move from place to place, or if they live in one place they are more like wild animals' caves or animal cages'. 'The majority of those living in Brazil', he added, 'and almost all those living in Florida are like that.'[69] Clearly, these people, who for Acosta included the natives of the northern parts of America, could not be dispossessed because they did not possess. They had no *meum* and *tuum*, no mine and yours. In contrast to the second class of barbarians, they had failed to create dominion through the exploitation of the laws of nature.

From 1609, Virginia was redescribed in these terms and this redescription employed Acosta's writings. The reception of Acosta's writings made it possible to embrace Vitoria's attack on the Spanish conquests for the reason that the societies conquered had already at the time of conquest been 'taken' (to use the terms of *ferae bestiae*), and at the same time they made it possible to describe the land in which North American Indian peoples lived as open to the first taker and therefore justly colonised. In 1604, Acosta's *Historia natural y moral de las Indias* was translated into English by Edward Grimstone with the title *The naturall and morall historie of the east and west Indies*. Acosta's *Historia* was a work in which the progressive theory of barbarity established in *De procuranda Indorum* was demonstrated through an account of America in terms of its nature and, importantly, its people and their 'manners, ceremonies, lawes, governments, and warres'.[70] In this work Acosta argued that there was a great diversity of peoples in the Americas and he showed how each corresponded to one of his classifications of barbarity through analyses of their political structures, commerce, customs, physical environment and (the most telling sign) religions. This work, the original and translation, was enthusiastically received by promoters of early modern English colonisation. It was first recorded to have been employed in 1596 to support Walter Raleigh's voyages to Guiana and in particular to help prove the existence of El Dorado. In July of that year, Thomas Hariot, the Elizabethan scientist and employee of Raleigh, wrote to Sir Robert Cecil, the Secretary of State, concerning 'El Dorado which hath been showed your Honor out of the Spanish book of Acosta'.[71] Here we see Acosta's text employed not merely in curiosity or the pursuit of knowledge but, in the attempt to sway Cecil, as an instrument in the councils of state and as a tool of colonial expansion.

69 *Ibid.*

70 José de Acosta, *The natuall and morall historie of the east and west Indies* (London, 1604), title page.

71 See Fitzmaurice, *Humanism and America*, p. 52.

In the years after the foundation of Jamestown, Acosta's *Historia* was cited on matters of nature and custom in ways which supported his theory of progressive barbarism. Moreover, it was cited specifically in order to employ that theory to redescribe Algonquian peoples of the Chesapeake as belonging to the third class of barbarism and so to justify the dispossession of those people or, rather, to justify the possession of the lands on which those people lived, but from which they could not be dispossessed, having no or few possessions. William Strachey's *Historie of travell into Virginia Britannia* was typical of this use of Acosta. Strachey wrote his *Historie* during his time in Virginia as Secretary of the colony between 1609 and 1612. It is thought that he had a copy of Acosta's *Historie* with him in the Jamestown fort.[72] If this was the case, it again reveals Acosta's *Historie* in a pragmatic light: namely, as an instrument of a colonial secretary. We shall see this relationship between texts and action, and the breakdown of the border between the two, repeated over centuries. Acosta's text served as an authority on New World cosmology and was therefore particularly useful in negotiating with the people and nature of that world.

What Strachey learned from that cosmology is evident in his own *Historie*. Importantly, he employed Acosta in his chapters 'De origine, populi' and 'Of the religion amongst the inhabitaunts'. For Acosta, religion was the best measure of the state of a civilisation. Strachey observed that the Virginian Indians were not so base that they were without religion: 'There is as yet in *Virginia* no place discovered to be so savage and simple, in which the Inhabitants have not a religion.'[73] They were all the same, he argued, committed to devilish practices such as sacrifices, and it is clear that he thought that the Virginian Indians, along with most Americans, belonged to the third class of barbarians. On this matter, he referred the reader to Acosta: 'that the Devill hath obteyned the use of the like offering in many other parts of *America, Acosta* hath observed and related in his morrall and naturall History'.[74] In the chapter on the origin of New World peoples, Strachey stated even more emphatically his view that those peoples belonged to the lowest category of barbarians, asking 'what difference may be betweene them and bruit beasts, nay things more vyle, and abhorring the inbredd motions of Nature yt self'. Explaining how this 'vagabond race of Cham' could have got itself into the New World, Strachey declared: 'Lett me referre the reader to the search of *Acosta* in his [space] booke, Chap: [space] of his morall and naturall History of the West-Indies.' And he left no doubt about his estimation of Acosta, who, he

[72] Strachey, *Historie of travell into Virginia Britannia*, p. xxvii. [73] *Ibid.*, p. 88. [74] *Ibid.*, p. 90.

continued, 'hath so officiously laboured herein, as he should but bring Owles to Athens, who should study for more strayned, or new Aucthority Concerning the same'.[75]

Samuel Purchas and Acosta

The English author who most enthusiastically employed Acosta was Samuel Purchas. Indeed, Purchas was more indebted to Acosta (and more indebted to Acosta than he was to Vitoria) than was any other early modern English writer. In *Hakluytus posthumus*, Purchas used Acosta's *De temporibus novissimus* (first published in 1590) and *De procuranda Indorum* to argue that the northern parts of the Americas were 'thinly inhabited, and indeed in great part not at all'.[76] Chapters 2, 4, 5 and 6 of Book 5, Part 2 of *Hakluytus posthumus* reprinted much of the first six books of Grimstone's translation of Acosta, from a total of seven. But it was in *Purchas his pilgrimage* that this debt was most clear, particularly in Books 8 and 9 concerning the Americas. Nor did Purchas hide his debt to Acosta. In the first sentence of Book 8, he acknowledged that his subject would allow contemplation of 'such Philosophical Subjects, as [b] the best Authors have thought worthie the first place in their Histories of these parts'. The marginal note 'b' cites 'Joseph Acosta de procuranda Indorum salute, & hist indie [*The natuall and morall historie of the east and west Indies*]', as well as Giovanni Botero, *Relationi universali* and Francisco López de Gómara. The following two books of *Purchas his pilgrimage* are abridgements of Acosta, Botero and Gómara's histories. Purchas laboriously cut and pasted from the three texts, with assistance from many more minor sources, to weave a relatively seamless narrative of the history and customs of the New World. With Acosta, Purchas drew most heavily upon the books of moral history in the *Natuall and morall historie*: that is, the books concerned with custom – 'manners, ceremonies, laws, governments'. Unravelling this complex fabric is extremely difficult, but it is clear, for example, that of the 100 pages in Acosta's fifth book, Purchas reproduced at least thirty, and in the 150 pages of Books 8 and 9 of the *Pilgrimage*, Acosta was cited sixty-three times.[77] Purchas repeatedly and explicitly reverts to

[75] *Ibid.*, p. 55. For the use of Acosta, see also, for example, *A true declaration of the estate of the colonie in Virginia*, pp. 8 and 23. On Acosta, see also Joyce Chaplin, *Subject matter: technology, the body, and science on the Anglo-American frontier, 1500–1676* (Cambridge, MA, 2001), pp. 120 and 177.

[76] Purchas, *Hakluytus posthumus*, bk. 1, ch. 2.7, pp. 58–60, 'Of America whether it were then peopled'.

[77] Book five of Acosta is numbered 329–430; the following thirty pages are reproduced in Books 8 and 9 of Purchas' *Pilgrimage* (cross-referenced page numbers in the *Pilgrimage* are given in brackets):

Acosta's voice: 'They shewed me, (it is *Acostas* speech)...'; 'But to return to Acosta, h he telleth...'[78]

The availability and impact of Acosta's work in seventeenth-century England is evident from the fact that Purchas used Grimstone's 1604 translation of the *Natural and moral history* and not the original in Spanish or De Bry's 1590 Latin version (although he did use the Latin version of *De procuranda Indorum*, which was not translated into English until the twentieth century). The fact that it is Grimstone's translation and not Purchas' is rapidly evident from a comparison of any of the numerous transcribed passages. In the pages of the *Pilgrimage*, Grimstone almost achieved a second edition (which would come later), although in contrast to Acosta, he received no acknowledgement. Through Purchas we see Grimstone's text at work, but we also see Purchas at work with Grimstone's text. It was necessary to make adjustments to Acosta's account. It was important, for example, both for the Protestant Purchas and the Catholic Acosta that heathen religion could corruptly imitate true Christian religion. In Acosta's progressive history, a people who believed in one god was more advanced than a people who followed numerous gods. Book 5, Chapter 25 of Acosta's *Historia* accordingly recorded the encouraging ways in which Mexican religious rites 'laboured to imitate and counterfeit the sacraments of the Holy Church', albeit in ways corrupted by the Devil. Purchas reprinted this chapter. But where Acosta concluded that 'the Gospel of our Lord Jesus Christ thrust out all these superstitions' (to which Grimstone apparently did not object), Purchas felt obliged to adapt this conclusion with 'till the Spaniards substituted in place thereof their Masse, a masse of more monstrous absurdities, (in their transubstantiation, bread-worshipping, God-eating...) then the former, notwithstanding the fairer pretexts of Christian and Catholike titles'.[79] Here Acosta's progressive theory of history is given a Protestant teleology.

Acosta's importance to Purchas is not, however, revealed simply by the extent to which Purchas borrowed from Acosta's narrative of American history and culture. On the level of narrative, he was almost equally indebted to Botero and Gómara. There was a more profound link between the puritan Purchas and 'that learned and iudicious Author, *Josephus Acosta*', a Jesuit.[80] The *Pilgrimage*, first published in 1613 and the

340–1 (718); 345–7 (736); 348–50 (674); 360–1 (730); 365–6 (672); 368–9 (671); 391–3 (734–5); 393–6 (679); 398–400 (732); 402–6 (673); 406–7 (731); 408 (673). This list is not exhaustive.

78 Purchas, *Purchas his pilgrimage*, pp. 728 and 727.

79 *Ibid.*, pp. 734–5; Edward Grimstone, *The naturall and morall historie of the east and west Indies* (London, 1604), pp. 391–3.

80 Purchas, *Purchas his pilgrimage*, p. 610.

foundation of Purchas' subsequent work, was to a large degree *modelled* on Acosta's *Historia*, although Purchas was more ambitious than Acosta in scope, taking all time and all the world as his subject. Above all, Purchas conformed to Acosta's classes of barbarity and used Acosta's signs of classification to conduct his analysis, often citing Acosta to establish authority. Purchas' full title was illustrative of this debt: namely, *Purchas his pilgrimage, or relations of the world and the religions observed in all ages and places discovered, from the creation to the present*. Religion was the focus of Purchas' history of the world in part because, as for Acosta, the state of religion was the best indicator of a culture's state of civilisation or barbarity. As Purchas stated in dedicating the book to Archbishop George Abbott, one of the two 'lessons' of his work was 'that law of Nature [has] written in the practise of all men (as we here in the particulars doe shew) the profession of some Religion'.[81] Books 8 and 9 of the *Pilgrimage* were concerned with the second and third classes of barbarians in the Americas (there being no barbarians of the first class). Citing Acosta, Purchas observed that the Mexicans belonged at first to the third class of barbarity: 'very barbarous and savage, which lived only by Hunting ... They lived naked, solitarie in the Mountaines, without Tillage, Policie, or any Religious Ceremonies'.[82] He then went on, again employing Acosta, to describe the development of a complex religion, the following of an idol who led them to create Tenochtitlan, the creation of temples, ceremonies, priests, new idols, feasts, sacrifices, baptism, marriages, burials, colleges, schools, picture writing and beliefs concerning life after death and the soul.[83] By contrast, the Brazilians, who clearly conformed to the lowest form of barbarity, were later summarised with the sentence: 'They have no use of three letters in the Alphabet, L, F, R, a reason whereof some have wittily given, they have no Law, Faith, nor Ruler.'[84] In this sense they could possess no dominion, let alone sovereignty, and were 'in summe, more like beastes then men'.[85]

It was when Purchas turned to Virginia that he had the least need for Acosta's narrative. Acosta had not written on this region. And yet it is at this point that Acosta's impact upon Purchas is most evident. The Virginian Indians were described in terms of the lowest form of barbarians. The evaluation was again made by appealing to Acosta's signs of civilisation. Purchas found significance, for example, in the fact that native Virginians, 'having no letters', have no records.[86] Their understanding of

[81] *Ibid.*, Epistle dedicatory. [82] *Ibid.*, p. 659. [83] *Ibid.*, pp. 660–84. [84] *Ibid.*, p. 705.
[85] *Ibid.* [86] *Ibid.*, p. 636.

religion was presented as crude: 'I may also here insert the ridiculous conceits which some Virginians hold, concerning their first originall ... that a Hare came into their countrey and made the first men. . .'.[87] He was therefore able to propose that 'the Savage inhabitants, [are] unworthie to embrace with their rustike arms so sweet a bosome [as Virginia]'.[88] These judgements were echoed seventy years later in John Locke's famous dismissal in the *Second treatise of government* of the natural law rights of Native Americans. As we shall see in the next chapter, Locke also echoed the use of Acosta's anthropology to justify that dismissal, declaring: 'If *Josephus Acosta's* word may be taken, he tells us, that in many parts of *America* there was no Government at all.'[89] Locke was drawing upon the intellectual innovation of the previous generations of English colonisers.

In company with many of his contemporaries, Purchas employed natural law assumptions derived largely from Vitoria's defence of Indian rights to demonstrate that native Virginians do not possess rights. And he did this by employing Acosta's writings to redescribe the state of the Virginians. One could conclude that English promoters of the Chesapeake colony therefore succeeded in completely reversing the force of the Salamanca theologians' defence of indigenous rights. This statement would be only partially true. The redescription was not coherent. In his 1617 expanded edition of the *Pilgrimage*, Purchas repeated his reliance upon Acosta and again described North American Indians in terms of the lowest form of barbarity. He added, however, a further chapter to this edition, 'On the present state of Virginia', which was largely an edited version of John Rolfe's *Relation of the state of Virginia* (1616), observing: 'This peace hath yeelded many benefits, both opportunitie of lawfull purchase of a great part of the Countrey from the Natives, freely and willingly relinquishing and selling the same for Copper, or other commodities (a thing of no small consequence to the conscience, where the milde Law of Nature, not that violent Law of Armes, layes the foundation of their [the colonists'] possession.'[90] Here native dominion was assumed in the act of selling the land. The Indians were acknowledged to have rights arising from the law of nature and the author confessed to a troubled conscience on the part of the English.

This question of conscience is vital to the contradictions in the legal descriptions of native peoples. Indeed, *Purchas his pilgrimage* is not the

87 *Ibid.*, p. 641. 88 *Ibid.*, p. 631.
89 John Locke, *Two treatises of government*, ed. Peter Laslett (Cambridge, 1960), II, §103.
90 Purchas, *Purchas his pilgrimage*, p. 946.

only place where contradictions and conscience were evident in discussions of these questions. The glaring contradictions in the tracts concerning colonisation need hardly be pointed out. Almost routinely, the authors claimed, on the one hand, that the colony had purchased land from the natives and that, on the other hand, the land was possessed by no one (and therefore presumably could not be sold). How can it be possible, on the one hand, to trade with people who, on the other hand, have no mine or yours, no concept of property? These contradictions were not merely between authors, they were also frequently embraced by the authors individually, in individual tracts and on a single page. In his *History of travell into Virginia Britannia*, Strachey, for example, in response to the anxiety that 'surely Christian men, should not shew themselves like Wolves to devoure...', answered with the argument that the land would not be forcibly possessed: 'and therefore even every foote of Land which we shall take unto our use, we will bargayne and buy of them for copper, hatchets, and such like commodities'.[91] Land would be purchased, and yet, as we have heard, Strachey also claimed that the Indians neither 'use or know how to turne to any benefit' the environment in which they live and therefore have no possessions, not even land, to trade. The tension is nowhere more evident than in Robert Gray's *A good speed to Virginia*. Gray raised the customary anxiety over possession: 'The first objection is, by what right or warrant we can enter into the land of these Savages, and plant ourselves in their places.' In accordance with Company policy, he disavowed any such intention: 'the answer to the forsaid objection is, that there is no intendment to take away from them by force that *rightful inheritance* they have in that Countrey'.[92] Yet, having noted this rightful inheritance, a property right, it was Gray who described the Indians as 'beasts and brutish savages, which have no interest in it [the land], because they participate rather of the nature of beasts than men'.

These tensions underline the ideological pressure on the promoters. Their inversion of the natural law defence of the Native Americans was political rather than philosophical. It was in this quotidian and pragmatic context, rather than in philosophical discourse, that the natural law tradition began to be turned to the purposes of dispossession. The moral certainty and relative coherence found in Locke's discussions of aboriginal rights were not characteristic of the vast majority of discussions of the legal status of Indians. One of the principal tools in overcoming the rights of

[91] Strachey, *Historie of travell into Virginia Britannia*, p. 26.

[92] Gray, *A good speed to Virginia*, sig. [C4]r, emphasis added.

Indians was the inversion of the polemical force of the natural law arguments of the Spanish theologians. But it was precisely the use and knowledge of that natural law tool that nourished uncertainty and troubled consciences. Natural law assumptions could be turned back in favour of indigenous peoples as easily as they had been turned against them. In the subsequent history of European discussions of indigenous legal rights, that troubled conscience would be more often apparent in justifications of dispossession than in Locke's philosophical rigour.

CHAPTER 4

Occupation and convention

Chapter 2 revealed the way in which Spanish theologians used the idea of occupation to argue that Native Americans had rights. I then showed that this argument was reversed by the first English colonisers of America through a trope of empirical redescription. At the same time, employing Acosta's works, those English colonisers began to conceive of occupation in terms of different stages of society and not simply as an argument concerned with rights, as it had been for Vitoria. Whereas occupation was understood to mean that the potential of nature must be released in order for property to be established, the English, conscious of Vitoria's defence, simply claimed that the natives of the northern parts of America had not exploited nature and so they did not possess the land upon which they roamed like deer. Such people therefore belonged to an earlier moment in history.

While the English colonists in America sent reports back to the Virginia Company on their experiences and elaborated theories about Native American and English peoples living in different stages of history, a young Thomas Hobbes sat, as secretary to William Cavendish, later the second Earl of Devonshire, in Virginia Company meetings during the early 1620s. Similarly, the precocious young humanist scholar Hugo Grotius worked for the Dutch East India Company, also during the first decades of the seventeenth century. Both Grotius and Hobbes would refine the ideas distinguishing the natural and civil states that had been employed in the process of overseas expansion. Both represented the natural state as dangerous and emphasised the necessity of survival. Both took the humanist idea of self-preservation to be fundamental to the possession of a right. In developing these arguments, they were followed by other seventeenth-century natural law writers, notably Samuel Pufendorf and John Locke (who was also deeply engaged in colonial enterprise). For these seventeenth-century writers on natural law, with the exception of Hobbes, occupation was a means of survival as well as a means for distinguishing different stages of historical progress. What these writers on natural law succeeded in creating, therefore, was a theory of property in which occupation was essential not only to the self-preservation of individuals but also to states and, as such, it was a right that could be exercised both by individuals and states. This theory provided a powerful justification of expansion.

This is not to say that seventeenth-century natural law theorists presented a harmonious account of property. One of the most important issues dividing them was whether property was the creation of convention, or compacts, or whether it arose from individual acts.[1] Remarkably, occupation was used to explain both these theories. We have seen that medieval jurists and theologians adhered to diverse theories of private property. They disagreed about whether private property could be created in a state of nature, through occupation or whether it was a creation of a civil state. These contrasting positions shaped discussions of property during the following centuries. In the seventeenth century a theory of property developed which drew upon elements of both these positions. This was the notion that rights in things are created by occupation, or the taking of things, in a pre-civil state, but that the institution of private property is only secured in civil society through consent and agreement to the principle of occupation. Grotius and Pufendorf were the foremost adherents of this view. Their arguments contrasted with Hobbes, who agreed that a pact was necessary to establish property, but that the state of nature was so dangerous that the necessary conditions for property could only be met in a civil state. John Locke, on the other hand, argued in his *Two treatises of government* that private property could be created by the actions of individuals in a state of nature and he expanded upon the idea of occupation to explain how, and he did not agree that consent was necessary in that process.

With the exception of Hobbes, therefore, occupation played a central role in seventeenth-century jurists' and philosophers' understandings of property, but it was an understanding of occupation that was very different from medieval accounts of the concept. The theory of occupation as a right of property driven by self-preservation and creating a path out of the state of nature drove the development of the European powers' territorial

[1] For convention and 'unilateralism' in seventeenth-century accounts of property, see Kiyoshi Shimokawa, 'The origin and development of property: Conventionalism, unilateralism, and colonialism', in Peter Anstey (ed.), *The Oxford handbook of British philosophy in the seventeenth century* (Oxford, 2013).

empires in the Americas and their commercial interests in the East. These empires were focused not simply upon taking control of foreign lands and peoples, but with appropriating the land and goods of those places and frequently with pushing away or even exterminating their populations. Their concerns therefore embraced both the seizure of sovereignty and the appropriation of property. The theory of occupation was one of the most effective means with which to address these questions and was used to argue opposite viewpoints: namely, either it left little or no place for inhabitants of the lands concerned, or it was used by opponents to claim that these peoples did have rights. This understanding of property in terms of occupation was perfectly adapted to the foundation of the territorial empires. Moreover, the concern with the pre-civil condition was particularly well adapted to, and partly illustrated by, European colonisers' descriptions of the Americas as existing in such a state, just as it was also well fitted to the rejection of that argument.

Hugo Grotius on sociability and self-preservation

As we have seen, Francisco de Vitoria and Domingo de Soto lectured during the Reformation and, indeed, were concerned with questions of religious orthodoxy. Vitoria questioned whether the Conquistadors' justifications for their conquests had been heretical. However, even while teaching during the Reformation, Vitoria and Soto remained relatively optimistic about human sociability, albeit that they conceded a role for self-preservation in the formation of civil society. In the following generations, Europeans' understandings of human nature were to be challenged by the extraordinary violence that gripped Europe in the wake of the Reformation and the wars of religion. This challenge was felt by humanist writers and natural law writers alike and it changed their understandings of the state of nature and their notions of human sociability.

These changes were first evident in the writings of sixteenth-century humanists. Increasingly over the course of the sixteenth century, followers of the *studia humanitatis* from Niccolò Machiavelli to Giovanni Botero questioned the notion that virtue, narrowly understood as goodness, governed, or should govern, human behaviour. At the same time, these writers, and contemporaries such as Michel de Montaigne and Justus Lipsius, increasingly emphasised the self-interested nature of human behaviour. These concerns were adopted by Hugo Grotius, one of the most precocious humanist scholars of the early seventeenth century. Grotius was profoundly influenced by the late humanist concern with unsociable, interested behaviour. While trained in the *studia humanitatis*, Grotius became recognised as one of the greatest writers on natural law in the seventeenth century, and he was subsequently and anachronistically credited with creating international law.[2] Just as humanist scholars had been led by the violence and instability of the world in which they lived to question the role of virtue in human conduct, Grotius brought the analysis of interest to question the idea of sociability in scholastic natural law writings.[3]

Grotius too was personally familiar with the dangers of the wars of religion and civil conflict. He was born in Delft in 1583, at that time a leading city in the Dutch Revolt against Spain. His early work, *De jure praedae*, the *Commentary on the law of prize and booty* or, as he called it, *De Indis*, was written to address 'the safety of our country' in the conflict between the Dutch and the Portuguese in trade to the East Indies.[4] He took an active role in politics as the advisor to Jan van Oldenbarnevelt, the Advocate (or chief minister) of the States of Holland, but his political career was cut short when he and Oldenbarnevelt were arrested in 1618. While Oldenbarnevelt fell victim to internal divisions within Holland and was beheaded in 1619, Grotius was imprisoned for life. He escaped prison and fled to exile in France in 1621. Following such experiences, it is hardly surprising that he devoted so much of his literary energy to writing upon war. It was in exile that he wrote his major work *On the laws of war and peace*. According to one account of the development of natural law and the emergence of the so-called 'modern' school of natural law, it was Grotius who transformed the assumptions underlying the understanding of the natural state of humans.[5] Drawing on the humanist emphasis upon self-preservation and self-interest, he argued in *De Indis* that states, like individuals, are motivated by survival and self-interest, and that the conventions which regulate the behaviour of states must begin with this

[2] For a critique of Grotius as the founder of international law, see Peter Haggenmacher, *Grotius et la doctrine de la guerre juste* (Paris, 1983).

[3] On Grotius and late humanism, see Richard Tuck, *Philosophy and government 1572–1651* (Cambridge, 1993), pp. 154–69; Tuck, *Rights of war and peace*, p.78.

[4] Hugo Grotius, 'Defence of Chapter V of the Mare Liberum', in Grotius, *The free sea*, p. 77. On the conflict in the East Indies as the context for *De jure praedae*, see Borschberg, 'Hugo Grotius, East India trade and the King of Johor'; Borschberg, 'The seizure of the Sta. Catarina revisited'; van Ittersum, *Profit and principle.*

[5] Richard Tuck, 'The "modern" theory of natural law', in Anthony Pagden (ed.), *The languages of political theory in early modern Europe* (Cambridge, 1987), pp. 99–119. For a critique of the claim that Grotius marks the development of a 'modern' theory of natural law, see Tierney, *The idea of natural rights*, pp. 316–22.

assumption. The radical assumption underlying this claim was that 'an individual in nature is morally identical to a state'.[6]

It is easy to overdraw the distinction between scholastic and seventeenth-century natural law, and also to over-state Grotius' role in the development of a natural law based upon self-preservation rather than sociability.[7] Medieval canonists, and even Aquinas, identified self-love as a key part of the natural order.[8] Vitoria emphasised that although humans are naturally sociable, they create civil societies in order to protect themselves. Families, Vitoria observed, are capable of providing their members with the services that they need, but they cannot provide adequate 'defence against violent attack'. This need for security was the 'chief reason' that led Cain and Nimrod to 'compel the first men to live together in cities'.[9] He therefore concluded that the 'primitive origin of human cities and commonwealths' was a 'device implanted by Nature in man for his own safety and survival'.[10] For Vitoria, human sociability is not the cause of cities, or civil society, but rather a happy aid to the necessity of creating cities for the purposes of survival. Similarly, Grotius acknowledged human sociability as well as unsociability. One reason why we ought to be sociable, argued Grotius, is precisely because it is in our self-interest, such that 'expediency might perhaps be called the mother of justice and equity'.[11] It is through being sociable and, ultimately, creating civil society that we are most likely to guarantee our preservation. This was a kind of self-interested sociability: 'love, whose primary force and action are directed to self-interest, is the first principle of the whole natural order'.[12]

In *De Indis*, self-interested sociability was for Grotius the cause of society. In this he differed from Vitoria's dual emphasis upon self-preservation and sociability only in that for Vitoria, sociability was a natural fact that happily coincided with the necessity of creating cities. In his later and famous *De jure belli ac pacis*, however, Grotius retreated to a position on sociability that was much closer to Vitoria in his understanding of sociability as a cause of civil society; that is, he conceded a natural 'mutual desire of society', an *appetitus societatis* or, for the Stoics, *oikeiosis*,

[6] Tuck, *Rights of war and peace*, pp. 82–5.
[7] Tierney, *The idea of natural rights*, p. 322 makes a similar point comparing Grotius' thoughts on self-preservation with medieval political thought.
[8] Tierney, *The idea of natural rights*, p. 322. [9] Vitoria, *On civil power*, p. 9.
[10] *Ibid.*; see also Vitoria, *On the law of war*, in Pagden and Lawrence (eds.), *Vitoria: political writings*, p. 299 on the right of each individual to declare war for self-preservation.
[11] Hugo Grotius, *Commentary on the law of prize and booty*, ed. Martine Julia van Ittersum (Indianapolis, 2006), p. 21.
[12] *Ibid.*

which would of itself cause society.[13] 'Among the traits characteristic of man', argued Grotius, 'is an impelling desire for society' so that 'the assertion that every animal is impelled by nature to seek only its own good cannot be conceded.'[14] Rejecting Carneades' and others' views that expediency is 'the mother of what is just and fair' (with which he had agreed in 1604), Grotius responded that 'the very nature of man . . . even if we had no lack of anything would lead us into the mutual relations of society'.[15] But he added that 'the law of nature has the reinforcement of expediency' because our weakness obliges us to seek the help of others in order to 'live properly'.[16] In this account, expedience worked to the same effect as the desire for society, just as justice and self-preservation worked to the same end.[17] For Grotius, therefore, society was a creation of what is both just and what is expedient, and ideally was the consequence of a harmony between these two.[18] In this sense the impact of humanism on his account of natural law is apparent from the concern with self-preservation in the work of Montaigne, Lipsius or Pierre Charron. In addition, the calculus of justice (and honour) versus expedience was an older and central concern of humanism inherited from classical sources generally and was particularly marked in Cicero's moral philosophy, including his rhetorical works.[19]

Grotius not only changed his views on sociability over the course of his career, he also changed his theory of property. He has been seen as the first of the seventeenth-century theorists of property as the creation of convention, or a social pact. He provided two different accounts of property: one

[13] On Grotius and the *appetitus societatis*, see: Benjamin Straumann, *Hugo Grotius und die Antike* (Baden-Baden, 2007), pp. 143–57; Benjamin Straumann, '*Oikeiosis* and *appetitus societatis*: Hugo Grotius' Ciceronian argument for natural law and just war', *Grotiana*, 24–5 (2003–4), 41–66; Jon Miller, 'Stoics, Grotius and Spinoza on moral deliberation', in Jon Miller and Brad Inwood (eds.), *Hellenistic and early modern philosophy* (Cambridge, 2003), p. 137; Christopher Brooke, *Philosophic pride: stoicism and political thought from Lispsius to Rousseau* (Princeton, 2012), pp. 37–58.

[14] Hugo Grotius, *De jure belli ac pacis libri tres*, 2 vols. (Oxford, 1925), vol. 2, p. 11.

[15] *Ibid.*, p. 15.

[16] *Ibid.*

[17] Straumann, *Hugo Grotius und die Antike*, pp. 143–57; Straumann, '*Oikeiosis* and *appetitus societatis*', p. 66; Miller, 'Stoics, Grotius and Spinoza on moral deliberation', p. 137.

[18] Richard Tuck has been criticised for over-emphasising the role of self-love in Grotius' understanding of sociability: Brooke, *Philosophic pride*, p. 37; Tierney, *The idea of natural right*, p. 323; Robert Shaver, 'Grotius on scepticism and self-interest', *Archiv für Geschichte der Philosophie*, 78(1) (1996), 27–47, at 28. Tuck's emphasis is upon Grotius' 'continued attempt to integrate the laws of nature into a system based on the principle of self-preservation' (Tuck, 'The "modern" theory of natural law', p. 113), although he does acknowledge that in *De jure belli ac pacis*, Grotius changed his position on sociability to allow that 'the universal desire to live with his fellows' would lead men to society regardless of the desire for self-preservation.

[19] See Annabel Brett, 'Natural right and civil community: the civil philosophy of Hugo Grotius', *Historical Journal*, 45(1) (2002), 31–51 on Grotius and civil science, and the need to include Cicero's rhetorical works in the understanding of expedience.

that saw it as a direct product of occupation and a second in which he argued that occupation must be sanctioned by consent.

Property in *De Indis*

Grotius portrayed occupation as the direct cause of property in his early and unpublished *De Indis*. *De Indis* was written in 1604–6, but was only published, as *De jure praedae*, in 1868 four years after it was found in Grotius' family papers. Only the twelfth chapter was published in Grotius' lifetime, in 1609, as the celebrated *Mare liberum*, or *Free sea*. In what is now a well-known story, *De Indis* was written to address fierce, and sometimes deadly, competition between the Dutch and the Portuguese in the East Indies.[20] Grotius' family was heavily involved in the trade to the Indies and, like his fellow countrymen, he understood that success in that trade would be key to success in the revolt against Spain. Dutch expansion in the East Indies perhaps exceeded what was necessary for defence at home, although Grotius argued that the two were inextricably linked in his *Antiquitate Reipublicae Batavicae* published in 1610.[21]

Grotius wrote *De Indis* in response to the controversy following Jacob van Heemskerk's capture of the Portuguese ship, the *Santa Catarina*, in the Singapore Straits in 1603. The *Santa Catarina* held a fabulously rich cargo of Chinese silk and porcelain, camphor, sugar, aloes and American gold.[22] The total value was over three million guilders, almost as much as the English government's annual budget at the time.[23] Unsurprisingly, the Portuguese immediately demanded restitution of their property. The newly formed United Dutch East India Company asked Grotius to write a defence of Heemskerk's actions. Grotius published the twelfth chapter of that defence in 1609 at the request of the Company which at that time feared the Spanish demand that Dutch traders withdraw from the East as part of the negotiation that resulted in the Twelve Years' Truce from 1609 to 1621.[24]

20 Grotius, *Commentary on the law of prize and booty*, pp. xiii–xxi; Borschberg, 'Hugo Grotius, East India trade and the King of Johor'; Borschberg, 'The seizure of the Sta. Catarina revisited'; Ittersum, *Profit and principle*.

21 Romain Bertrand, *L'histoire à parts égales: Récits d'une rencontre Orient-Occident XVIe–XVIIe siècle* (Paris, 2011), pp. 296–7; Jan Blanc, 'Grotius, historiographe des Bataves au XVIIe siècle', in Chantal Grell (ed.), *Les historiographes en Europe de la fin du Moyen Age à la Révolution* (Paris, 2006), pp. 296–312.

22 Ittersum, *Profit and principle*, p. 36.

23 Tuck, *Rights of war and peace*, p. 79.

24 Borschberg, 'Hugo Grotius, East India trade and the King of Johor', 227; Ittersum, *Profit and principle*, p. xxii.

In *De Indis* and *Mare liberum*, Grotius made three important claims in response to the capture of the *Santa Catarina* and the Iberian claim to monopoly over trade to the East. First, he argued that individuals in a state of nature have the right to punish breaches of natural rights, particularly insofar as those breaches impede an individual's right to self-preservation. Second, he used the idea of occupation to claim that the first person to seize something becomes its owner – this argument could be applied to booty in war, even a war between individuals in nature, as much as it could apply to wild beasts. At the same time, he argued that the Portuguese and the Spanish could not apply this claim to occupy to the territories of the East or West Indies because they had already been taken. Third, he used the idea of occupation in a negative sense to argue that things which could not be seized, things which are inexhaustible such as the sea and the air, remain common property. He employed the first argument, concerning the right to punish, to argue that Heemskerk was responding to Portuguese aggressions against Dutch traders – and this was certainly the defence that Heemskerk used himself.[25] Whether Heemskerk's actions were private or public was unclear, but in both cases punishment of wrongs would be permitted.[26] It was debatable whether the capture of the *Santa Catarina* was necessary either to Heemskerk's self-preservation or the self-preservation of the Dutch States-General, particularly at a time when peace with Spain was increasingly likely, but the broader context of the revolt against Spain certainly aided the case.

In *Mare liberum*, Grotius had not yet developed his understanding that property is based upon contract. In attacking the Portuguese case, he argued that exclusive rights to trade in the East could only be based upon dominion, or property, in the seas and sea routes used for trading. Such a claim, he argued, would be absurd because property can only be based upon occupation, and occupation of the sea is impossible.

This renowned argument of *The free sea* would remain central to his thought: namely, the argument that the sea is the common property of all and that it cannot be made the particular property of any state or person. His success in elaborating this argument rested upon making extensive use of the Roman law of occupation except that, in this instance, he used the principles of occupation to make a negative case, a case when particular property does not exist. Particular property, he pointed out, is something that only comes to be extended over those things that will be damaged by their use; that is, not over those things, such as the air and the sea, which

[25] Ittersum, *Profit and principle*, p. 6. [26] *Ibid.*, pp. 43–52.

can be shared without being diminished.[27] Nor could particular property be extended over things which cannot be occupied either because they are so vast or because of their nature. Again, here the sea was the best, and most pertinent, example; although it could be exploited, it could not be occupied other than in very limited ways (as the Dutch jurist Cornelius van Bynkershoek would later argue, a cannon in a fort, for example, could extend territorial sovereignty over a limited area of the sea). Land, on the other hand, cannot be used by all people without conflict occurring and this is the reason why it became necessary to have property: 'If any things could not remain common, they became the property of the first taker.'[28] The sea was not susceptible to occupation in this way. It could and did remain common. He therefore warned of the importance of distinguishing between different kinds of things that had not been taken: 'even though the said things are correctly called *res nullius* in so far as private ownership is concerned, they are very different from those which are also *res nullius* but which have not been assigned for common use: e.g. wild beasts, fish, and birds. Items belonging to the latter class can be made subject to private ownership.'[29] Some things remain common because they cannot be seized, while others remain common because, although they can be, they have not been seized. Grotius' argument concerning property that remains common because it cannot be taken proved to be particularly influential in the following centuries. It propelled the law of occupation, stated negatively, to a position vital to the understanding of the freedom of the seas.

Grotius argued in *De Indis* that private property was first gradually established through use: '"What had been seized as his own" by each person should become the property of that person. Such seizure is called *possessio* [the act of taking possession], the forerunner of *usus* [use], and subsequently of *dominium* [ownership].'[30] Once established, private property was cemented in law: 'The recognition of the existence of private property led to the establishment of a law on the matter, and this law was patterned after nature's plan.'[31] This process was legal recognition of the natural law right of occupation: 'For just as the right to use the goods in question was originally acquired through a physical act of attachment, the

[27] Grotius, *The free sea*, p. 116. [28] *Ibid.*

[29] Grotius, *Commentary on the law of prize and booty*, p. 322. The term 'res nullius' here was imposed on Grotius' text. It is absent in the original Latin manuscript of *De jure praedae* or *De Indis*. On this question, see Chapter 8.

[30] Grotius, *Commentary on the law of prize and booty*, p. 24.

[31] *Ibid.*, p. 318. Compare Grotius, *The free sea*, p. 22: 'Property being found out, there was a law set down which should imitate nature.'

very source (as we have observed) of the institution of private property, so it was deemed desirable that each individual's private possessions should be acquired, as such, through similar acts of attachment. This is the process known as "occupation" [*occupatio*].'[32] In summarising his argument, he declared in *Mare liberum* that 'all propriety hath his beginning from occupation'.[33] He later amplified this argument when he responded in 1615 to an attack on *The free sea* by William Welwood, the Professor of Civil Law at the University of St Andrews. In *Defence of Chapter V of mare liberum*, Grotius declared that 'property does not occur except through occupation'.[34] Again, in this early version it was clear that use and not agreement was the origin of property: 'in order that this thing become the property of that man, some deed of the man should intervene'.[35] That deed was the 'taking' set down in the Roman law of occupation and Grotius paraphrased the Roman law to make his case. Fish 'become property', he argued, employing the example from *ferae bestiae*, 'in such a way as all things which belong to no one (*res nullius*), namely by occupation'.[36]

Property in *De jure belli ac pacis*

Thirteen years later, in *De jure belli ac pacis* or *On the law of war and peace*, Grotius introduced consent into his account of the origin of private property. He argued that following the creation of the world, and again after the Flood, all things belonged equally to all people, all property was common. This state of community of property, he added, 'may be seen among certain tribes in America'.[37] As we have seen in the previous chapter, such a description of Native Americans had already become common prior to the time at which Grotius wrote *On the law of war and peace* in 1625. Moreover, Grotius was familiar with the work of José de Acosta, in particular *De procuranda Indorum salute*, which, as we have seen, was one of the most useful tools for the redescription of Native Americans as living in a natural or pre-civil state. He cited Acosta in precisely this context; that is, in his discussion of whether it is possible, as Pope Innocent IV had argued, to wage war as a punishment against those who sin against nature – in other words, against those who are 'wild beasts rather than men'.[38] For Vitoria, as Grotius noted, punishment for transgressions of the

[32] Grotius, *Commentary on the law of prize and booty*, p. 318. [33] Grotius, *The free sea*, p. 24.
[34] *Ibid.*, p. 85. [35] *Ibid.*
[36] *Ibid.*, p. 116. Note that the term 'res nullius' was again inserted into this text by the nineteenth-century translator of Grotius' *Defence* against Welwood.
[37] Grotius, *De jure belli*, pp. 186–7. [38] *Ibid.*, p. 506.

law of nature rested with a civil jurisdiction and so no state could take it upon itself to punish the subjects of another state on that ground. But Grotius agreed with Acosta that such transgressions may be punished in the same way that they can be punished in a state of nature.

For Grotius, the natural state of common property was prelapsarian, although his sources for that state, as he himself emphasised, were as much pagan as biblical. He cited Seneca, Porphyry, Diogenes Laertius, Tertullian and Philo alongside Proverbs and the apostle Paul. The state of nature was a condition in which there was 'no knowledge of evil' or of virtue.[39] In this state, people 'lived easily on the fruits which the earth brought forth of its own accord, without toil'. It was the beginning of knowledge, the knowledge of good and evil, symbolised by the tree of the knowledge of good and evil that brought people out of their state of innocence and harmony. Ambition, a vice, and industry led to the abandonment of common property, first in movable goods and later in immovables. This relationship between vice and the origin of private property is important. In his perception that property arose from our fallen nature, Grotius developed a theory of property that was harmonious with Reformation theology: namely, with the Protestant emphasis upon the inherent sinfulness of humankind and the consequent conclusion that we can be justified in the eyes of God through faith alone.

The reconciliation of the understanding of property with the theory of justification through faith alone was important for Protestant natural law philosophers throughout the seventeenth century. The association of property with sinfulness underlay ambivalence towards private property that had deep roots in Christian theology.[40] This ambivalence was extended towards colonised peoples who were sometimes believed to be living in a natural and innocent state and thus could be perceived to have fallen victim to the European vice of ambition which drove the acquisition of colonial property. Indeed, in explaining how property first became possible from our fallen nature, Grotius cited 'certain tribes in America' in order to illustrate the 'great simplicity' and 'mutual affection' which prevailed in societies prior to the introduction of property.[41] But the perception of property in terms of sinfulness, as we shall also see, would become contentious with some eighteenth-century Protestant

[39] *Ibid.*, p. 187.
[40] See, for example, on Franciscan poverty, Tierney, *The idea of natural rights*, pp. 93–130.
[41] Grotius, *De jure belli*, pp. 186–7.

philosophers, who, despite their own Reformed theology, sought to recover a theory of human sociability.

Grotius argued that as people first left the state of nature, but without having come to a fully civil state, they began to take things for their own individual use, which was necessary for their self-preservation. They thus developed a right in these things that derived from their right to self-preservation. The taking of things for use, or our 'attachment' to them, as he put it, was occupation and in this sense there is no difference in Grotius' account of the origin of individual property between *On the law of war and peace* and *De Indis*. He stated the doctrine of occupation in its conventional formulation as applying to 'wild animals, fish and birds' and observed that this principle is 'not at variance with what we often read in the Roman law'.[42] Importantly, he also applied this doctrine to land (although land was notably absent from the Roman law statements of occupation): 'Unoccupied lands become the property of the individuals who become occupants of them, unless they have been taken over as a whole by a people.'[43] He repeated this Roman law doctrine throughout his work: 'Things which are ownerless, to be sure, become the property of those who take them.'[44] In stating this doctrine, he was therefore establishing an origin for property that, so far, was entirely familiar.

The difference beween *De Indis* and *On the law of war and peace* is apparent when Grotius explains that 'as soon as community of ownership was abandoned . . . all agreed, that whatever each one had taken possession of should be his property'.[45] The number of people in a country becomes so abundant, he argued, that private property in land is necessary in order to avoid conflicts over the use of land and goods. The 'kind of agreement' among people over the creation of property was 'either expressed, as by division, or implied as by occupation'.[46] Therefore, it was no longer simply the taking of things or their use that was the origin of property, but compact. People recognised, however, the natural justice that each person should own those things to which they had become attached for their survival, so their agreement on what would constitute property was precisely the principle that the first person to take something should be the owner. Nevertheless, in this analysis, Grotius had placed occupation, or taking, at one step removed from the origin of property. First, consent was necessary.

[42] *Ibid.*, p. 192. [43] *Ibid.*, p. 191. [44] *Ibid.*, p. 670. [45] *Ibid.*, pp. 189–90.
[46] *Ibid.*, p. 189.

This emphasis upon compact in the understanding of property was later followed by both Thomas Hobbes and Samuel Pufendorf. For Hobbes, however, such pacts could only be made in civil society. In both *De Indis* and *On the law of war and peace*, Grotius presented the origin of private property in terms of the evolution of human society. He refers to 'stages' in the 'evolution of property'.[47] Private property did not exist in the first state of nature, but rights in things necessary for survival preceded the fully civil state, while the institution of dominium belonged to the civil state and was modelled upon nature.[48]

For Grotius, peoples who did not practise intensive cultivation could nevertheless be regarded as having established sovereignty and could be perceived as the possessors of their own countries. He explicitly stated the principle that uncultivated land could be held sovereign. He regarded occupation as an act that could be performed both by individuals in creating particular property and by peoples in creating sovereignty. For this reason, he argued that foreigners have a right to occupy and take possession of the desert places in a country, but this did not grant them sovereignty to that soil: 'uncultivated land ought not to be considered as occupied except in respect to sovereignty, which remains unimpaired in favour of the original people'.[49] Although Grotius described some Native American peoples as living in a state of nature, here he provided a potential critique of the conquest of non-European peoples. While many non-European peoples were not perceived to have achieved the same level of land exploitation as found in some parts of Europe, they could nevertheless be understood to possess sovereignty.

Grotius' thoughts on freedom of the sea in *On the law of war and peace* substantially repeated his argument in *De Indis* and *Mare liberum*. This restatement of the doctrine of sea as common property is striking, however, because it is now placed in the different context of a theory of private property in terms of consent. In the beginning of human society, Grotius argued, 'when the human race could assemble', 'primary acquisition' was made by 'division', that is, agreements amongst the assembled people.[50] Thereafter, he added, 'it takes place through occupation only'. In the

[47] Grotius, *Commentary on the law of prize and booty*, p. 319.

[48] On the origins of private property in Grotius' writings, see Stephen Buckle, *Natural law and the theory of property: Grotius to Hume* (Oxford, 1993), pp. 10–14 and 35–44; Tuck, *Natural rights theories*, p. 61; Keene, *Beyond the anarchical society*, pp. 52–3; Garnsey, *Thinking about property*, pp. 136–9; Karl Olivecrona, 'Appropriation in the state of nature: Locke on the origin of property', *Journal of the History of Ideas*, 35(2) (1974), 213–15.

[49] Grotius, *De jure belli*, p. 202; see also p. 207.

[50] *Ibid.*, p. 206.

original division of things, however, the peoples who made the division were separated by the sea and so it was impossible for them, Grotius observed, to make any division of the sea itself.[51] For this reason, as well as its inexhaustible nature, and the difficulty of occupation, the sea rested in common. It is precisely through the sea's inexhaustibility and insusceptibility to occupation that the principle of occupation, in a negative sense, applies to it and was the principle determinant of property in it. Here, therefore, in order to explain freedom of the sea, Grotius appeared to have resorted to an understanding of property that precluded consent and relied, as he had in *Mare liberum*, on the direct application of the Roman law of occupation, specifically the impossibility of occupation, as the only possible explanation of the origin of property, or lack of property, in the seas. While Grotius' theory of property as the creation of convention could conceivably have dispensed with the idea of occupation, his understanding of the freedom of the sea made it necessary for him to continue to employ the Roman theory of occupation as an explanation of why it was not possible to take property in the sea.

Grotius on empire

There is a further reason why Grotius needed the idea of occupation when his theory of contract might have dispensed with it (as Hobbes later did). Occupation, as Grotius knew from Vitoria, was useful for thinking about empire. There are contrasting scholarly views on the role Grotius played in the justification of empire. In the 1960s, C.H. Alexandrowicz, the eminent historian of international law, praised Grotius for an enlightened attitude towards non-European peoples. Edward Keene comments that this is a view that has 'some merit', although it is not his own.[52] In contrast to many contemporaries, Grotius asserted the validity of treaties with non-European rulers. In the unpublished treatise *De societate publica cum infidelibus* (*On public society with non-Christians*), he argued, in common with Thomas Aquinas and Vitoria, that the sovereignty of non-Christian rulers is not compromised by 'errors of faith'.[53] His papers include draft treaties that he wrote on behalf of the East India Company with Southeast Asian rulers in Borneo, Siau, Tidor and Ternate, and with the King of

[51] *Ibid.*, p. 191. Here Grotius anticipated a criticism that would later be made more generally of the notion that the origin of property was in explicit consent or contract; that is, how could it be possible to make a universal division of things when peoples were separated by vast oceans.

[52] Keene, *Beyond the anarchical society*, p. 51.

[53] Borschberg, 'Hugo Grotius, East India trade and the King of Johor', 238.

Johore on the Malay Peninsula, who was central to the dispute over the *Santa Catarina* and an important ally against the Portuguese.[54]

Recent studies of Grotius have argued not only that he was the founder of international law but also that he was an apologist for the expansion of Europe, an 'imperialist thinker'.[55] Thus, the foundations of international law (for those scholars who understand Grotius' work in terms of the foundations of international law) were cast in an imperial mould. These claims need to be measured against what we understand by 'imperial'. If empire is understood in terms of the landed empires that were being established by Europeans at the time Grotius wrote, it is difficult to cast him as an apologist for that enterprise. His main concern with the Americas was in criticising Spanish and Portuguese claims to *imperium*. Unlike his contemporary Johannes de Laet, who like Grotius had been a student of Joseph Scaliger in Leiden, he was not engaged in the Dutch West India Company efforts to promote and justify the Dutch attempts to establish a colony in Brazil.[56] If by empire we understand what came to be called 'informal empire', commercial or trading empires, then Grotius certainly did provide an ideology for aggressive Dutch commercial expansion in the East, albeit that he did so by calling for equal recognition of non-European sovereignty, a bulwark against the Portuguese and Spanish, and the formation of equal treaties.[57] His call for 'trade supported by force of arms' was directed primarily against rival European powers in the East, but it was also used against local powers.[58] The stronger argument, however, for Grotius as an imperialist thinker may be his claim that the laws of nature, and in particular his understanding of property and sovereignty, provided a universal standard by which relations between all peoples could be judged. The imposition of Grotian values in the law of nations could well be said to have contributed to the imposition of European cultural and political hegemony upon much of the non-European world. Such a claim, however, assumes that the European ideas of property

[54] *Ibid.*, 225–48.

[55] Keene, *Beyond the anarchical society*; Muthu, *Enlightenment against empire*, p. 277 and see also pp. 7, 17 and 268; Tuck, *Natural rights theories*, p. 62; Tuck, *War and peace*; Arneil, *John Locke and America*, pp. 46–54.

[56] Johannes de Laet, *Nieuwe Wereldt ofte Beschrijvinghe van West-Indien* (Leiden, 1625). On de Laet and the comparison with Grotius, see Arthur Weststeijn, 'Republican empire: colonialism, commerce and corruption in the Dutch Golden Age', *Renaissance Studies*, 26(4) (2012), 491–509, at 496.

[57] On the limits of the concept of empire, see Frederick Cooper, 'Modernizing colonialism and the limits of Empire', in Calhoun, Cooper and Moore (eds.), *Lessons of empire*, pp. 63–72.

[58] Borschberg, 'Hugo Grotius, East India trade and the King of Johor', 243–4.

and sovereignty could not be used (by Europeans or non-Europeans) to oppose imperial projects.

As we have seen in the case of the Virginia Company, European colonisers and trading empires were acutely conscious of the writings of the Salamanca theologians and the problems they presented for the legitimacy of continuing conquest and colonisation. Grotius, while not trained as a Scholastic philosopher, was a close reader of Vitoria's lectures. Following Acosta, his understanding of America was that the continent was sparsely inhabited and under-exploited, although he condemned the conquest of societies that appreciate the operation of natural law. In his writings on the East Indies, however, particularly in *The free sea* and also in *De societate publica cum infidelibus* (more obliquely addressing the issues arising in the East), his views were hardly distinguishable from Vitoria's polemic.[59] Following Vitoria, Grotius demolished each of the Portuguese and Spanish claims to *dominium* and *imperium* in the Indies, devoting a chapter to each claim: first, the claim to dominion based upon discovery, then by the 'Pope's gift', then 'by title of war' or conquest and finally by religion. In response to the claim to 'title by invention', or discovery, Grotius followed Vitoria's reasoning that the 'Indians' 'have, and always had, their kings, their commonwealth, their laws, and their liberties'; that is, lawful society was already constituted in a manner demonstrating that the 'Indians' understood the operation of natural law.[60] But he then extended Vitoria's analysis and departed from it, arguing that discovery never provides title 'for to find [i.e., possess] is not to see a thing with the eyes but to lay hold of it with the hands'.[61] 'Finding' is used here in the sense of the Roman law of occupation, to take, and it is in this sense that finding could be possession. Grotius concluded: 'Vitoria therefore rightly saith that the Spaniards got no more authority over the Indians for this cause [i.e., Discovery] than the Indians had over the Spaniards if any of them had come formerly into Spain.'[62]

European discussions of discovery were often represented as claims based upon seeing or visiting, but could only be serious, according to Grotius, if they were based upon taking with the hands. He therefore opened up a distinction between discovery and occupation which would become fundamental to the law of nations: with the former seen as a very weak basis for title, or no title at all, and the latter as the strongest claim. He established this distinction between discovery and occupation precisely

[59] On *De societate publica* and Vitoria, see *ibid.*, 237–8. [60] Grotius, *The free sea*, pp. 13–15.
[61] *Ibid.*, p. 13. [62] *Ibid.*, p. 15.

for the purpose of combating the huge claims of the Portuguese and Spanish empires. He understood that recognition of the right of discovery in the law of nations would impede rather than facilitate European expansion. To permit European powers to claim sovereignty, by right of discovery, over large areas of territory which they did not exploit would greatly reduce the territory that could be exploited by other powers. The right of discovery was an impediment to empire and its critics recognised this problem over a number of centuries (although it does not follow that every critic of the right of discovery was an apologist for colonisation). Grotius' distinction between discovery and occupation was seminal to these critiques.

After his dismissal of the right of discovery, Grotius moved on to the other bases of title that Vitoria had itemised. He offered the possibility, raised by Vitoria, that the Indians could be 'out of their wits and unsensible', but concluded that they were 'ingenious and sharp witted'.[63] On Pope Alexander VI's donation of the East Indies to the Portuguese, Grotius noted (paraphrasing Lorenzo Valla on the Donation of Constantine) first of all that 'our Lord Christ had rejected all earthly government' so that he could not have 'translated' temporal power either to 'Peter or the Church of Rome'. Again he concluded by the authority of 'the opinion of Cajetanus and Vitoria ... that it is not a sufficient title against the Indians ... [simply] because the Pope gave those provinces'.[64] On the question of just war, Grotius declared:

> there were no cause truly that they should pretend war. For they who pursue the barbarians with war, as the Spaniards do the people of America, are wont to pretend two things: that they are hindered from trading with them, or because they will not acknowledge the doctrine of true religion. As for trading, the Portugalls obtained it of the Indians, so that in this behalf they have no reason to complain.[65]

Here Grotius was paraphrasing Alberico Gentili, who, as we have seen, condemned such pretences. On 'the other pretence', namely that of conquest in the name of religion, he cited Cajetan on the doctrine that Vitoria adopted: namely, that for infidel countries, 'the lords thereof, although infidels, are lawful lords, whether they be governed by regal or political government, neither are they deprived of dominion of the lands or goods for their infidelity'.[66]

[63] *Ibid.* [64] *Ibid.*, pp. 16–17. [65] *Ibid.*, p. 18.
[66] *Ibid.*, pp. 18–19. See also Vitoria, *On the American Indians*, pp. 263–4.

Thomas Hobbes' rejection of occupation

Thomas Hobbes, like Grotius, trained as a humanist. Of all the seventeenth-century natural law theorists, Hobbes made the most forceful and the most notorious articulation of the principles of self-preservation as the basis of civil society. He too wrote against the background of religious and civil wars in Europe and, particularly, the devastating Civil War in England in the 1640s.[67] Like Grotius, fearing for his safety, he wrote in exile during the civil wars in his own country. This examination of rights in the context of European wars is key to understanding later observers' concerns over the status of rights in colonised lands.

Hobbes rejected the Aristotelian notion of natural human sociability, going far beyond Grotius' thoughts on self-preservation in this respect. He declared that 'men have no pleasure, (but on the contrary a great deale of griefe) in keeping company, where there is no power to over-awe them'.[68] He saw the state of nature, whether between individuals or states, as a state of war, a brutal competition for survival: 'they are in that condition which is called Warre; and such a warre, as is of every man, against every man'.[69] He added that in this state of nature, 'nothing can be Unjust. The notions of Right and Wrong, Justice and Injustice have there no place'.[70] Justice and injustice, he argued, were 'none of the Faculties' of body or mind, but rather of society.

Hobbes conceded that it was unlikely that the whole world had ever been in the state of nature he described. He clearly believed that self-interest would quickly push most peoples into society. But he equally clearly believed that civil war, such as the Civil War in England against which he wrote *Leviathan*, was close to such a state of nature. And he also observed that 'there are many places' in the world in which people now live in a state of natural war such as he described, notably 'the savage people in many places of America . . . have no government at all; and live at this day in that brutish manner, as I said before'.[71] Moreover, he added, 'in all times, Kings and Persons of Soveraigne authority' have been in a posture of gladiators 'their eyes fixed on one another'.[72] Thus, an ironic consequence of creating states was the creation of a state of nature between states.

67 Quentin Skinner, 'Hobbes' life in philosophy', in *Visions of politics, volume* III: Hobbes and civil science (Cambridge, 2002), pp. 8–37; Noel Malcolm, 'A summary biography of Hobbes', in *Aspects of Hobbes* (Oxford, 2002).

68 Thomas Hobbes, *Leviathan*, ed. Richard Tuck (Cambridge, 1991), p. 88. 69 *Ibid.*

70 *Ibid.*, p. 90. 71 *Ibid.*, p. 89. 72 *Ibid.*, p. 90.

From the premises of natural unsociability, Hobbes argued that each individual was driven by 'Fear of Death' and sought above all her or his own preservation.[73] As long as the state of nature endured in which each person had the right to all things, including the life of others, there was no security for any person.[74] Individuals, he argued, chose to leave this dangerous and uncertain natural world and to pursue the only means to ensure their preservation by creating the security of society and sovereignty. For this reason, he concluded that the 'Fundamental Law of Nature' is 'to seek Peace, and follow it'.[75] But, he quickly observed, no person can find peace from others unless they divest themselves of their right in nature to all things, including the lives of others. In other words, in order to find peace from others, we must ourselves give up our power over others. Here he found authority in scripture to support his argument: 'This is the Law of the Gospell; Whatsoever you require that others do to you, that do ye to them.'[76] Thus, each individual transfers her or his rights to others in return for the reciprocal act in which the others also transfer their rights. Through these contracts, society is formed. The motive for these contracts 'is nothing else but the security of a man's person, in his life, and in the means of so preserving life'.[77]

Given his grim view of the natural state, Hobbes disagreed with Grotius that property could be created prior to civil society. Indeed, such was Hobbes' view of nature that he argued that contract was the basis of all social relations. For this reason, the right of the first taker in Roman law had a correspondingly minor role to play in Hobbes' thought; he did not retrieve a doctrine of occupation as the first basis for property agreed upon by the people covenanting a civil order. According to Hobbes, in the state of nature there is no law and so no justice, and where there is no justice, there can be 'no Propriety, no Dominion, no *Mine* and *Thine* distinct'.[78] He later repeated 'where there is no Common-wealth, there is no Propriety', just as he had earlier stated in *De cive* or *On the citizen*: 'Property and commonwealths come into being together.'[79] Having said this, Hobbes' views on property being created in a civil state are not as far from other seventeenth-century natural law writers as first appears. Grotius and Pufendorf argued that property could be created in the state of nature when, in an important step in the direction of civility, small groups of people, such as families, were able to agree amongst themselves on the rules

[73] *Ibid.* [74] *Ibid.*, p. 91. [75] *Ibid.*, p. 92. [76] *Ibid.* [77] *Ibid.*, p. 93. [78] *Ibid.*, p. 90.
[79] *Ibid.*, p. 101; Thomas Hobbes, *On the citizen*, eds. Richard Tuck and Michael Silverthorne (Cambridge, 1998), p. 85.

establishing property. Hobbes acknowledged that 'fathers of families' could create property before the institution of commonwealths, but he neatly defused this question by responding that 'the family is a small commonwealth', thus leaving his position very close to Grotius and Pufendorf.[80] His account of the state of nature was, nevertheless, more brutal than those of his contemporaries.

It is no accident that the modern philosopher most committed to the notion that the pre-civil condition contains none of the benefits of social life was also the author with the least to say on property acquired through occupation. This fact reveals much about later discussions of occupation. As we shall see, occupation remained powerful in Western political thought, even amongst natural law writers who believed that private property was a product of civil society. Most writers, with the exception of Hobbes, maintained a notion of primitive acquisition through occupation which itself provided the principles for more advanced forms of ownership. Primitive acquisition could be maintained by writers such as Grotius because they did not share the unremittingly bleak understanding of the possibilities of life in a natural state to which Hobbes subscribed. It is through Hobbes, therefore, that we find one explanation for why Grotius maintained such an important role for occupation in his theory of property. While agreeing with Grotius about self-preservation, Hobbes completely dismissed the notion of natural sociability to which Grotius had clung. As far as Hobbes was concerned, society was entirely based upon a contract and natural unsociability. He provided no parallel account of human sociability leading in the same direction as necessity and so there was absolutely no reason for him to use the idea of occupation as a part of his explanation of the origin of private property if the possibility arose, which Grotius had raised, that a society was formed merely through sociability rather than contract.

The more important point that is absent from Hobbes' account of property, but present in those of Grotius, Pufendorf and Locke, is the understanding of occupation as an act of self-preservation and therefore as a right of expansion. As Istvan Hont has observed, Hobbes was sceptical of early modern states' 'vain-glory', and he derided 'the insatiable Appetite, or bulimia, of enlarging Dominion' that was so characteristic of contemporary states.[81] He did not subscribe to the idea that the pursuit of the

80 Hobbes, *On the citizen*, p.85.

81 Hont, *Jealousy of trade*, pp. 17–22. For Hobbes' familiarity with the literature on greatness and reason of state and his sympathy with some of its themes, despite his disdain for 'pretenders to Political Prudence', see Noel Malcolm, *Reason of state, propaganda and the Thirty Years' War: an unknown translation by Thomas Hobbes* (Oxford, 2007), pp. 109–23.

greatness of the state entailed an obligation to secure its preservation through outward expansion as well as internal control. While the idea of occupation could be used to critique expansion, it may be Hobbes' recognition that it was such a powerful argument for self-preservation through overseas expansion that persuaded him to remain silent on the idea in his account of property. The internal peace of the state was his paramount concern and this may be why he brought so little of his experience in the Virginia Company to his political thought.[82]

Occupation as contract: Samuel Pufendorf

In the development of a theory of natural law based upon interests rather than sociability, Grotius and Hobbes were joined by a third great seventeenth-century natural law theorist, Samuel Pufendorf, who agreed that self-preservation moved people to contract together to form civil society. Pufendorf (1632–94) was a native of Saxony educated in the Grotian school of moral and political philosophy. He too wrote against the background of the Thirty Years' War that had decimated his native country. As a child, Pufendorf, like Hobbes and Grotius when adults, was forced to flee war. As a tutor to the family of the Swedish ambassador to Denmark, Pufendorf was imprisoned, along with the ambassador and his family, for more than eight months when war broke out between the two countries.[83] He directed his political philosophy towards the establishment of principles that would bring stability and order to political life, and would be blind to theological and cultural differences that had been the causes of conflict.

Pufendorf could be almost as bleak as Hobbes about the natural inclinations of humans, although he distanced himself from Hobbes' account of the state of nature. In his textbook for students, *De officio hominis et civis* (1675) translated as *The whole duty of man, according to the law of nature*, he described the person in a natural state as '*malicious, insolent*, and easily *provok'd*' as well as both '*capable*' and '*prone* to do Mischief to his Fellow'.[84] Of the natural state itself, he concluded: 'There the *Passions* rule, and there is a continual Warfare, accompanied

[82] Noel Malcolm, 'Hobbes, Sandys and the Virginia Company', *Historical Journal*, 24(2) (1981), 297–321 speculates on why Hobbes' Virginia Company experience made little apparent mark on his thinking.

[83] Samuel Pufendorf, *De jure naturae et gentium libri octo*, vol. 2, translation of the edition of 1688 by C. H. Oldfather and W. A. Oldfather (Oxford, 1934), p.13a.

[84] Pufendorf, *The whole duty of man, according to the law of nature*, edited and with an introduction by Ian Hunter and David Saunders (Indianapolis, 2003), p. 55.

with Fears, Want, Sordidness, Solitude, Barbarity, Ignorance, and Brutishness.'[85]

In his epic account of the law of nature and nations, *De jure naturae et gentium* (1672), Pufendorf critiqued Hobbes' account of the natural, or pre-civil, state, which Pufendorf argued had never existed for all humans at one particular time.[86] Hobbes' account of the state of nature was too extreme: 'the reasons adduced by Hobbes for the desire of men to do harm to one another are only particular ones . . . and are by no means important enough to make a universal war of all men against all others inevitable'.[87] 'Man', Pufendorf argued, 'cannot avoid naturally inclining to peace': 'the natural state of men, even when considered apart from commonwealths, is not one of war, but of peace; a peace founded on the following laws . . . he shall allow every one to enjoy his own possessions'.[88] Why, he asked, 'undertake a war without provocation?' He conceded that 'it must be confessed that this natural peace is but a weak and untrustworthy thing, and . . . but a poor custodian of man's safety'.[89] Thus, the law of self-preservation impelled people to the creation of civil society.

Reflecting on the dangers inherent in the pre-civil state, Pufendorf agreed with Grotius and Hobbes that 'Man is an Animal very desirous of his own *Preservation*'. Although man is 'of *himself* liable to many *Wants*', he is, unlike other animals, '*unable* to Support himself without the Help of *other* of his Kind'.[90] This need for others was a remnant of natural sociability found in earlier natural law writers. While Pufendorf agreed with proponents of natural sociability that 'man' 'earnestly seeks after Civil Society', the reason was not affection for others, but 'a most tender Affection for himself and his own Good'.[91] It was, according to Pufendorf, the '*fundamental Law of Nature*, That EVERY MAN OUGHT, AS FAR AS IN HIM LIES, TO PRESERVE AND PROMOTE SOCIETY'.[92] The reason, that is, that we ought to be sociable is precisely because it is in our self-interest: in order to secure 'his Preservation, 'tis absolutely

[85] *Ibid.*, p. 171.

[86] Hont, *Jealousy of trade*, p. 171. Pufendorf distinguished three different kinds of natural states (see Buckle, *Natural law and the theory of property*, pp. 86–91). The first related to the nature of human beings as certain kinds of creatures and so could be discovered in civil, or 'adventious', states. The other two related to the sense Hobbes used of a pre-civil state. In order to avoid confusion, here I will use the term 'pre-civil'.

[87] Pufendorf, *De jure naturae et gentium*, p. 171. [88] *Ibid.*, p. 172. [89] *Ibid.*, p. 176.

[90] Pufendorf, *The whole duty of man*, p. 55.

[91] *Ibid.*, p. 187. See Hont, *Jealousy of trade*, p. 173 on Pufendorf's rejection of Grotius' *appetitus societatis*.

[92] Pufendorf, *The whole duty of man*, p. 56.

necessary, that he be *sociable*'.[93] Humans were unable to provide all their needs when alone, they needed commerce with others in order to be able to survive. This was self-interested sociability or, as Kant would later label it, 'unsocial sociability'.[94] It is through being sociable and, ultimately, creating civil society that we are most likely to guarantee our preservation. For eighteenth-century writers such as Adam Smith, Pufendorf's understanding of the state of nature created an explanation for commercial society.[95] Relations of exchange between people were not merely desirable but also necessary to their survival.

Civil society is created, according to Pufendorf, again agreeing with Grotius and Hobbes, through agreements.[96] He stressed that it was necessary to establish '*perfect Consent and Agreement*' in creating civil society. Any group of people 'if they do not *agree* among themselves ... will be capable of effecting but very little'.[97] The covenant that creates civil society must be lasting and every member of that society must give their 'consent' to be 'Fellow Members of the same Society'.[98] Any person who does not consent is excluded from that society. All members must also covenant to choose a constitution for this society.

Pufendorf on property

Pufendorf began *De jure naturae et gentium* by distinguishing between physical and moral entities. While physical entities were, he argued, brought about by the original creation of God, moral entities are 'superadded' to physical things and are produced by 'the will of intelligent entities', and 'come into existence only by the determination of their authors'.[99] Moral entities come to exist as a result of the purposeful actions of humans in the physical world. They do not exist by themselves and they are instituted in order to 'bring order into the lives of men'. Amongst the categories of moral entities are moral qualities, which may be 'active' or 'passive', and amongst the 'noble' species of active moral qualities were power, right and obligation.[100] The power over one's own possessions, Pufendorf claimed, is ownership, or property.[101] Thus, Pufendorf's understanding of the origin of property was part of an account of ethical voluntarism and he placed this human power to shape the world, and the ability to create property, within an account of history.

[93] *Ibid.*, p. 55. [94] Hont, *Jealousy of trade*, p. 175. [95] *Ibid.*, p. 45. [96] *Ibid.*, p. 177.
[97] Pufendorf, *The whole duty of man*, p. 193. [98] *Ibid.*, pp. 193–5.
[99] Pufendorf, *De jure naturae et gentium*, p. 6. [100] *Ibid.*, p. 18. [101] *Ibid.*, p. 19.

Pufendorf disagreed with Grotius that all things were in the first instance common to all people after the creation. Grotius' assumption implied that private property necessitated taking things that belonged in common to others, a fact that was justified by their abundance but was nevertheless awkward. Pufendorf described the initial state as 'negative community'; that is, things rested in a property-less state for the negative reason that they had not been acted on in any way.[102] However, this negative community was 'inherently unstable' because humans were always looking to appropriate things.[103] Such appropriation could lead in two directions: either to 'positive community' or to private property. Positive community was a state in which things are held in common due to positive agreements to do so. A further departure from negative community was private property, or dominion. For Pufendorf, the attachment to private property was initially possible prior to a fully civil state, although the protection of property, property in one's things as well as oneself, was a motivation for creating civil order.[104] Property could exist prior to civil society because, in contrast to Hobbes, the pre-civil state was relatively peaceful and was not prone to 'promiscuous thieving and robbery'. Nor would Pufendorf allow Hobbes' assertion in *De cive* that '[robbery] is not contrary to the Law of Nature'.[105]

For Pufendorf, private property came to exist as part of an extended and progressive transition from a state of nature to a fully civil state.[106] In the various stages between these two states, humans increased in number and divided into separate groups. Discussing the 'causes for things passing into proprietorship, and the order which they followed', he reasoned that most things which are of use to humans were sufficiently scarce for more than one person to lay claim to them and thus for conflicts to arise over the possession.[107] Moreover, many useful things were brought about by cultivation and therefore by labour, and it was 'improper' that others should have a claim to the fruits of a person's labour. To settle these issues, in order to have 'peace among men', particularly 'as men multiplied', dominion was introduced.

[102] Buckle, *Natural law and the theory of property*, pp. 93–7.
[103] Garnsey, *Thinking about property*, p. 117.
[104] Buckle, *Natural law and the theory of property*, pp. 97–9.
[105] Pufendorf, *De jure naturae et gentium*, p. 175.
[106] See Hont, *Jealousy of trade*, pp. 178–9 and Buckle, *Natural law and the theory of property*, p. 99 on the historical character of Pufendorf's account of property; see also Garnsey, *Thinking about property*, p. 141 on Pufendorf spinning out the transitional process.
[107] Pufendorf, *De jure naturae et gentium*, pp. 539–40.

In common with Hobbes, however, Pufendorf insisted that 'the *Property* of Things flow'd immediately from the Compact of Men'.[108] It was not labour, therefore, that created property, as it would be for Locke, but the agreement to recognise the fruits of labour.[109] Property was a moral entity and must be the product of a moral action: namely, an agreement. For Hobbes, the making of a compact to recognise property was the end of the matter; he saw absolutely no need to address the question of occupation which had been the foundation of the Roman and medieval understanding of property. It is striking, therefore, to find that Pufendorf, who insisted that property derives from contract, immediately turned from the proof of this argument to a discussion of occupation as the basis of the first contracts and therefore as the origin of property. He conducted this analysis over three chapters of *De jure naturae et gentium*. The right of the first taker, or first occupier, was the subject, he argued, of the first agreement to establish property: 'Hence we apprehend the first Agreement, that Men made about this Point, to have been, that what any Person had seiz'd out of the common Store of Things, or out of the Fruits of them, with design to apply to his private Occasions, none else should rob him of.'[110] Occupation accordingly marked the first step in the progress of history away from the state of nature.

One reason for this return to the theory occupation was an awareness of how powerful it was as an alternative to the contract theory of property. Pufendorf addressed the possible tensions between the rival theories at length. He argued against the possibility that simple occupation, occupation alone, was the basis of property by declaring 'we cannot apprehend how a bare corporal Act, such as Seizure is, should be able to prejudice the Right and Power of others, unless their Consent be added to confirm it; that is, unless a Covenant intervene'.[111] 'First occupancy of itself', he argued, 'before the existence of pacts, does not confer any right.'[112] Much of his discussion of occupation was therefore a sustained attack on the theory as the first cause in the explanation of property. In his chapter 'Of occupancy', Pufendorf was largely concerned with the property in wild beasts which had been the focus of the Roman law. By addressing himself

[108] *Ibid.*, p. 366; see also p. 365, arguing that property was the creation of 'some Covenant either tacit or express'. Garnsey, *Thinking about property*, pp. 141–2.

[109] On this contrast with Locke, see Buckle, *Natural law and the theory of property*, pp. 101–2.

[110] Pufendorf, *De jure naturae et gentium*, p. 367.

[111] *Ibid.*, p. 368; see also p. 375: 'before Occupancy can produce Dominion, it is necessary that some Compact (a tacit one at least) should have been first settled'.

[112] *Ibid.*, p. 538.

to wild beasts and not to the broader applications of the law of occupation, he went to the heart of the Roman law. He entered into great detail on questions such as who should be allowed the privilege of hunting, on whether a beast is occupied if it is only wounded and also whether game taken by a poacher belongs to the poacher or the sovereign. Pufendorf's attention to these details was always conducted with regard to the claim that all rights of occupancy are derived from a covenant. 'Taking', he indignantly declared in this discussion, 'must not presently be construed *acquiring*: The former being a bare natural Action, whereas the latter includes a moral Effect.'[113] Again, his emphasis was upon property as a moral entity created by human agency. Therefore, his response to the problems posed by hunting wild beasts was that 'it is apparent, that it depends on the Will of the Sovereign, and not on any natural and necessary Law, what Right the private Members of a State shall enjoy, as to the gathering of Moveables not yet possessed'.[114]

Turning to the matter of the occupation of territory, Pufendorf argued that: 'Men have, indeed, a Privelege of making waste Places their own, by first seizing upon them.'[115] But this law of occupation was only possible because of the 'tacit Convention between the first Introducers of *Property*', which assigned the 'Right of those things which did not fall under their prime division' and gave those things to 'the Persons who should first take Possession of them' or, as he succinctly put it, 'whatever did not come out of this grand Division, should pass to the first Occupant'.[116] We are judged, he argued, to have occupied a thing when we have taken possession of it and this means 'joining Body to Body, either immediately, or by a proper Instrument'. Joining must be either 'with the Hands' in the case of movable goods and 'the Occupancy of the Soil with the Feet, together with an Intention of manuring it'.[117] By contrast, he dismissed the so-called right of discovery employed by many European colonisers, as had Gentili and Grotius. Indeed, the 'doctrine' of discovery had a very tenuous position in the law of nations. As Pufendorf declared, 'the bare seeing a thing, or the knowing where it is, is not judged a sufficient Title of Possession'.[118] He also largely agreed with the Roman law of prescription: namely, that once our connection with something is broken, for example, if we lose a beast that has been in our custody, it is no longer our

[113] *Ibid.*, p. 390. [114] *Ibid.*, p. 388. [115] *Ibid.*, p. 383.

[116] *Ibid.*, pp. 384–6. At this point he cited the Roman law of the first occupant from the *Digest*: 'Quod enim nullius est, id ratione naturali occupanti conceditor.'

[117] *Ibid.*, p. 391. [118] *Ibid.*

property.[119] Similarly, according to this law, if we abandon land, it once again becomes waste and will become the property of the first occupier. In Roman law there was only one form of property that could never cease to be property even if it was completely separated and lost to the owner, and this was the slave.[120] Clearly the law of occupancy and, more specifically, the law of prescription applied to slavery would be a strong incentive for slave rebellion.

It is important to ask why Pufendorf returned to the theory of occupation after Hobbes had abandoned it, even while he agreed with Hobbes that compact was the origin of property. The explanation lies in Pufendorf's understanding of moral entities, such as property and sovereignty, arising from voluntary human acts. Beginning with these assumptions, the idea of use, a form of action, combining with compact was a powerful explanation for property. He conceded that 'many Things stand in need of human Labour and Culture, either for their Production, or to fit and prepare them for Use'. For this reason, in the pre-civil state, it was:

> very inconvenient that a Person, who had taken no Pains about a Thing, should have an equal Right to it when another, by whose Industry it was either first raised or exactly wrought and framed, to render it of farther service. It was highly conducive then to the Common peace, that immediately, upon the Multiplication of Mankind, Properties should be appointed in moveable Things, especially such as require the Labour and Improvement of Men, and in those Immoveables, which are of immediate and necessary Use.[121]

Here Pufendorf accepted that not only taking and use but labour and improvement were the most likely means by which things would be removed from the common and made particular. The problem, as he saw it, was simply that this process had to be recognised by agreement. Not to recognise the role of occupancy would be to ignore the right that use and industry bestow in our relation to things.

Despite arguing for the importance of use as a basis of right, Pufendorf claimed that there is no preferable and universal manner of using things: 'Neither doth that Divine Grant, express'd in holy Scripture, describe any determinate Manner of Property, but only an indefinite Right of applying Things to such Uses as should be agreeable to the Wisdom, and to the Occasions of Men.'[122] He continued: 'The Divine Donation conferred on Man a Right of applying other Creatures to his Use; which Right was

[119] *Ibid.*, p. 394. [120] *Ibid.*, p. 395. [121] *Ibid.*, p. 368.
[122] *Ibid.*, p. 373; see also pp. 365, 366 and 369 (on More and Campenella).

indifferent to positive Communion, or to Property.'[123] His relativism on this question recognised the different needs of different societies: 'we pretend not that it was necessary all Things should be appropriated in the same Moment; but, according as the Temper or Condition of Men, the Nature of the Things themselves, and the Difference of Place required'.[124] He concludes from this that 'neither are we, who are utterly banish'd [from] the primitive Communion, nor those barbarous Nations, which still retain many Foot-steps of it, guilty, in this Respect, of a Breach of the *Law of Nature*'.[125] Indeed, at times Pufendorf associates the state of positive community with the virtue early modern people often attached to the '*German* nations' described by Tacitus. Amongst these peoples was found 'the ancient Simplicity of Life, so unacquainted with Avarice and Luxury'. Driven, however, by a belief in historical progress, Pufendorf, unlike God, was unable consistently to remain indifferent to the form in which property was held, nor could he remain positive about primitive virtue.

Pufendorf on empire

The critique of European colonial practices becomes more pronounced when we turn from Grotius to Pufendorf.[126] One of the striking differences between the two philosophers is in how they read Vitoria. Whereas Grotius understood Vitoria to have been condemning the Spanish conquests, Pufendorf interpreted Vitoria as an apologist for empire and developed his own critique of colonial rationalisations. According to Pufendorf: 'Franciscus a Victoria, *Relectiones de Indis*, Pt.V, § 3, does not win many to his position when he discusses the adequate grounds on which the Spaniards felt themselves entitled to subdue the Indians.'[127] He continued: 'It is crude indeed to try to give others so indefinite a right to journey and live among us, with no thought of the number in which they come, their purpose in coming, as well as the question of whether . . . they propose to stay but a short time or settle among us permanently.'[128] Pufendorf was able to put Vitoria's discussion of the rights of 'natural communication' in doubt because his understanding of natural law rested

[123] *Ibid.*, p. 374.
[124] *Ibid.*, p. 376. Tuck, *Rights of war and peace*, pp. 155–65 notes Pufendorf's relativism regarding property (and also his critiques of the Spanish treatment of 'Indians').
[125] Pufendorf, *De jure naturae et gentium*, pp. 376–7.
[126] See Tuck, *Rights of war and peace*, pp. 155–65 on Pufendorf's critique of empire.
[127] Pufendorf, *De jure naturae et gentium*, p. 364. [128] *Ibid.*, pp. 364–5.

less upon the supposition of a universal human fellowship and more upon the notion of the universal rule of self-interest and self-preservation.

He had little further to say in explicit reference to peoples conquered by Europeans, but he proceeded to critique the legal arguments based upon 'use' that had come to support European colonial ventures. God's command that men should 'use the products of the earth' (which was a staple justification of colonial ventures) was not, he argued, the 'immediate cause of dominion'.[129] Dominion, as we have seen, arises from consent, from the agreement of the community about the nature and limits of ownership. Thus, he pointed out, a community may decide legitimately to employ proprietorship whereby individuals possess things for their own use, or they may rather hold some or all of the goods and land in 'positive community' – that is, in a communal ownership. In *both* cases, Pufendorf insists, all claims by outsiders to those goods are excluded. He implicitly rejected here the argument used by colonisers that native peoples who had not established individual proprietorship had failed to establish dominion. Following this argument, he extended his defence of cultural difference, arguing that ownership and sovereignty could be based upon a variety of different relationships to the land. God, he declared, 'gave men an indefinite right' to the 'earth and its products':

> yet the manner, intensity, and extent of this power were left to the judgement and disposition of men; whether, in other words, they would confine it within certain limits, or within none at all, and whether they wanted every man to have a right to everything, or only to a certain and fixed part of things, or to be assigned his definite portion with which he should rest content and claim no right to anything else.[130]

He added: 'Yet it was far from God to prescribe a universal manner of possessing things, which all men were bound to observe. And so things were created neither proper nor common (in positive community) by any express command of God, but these distinctions were later created by men.'[131]

It is true that Pufendorf argued that 'Men have, indeed, a Privelege of making waste Places their own, by first seizing upon them', and this claim would appear to be have been consistent with the judgement of contemporary colonising powers that the places inhabited by many non-European peoples were waste places.[132] But he later clarified this issue by stipulating that 'if in a Region thus possessed [that is, in positive community], any

[129] *Ibid.*, p. 536. [130] *Ibid.* [131] *Ibid.* [132] *Ibid.*, p. 383.

thing should be found, which is not ascertained to a private Owner, it must not presently be looked on as *void* and *waste*, so that any one Person may seize it as his *Peculiar*; but we must suppose it to belong to the whole People'.[133] Despite his endorsements of progressive history, here Pufendorf made a claim for freedom from incursion of non-European peoples who were at this time often believed to be living in a state of positive community. Importantly, he based this claim on the contract theory of property and his understanding of the different forms that property could take, all of which were moral entities.

While he rejected a lack of use, or the kind of use, as a justification for conquest, Pufendorf also pointed out that just as self-preservation was the cause for creating civil society, it was also the basis of its legitimacy. He criticised Aristotle for arguing that the law of nature was based upon the 'general agreement of all men or nations . . . and of civilized mankind'.[134] 'What people', he asked, 'endowed with enough judgement to preserve its existence, will be willing to acknowledge that it is barbarous?'[135] To the same end, he cited Pierre Charron and Michel de Montaigne on the great diversity between cultures and the 'foolish' habit of condemning customs as barbarous or base 'for the simple reason that it does not agree with our own general customs and ideas'.[136] This is not to argue that Pufendorf was a sceptic or moral relativist.[137] On the contrary, he rejected custom as a basis for the law of nature because he saw its true basis as reason, but his understanding of human action in terms of self-preservation embraced a great diversity of cultures. If a people demonstrated sufficient judgement to preserve its own existence, it was legitimate. Upon such a test, all societies in the world might be deemed to be legitimate, although, tellingly, later generations of Europeans would argue that certain indigenous peoples, for example, in Australia, were a 'dying race', unable to preserve their own existence.

Occupation as labour: John Locke

How did Pufendorf arrive at this potentially radical understanding of the implications of natural law for colonisation? And how did he come to see Vitoria as an apologist for European expansion (an interpretation of Vitoria that has become widely shared in the late twentieth and

133 *Ibid.*, p. 387. 134 *Ibid.*, pp. 188–9. 135 *Ibid.*, p. 189. 136 *Ibid.*, pp. 189–93.

137 See Hont, *Jealousy of trade*, pp. 167–8 on Pufendorf's rejection of scepticism through the opposition between cultural diversity on the one hand and non-civil society on the other.

twenty-first centuries)? Between the writing of Grotius' *Mare liberum* (1609) and Pufendorf's *De jure naturae et gentium* (1672), the character of European colonisation and the ideological justifications for colonisation had undergone dramatic change. Nowhere was this change more evident than in the English colonisation of America. English colonisers had absorbed the implications of the Salamanca theologians, and of Vitoria in particular, and as a result they had radically altered the polemical force of those writers. I have shown how this transformation of Vitoria into an apologist for empire was made partly through the use of Acosta's writings, and this is the Vitoria whom Pufendorf was reacting against.

The person who took this transformation of use as an argument against the rights of indigenous peoples furthest (and used Acosta to do it) was John Locke. Locke was less concerned than Hobbes and Pufendorf with the grounds of political obedience, which had been central to the wars of religion. In the years after the succession of the Catholic James II in England, and preceding his overthrow in the Glorious Revolution of 1688, Locke focused rather upon the question of resistance to absolutism and legitimate government.[138] But he was not only motivated by the political calamities of seventeenth-century Europe, he was also deeply interested in the world outside Europe and in particular in the colonisation of America. His writings have excited great interest amongst historians of empire not only because he made strident statements upon the status of American 'Indians', but also because he made those observations in the context of his own deep professional involvement in the colonisation of Carolina to the point that he helped draft, and repeatedly revise, the constitution for that colony.[139] He brought his reflections on America to the problems that absolute rule at home posed for the nature of property.

In his *Two treatises of government*, and in common with Grotius, Hobbes and Pufendorf, Locke understood self-preservation to be the motive for the creation of civil society.[140] He also agreed with Grotius and Pufendorf in his notion that property can exist before civil society. Indeed, for him, civil society is created only to preserve our property in our

[138] Peter Laslett, 'Introduction', in Locke, *Two treatises of government*, pp. 45–66.

[139] Arneil, *John Locke and America*; Tully, *An approach to political philosophy*; Armitage, 'John Locke, Carolina, and the two treatises of government'; Duncan Ivison, 'The nature of rights and the history of empire', in David Armitage (ed.), *British political thought in history and literature, 1500–1800* (Cambridge, 2006), pp. 191–211. For scepticism on this scholarship, see Paul Corcoran, 'John Locke on the possession of land: native title vs. the 'principle' of vacuum domicilium', *Proceedings, Australasian Political Studies Association Annual Conference*, 2007.

[140] See Buckle, *Natural law and the theory of property*, pp. 143–4 and 149 for differences on the issue of self-preservation between Locke's *Two treatises* and his earlier *Essays on the law of nature*.

lives, our liberty and our estates. In at least one sense in which he used the term 'property', his understanding of the concept was not far removed from that of Pufendorf or Grotius. This was the sense in which the property of something could be understood as a relation to it. Thus, property 'in' something indicated our relation to it. This relational understanding, and not the idea of property as an object, was what property had signified prior to Locke, although the reification of property was an almost inevitable consequence of its understanding as a subjective right. The relational meaning of 'property' was evident in the overlap between the English words 'property' and 'propriety'.[141] The classic example of the relational understanding of property was Cicero's claim that we have property in a theatre seat due to our occupation of it. Grotius cited Cicero on occupation, using the comparison of a theatre seat: 'Although the theatre is a public place, yet it is correct to say that the seat which a man has taken belongs to him.'[142] Implicit in this understanding of occupation is that abandonment of the seat cedes propriety in relation to it and, indeed, the law of prescription was based upon an acceptance of that assumption. For Grotius and Pufendorf, the example of the theatre seat underlined the relationship between property resting in occupation and property originating in an agreement; that is, the seat must be taken and other theatre-goers agree that the seat belongs to the occupant. Locke, however, transformed the meaning of occupation and taking from signifying a mere presence to the improvement of the thing which becomes property. In this understanding, property could no longer remain as a simple relation to something. The thing itself was transformed and the meaning of property had to change accordingly, with emphasis upon the nature of the thing itself and not just one's relation to it.

Locke distinguished two senses of property over things: common property is the right we have to all things in order to sustain ourselves. Common property for Locke, as for Grotius, was the consequence of God's donation of the earth to all people for their enjoyment. The second sense of property is particular property, property in a thing, which we gain by removing the particular from the common through its use.[143] However, whereas for Grotius in *On the law of war and peace*, all people could take

[141] See David Armitage, 'Shakespeare's properties', in David Armitage, Conal Condren and Andrew Fitzmaurice (eds.), *Shakespeare and early modern political thought* (Cambridge, 2009), p. 32.

[142] Grotius, *De jure belli*, p. 186. This example of the theatre seat is also found in Pufendorf, *De jure naturae et gentium*, pp. 371–3 and also in passages from Cicero cited there.

[143] On common and particular property in Locke, see James Tully, *A discourse on property: John Locke and his adversaries* (New York, 1980), pp. 3–4.

from the common what they needed for self-preservation, for Pufendorf, there was no natural right to private property, not even for the purpose of self-preservation. For him, all such rights arise from agreement. Locke, who admired Pufendorf's *De jure naturae et gentium*, used his labour theory of property to counter Pufendorf's denial of the natural right to consumption.[144]

Locke understood the state of nature to be to some degree sociable and it was on this basis that property could exist, so long as sociability endured. To this end he argued that there is a 'plain difference' between the state of nature and the state of war, even though 'some men' have maintained otherwise.[145] Those 'some men', as Peter Laslett observes, were clearly the Hobbesists. Locke was here opposing his theory to Hobbes because he appreciated Hobbes' point that, given that the state of nature is a state of war, property can only exist in society, and in that case Locke's reason for establishing society, the preservation of property, would be lost. In his understanding that property can be created outside civil society through the exploitation of nature, Locke was in agreement with Grotius and Pufendorf, although he surpassed both in his understanding of how use creates not only property but also value. He had not always held that position: as late as 1688, he had agreed with Grotius that individual property was created in the pre-civil state through conventions, or contracts.[146] As David Armitage has pointed out, this shift from a contractual to an individualist understanding of the creation of property corresponded with Locke's engagement with Carolina and a reluctance, explicit in the *Fundamental constitutions* for Carolina (which Locke helped draft), to acknowledge property relations arising from compacts between settlers and Native Americans.[147] Moreover, for Locke, value was the basis of a progressive understanding of history, and its addition to the understanding of property further distanced the world of settlers from that of the Native Americans. Acosta, as we have seen, furnished a progressive theory of history on the basis of his observations of American societies. Acosta's history was 'a popular book with Locke, and by his side in 1681'.[148]

According to Locke, the more intensively we labour on nature, the more value we add to our property. Through this process, a particular person and a particular society surpasses others in the degree to which the

[144] Tuck, *Rights of war and peace*, pp. 173–4; Garnsey, *Thinking about property*, p. 143. On Locke's admiration for Pufendorf's *De jure naturae*, see Laslett, 'Introduction', p. 75.

[145] Locke, *Two treatises of government*, p. 280.

[146] David Armitage, *Foundations of modern international thought* (Cambridge, 2013), pp. 109–10.

[147] *Ibid.*, p. 110. [148] Locke, *Two treatises of government*, p. 335.

?

potential held in nature is released. What Locke achieved with this theory was an explanation of progressive history that Acosta had only intuited.[149] Crucially, Locke adopted the theory of particular, or private, property based upon occupation, or the right of the first taker. But he explained, through using labour and value, *how* it is that to take or occupy, or as he said '*to appropriate*', makes something our property. The fruit or venison, he argued, that which is taken by the 'wild *Indian*, who knows no Inclosure, and is still a Tenant in common' must be the property of that Indian.[150]

It is not generally acknowledged that the famous passage in which Locke outlined this theory of the origin of particular property was a gloss on the Roman law of the first taker that was to some degree hidden by having had the language of labour superimposed upon it. Indeed, Locke's theory of property has often been contrasted with the occupation theory of property.[151] By contrast, in the century after he published the *Two treatises of government*, his theory of labour was often understood to be a theory of occupation. As we shall see, Sir William Blackstone, for example, declared: 'There is still another species of property, which, being grounded on labour and invention, is more properly reducible to the head of occupancy than any other; since the right of occupancy itself is supposed by Mr Locke, and many others, to be founded on the personal labour of the occupant.'[152] The contrast between Locke's theory and 'occupation theory' has been made on the basis that his theory of labour and value goes well beyond what was proposed in the raw Roman law doctrine. While this is true, the contrast overlooks the fact that his theory of labour and value begins precisely in a close analysis of what it means to occupy. Locke asked when an acorn 'pickt up under an Oak', or apples from trees, become the property of the persons who take them: 'When did they begin to be his? When he digested? Or when he eat? Or when he boiled? Or when he

149 See Buckle, *Natural law and the theory of property*, p. 147 on Locke distinguishing two historical stages, primitive and civil, but recognising steps within these: namely, hunting and gathering, pastoral, agricultural and commercial. Locke did not have a strong sense of an evolutionary sequence between these steps.

150 Locke, *Two treatises of government*, pp. 287–91.

151 Karl Olivecrona, 'Appropriation in the state of nature: Locke on the origin of property', *Journal of the History of Ideas*, 35(2) (1974), 211–31 makes no acknowledgement of the Roman law basis of Locke's theory of the origin of property. Jeremy Waldron has pointed out that the labour theory of appropriation has been contrasted with what he describes as 'First Occupancy Theory', but he agrees that in Locke's explanation of the origin of property, the two are coextensive insofar as they concern the 'fruits and animals of the earth'; Waldron, *The right to private property*, p. 173.

152 Sir William Blackstone, *The commentaries on the laws of England*, 4 vols. (London, 1765–9), vol. 2, p. 405.

brought them home? Or when he pickt them up? And 'tis plain, if the first gathering made them not his, nothing else could.'[153] He then added 'That *labour* [i.e., the taking or gathering] put a distinction between them and common.' So 'gathering', or what in Roman law was 'taking', is equated with 'labour'. The addition of labour to this understanding of the origin of particular property, or property in something, certainly allowed Locke to develop a theory of property which had greater depth than simply the matter of taking because it allowed him to introduce the notion of value and so develop his stadial theory of history. But the addition of labour does not disguise the fact that Locke's theory of the origin of property is based upon the law of the first taker in Roman law.

Underlining his gloss on the Roman law of occupation, Locke expanded on his explanation of the origin of property by using precisely the two kinds of example to which Roman law directly referred: namely, wild beasts and 'pearls' of the sea. He continued:

> And amongst those who are counted the Civiliz'd part of Mankind, who have made and multiplied positive Laws to determine Property, this original Law of Nature for the *beginning of property*, in what was before common, still takes place; and by vertue thereof, what Fish any one catches in the Ocean . . . or what Ambergriese any one takes up here, is *by* the *Labour* that removes it out of that common state Nature left it in, *made* his *Property* who takes that pains about it . . . For being a Beast that is still looked upon as common, and no Man's private Possession; whoever has imploy'd so much *labour* about any of that kind, as to find and pursue her, has thereby removed her from the state of Nature, wherein she was common, and has *begun a Property*.[154]

Clearly, Locke was here explicitly referring to the account of the origin of property in civil law; that is, to the Roman law of the first taker. He does so not only through his examples, wild beasts and pearls of the sea, but also through declaring that this law of the first taker was the positive law of civilised societies. He agrees, therefore, with the Roman law account of the origin of property and he builds his theory of property on that foundation. It is from his analysis of this Roman law theory that he derives the crucial principle of use, which is in turn the basis of his notion of labour and value. For him, labour becomes the mechanism by which something is first 'taken' from the common; that is, his analysis of Roman law leads him to name the crucial act of 'taking' as 'labour'.

[153] Locke, *Two treatises of government*, p. 288. [154] *Ibid.*, pp. 289–90.

Continuing his commentary on the Roman law of occupation, Locke points out that 'Fruits of the earth' and the 'Beasts that subsist on it', the two explicit subjects of the Roman law of *ferae bestiae*, are no longer 'the *chief matter of property*'. Rather, the chief matter of property is now 'the *Earth it self* and it is property in land, governed by the principle of possession belonging to the first taker, that absorbs the remainder of Locke's essay 'On property'.[155] Here, according to Jeremy Waldron, a gap opens between the 'mere taking of occupancy' and Locke's labour theory of property, because for a person 'merely' to occupy land does not necessarily mean that the person applies labour to it.[156] It is true that merely marking off land or enclosing it had sometimes been treated as a sufficient sign of occupancy and therefore as property, although such acts had been contested, amongst other occasions, in widespread rejection of European discoverers' symbolic acts of possession.[157] For example, as we have seen, writing about Portuguese claims to the Moluccas, Grotius argued that 'to find is not to see a thing with the eyes but to lay hold of it with the hands'. It is for this reason that 'the grammarians use the words *invenire* [to find or discover] and *occupare* [to occupy/to take possession] for words of one signification, and all the Latin tongue saith, "we have found that which we have gotten"'.[158] For Grotius, this did not mean that discovery amounted to property, but, on the contrary, that something had been discovered only when it had truly become the property of an occupant; it had to be seized to be found. Movable things had to be 'laid hold on' and immovable things, such as land, had to be 'bounded and guarded'.[159]

Locke rejected entirely the understanding of occupation as symbolic acts and it is clear that his essay on property insists on a definition of occupation *as* labour. In this sense there is no gap in his account between the theory of occupation and the labour theory of property, including landed property. Locke gave temporal depth to his notion that land is 'now' the chief matter of property rather than the beasts and fruit of the land. Although, according to his theory, there is no reason that property in land

155 *Ibid.*, p. 290.
156 Waldron, *The right to private property*, p. 173. Moreover, it is not clear why 'labour should give rights to the land itself and not merely to its product': Garnsey, *Thinking about property*, p. 146.
157 Contrast Patricia Seed's emphasis upon such acts in arguments for title: Patricia Seed, *Ceremonies of possession in Europe's conquest of the New World 1492–1640* (Cambridge, 1995).
158 Grotius, *The free sea*, p. 14.
159 *Ibid.* For Locke, even enclosure was not a sufficiently rigorous form of occupation to ensure the existence of property because somebody could enclose land, but not labour upon it. See Waldron, *The right to private property*, p. 173; and Locke, *Two treatises of government*, p. 295.

could not be acquired in a state of nature, he clearly wished to distinguish the chief object of particular property in civil society from a state of nature. He may also have wished to distinguish higher stages in the progressive theory of history from the earlier stages that the Roman law of the first taker addressed. He stressed, however, that labour in the Earth, or land, is 'acquired as the former' (by which he refers to the former subjects of property, fruits and beasts): namely, through 'appropriation', taking, or, as he analysed it, 'labour'.[160] From this foundation of the Roman law explanation of the origin of property applied to land, he goes on to develop his extensive analysis of how the degree of intensity in which land is used, or cultivated, establishes a correspondingly strong title to land as well as more sophisticated societies. In his analysis of the origin of property in land we find the most extensive application yet of the principles of the Roman law of occupation to property in land. Both Vitoria and Grotius had used the law of occupation to refer to property in land, but neither had developed that analysis as extensively as Locke to explain the origin, nature and central importance of property in land.

How does the fact that Locke based his theory of property upon the Roman law theory of occupation change our understanding of his work? What did the Roman law provide him? As we have seen, Locke agreed that society was based upon a contract that was inspired by each person's desire for self-preservation. But he was not convinced by the arguments of Grotius, Hobbes and Pufendorf that property is also a product of agreement. Labour, on Locke's analysis, was a sufficient cause of property. And he did not share Hobbes' unremittingly bleak view of the state of nature which was the only way of ensuring that contract must be the only origin for property.

For Locke, property could not be the creation of an agreement because the protection of property was precisely the reason we need to make agreements. Property necessarily had to exist prior to contracts. 'Government', he repeatedly claimed, 'has no other end than the preservation of property', and government could only be the creation of consent or contract.[161] The Roman law theory of occupation provided the most powerful account of the origin of property outside of the theories of the contract theorists. Upon this foundation, Locke was able to build his labour theory of property in a way that was consistent in both natural and civil states.

[160] Locke, *Two treatises of government*, p. 291: '*appropriation* of any parcel of *Land*'.
[161] Locke, *Two treatises of government*, p. 329.

The powerful union of the theory of property and the progressive theory of history largely explains the extraordinary power that the idea of occupation as a theory of property would have for the rationalisation of European landed empires. Through being combined with the progressive theory of history, the Roman law of occupation had become tied to Europeans' sense of their own destiny and it was John Locke, more than any other theorist, whose work embodied the intellectual platform for landed European expansion.

Conclusion

On the face of it, the theory of property as compact could have dispensed with the theory of occupation. Grotius, Hobbes and Pufendorf were concerned with developing a theory of rights that fitted the modern state – that is, a theory in which rights were derived from the state. In this sense they sought to restrict the appeal to authority outside the state that had been at the heart of the wars of religion. For Grotius and Pufendorf, however, the theory of occupation was not so easily dispensed with – the voluntarism of property arising from use meshed with the idea of contract. For Locke, the sovereignty of the state was less his concern than the limits upon that sovereignty, and he turned back to the theory of occupation in order to define those limits. Between them, Grotius, Pufendorf and Locke (and, in a negative sense, Hobbes) had set the terms for a debate over the relation between occupation, property and sovereignty which would endure throughout the eighteenth century and, largely, through to the present day. This debate divided those who argued for the absolute nature of sovereignty (even if they were not absolutists) and those who argued for limits upon sovereignty.

From Hobbes' point of view, or a theorist arguing for the absolute power of the state, Locke might be said to have mortgaged *imperium* to *dominium*; that is, to have mortgaged sovereignty to property. From this point of view, it was unacceptable that a basis for right, in this case the right of property, could arise from something outside of and prior to sovereignty. For Hobbes, this would simply be a recipe for rebellion. But for Locke, it was crucial that sovereignty should not be absolute. Indeed, this was the polemical purpose for his writing the *Two treatises of government* against Robert Filmer, the apologist for the divine right of kings (and probably against Hobbes as well).[162] He insisted that sovereignty should be understood not only as

162 Laslett, 'Introduction', pp. 67–92; Buckle, *Natural law and the theory of property*, pp. 161–79.

arising from a social contract, as Hobbes and Pufendorf agreed, but also as not having been alienated from the power of subjects. The mortgage that property, and particularly occupation, placed on sovereignty was the limit of sovereign power. The theory of occupation provided Locke with a tool with which to place this limit upon sovereignty.

The division over whether the state needed to exist before occupation could create property would be central to discussions of colonial property over the following two centuries. The surprising aspect of these discussions is that both philosophical positions – that which held that property and rights are created prior to the state and vice versa – were employed to argue that colonised peoples had rights and that they did not. Hobbesian ideas were employed to argue that indigenous peoples did not live in states and so did not possess rights, but they were also employed to argue that indigenous political communities were legitimate because each society organises property and other social relations as it deems appropriate to its circumstances. Similarly, the argument that rights pre-exist the state was used to argue that indigenous peoples had not exploited nature and so did not possess property, but it was also employed to argue that even if indigenous peoples did not live in recognisably sovereign states, they still possessed property rights.

In each of these cases, what was at issue for Europeans, even when discussing colonial property, was the relation between property and the European state. At stake was both the territorial foundation of states as well as the question of the security of property for the subjects of those states. The discussion of occupation revolves around questions of land for Grotius, Pufendorf and Locke. By contrast, the Roman law discussion of occupation makes no mention of land. The key context for the seventeenth-century discussions of occupation is the development of the state – that is, the development of a form of political organisation that focused upon territorial competence and placed property in land at the centre of political life. Indeed, for Locke, property in land was a prior condition for the creation of sovereignty.[163] Some of these states were built from empires, others were the platform for empires, but they all existed in some degree of tension with empire.[164] When these writers considered the justice of occupation in empires, they were immediately forced to reflect on the implications for the territorial states of Europe.

state

[163] Tuck, *Rights of war and peace*, p. 176.

[164] On tensions between states and empires, see Elizabeth Mancke, 'Empire and state', in Armitage and Braddick (eds.), *The British Atlantic world.*

A point underlined by the work of Grotius, Hobbes, Pufendorf and Locke is that, as we have seen, all four were touched by the great instability caused in Europe by the Reformation and the wars of religion. They were deeply concerned by the need to impose order on a disordered and dangerous world. People will ask, Locke observed, where did this state of nature ever exist? His answer, that in the beginning all the world was America, has captured the attention of many recent readers. But the contemporary readers of these natural law writers would never have been in any doubt that the dangerous state of nature they described was the state they had experienced in Europe when civil society dissolved into civil war or into the bloody wars between European states. Pufendorf's description of the pre-civil state as 'a continual Warfare, accompanied with Fears, Want, Sordidness, Solitude, Barbarity, Ignorance, and Brutishness' would for many have resembled their experiences of the wars of religion.[165] When these natural law writers wrote about property, they were concerned with property over life and liberty as well as estates. They had a strong sense of the fragility of civil society and of their own states. These lessons were not easily forgotten and it is important to keep in mind when we turn to writers on property and occupation in the eighteenth and nineteenth centuries that concerns about order, liberty and the rule of law in Europe remained priorities even when discussions turned on questions of colonial or imperial occupation.

[165] Pufendorf, *The whole duty of man*, p. 171.

CHAPTER 5

Theories of occupation in the eighteenth century

Eighteenth-century theorists of property were split between those, such as Jean Barbeyrac, who agreed with Locke that occupation in a state of nature created rights of property through labour and those who argued that compacts created property.[1] Amongst those philosophers who favoured convention as the origin of property, some agreed with Grotius and Pufendorf that such agreements could be established prior to the creation of civil society, while others, such as Kant, agreed with Hobbes that it was in a civil state that agreements create property, although, unlike Hobbes, for Kant, the form such agreements took was that the first person to take something would become the owner. Whether siding with Locke or favouring convention, all these writers agreed that occupation was instrumental in creating not only rights in property but also in elevating the occupiers in the progress of history. This concept of occupation as a force of stadial history was strongest in the writers of the Scottish historical school, who explained the creation of property not as the product of natural laws, but as part of an historical evolution. In their theories, occupation became a positive and historical phenomenon more than a law of nature.

Many of these eighteenth-century writers on occupation were also concerned with the ways in which the idea had been used to justify European expansion. As we shall see in the next chapter, the Lockeans found an enthusiastic audience amongst the land speculators in eighteenth-century North America, although the understanding of occupation in terms of labour has been over-stated both in terms of its impact upon colonisation and, as I argue in this chapter, as a peculiarly English doctrine. Moreover, due to their concerns about colonial appropriations,

[1] For the conventionalist versus the 'unilateral' account of property in the eighteenth century, see Kiyoshi Shimokawa, 'A brief history of post-Lockean unilateralism: Barbeyrac, Carmichael and Hutcheson on property', *Humanities: Christianity and Culture*, 43 (2012), 1–26.

some writers argued that non-European peoples' occupation of their territories not only gave them a right in those territories but also showed that they were worthy of being regarded as civilised peoples. At the same time, a number of these critics argued that European interests would be better served by commercial expansion, or the creation of trading empires, rather than by the territorial empires that had been created in the Americas and, increasingly, by the British East India Company in the East.

The eighteenth-century Lockeans: Gottlieb Gerhard Titius, Jean Barbeyrac and Gershom Carmichael

Locke's understanding of the origin of property arising from occupation and labour rather than contract immediately found supporters in continental Europe, including Gottlieb Gerhard Titius (1661–1714) and the philosopher Jean Barbeyrac (1674–1744), who edited Pufendorf's *De jure naturae et gentium.*[2] In 1702 Locke began correspondence with Barbeyrac.[3] Like so many seventeenth-century natural law writers, Barbeyrac lived with the instability and danger caused by the Reformation and he sought the principles of a political order that would address those troubles. He was from a French Huguenot family that had been forced into exile, first in Lausanne and then in Berlin, following the revocation of the Edict of Nantes in 1685. Barbeyrac announced to Locke his intention to translate the works of Pufendorf into French, and it would be Barbeyrac more than any other author who served to popularise Pufendorf's philosophy.[4] On the important question of the origin of property, however, Barbeyrac

[2] In *The religion of nature delineated*, William Wollaston (1659–1724) also agreed that occupation was the origin of property. Wollaston was a popular philosopher in England in the first half of the eighteenth century, although his success was largely posthumous. According to his biographer, John Clarke, *The religion of nature delineated* sold 10,000 copies between 1722 and 1750: see Clarke's biography prefacing the 1750 edition of *The religion of nature delineated.* It went through eight editions in that time. In this work Wollaston echoed the social contract theorists of the seventeenth century, agreeing that 'Men may become members of a society . . . by giving their consent' (p. 151). Three years after the publication of *The religion of nature delineated*, Barbeyrac noted Wollaston's agreement that property arises from use in his notes on Pufendorf (p. 368, n. 1). It was Barbeyrac and not Basil Kennet, his English translator, who made this reference to Wollaston; see Samuel Pufendorf, *Le droit de la nature et des gens, ou système général des principes les plus importans de la morale, de la jurisprudence, et de la politique* (London [Paris?], 1740), vol. 2 of 3, p. 251, n. 7 for Barbeyrac's note on Wollaston. While for Wollaston property was founded in nature, in civil society it was 'founded not only in *nature*, but also in *law*' (p. 152).

[3] Locke, *Two treatises of government*, p. 75.n.

[4] Knud Haakonssen, *Natural law and moral philosophy: from Grotius to the Scottish Enlightenment* (Cambridge, 1996), pp. 58–9; Tully, *An approach to political philosophy*, pp. 109–11; T. J. Hochstrasser, *Natural law theories in the early Enlightenment* (Cambridge, 2000), p. 15.

decided in favour of his correspondent Locke and disagreed with Pufendorf. In a note to Pufendorf's claim that 'it was agreed' when the human race were but a small number that occupancy or, rather, 'seizing' would be the means by which something became property, Barbeyrac said that this principle required no agreement at all. 'There was no need of any Convention', he argued, 'either express or tacit for this purpose. The Right of the first Occupant is necessarily concluded to be conformable to his Intention who bestows any Thing in common to many.'[5]

Barbeyrac's support for Locke's understanding of property has been well documented. Less well known is the role of Titius, a prolific civil lawyer and also editor of Pufendorf's *De jure naturae et gentium*, and yet Barbeyrac clearly relied to a very large degree on Titius' work to form his own views on Pufendorf. Titius was the author of *Jus privatum Romano German* (1709) and a professor of Roman law at the University of Leipzig.[6] He was one of the most prominent civil lawyers of his generation. He had been a student of the rationalist philosopher Christian Thomasius and shared Thomasius' views on the separation of church and state. However, whereas Thomasius has been seen as having left individual rights out of his theory of state sovereignty, Titius used Pufendorf in order to deny that property rights come from the state. Many of Barbeyrac's notes on Pufendorf 'consist of references to the *Two Treatises* [by Locke]'.[7] But the occasions on which Barbeyrac turned to Titius were far more numerous.[8] Barbeyrac's reliance on Titius, particularly on the questions of property and the state of nature, reveals the civil law foundation for the revival of the theory of occupation after Locke.[9] Indeed, as we shall see, discussions of the civil law as much as philosophy were the context in which the theory of occupation was employed throughout much of the eighteenth century. During this period, Locke's arguments on property were criticised by philosophers including David Hume and Immanuel Kant, but the principle of occupation as the origin of property was widely accepted in discussions of property in civil law and the law of nations.

5 Samuel Pufendorf, *The law of nature and nations*, trans. Basil Kennet, 5th edn (London, 1749), p. 128.
6 James Moore and Michael Silverthorne (eds.), *Natural rights on the threshold of the Scottish Enlightenment: the writings of Gershom Carmichael* (Indianapolis, 2002), p. xiv.
7 Tully, *An approach to political philosophy*, p. 109.
8 Most modern commentators on Pufendorf have ignored Titius, but for an important discussion, see Moore and Silverthorne (eds.), *Natural rights on the threshold of the Scottish Enlightenment.*
9 See, for example, Pufendorf, *The law of nature and nations*, p. 364 n. 2, p. 366, n. 2, p. 379, n. 2, p. 385, nn.1 and 2, p. 386, n. 2, p. 391, n. 3.

Consistent with his civil law perspective, Titius argued that: 'All Possession, according to the Will of the Donor [i.e., God], hath in it an effectual Virtue to make the first Occupant appropriate to himself lawfully any thing before held in common.'[10] He made this claim in his own edition of Pufendorf's *De jure naturae et gentium.* Barbeyrac also cited this passage from Titius in a footnote to Pufendorf's claim that possession proceeds from 'mutual Agreement'.[11] 'Not at all', responded Barbeyrac to Pufendorf in his annotated conversation.[12] He went on to explain that the 'immediate Foundation of all particular Right', that is, of private property, 'is the first Possession'. Barbeyrac was, like almost all early modern philosophers, familiar with and cited the Roman law foundation of this doctrine – *quod enim ante nullius est, id naturali ratione occupanti conceditur* (that which belongs to nobody becomes by natural reason the property of the occupier).[13] He pointed out that Locke had arrived at his conclusions regarding occupation as the origin of property prior to Titius and, moreover, that Locke 'cleared up the Manner' of *how* property is created – namely, through occupation and labour. He accordingly paraphrased at length Locke's discussion of how acorns become property through being taken; that is, he returned precisely to that passage in which Locke most closely echoed the Roman law of occupation.[14] In a subsequent discussion of property, Barbeyrac again responded to Pufendorf, arguing that 'Agreement is no wise necessary' and adding: 'The *Roman Lawyers* do not suppose any [agreement].'[15] Barbeyrac ridiculed as a 'meer Chimera' Pufendorf's argument that on the foundation of civil society, property was divided into that which was particular and private, and that which would be left common and open to appropriation through occupation. Ignoring Pufendorf's observation that the original agreement could be explicit *or* tacit, Barbeyrac declared that 'Mankind never met together' for such a purpose.[16]

An important modification by Titius and Barbeyrac from Locke and previous writers on occupation was the claim that occupation is constituted by an intention, not taking with the hands or feet (a point, as we shall see, that would be taken up by Kant). When Pufendorf argued that occupation must be achieved 'with the Hands' in the case of movables and 'with the Feet' in the case of land, he posed a problem for this physical

[10] Pufendorf, *The law of nature and nations*, p. 366, n. 2, quoting Titius.

[11] *Ibid.*, pp. 366–7. See also Laslett's note to Locke's discussion of this aspect of property for recognition of Barbeyrac's acknowledgement of Titius; Locke, *Two treatises of government*, p. 288.

[12] Pufendorf, *The law of nature and nations*, p. 366, n. 2.

[13] *Ibid.*, p. 388, n. 3.

[14] *Ibid.*, p. 366, n. 2.

[15] *Ibid.*, p. 367, n. 1.

[16] *Ibid.*, p. 373, n. 2.

taking of a thing by recounting a story from Plutarch. In this story the people of two Greek cities were forced into Thrace to 'find out new seats'. They heard that the city of Ancanthus was deserted and so by the law of prescription sent two spies, one from each community, to establish the truth of the claim. On discovering from afar that the rumour was true, namely that the city was deserted, each spy rushed to claim the city for his own community. The Chalcidian Spy was winning the race to possession, so the Andrian, 'seeing himself outrun', threw his spear at the city gate and, when it stuck there, cried out that 'he had taken the prior Possession in Behalf of his Countrymen'.[17] The dilemma to be solved, given that occupation rests in taking with the hands, is which spy had the first occupancy of Ancanthus? Barbeyrac commented that Plutarch's story was beside the point, because Titius had shown that occupation is established not by taking with the hands but by an intention.[18]

This distinction, between physical occupation and intention to occupy, had important implications for the justifications of European colonisers. Pufendorf's recounting of Plutarch's story about two Greek communities vying for a barbarian territory regarded as deserted was reminiscent of the race between European colonial powers, at the time when Pufendorf was writing, to claim various parts of the Americas (not to mention subsequent contests). The rules of that race were regarded as crucial to establishing legitimacy and, as far as possible, avoiding conflict. Occupying a territory with hands and feet was no easy task, and yet this is what Vitoria, Grotius, Locke and Pufendorf insisted upon if territorial claims were to be legitimate. Having the intention to occupy was another matter and this intention, rather than the reality of occupation, was often employed to justify European claims to non-European lands. The Monroe Doctrine in North America, the principles on intention accepted at the Berlin Conference in 1884/5 and the British claim to sovereignty over the continent of Australia, when it occupied only a small percentage of the landmass by the middle of the nineteenth century, are just a few examples of how important this distinction could be.[19] At the same time, Barbeyrac agreed with Grotius that: 'The meer Sight of a Thing can't have the same Effect [of occupation].'[20]

[17] *Ibid.*, p. 391. [18] *Ibid.*, p. 391, n. 3.

[19] On the gap between the power of jurisdiction and broader geographical claims to sovereign authority in the history of European empires, see Benton, *A search for sovereignty*.

[20] Pufendorf, *The law of nature and nations*, p. 367, n. 6.

Prior and necessary to Barbeyrac and Titius' discussion of property was Titius' attack on Pufendorf's understanding of the state of nature. In his chapter 'On the natural state of man' in *De jure naturae et gentium*, Pufendorf had, as we have seen, been influenced by Hobbes, observing that '*Hobbes* has been lucky enough in painting the inconveniences' of the state of nature and citing Hobbes from *De cive*:

> Out of Society (says he) we are defended only by our single Strength; in Society, by the Strength of all. Out of Society no Man is sure to keep Possession of what his Industry has gained; in Society every body is secure from that Danger. To conclude, out of Society we have the Tyranny of Passions, War, Fear, Poverty, Filthiness, Barbarity, Ignorance, and Wildness; in Society we have the Sway of Reason, Peace, Security, Riches, Decency of Ornament, Company, Elegancy, Knowledge, and Benevolence.[21]

Although Pufendorf moderated Hobbes' account of the pre-civil state, Barbeyrac responded that: 'Our Author [i.e., Pufendorf] ought not to have approved Mr *Hobbes's* words so generally, as Mr *Titius* has observed (*Obs*. 460, 461.) as I shall shew in this and the following notes.'[22] Barbeyrac then conducted an extended, point-by-point, refutation of Hobbes' and Pufendorf's understandings not only of the state of nature but also of the benefits of civil society. Following Titius' example, Barbeyrac rhetorically redescribed the 'sway of reason' in civil society as 'those Monsters of Ambition, Covetousness, Pleasure, Cruelty and Inhumanity, which ordinarily reign in the courts of princes'.[23] Similarly, in response to the remainder of Hobbes' list of the benefits of civil society, including peace, security, riches, company, elegancy and knowledge, he observed that: 'Under these fine Names are often hidden Vanity, Weakness, Folly, Pedantry, irregular Passions, and artful Intrigues.'[24] He dismissed the 'false Hypothesis of Mr Hobbes that A State of Nature is A State of War'.[25] Any vice or virtue found in civil society, he argued, can also be found in the state of nature: 'The horrible Persecutions which the Subjects sometimes suffer, and the bloody Wars which often harrass the most flourishing States and Empires, prove, that Peace and Tranquillity do not more ordinarily reign in civil Societies, than in the state of nature.'[26] Indeed, he added, wars in the civil state are worse than in the natural state because they are on a larger scale and this is true of most vices. While not dismissing the advantages of civil society altogether and not adopting a primitivist position, Barbeyrac

[21] *Ibid.*, pp. 101–2. [22] *Ibid.*, p. 101, n. 2. [23] *Ibid.*, p. 102, n. 1. [24] *Ibid.*, p. 102.
[25] *Ibid.*, p. 101, n. 8. [26] *Ibid.*, p. 102, n. 2.

argued that the civil state was capable of greater brutality than the state of nature. He concluded that: '*Hobbes*, and our Author too [i.e., Pufendorf], far exaggerate the Advantages of *Civil Society* over a *State of Nature*.'[27]

Here again Titius and Barbeyrac remind us that the occupation theory of property was closely tied to the theory of natural sociability. If we believe that human nature is brutish, fallen, sinful and nasty, then it is almost inevitable that property cannot, as Hobbes argued, exist in a natural state, or it may only do so tenuously. It must be a product of civil society, as for Hobbes (because in nature there is no *meum* or *tuum*, no mine or yours), or the product of a progression toward civil society, as for Pufendorf, and it is therefore a product not of use but, in the first instance, contract and consent. The contrary also holds true. For those theorists who believed that occupation alone was the origin of property, it was also necessary to subscribe to an understanding of the natural state, or pre-civil state, that would make it possible to hold property. There was no point in having a theory by which property could be created only for it to be impossible to hold. It was therefore necessary when occupation was seen as the origin of property to also argue that the natural state was sociable and therefore amenable to the holding of property in some degree. This, as we have seen, was Locke's position, although he understood that civil society could improve the conditions in which property could be developed.

The question of whether property was linked to natural sociability had a far-reaching impact upon understanding of the justice of colonising non-European lands. Those writers who saw humans as naturally sociable also believed that the conditions existed in the natural state which made it possible to create property without any need for states or even civil society. It was therefore clear that such political forms were not necessary for a people to have a right in their lands and goods. Of course, the same assumptions, which based the origin of property in use, could also be employed to argue that non-European peoples had not exploited their environment and therefore possessed no rights over it. For writers who saw all rights arising from sovereignty and civil society or from a stage in the progression towards civil society, it was clear that non-European peoples who were believed not to live in states did not have any rights. But again, similar assumptions could be employed to pose the inverse case (as we shall see shortly in the work of Christian Wolff): namely, that the level of a people's civilisation was not the basis of their rights, but that they possessed rights merely by disposing with their world as they saw fit.

[27] *Ibid.*, p. 102, n. 4.

Debates deploying these tools were conducted over the centuries separating Vitoria in the sixteenth century, Grotius in the seventeenth century and the international lawyers of the nineteenth century. Those debates were dramatised in divisions over the conquests of North America in the eighteenth century, Africa in the nineteenth century and the Poles in the twentieth century.

Locke's theory of property found support in Britain as well as on the Continent.[28] Gershom Carmichael (1672–1729) was prominent amongst these Lockean enthusiasts. Carmichael, like Titius and Barbeyrac, was a commentator on Pufendorf, although his commentary was upon Pufendorf's abridged *On the duty of man and citizen* and not upon his *De jure*. He was the first Professor of Moral Philosophy at the University of Glasgow and he introduced the writings of the seventeenth-century natural law theorists, particularly Grotius, Pufendorf and Locke, to the Scottish universities.[29] In the wake of the Glorious Revolution, the writings of Grotius, Pufendorf and Locke permitted Carmichael to present an understanding of political authority based upon contract and consent rather than divine right and patriarchalism.[30] Moreover, the principles of those natural law writers drew upon Roman law, which was itself the basis for Scottish civil law.

Carmichael sought to improve Pufendorf along Lockean lines.[31] He disputed Pufendorf's conclusions on the necessity of political obedience and, like Titius and Barbeyrac, he took exception to Pufendorf's understanding both of the pre-civil state and property. Titius was an important influence upon Carmichael, who insisted, like Titius, upon the natural sociability of humans.[32] For Carmichael, the first, second and third laws of nature demanded respect for God and God's creation, which meant an obligation to respect others and to be sociable. He observed that: 'Titius remarks that the state of *solitude* is quite improperly called *natural*, that in fact such a condition is supernatural inasmuch as God has destined man for sociability.'[33] In commenting upon Pufendorf's account of the brutality of the pre-civil state, Carmichael argued:

[28] Compare Dunn, 'The politics of John Locke' on the limited influence of Locke amongst eighteenth-century philosophers.

[29] Moore and Silverthorne (eds.), *Natural rights on the threshold of the Scottish Enlightenment*, pp. x–xi.

[30] *Ibid.*, pp. ix–x.

[31] Buckle, *Natural law and the theory of property*, p. 195; Tuck, *Rights of war and peace*, pp. 182–3.

[32] Moore and Silverthorne (eds.), *Natural rights on the threshold of the Scottish Enlightenment*, p. xiv.

[33] Gershom Carmichael, *Supplements and observations upon Samuel Pufendorf's On the duty of man and citizen*, in Moore and Silverthorne (eds.), *Natural rights on the threshold of the Scottish Enlightenment*, p. 125.

Pufendorf follows Hobbes, perhaps too boldly; certainly he has been criticized on this account by the distinguished Titius and Barbeyrac. I would not want to make my own criticism of this passage more severe than theirs; much less would I doubt that the condition of citizens under a government that is not utterly evil (for I dare not affirm more) is much preferable to the condition of individual men or even of individual families living in the natural state. But one should not conceal from the reader, as the Hobbesian words which Pufendorf adopts do, that the worst condition of the natural state is being compared with the civil state as it ought to be, rather than with the civil state as we find it all around us in man's present fallen condition.[34]

For Carmichael, as for Titius, unsociability is little more to be expected of the state of nature than of civil society. Clearly, moreover, humans are not only obliged to be but also are sociable in the state of nature.

As we have seen with Grotius, Locke, Barbeyrac and Titius, this natural sociability makes possible the possession of property in a pre-civil society through occupation. Carmichael, too, explicitly and forcefully rejected Pufendorf's argument that property arises from compact: 'the acquisition of ownership consists in an act of the acquirer alone, and should not therefore be made dependent, as the author contends, on a general human agreement'.[35] In accounting for the 'Original modes of acquisition', Carmichael declared 'Occupation of territory' and 'Occupation of moveables' to be the premier modes.[36]

While agreeing with Locke, Titius and Barbeyrac on the origin of property, Carmichael took Locke's part where those authors differed, notably on the question of intention. He argued that we cannot agree 'with the distinguished scholars' who argue that 'a declaration of will alone suffices for acquiring ownership of a thing which belongs to no one, without any taking direct or indirect'.[37] He cited Barbeyrac as the source of this argument and noted that it was impossible to reconcile with Locke's principle of 'origin of ownership', with which Barbeyrac otherwise concurred. Like Locke, Carmichael declared that property arose from labour: 'most earthly things which are useful to man can provide little or no use to several men at the same time, and many of them are consumed by use; but they can be developed, and they need to be developed, by human labor and more closely adapted to human purposes'.[38] He directly acknowledged his debt to Locke on this question: 'We conclude therefore that in all the cases mentioned, private ownership of things which have limited use can

[34] *Ibid.*, p. 127. [35] *Ibid.*, p. 94. [36] *Ibid.*, p. 97. [37] *Ibid.*, p. 99. [38] *Ibid.*, p. 94.

be acquired solely by the expenditure of labor in appropriating them or in preparing them for use, with the intention of keeping them for oneself; we need not ask or await the suffrages of others. For a more thorough discussion of this matter, read the celebrated Locke, *Second Treatise of Government*, chapter 5 [I.12.2.i].'[39] As had Locke, Carmichael virtually equated labour with occupation: 'if other men attempt to take away a thing so occupied from the occupier or prevent him from using it for his own purposes, and at the same time deny it to others for all of whom together it would not be adequate, they would be stealing the fruit of his labor, and this would be a wrong'.[40] In this account, occupation was identified not only with labour but also with a labour theory of value.

The compact theory of property in the eighteenth century: Christian Wolff, Jean-Jacques Rousseau, Emer de Vattel and Immanuel Kant

The Lockean understanding was by no means dominant amongst eighteenth-century philosophers. The compact theories of property developed by Grotius, Hobbes and Pufendorf were taken up by some of the most eminent philosophers of the eighteenth century. They were adopted despite and, to some degree, in reaction to Titius and Barbeyrac's arguments for occupation as the sole origin of property. The philosophers Christian Wolff, Jean-Jacques Rousseau, Emer de Vattel and Immanuel Kant developed the compact theory of property in different ways, but they did not, like Hobbes, dismiss occupation from their accounts of property. Rather, like Pufendorf, they understood occupation to be a law flowing from the agreements which formed communities. Three of these philosophers, Wolff, Rousseau, and Kant, extended the critique of European empire that had been largely implicit in Pufendorf's account of property.

These eighteenth-century critiques of empire were frequently inspired by the idea of human perfectibility, and in this respect they looked to the philosophy of Christian Wolff (1679–1754). Wolff was the most celebrated German philosopher of his time and the most eminent writer on the law of nations in the first half of the eighteenth century. He was notoriously dismissed by Frederick William I of Prussia from his post at the University of Halle in 1723. Frederick II, or Frederick the Great, however, was one of Wolff's great admirers. He was steeped in Wolffian philosophy, and when

[39] *Ibid.*, p. 96. [40] *Ibid.*, p. 94.

he replaced his father on the Prussian throne in 1740, he recalled Wolff from exile to be Chancellor of the University of Halle.[41]

The central concern of Wolff's political philosophy was human perfectability. According to Wolff, natural law commands all humans to use their natural abilities to achieve the highest state of happiness and harmony with others.[42] While the state of nature, or the 'original state', was social, it did not provide the full potential for human perfection. People therefore gave up their rights over themselves and the free use (but not ownership) of the world around them in order to participate in society and to possess property.[43] Following the original state, or 'status originarius', was a 'status adventitus', in which social authority and private property were established.[44] The communities that constitute the adventitious state in time follow the duty to pursue perfection further and surrender their rights in order to establish the 'status civilis', or civil state.[45] Importantly, for Wolff, like Pufendorf, we are obliged to make our own decisions about how to govern ourselves and restrain our passionate nature, and for this reason each society has to be left to itself to make decisions about how to achieve these goals. For Wolff, the purpose of the state is to aid that pursuit.[46] According to him, therefore, there is an obligation not only to respect the choice each society makes about its own organisation but also to respect its pursuit of the perfectibility of human nature. He was adamant, in this respect, that any society is capable of using human reason to achieve those ends. Indeed, it was in part as a consequence of him making precisely this claim about Confucian societies that he found himself exiled by Frederick I.[47]

Wolff's concern with human perfectability led him to embrace historical progress and enthusiastically to endorse the virtues of civilisation. 'It is plain', he argued, 'because it has to be admitted, that what has been approved by the more civilized nations is the law of nations.'[48] While he granted this custodial role in the law of nations to civilised powers (which he did not limit to European nations), he defended the rights of non-European peoples in the societies, adventitious or civil, they had established. Whereas Vitoria had been at pains to defend the subjects of Spanish

[41] See Knud Haakonssen, 'German natural law', in Mark Goldie and Robert Wokler (eds.), *The Cambridge history of eighteenth-century political thought* (Cambridge, 2006), pp. 257 and 268–9.

[42] *Ibid.*, p. 270. [43] *Ibid.*, p. 272. [44] *Ibid.* [45] *Ibid.*, pp. 272–3. [46] *Ibid.*

[47] Tuck, *Rights of war and peace*, p. 191.

[48] Christian Wolff, *Jus gentium methodo scientificia pertractatum*, trans. Joseph H. Drake, 2 vols. (Oxford, 1934), vol. 2, p. 17 . See also Tuck, *Rights of war and peace*, p. 188; and Brett Bowden, *The empire of civilization: the evolution of an imperial idea* (Chicago, 2009), pp. 118–19.

conquest, he did so because he believed them to be civil. Wolff diminished the question of civility as a basis for rights and thereby diminished the power of the trope whereby non-European peoples could be redescribed as uncivil. He established first that 'unknown lands inhabited by a nation may not be occupied by foreign nations'.[49] He then acknowledged that: 'Certainly separate families dwelling in the same land are to be distinguished from nations, nor can those things be applied to them which have been proved concerning the right and duties of nations.'[50] For him, family authority belonged to the adventitious state. He then turned to the question 'Of separate families dwelling together in a certain territory'. He repeatedly argued that:

> if the families have no settled abode but wander through the uncultivated wilds, in that case, nevertheless, they are understood to have tacitly agreed that the lands in that territory in which they change their abodes as they please, are held in common, subject to the use of individuals, and it is not to be doubted but that it is their intention that they should not be deprived of that use by outsiders. Therefore they are supposed to have occupied that territory as far as concerns the lands subject to their use, and consequently to have jointly acquired ownership of those lands, so that the use of them belongs to all without distinction. Therefore those lands are subject to a mixed community-holding.[51]

He conceded that 'things are occupied for the sake of their use', but responded that: 'if, indeed, separate families should be accustomed to wander about after the manner of the Scythians [the classic early modern example of barbarity] through uncultivated wilds ... the intention of wandering, which is governed by that intended use gives sufficient evidence of the occupation of the lands subject to their use, although they have not established a permanent abode on them'.[52]

Wolff questioned the centrality of 'use' (so important for Locke) in the understanding of property, agreeing with Pufendorf that ownership has its basis in consent. Having said that things are occupied for their use, he was then able to declare, in complete opposition to Locke, that 'ownership is not lost by a non-user'.[53] In what was an implicit critique of seventeenth- and eighteenth-century colonial practice, he argued that the lands of 'separate wandering families' 'can be occupied by no one coming into the territory inhabited by these families, even if at the time those who

[49] Wolff, *Jus gentium*, p. 156. Henry Reynolds has noted Wolff's concerns about the justice of colonisation; see Henry Reynolds, *The law of the land* (Melbourne, 1987 and 2003), pp. 19–22.
[50] Wolff, *Jus gentium*, p. 157. [51] *Ibid.*, p. 158. [52] *Ibid.* [53] *Ibid.*, p. 159.

inhabit the territory are not using those lands'.[54] He reached the inevitable conclusion that the *imperium*, or sovereignty, claimed by contemporary colonisers was invalid insofar as it was based upon what we have come to call the agriculturalist argument.[55] In the chapter 'Whether separate families can be subject to civil sovereignty', he simply concluded that 'no one has the right to subject separate families to civil sovereignty'. 'By nature all men are free', he observed, and 'therefore, since a right born with him can be taken from no man, but since it certainly is taken away in part, if any are subjected to civil sovereignty against their will; in either hypothesis no one has the right to subject to civil sovereignty separate families dwelling in a certain territory'.[56]

These arguments developed the recognition, already found in Pufendorf, that each society's claims to ownership had to be measured at least to some degree in terms of their own cultural practices (even if all societies, according to Wolff, must be guided by natural reason). This natural law defence of the rights of non-European peoples – with its appeal to cultural, but not epistemological, relativism – was to be developed into a late eighteenth-century attack on European empire which would continue to resonate throughout the nineteenth century. Vitoria, and many of those he influenced, had challenged the justice of European empire on the basis that universal laws of behaviour exist and that, according to those laws, non-European peoples conformed sufficiently to the norms of humanity such that it would be unjust to dispossess them. Eighteenth-century theorists of property as compact developed the natural law critique of Empire into something very different. They opposed empire on the basis of cultural relativism: that is, on the basis that humanity is culturally constituted and that cultures are incommensurable. The shift from universalism to cultural relativism had begun in Pufendorf and Wolff's writings and, importantly, their toleration was based upon the experience of the European wars of religion and the desire to establish a political order that was indifferent to religious and cultural difference. This was not relativism of a kind we might recognise today: namely, a rejection of universal or metaphysical values. It was, on the contrary, based upon the idea of free human action within the limits of human reason in Pufendorf's case, and upon free action within the limits of the pursuit of perfection in the case of Wolff.

54 *Ibid.*

55 For Wolff's 'implicit criticisms of the international behavior of the commercial empires', see Tuck, *Rights of war and peace*, pp. 187–91.

56 Wolff, *Jus gentium*, p. 159.

Wolff's notion of human perfectibility had a great impact upon subsequent philosophers, including Jean-Jacques Rousseau and Emer de Vattel. But while Wolff pursued his notion of perfectibility to speculate on progress to a future world society, or *civitas maxima*, both Rousseau and particularly Vattel, while they were contemporaries who openly disagreed on many issues, contained their political thought within the bounds of state sovereignty.[57] This attachment to sovereignty had implications for their understandings of occupation, which, for both, focused upon sovereignty as well as property. The immediate context for Rousseau and Vattel's focus upon sovereignty was their citizenship of Geneva and Neuchâtel respectively. Both cities were associated with the Swiss Confederacy during the eighteenth century, although they did not enter the Swiss Confederation until after the Napoleonic Wars. At the same time, both cities were strongly influenced by their powerful neighbours, France and Prussia. The Swiss Confederation, and neighbouring cities such as Geneva and Neuchâtel, were fragile republics, principalities and monarchies, drawn together in order to protect themselves from the turbulent and treacherous states by which they were surrounded. Both Rousseau and Vattel, albeit in different ways, responded in their political writings to the problems faced by these vulnerable cities and, in particular, both sought ways to justify a system of smaller sovereign states rather than favouring the universal claims of certain European sovereigns. Accordingly, both would articulate an understanding of occupation not only as a matter for sovereigns and nations but also as a basis for sovereignty.

Rousseau argued that occupation gave a kind of primitive right in the state of nature. This right was superior to the right that came from force, which he dismissed as no right at all. But the right of occupation in nature was susceptible to the insecurity of a pre-civil state, even if the condition of natural man was more solitary than brutish in the Hobbesian sense.[58] The creation of civil society transformed the right of occupation in the natural state into property, although in the early stages of civil society, the right of occupation remained weak and was a cause of constant conflict: 'Between the title of the strongest and that of the first occupier, there arose perpetual conflicts, which never ended but in battles and bloodshed. The new-born state of society thus gave rise to a horrible state of war.'[59] Even at this stage

[57] On the disagreements between Vattel and Wolff, see Tuck, *Rights of war and peace*, pp. 191–7.
[58] *Ibid.*, p. 199.
[59] Jean-Jacques Rousseau, *Discourse on inequality* in *The social contract and discourses*, trans. G. D. H. Cole (London, 1973), pp. 87–8.

of society, occupation, while the origin of property, was little more than usurpation. Indeed, the *Discourse on inequality* began with the dramatic claim that: 'The first man who, having enclosed a piece of ground, bethought himself of saying "This is mine", and found people simple enough to believe him, was the real founder of civil society.'[60] This was the last stage of the state of nature, similar to Wolff's adventitious state. 'The idea of property', Rousseau argued, 'depends on many prior ideas, which could only be acquired successively.'[61] It was in order to secure and also disguise their usurpation that property owners encouraged others to join with them in further developing laws.[62] It was only in an idealised future state that true occupation would be the basis to property.[63] True occupation, in this context, was consistent with accounts of occupation in the law of nations for more than 100 years – namely, it could only occur where no land had already been taken, it could not include more than was necessary for self-preservation, and the land would need to be used.

For Rousseau, the creation of a right to property was reinforced by sovereignty. Although he agreed with Locke that property could be created prior to the civil state, in contrast to Locke, he did not perceive the right of property to be mortgaged against sovereignty. Individual property rights would always be subordinate to the rights of the community, for otherwise there would be no 'real force in the exercise of Sovereignty'.[64]

Rousseau took the connection between occupation and sovereignty further than previous philosophers in his portrayal of the rights of a state itself, when considered in relation to other powers, being founded upon 'the right of the first occupier, which it holds from its members'.[65] He thus endorsed Grotius' idea of the occupation of sovereignty which Pufendorf had rejected. Rousseau, however, extended this idea which Grotius had discussed in relation to conquest, arguing that the occupation of sovereignty was the origin of sovereignty just as the occupation of property was the origin of true property. With this insight, Rousseau developed Hobbes' argument that states exist in relation to each other as individuals do in the state of nature. If in the state of nature individuals establish a right to something not by force but by occupation, then states too gain their right of sovereignty, in relation to other states, not by the power of force but by their occupation of the rights of their members.

[60] *Ibid.*, p. 76; Garnsey, *Thinking about property*, p. 164.
[61] Rousseau, *Discourse on inequality*, p. 76. [62] *Ibid.*, pp. 88–90.
[63] Garnsey, *Thinking about property*, p. 165.
[64] Rousseau, *The social contract* in *The social contract and discourses*, p. 180. [65] *Ibid.*, p. 179.

Importantly, Rousseau also understood occupation not only to be a right that defines what we may possess but also what we may not possess: 'the positive act which makes him proprietor of one thing excludes him from everything else. Having his share he ought to keep to it, and can have no further right against the community'.[66] Accordingly, 'to establish the right of the first occupier over a plot of ground', it was necessary that the ground be 'uninhabited', that only what was necessary was taken and that 'possession must be taken, not by an empty ceremony, but by labour and cultivation, the only sign of proprietorship that should be respected by others, in default of a legal title'.

If these principles of occupation were applied to states as well as individuals, as Rousseau had argued, it became clear that many of the claims of the European imperial powers would appear unjustifiable. 'How', he continued, 'can a man or a people seize an immense territory and keep it from the rest of the world except by a punishable usurpation, since all others are being robbed, by such an act, of the place of habitation and the means of subsistence which nature gave them in common?' Such an argument had been used to justify imperial expansion, but Rousseau immediately showed that the polemical direction of his thoughts applied as much to Europeans as non-Europeans: 'When Nuñez Balboa, standing on the seashore, took possession of the South Seas and the whole of South America in the name of the crown of Castile, was that enough to dispossess all their actual inhabitants.' He added ironically: 'If this was the case, it was quite unnecessary to multiply those ceremonies, and all the King of Spain had to do was, from his apartment, to take possession all at once of the whole universe.'[67]

Rousseau's understanding that occupation was not only a right that came from sovereignty but also a foundation of sovereignty and a thing that sovereign powers did was to be further developed by Emer de Vattel, his Swiss contemporary and critic. Vattel was educated in the self-preserving city-states of Neuchâtel, Basel and Geneva, and although he was a Prussian subject by birth, he was 'first and foremost Swiss'.[68] His understanding of the community of nations in his monumental *The law of nations*, or *Droit des gens* (1758), was framed by the fragile environment of the Swiss republics and principalities. He agreed with Wolff that in addition to pursuing self-preservation and self-perfection, all persons and

[66] *Ibid.* [67] *Ibid.*, p. 180.

[68] Emer de Vattel, *The law of nations*, edited and with an introduction by Bela Kapossy and Richard Whatmore (Indianapolis, 2008), p.xii.

thus all states, which are fictional persons, should seek the preservation and perfection of others. Just as the seventeenth-century natural law theorists had shown that self-preservation needed others in order to succeed, self-perfection similarly needed the help of others because nobody is born with all that they need in order to perfect themselves. For nations, this meant that they must pursue commerce and society with other nations, not out of mutual love, as Vitoria had argued, but out of the need to survive. Unlike Wolff, however, Vattel could not agree that these principles should lead to the creation of a universal republic, or *civitas maxima*.[69] Rather, he believed that the preservation of state sovereignty was fundamental to the preservation of the self of the nation and he placed the interests of the nation above all else. At the same time, he saw that competing sovereign states would be drawn into conflict, as they were in the Seven Years' War, when his *Droit des gens* was published. He directed his law of nations towards minimising conflict at the same time as preserving the principles upon which sovereignty rested.

Vattel has often been compared with Locke, particularly because he is understood to be articulating Lockean principles when he denied rights to peoples who did not cultivate the land. Indeed, Richard Tuck places Vattel in the 'tradition of Locke, Carmichael and Barbeyrac' due to his vigorous endorsement of principles of exploitation of the earth which underlay aggressive European 'adventurism'.[70] Where Locke, however, focused upon the individual, Vattel focused upon the nation, and while Locke placed property and sovereignty in a delicate balance, for Vattel, the rights of sovereignty trumped those of individuals.[71] Indeed, for him, the rational self-love of an individual drives his obedience to the state because 'his own happiness is connected with that of his country'.[72] These differences are clear in his account of the rights of occupation and they place him, on these terms, closer to Pufendorf and Wolff and even Rousseau, whose *Discourse on inequality* Vattel criticised.[73]

Vattel argued that God gave the world to 'all men in general', but as they multiplied, it was no longer possible for the earth to sustain the number of people without more intensive cultivation.[74] People accordingly appropriated to themselves particular parcels of land in order not to be

[69] Emmanuelle Jouannet, *Emer de Vattel et l'émergence doctrinale du droit international public* (Paris, 1998); Tuck, *Rights of war and peace*, p. 192.
[70] Tuck, *Rights of war and peace*, pp. 191–5.
[71] Jouannet, *Emer de Vattel*.
[72] Vattel, *The law of nations*, p. xvii.
[73] On Vattel and Rousseau, see Tuck, *Rights of war and peace*, p. 191.
[74] Vattel, *The law of nations*, p. 158.

'disturbed in their labour'. 'Such must have been', he asserted, 'the origin of the rights of *property* and *dominion*, and this fully justifies their establishment'.[75] At the same time as the creation of these rights, these people 'formed themselves into the body of a political society'. In this account, the rights of property and what Wolff described as adventitious rights were established almost simultaneously. Vattel, like Wolff and Rousseau, believed that property was dependent upon a kind of community compact, or upon political authority. He agreed with Wolff that 'free families' coming together to form a sovereign 'nation or state' could previously have been in possession of 'domain', or property, as a form of adventitious rights in the same territory.[76] Importantly, for Vattel, occupation conferred not only a right but also elevated the occupiers in their progress towards a more civilised state.

Vattel stated the right of the first occupier in relation to the claims of nations, in contrast to Locke, who stated the same right in relation to individuals. 'All mankind', he argued, 'have an equal right to the things that have not yet fallen into the possession of any one; and these things belong to the person who first takes possession of them.' In the following sentence he deduced: 'When therefore a nation finds a country uninhabited and without an owner, it may lawfully take possession of it.'[77] He was quick to add that a 'nation' may not 'appropriate to itself' a country 'which it does not really occupy'.[78] Here he concurred with the long-standing scepticism of the pretentions of many colonising powers which extended beyond their power and he was, like Vitoria, Gentili and Grotius before him, particularly damning of the ceremonies of possession which underpinned such claims: 'In effect, when navigators have met with desert countries, in which those of other nations had . . . erected some monument to shew their having taken possession of them, they have paid as little regard to that empty ceremony, as to the regulation of the popes.'[79]

Vattel's scepticism also extended to peoples who did not sufficiently exploit the land. 'There is another celebrated question', he ruminated, 'to which the discovery of the new world has principally given rise.'[80] This question was whether a nation may 'take possession of some part of a vast country' in which there are 'none but erratic nations'. His answer was that all humans are under an 'obligation to cultivate the earth' and, as with colonising powers, no nation can appropriate more land than they can 'settle and cultivate'.[81] His now notorious conclusion from these premises

[75] *Ibid.*, p. 213. [76] *Ibid.*, p. 214. [77] *Ibid.* [78] *Ibid.*
[79] *Ibid.*, p. 215. Compare Seed, *Ceremonies of.* [80] Vattel, *The law of nations*, p. 216. [81] *Ibid.*

was that peoples like the 'ancient Germans' and 'modern Tartars' who 'disdain to cultivate their lands', living instead by 'plunder', 'deserve to be extirpated as savage and pernicious beasts'.[82] He did not share the nostalgia for martial virtue that had characterised early modern discussions of the Ancient Germans, influenced by Tacitus' *Germania*, or the similar sentiments articulated by his contemporary Rousseau.[83] Others, who 'avoid labour' and live by hunting, have 'no reason to complain' if colonisers from countries 'too closely confined' come to possess a part of their territory.[84] Indeed, the duty of all men to pursue the preservation and the perfection of others would oblige those people to make way for the colonisers, even if they remained indifferent to their own perfection. Vattel then effectively endorsed Acosta's history and anthropology when he concurred that the conquest of Peru and Mexico was 'a notorious usurpation', but that the establishment of 'many colonies on the continent of North America' was, if they remained within 'just bounds', 'extremely lawful'.[85] In these observations he was at odds with Wolff's argument that separate families living in a land could possess a kind of sovereignty that demanded respect.

While Vattel was disdainful of the rights of nomadic peoples, he was not entirely consistent on the question. His recognition that property could be established outside a state left open the problem that states could not colonise territories where a person or people had not established sovereignty, but had established property. This possibility widened the implications of Vattel's account of property for people who were believed not to possess sovereignty. He addressed this question, arguing that 'an independent private person', whether he was driven from his country or whether he willingly quitted it, 'may settle in a country which he finds without master, and there possess an independent domain'.[86] This person may then proceed, if 'he' wished, to establish a state by attracting other people to him. But if he did not, any subsequent coloniser who settled the whole country could not do so 'without respecting the rights and independence of this person'.[87] Vattel then expanded this premise regarding the individual settler to encompass 'many independent families' or tribes. Such peoples 'possess the free domain', or property, 'but without empire', or sovereignty, 'since they do not form a political society'.[88] He then argued that: 'Nobody can seize the empire of this country' because this would be to subject these peoples to civil society against their will. Here Vattel recalls

[82] *Ibid.*, p. 129. [83] On early modern uses of *Germania*, see Fitzmaurice, *Humanism and America.*
[84] Vattel, *The law of nations*, p. 130. [85] *Ibid.*, p. 94. [86] *Ibid.*, p. 233. [87] *Ibid.*
[88] *Ibid.*, p. 234.

Wolff's argument that each society determines the terms upon which it pursues self-perfection. We cannot, he argued, 'without injustice' deprive 'families wandering in a country' of the land that they need. Perhaps conscious of the growing incoherence in relation to his earlier comments regarding the North American Indians, Vattel hastily added that it was necessary to recollect what he had said 'more than once' – namely, that 'the Indians of North America had no right to appropriate all that vast continent to themselves'.[89] As in so many discussions of occupation and colonisation, however, the criteria of use immediately rebounded on Vattel's argument, deepening the ambiguity. He turned from the American Indians to the 'Arabian shepherds' and here he conceded that while the Arabs did not pursue agriculture, they nevertheless 'possess their country' and 'make use of it after their manner'.[90] Following Pufendorf and Wolff, Vattel here accepts that what constitutes legitimate use may be something that each people determine for themselves. These principles whereby each state determined its own internal concerns remained vital to post-Westphalian European societies who continued to distance themselves from the horrors of the wars of religion.[91]

Vattel left the political standing of the extra-European world in an ambiguous state. On the one hand, he observed that wandering peoples, while possessing dominion, do not 'form a political society'.[92] On the other hand, he insisted that while other peoples may settle in such countries and also establish property (provided they do not dispossess the native inhabitants), these settlers cannot 'seize the empire' of such places; that is, they cannot usurp adventitious rights. Despite the uncertainties created by adventitious rights, Vattel consistently asserted that the rights of sovereign nations always trump those of individuals. During the eighteenth century, a struggle was waged in North America over the rights of individuals against the state. But by the nineteenth century, this struggle, insofar as it concerned the right of occupation, was largely won in favour of sovereignty. Vattel's work, as we shall see in the dispute over the Oregon Territory, would prove to be an important tool in realising that outcome.

Whereas the pursuit of human perfectibility led Rousseau and Vattel to robust accounts of state sovereignty, Immanuel Kant used perfectibility to

[89] *Ibid.* [90] *Ibid.*

[91] Jouannet, *Emer de Vattel.* Compare Tuck, *Rights of war and peace*, pp. 195–6, who argues that Vattel presents a 'liberal' apology for empire.

[92] Vattel, *The law of nations*, p. 234.

critique the state. In particular, he developed an understanding of the relation between property, sovereignty and human perfectibility to critique the imperial ambitions of contemporary states. Kant was a Prussian subject of the enlightened absolutist Frederick the Great. However, Frederick died in 1786 and was replaced by Frederick William II, who suppressed religious free-thinkers and demanded that all preachers and professors subscribe to orthodox church views. Kant was himself a victim of Frederick William II's attempts to silence religious dissent. He was reprimanded for an essay he published on religion and coercion, and was obliged to promise not to write on religious matters again.[93] Kant's political views were also formed by the French Revolution at this time and, specifically, by the war waged against France by the surrounding European monarchies. The object of that war was to defeat the Revolution and reinstate the monarchy. In the ten years from the mid-1780s to the mid-1790s, in this climate of growing intolerance at home and revolutionary war abroad, Kant developed his most important contributions to political philosophy, including the *Metaphysics of morals* and *Towards perpetual peace.*

Like Hobbes, Kant understood civil constitutions to be the source of property rights, but he arrived at this point by radically different means.[94] He did not agree that the basis of rights was self-preservation, but rather reason and human dignity. In his youth he had been a student of the dominant Wolffian philosophical school, but he would take Wolff's emphasis on human perfectibility further. He agreed that human behaviour was excessively inclined to evil, but he understood rights in terms of the standards to which humans should aspire, not by how they behaved at their worst. For him, the creation of civil constitutions was a necessary duty in the realisation through reason of dignity and rights.

Like many of his seventeenth-century natural law predecessors, Kant maintained the Roman law idea of occupation as an explanation for the origin of property even while he insisted on a civil constitution as the only conclusive means to create property. He argued that original acquisition in a state of nature was achieved by people removing things, including land, from the original common possession of the world by bringing them under their control. For Kant, this original acquisition, while 'true', was only provisional because it must be accompanied by a duty to seek a civil

[93] Alan Wood, 'General Introduction' to Immanuel Kant, *Practical philosophy*, trans. and ed. Mary Gregor (Cambridge, 1996), pp. xxvii–xxviii.

[94] For Kant's theory of property, see Allen W. Wood, *Kant's ethical thought* (Cambridge, 1999), pp. 245–9; Garnsey, *Thinking about property*, pp. 165–173.

constitution.[95] It is only through the recognition in law of a civil constitution that the provisional acquisition achieved by an original occupation, or bringing under control of things, becomes 'conclusive': 'conclusive acquisition takes place only in the civil condition'.[96] Crucially, 'taking control' was Kant's interpretation of what was meant by 'occupation', or 'occupatio'. Here he explicitly referred to the Roman and civil law of occupation: 'So original acquisition of an external object, and hence too of a separate and specific piece of land, can take place only through taking control of it (*occupatio*).'[97] He also understood that this kind of original acquisition created a *right* of property: 'the act required to establish a right is taking control (*occupatio*)'.[98] Indeed, like so many philosophers before him, Kant effectively appropriated the Roman law understanding of the origin of property into his own philosophical system.

For Kant, while possession and occupation meant 'taking control', it did not require cultivation. In direct repudiation of Locke, he declared: 'in order to acquire land is it necessary to develop it (build on it, cultivate it, drain it, and so on)? No'.[99] Developing land, he argued, was 'nothing more than an external sign of taking possession, for which many other signs that cost less effort can be substituted'.[100] Whereas for Locke, the natural law theory of occupation, taking, seizing or bringing into possession, was understood as development, for Kant, taking and possession became a matter merely of control and they left the form of possession to each agent to determine. This principle that it was for each person, or people, to employ their own reason in determining how to employ their property was central to Kant's thinking.

His reflection on original acquisition led Kant to ask whether 'we should not be authorised to found colonies, by force if need be' in order to establish a 'civil union' with other peoples and to 'bring these human beings (savages) into a rightful condition (as with the American Indians, the Hottentots and the inhabitants of New Holland [Australia]'.[101] 'Or', he added, '(which is not much better), to found colonies by fraudulent purchase of their land, and so become owners of their land, making use of our superiority without regard to their first possession.'[102] He made the customary observation that such actions would surely be authorised because 'nature itself (which abhors a vacuum) seems to demand it'.[103]

Kant anti-colonial

95 Immanuel Kant, *The metaphysics of morals*, in Kant, *Practical philosophy*, p. 416. 96 *Ibid.*
97 *Ibid.*, p. 415. 98 *Ibid.*
99 *Ibid.*, p. 417. On Kant's repudiation of Locke's understanding of property, see also Muthu, *Enlightenment against empire*, p. 187.
100 Kant, *The metaphysics of morals*, p. 417. 101 *Ibid.* 102 *Ibid.* 103 *Ibid.*, p. 418.

This he pointed out had been the means whereby 'great expanses of land in other parts of the world' had become 'splendidly populated' when they would otherwise have remained unknown to 'civilised people' and continued 'forever uninhabited'. He then resoundingly rejected this standard colonial apology, declaring it to be a 'veil of injustice (Jesuitism)', which would sanction any means to achieve 'good ends' and which must be 'repudiated'.[104] Thus, for Kant, original acquisition was a barrier to colonisation and he echoed the sceptical use of the Roman law of occupation in regards to European imperial ambitions.

Kant developed this strident anti-imperial reasoning throughout his various works on moral philosophy.[105] He followed Hobbesian reasoning insofar as he argued that each civil constitution created a sovereign person whose autonomy must be respected.[106] But he was sufficiently concerned by the injustices of empire to condemn the appropriation of one state by another as his second preliminary article of perpetual peace, arguing:

> For a state (like the land on which it resides) is not a belonging. It is a society of human beings that no one other than itself can command or dispose of. Like a trunk, it has its own roots; and to annex it to another state as a graft is to do away with its existence as a moral person and to make a moral person into a thing, and so to contradict the original compact, apart from which no right over a people can be thought.[107]

In the *Metaphysics of morals* he asked: 'can two neighbouring peoples (or families) resist each other in adopting a certain use of land, for example, can a hunting people resist a pasturing people or a farming people, or the latter resist a people that wants to plant orchards, and so forth'.[108] This was the same question previously put by Wolff and Vattel, with opposed answers. Kant took Wolff's side in making his answer: 'Certainly, since as long as they keep within their boundaries the way they want to *live* on their land is up to their own discretion.'[109]

Kant extended his critique of empire to a consideration of the claim to the natural right of communication that had been used by Europeans to justify their incursions into non-European lands. Specifically, he analysed the question of hospitality to strangers considered in depth by Vitoria and Pufendorf. For Vitoria, as we have seen, while conquest was unjustifiable,

[104] *Ibid.* [105] Muthu, *Enlightenment against empire*, pp. 186–200.
[106] Tuck, *Rights of war and peace*, pp. 207–14.
[107] Kant, *Toward perpetual peace*, in Kant, *Practical philosophy*, p. 318.
[108] Kant, *The metaphysics of morals*, p. 417.
[109] *Ibid.*; Muthu, *Enlightenment against empire*, pp. 198–9.

no nation could deny entry to strangers because all people belonged to the same human community, reflecting their natural sociability, and no law could impede the natural communication of man with man. Subsequent commentators have argued that Vitoria used this qualification to his argument as a way of opening a back door for the Spanish conquests. Certainly, subsequent colonisers, notably the English in the seventeenth century (as we have seen), used this right of communication and right of hospitality to legitimise colonisation. Pufendorf rejected the right of hospitality partly because he left it to each state to determine such matters and partly, as he noted, because the argument had become a notorious excuse for conquest. However, it is anachronistic, as I have argued, to impute these motives onto Vitoria. Hospitality was a genuine concern for the Thomists and, particularly at the time of the wars of religion (which were only in their infancy when Vitoria wrote), the right of hospitality included the right for people to seek refuge.[110]

In his 'Third definitive article for perpetual peace', Kant entered into this debate firmly taking the position that 'universal hospitality' was a 'cosmopolitan right' and he accordingly rejected Pufendorf's position on the issue. For him, the possibility to seek commerce with others provided the opportunity for peoples to 'enter peaceably into relations with one another' and so bring 'the human race ever closer to a cosmopolitan constitution'.[111] Importantly, however, and in agreement with Pufendorf, Kant was able to reflect on the fact that the right to communicate with other peoples had been grossly abused by European colonisers: 'the injustice they show in *visiting* foreign lands and peoples (which with them is tantamount to *conquering* them) goes to horrifying lengths'.[112] And it was this abuse of the right of commerce that led to the perception of other lands as *res nullius* – that is, as lands belonging to no one. Kant immediately continued: 'When America, the negro countries, the Spice Islands, the Cape, and so forth were discovered, they were, to them, countries belonging to no one, since they counted the inhabitants as nothing.'[113]

Crucially, Kant linked the violation of the right of colonised peoples to the violation of all rights:

> Since the (narrower or wider) community of the nations of the earth has now gone so far that violation of right on *one* place of the earth is felt in *all*,

[110] Brett, *Changes of state*. [111] Kant, *Toward perpetual peace*, p. 329. [112] *Ibid*.

[113] *Ibid*. We know that Kant understood things belonging to no one to be *res nullius* because in *The metaphysics of morals*, p. 417, he paired the terms 'something *belonging to no one (res nullius)*' while discussing the origin of property (see also p. 421 on *res nullius*).

> the idea of a cosmopolitan right is no fantastic and exaggerated way of representing right; it is, instead, a supplement to the unwritten code of the right of a state and the right of nations necessary for the sake of any public rights of human beings and so for perpetual peace.[114]

The injustices visited on colonised peoples were an injustice to all and a threat to the peace of all. Here Kant pointed to one of the strongest motives for concern with the violation of property and sovereignty in empire from Vitoria through to the twentieth century: namely, the fear of many critics was that colonial injustice would be repatriated. Sovereigns who were permitted to behave outside the law in their colonies would inevitably bring such practices back to the metropolis or, in Kant's case, the entire cosmopolitan community.[115] These anxieties were greatest at precisely the time that Europeans were fighting for the rule of law in their own societies.

The historical theory of occupation and property: Francis Hutcheson, Adam Ferguson, David Hume and Adam Smith

Over the course of the eighteenth century, a new understanding of the relationship between occupancy and property developed out of the Scottish historical school, or what has been labelled the 'Scottish Enlightenment'. These philosophers moved towards an understanding of property as an attribute of historical evolution rather than a consequence of natural laws, whether of sociability or self-interest. This is not to say that these Scottish philosophers simply abandoned the understandings of property developed by previous generations of natural law writers. On the contrary, they engaged with those debates and took their own positions on matters of self-interest, sociability and sovereignty. Moreover, their understanding of property developing in historical time was indebted to the natural law writers' own stadial theories of history that had been partly inspired by the idea of a state of nature.

One of the central concerns for the writers of the Scottish historical school was the rise of commercial society that presented perhaps the most salient political challenges in eighteenth-century Britain.[116] They struggled with the ascendance of commerce, with its glorification of interest and

[114] Kant, *Toward perpetual peace*, p. 330.
[115] See Muthu, *Enlightenment against empire*, pp. 186–92 on Kant's cosmopolitan right and anti-imperialism.
[116] Hont, *Jealousy of trade*.

attempted to develop a moral philosophy which would restore civic and communal values or, at best, to find ways of reconciling commerce with civic life. It was in this context that these writers engaged with the problem of sociability and property. As private or particular property was a creation of self-interest, it could be difficult to reconcile with sociability. The discussions of occupation accordingly warned against the unlicensed and unrestrained appropriation of property without regard to the rights of others. Those others could include non-European peoples. Crucially, however, the reason for scepticism about the colonisation of other peoples' lands was motivated by fears concerning liberty at home.

Anxiety that foreign conquests could endanger liberty at home was not new. Since the sixteenth century, Europeans had understood their expansion beyond the European world in terms of Roman accounts of empire.[117] Roman historians, particularly Sallust, had argued that the luxury and wealth created by empire caused the effeminacy of the once martial people who had conquered distant lands. Thus, luxury caused the loss of martial virtues and the decline and collapse of empire. This idea that empires contain the seeds of their own destruction was powerfully reprised by Machiavelli at the beginning of the sixteenth century and subsequently became a central anxiety for all the early modern European empires. In the eighteenth century, this critique of empire pushed philosophers and historians, including Charles-Louis de Secondat, Baron de Montesquieu, David Hume and Adam Smith, to seek a political economy in which wealth and luxury would not be seen as causes of corruption and decline. That need was particularly pressing in societies engaged in rapid commercial growth. This was the work achieved by the Scottish historical school and by continental contemporaries such as Montesquieu.

In arguing, however, that wealth and interest could be beneficial for society, these thinkers opposed the 'softness' of commerce, as Montesquieu put it, to the violence of conquest and occupation which European states had used to acquire foreign territories in the early modern period.[118] The immediate context for these concerns was the Seven Years' War and the East India Company conquests in India from 1757 that, according to this

117 On the the pre-modern ideology of empire and its Roman heritage, see: Pagden, *Lords of all the world*; Armitage, *The ideological origins of the British Empire*; Pocock, *Barbarism and religion*, vol. 3; Fitzmaurice, *Humanism and America*. See also Fitzmaurice, 'Neither neo-Roman nor liberal empire'.

118 Hirschman, *The passions and the interests*, p. 60; Pagden, *Lords of all the world*, p. 115; although see also Spector, 'Was Montesquieu liberal?', p. 68 on Montesquieu's portrayal of the harmful aspects of commerce.

account, were an extension of the early modern martial approach to empire. The military mobilisation and taxes required for such conquests were a threat to stability and liberty at home. Philosophers such as Hume and Smith were happy to see European influence extended abroad through the use of commerce, but not through the export of large colonial populations that required large armies to protect them, as in North America.[119] The kinds of empires they envisaged were empires of commerce, not colonial empires, in which the sovereignty of foreign nations could be controlled and their populations used to produce goods for trade. This meant that they were hostile to the idea of appropriating property in other countries and they were accordingly against the idea of occupation insofar as it concerned the appropriation of property overseas. They argued, like Rousseau and Kant, that property could only be established under sovereignty, with the implication that it could no longer be possible for private interests to conduct unrestricted aggressive extra-European expansion as they had, for example, in the case of the East India Company in the East, and in the Americas, for example, in the case of land speculators west of the Appalachian Mountains. In the following chapter, I will explore the tensions between these understandings of occupation and property within and outside sovereignty in the case of American land speculation.

The scepticism of empire expressed in the writings of these historians and philosophers was partly realised in the commercial, and sometimes 'informal', empires of the nineteenth century.[120] Their ideas left open the possibility that the sovereignty of another land could be 'occupied' without the appropriation of property and it was precisely that understanding of occupation that would develop in the nineteenth century (while hostility to the occupation of property continued). With the loss of the French, British and Spanish American empires between 1763 and the 1830s, European powers established African and Asian empires which were based upon commerce and trade, control over sovereignty and, rather than exterminating indigenous peoples, local populations who were exploited as productive labour.

119 Pagden, *Lords of all the world*, pp. 161–2; Armitage, *Ideological origins of the British Empire*, pp. 189–191.

120 On the contrast between continental and commercial empire, see: Gallagher and Robinson, 'The imperialism of free trade'; Pagden, *Lords of all the world*; Pagden, 'Empire and its anxieties'; Fisch, 'Law as a means and an end', p. 28; Steinmetz, 'Imperialism or colonialism?', p.140 distinguishing modern territorial empires from 'imperial*ism*'; Maier, *Among empires*. For the specifically British instance, see P. J. Marshall, 'Britain without America – a second empire?', in P. J. Marshall (ed.), *The Oxford history of the British Empire: the eighteenth century* (Oxford, 1998).

One of the earliest figures in the Scottish historical school to express this discomfort with empire was Francis Hutcheson. Hutcheson's account of occupation and property drew as much upon Locke as it did upon Hobbes and Pufendorf.[121] Indeed, Hutcheson was a voice of moderation throughout his philosophical writings. He was born into a Presbyterian Irish family and he established a dissenting academy in Dublin in 1719, at which time he was drawn to the Whig cause. While his views were nonconformist, he was obliged to work under the approval of the Church of Ireland and he was unsurprisingly drawn to ideas of toleration and benevolence.[122] Like many contemporaries, particularly Whigs, he struggled with the ascendance of commercial society, with its glorification of interest, and he attempted to develop a moral philosophy that would restore civic and communal values. In 1729, he replaced Gershom Carmichael, whom he regarded as 'by far the best commentator' on Pufendorf, as the Chair of Moral Philosophy at the University of Glasgow.[123] However, he made a break with Carmichael's moral philosophy that would be important for the later development of an historical understanding of the origin of property. He expressed scepticism regarding the notion of a state of nature, particularly a self-interested natural state, which had been so central to the natural law theorists of the seventeenth century. Without the state of nature to provide the motives and, in some accounts, the conditions for the development of property, it would become necessary, as we shall see, for philosophers such as Adam Ferguson, Hume and Smith, to substitute the seventeenth-century natural law theorists' abstract and hypothetical basis for property with an account of the development property in historical time.

A year after gaining his Chair, Hutcheson delivered his inaugural oration, *On the natural sociability of mankind*, in November 1730. In this oration, he argued that 'political writers should unlearn the use of these words (*natural state*)'.[124] Instead, he argued, the state prior to the civil state should be referred to as a state of '*liberty from human government*'.[125] But,

[121] Buckle, *Natural law and the theory of property*, pp. 191–233; Shimokawa, 'A brief history of post-Lockean unilateralism'.

[122] Daniel Carey, *Locke, Shaftesbury and Hutcheson: contesting diversity in the Enlightenment and beyond* (Cambridge, 2006), pp. 152–4.

[123] Francis Hutcheson, *A short introduction to moral philosophy*, in *Philosophiae moralis instituion compendiaria with a short introduction to moral philosophy*, ed. Luigi Turco (Indianapolis, 2007), p. 3.

[124] Francis Hutcheson, *On the natural sociability of mankind*, in *Logic, metaphysics, and the natural sociability of mankind*, eds. James Moore and Michael Silverthorne (Indianapolis, 2006), p. 201.

[125] *Ibid.*

according to him, it was not simply this state of liberty, and its dangers, that gave rise to government and property, as the seventeenth-century natural law theorists had maintained. Certainly, he agreed, there are dangers in a state free from civil government, although those dangers had been greatly over-stated. He could not agree that 'man' could be 'depicted (may God forgive the thought!) as a mute and naked animal, poor, solitary, nasty, dirty, rude, ignorant, timid, rapacious, aggressive, unsociable, incapable of giving or attracting love'.[126] Hobbes and Pufendorf, the authors of such blasphemies, were followers of the doctrines of self-love professed by the Epicureans.[127] Rather, Hutcheson argued, humans are naturally sociable. To establish this claim, he built on critics of Hobbes' theory of unsociability, particularly the Earl of Shaftesbury and Richard Cumberland.[128] He also drew upon critics of Pufendorf, including Titius, Joseph Butler and Hutcheson's own predecessor, Carmichael.

Our natural sociability, Hutcheson claimed, was not based upon our behaviour in a pre-civil society, but upon the ends to which God had fitted us; that is, sociability is the realisation of what is best in our natures.[129] Bernard Mandeville satirised Hutcheson on this score, arguing along with Hobbes (and Machiavelli for that matter) that people must be judged according to the behaviour they exhibit and not how we would like them to behave.[130] Hutcheson responded that we must judge the purpose of things not according to how they are, as they are frequently corrupt, but by the ends for which they were intended. The purpose of our eyes, for example, is seeing. They may be damaged or degraded, and our sight impaired, but that cannot change our description of them as an organ for seeing.

We pursue society, Hutcheson argued, both for the reasons Hobbes and Pufendorf gave, namely for self-preservation, but also out of our moral sense.[131] Like Pufendorf and Locke, Hutcheson sought to explain what drives us to pursue moral actions. Shaftesbury's answer to why we act

[126] *Ibid.*, p. 198.

[127] *Ibid.*, p. 202. Compare Tuck's account of Grotius and Pufendorf's elevation of self-interest in natural law, which, Tuck argues, was a consequence of the influence of Carneades and the Academic Sceptics; Tuck, 'The "modern" theory of natural law', p. 113.

[128] Anthony, Third Earl of Shaftesbury, *Characteristicks of men, manners, opinions, times*, 3 vols. (Indianapolis, 2001), vol. 1, pp. 56–7; Richard Cumberland, *A treatise of the laws of nature*, translated, with introduction and appendix, by John Maxwell (1727), edited and with a foreword by Jon Parkin (Indianapolis, 2005).

[129] Hutcheson, *On the natural sociability of mankind*, pp. 195–6.

[130] *Ibid.*, p. 195.

[131] For Hutcheson's account of moral sense, see Buckle, *Natural law and the theory of property*, pp. 195–201.

virtuously was that virtue is innate in human minds. Hutcheson, while agreeing with Shaftesbury about our virtuousness, rejected the idea of innate virtue. He argued instead that our moral sense is driven by an appreciation of beauty that is natural to humans.[132] Our appreciation of beauty extends beyond the beauty of objects and includes the beauty of actions, which we understand as moral virtue. One of the main objects of our moral sense is our approval of benevolent actions in others and that approval also leads us to perform benevolent actions ourselves. The centrality of benevelonce to moral sense underlines our sociable and virtuous nature. Being sociable did not mean, he added, that we are like cows or sheep, happy to live in herds, but rather that we are 'inclined and naturally fitted to lead a harmless life, to give mutual assistance, to protect and preserve others'.[133] According to Hutcheson, therefore, civil society was a product of both the self-preservation described by Hobbes and Pufendorf and the desire to preserve others: 'Men therefor are justly called 'creatures [animals] fitted by nature for civil polity.'[134] He argued that 'not only the dread of injuries, but eminent virtues, and our natural high approbation of them have engaged men at first to form civil societies'.[135]

In providing an account of sociability and civil society to rival the seventeenth-century natural law theorists, Hutcheson was also establishing a parallel account of the origin of property. Property, he argued, is the creation as much of our virtues as our desire for self-preservation and it cannot therefore be the product of ambition, avarice and evil. For Hutcheson, as for earlier natural law theorists, property is a right, but his understanding of right was closely tied to his theory of human benevolence.[136] Thus, the 'right' to take possession of animals is motivated by prudence and mercy for those animals rather than avarice.[137] Perfect rights, he argued, must come from actions performed for the general good – the more we pursue the public good, the greater our right in that thing. His understanding of rights accordingly reflects Pufendorf's 'reconstruction of rights in terms of duties'.[138] At the same time, Hutcheson's instances of perfect right have a Lockean tone and include the right to life, the right

[132] See *ibid.*, pp. 201–11 for a detailed account of Hutcheson's understanding of the centrality of beauty to the moral sense.
[133] Hutcheson, *On the natural sociability of mankind*, p. 201.
[134] Hutcheson, *Short introduction to moral philosophy*, p. 235.
[135] *Ibid.*, p. 236.
[136] Buckle, *Natural law and the theory of property*, pp. 213–16.
[137] Hutcheson, *Short introduction to moral philosophy*, pp. 134–5.
[138] Buckle, *Natural law and the theory of property*, p. 214.

to liberty and the rights of acquisition or property and contract. He continued in this Lockean vein when he argued that property arises not from agreement, as Pufendorf had claimed, but from use and 'labour and industry' upon the materials of nature provided in the original negative community.[139]

This rival account of property made extensive use of the theory of occupation. Hutcheson's discussion of the origin of property in his *Short introduction to moral philosophy* concentrated on the seizing (occupation) of animals that was also, of course, the subject of the Roman law of occupation. Occupation was the origin of property: 'Our desire for self-preservation and our tender affections excite us to occupy or acquire things necessary or useful for ourselves and those we love.'[140] Civil society creates security in what has already become property through occupation. Writing at the height of anti-imperial sentiment in the 1730s in his *A system of moral philosophy*, he expanded this account in the chapter 'How property is acquired', revealing the link between the law of occupation as it applied to the capture of wild beasts, as in the examples given in Roman law, and as it applied to colonisation. A person, he argued, who tires 'any wild creature in the chace' would be wrongly deprived of that creature by the intervention of another person.[141] Similarly, he claimed, 'one who has fitted out ships for a descent upon unoccupied lands, towards the occupation of which no previous labour has been employed by others' would be wronged if another person, with greater speed, arrived at the same lands and 'refused to make a division'. The lesson to be drawn here largely concerned rival European colonial powers, but Hutcheson then continued with an attack on colonisers who claim rights over 'a vast tract of land quite beyond their power to cultivate'.[142] His words contrasted with Locke, who levelled the same criticism at Native Americans. Hutcheson was not defending Native Americans with this observation, he was simply sceptical of rights in property that were used to justify expansion. He also criticised private individuals who make expansive claims: 'it would be vain for a private man with his domesticks to claim a property, upon the circumstance of his having first discovered or arrived at it, in a country capable of maintaining ten thousand families'. Equally vain, he added, were the exorbitant claims of nations over vast tracts of land which they do not cultivate.

139 *Ibid.*, pp. 224–5. 140 Hutcheson, *Short introduction to moral philosophy*, p. 135.
141 Francis Hutcheson, *A system of moral philosophy*, 2 vols. (Glasgow, 1755), vol. I, pp. 325–6.
142 *Ibid.*, p. 326. See also Armitage, *Ideological origins of the British Empire*, p. 188.

Hutcheson's discomfort with empire became more apparent in the second volume of *A system of moral philosophy*, in the chapter on 'How civil power is acquired'. Here, in a discussion of 'the rights of mother-countries over colonies' which partly accounted for the popularity of Hutcheson's writings in pre-Revolutionary America, he argued that colonies could be maintained until such point as they became self-sufficient.[143] Remembering, he argued, that the point of all political unions 'is the general good of those thus united', there could be no point in maintaining a colony when it did not serve the good of either colonists or the mother country. 'There is something so unnatural', he claimed, 'in supposing a large society, sufficient for all the good purposes of an independent political union, remaining subject to the direction and government of a distant body of men.'[144] Moreover, such an empire was a burden to the mother country and a cause of misery: 'to extend civil power over distant nations, and form grand unwieldly empires, without regard to the obvious maxims of humanity, has been one great source of human misery'.

Hutcheson's critique of empire was taken up by Adam Ferguson (1723–1816). For Ferguson, as for Hutcheson, his understanding of occupation, property and sovereignty was again central to that critique. Like Hutcheson before him, Ferguson was concerned with the rise of self-interest that accompanied the triumph of commercial society.[145] He was a professor of moral philosophy at Edinburgh from 1764 and his publications spanned the second half of the eighteenth century, from his *Reflections previous to the establishment of a militia* (1756) and his *Essay on the history of civil society* (1767) to his *Principles of moral and political science* (1792). While trying to preserve the virtues of civil and sociable life, he sought to develop a moral philosophy that could accommodate the reality of self-interest and commerce. His attempt to do so had a profound impact upon his theory of property and occupation, and also upon his understanding of the property and society of non-European peoples.

Ferguson outlined his theory of sociability in his *Essay on the history of civil society*. He observed that some authors had represented the state of nature as a time of tranquillity, others as a state of war, some as a state from which we have declined, others as the point from which we progressed.

143 Hutcheson, *A system of moral philosophy*, vol. 2, p. 308. See also Armitage, *Ideological origins of the British Empire*, p. 188.

144 Hutcheson, *A system of moral philosophy*, vol. 2, p. 309.

145 Hont, *Jealousy of trade*, pp. 296–8; J. G. A. Pocock, *Barbarism and religion, volume 2: narratives of civil government* (Cambridge, 1999), pp. 330–7; Lisa Hill, *The passionate society: the social, political and moral thought of Adam Ferguson* (New York, 2006).

Building on Hutcheson's scepticism regarding the idea of a state of nature, Ferguson argued that all these theories have 'led to many fruitless inquiries, and given rise to many wild suppositions'.[146] Simply what we do in positing these claims, he argued, is select the supposition that supports the larger theory of political society we wish to construct. These efforts in speculation were all the more fruitless because the evidence regarding our 'natural' state (and 'natural' was a word he treated with great scepticism) is readily at hand from experience and history: 'in framing our account of what man was in some imaginary state of nature, we overlook what he has always appeared within the reach of our own observation, and in the records of history'.[147]

Ferguson's common sense regarding the hypothetical fabrications of natural law theory and his call for the development of theories based upon observation could be seen as a logical step between the natural law theorists of the seventeenth century and the triumph of positivism over natural law in the nineteenth century, although he may rather be seen as paving the way for a synthetic understanding of law which drew upon natural law, positivism and historicism. Importantly, however, for him, observation was not scientific positivism. Observation was history and he argued that: 'the earliest and the latest accounts collected from every quarter of the earth, represent mankind as assembled in troops and companies; and the individual always joined by affection to party, while he is possibly opposed to another'.[148] For him, therefore, history showed that humans are indeed sociable and they have always been attached to some 'party' as he put it, using peculiarly eighteenth-century British political language. By virtue of being attached to a 'party', people are always in potential conflict with members of other parties. Thus, Ferguson, again partly drawing on Hutcheson, reconciled Hobbes and Pufendorf's hypotheses of the state of nature as a state of conflict with theories of natural sociability. Each person, he argued (in Chapter 2 of *Essay on the history of civil society* on self-preservation), is motivated by two dispositions: one that tends 'to his animal preservation' and 'another which lead[s] to society'.[149] This was the sociability of ancient natural law, not the unsociable sociability described by Pufendorf; that is; sociability driven by self-preservation. Love and friendship, Ferguson argued, are the most powerful passions. They excite us more than any other motives and under their influence

[146] Adam Ferguson, *Essay on the history of civil society*, 6th edn (London, 1793), p. 3.
[147] *Ibid.*; Pocock, *Barbarism and religion, volume 2*, p. 333. [148] Ferguson, *Essay*, p. 4.
[149] *Ibid.*, p. 17.

humans often act with disregard for their self-interest. Indeed, where danger is most present, our feelings of love and friendship are stronger.[150]

Certainly, for Ferguson, 'mankind' had always been in a civil state, the state of nature having never existed: 'Mankind are to be taken in groupes, as they have always subsisted.'[151] In the chapter concerning the 'Principles of union among mankind', he argued that: 'Mankind have always wandered or settled, agreed or quarrelled, in troops and companies.'[152] At the same time, he claimed, the state of nature is a state in which we always remain – we are always creatures of our nature: 'If we are asked therefore, Where the state of nature is to be found? we may answer, It is here; and it matters not whether we are understood to speak in the island of Great Britain, at the Cape of Good Hope, or the Straits of Magellan.'[153] He embraced the idea of human progress, but argued that all human societies find the means of living that are appropriate to their circumstances: 'The admiration which Cicero entertained for literature, eloquence, and civil accomplishments, was not more real than that of a Scythian for such a measure of similar endowments as his own apprehension could reach.'[154] At the same time, no society is static; all are constantly moving toward perfection while each individual moves towards the perfection 'of which he is capable'.

For early rights theorists, the right to property was closely associated with the right to property in oneself, to the right to self-preservation, and to self-fulfilment. This association remained in Locke's movement between the two senses of property as material object and property in life and liberty. But Ferguson reminds us also that for many thinkers the right to property was one step removed from corruption. He traced the right to property to self-preservation and the pursuit of interest that, he argued, when taken by itself, was a mere path to corruption.[155] The right to property, and interest, had to be tempered and framed by duty and affection for others.

It was in the course of making a sustained attack upon that moral philosophy which was based upon a theory of interest and self-preservation (here Hobbes and Pufendorf were clearly in the foreground) that Ferguson came to the question of property. He rejected the Epicureanism that he believed underlay the modern philosophical rise of interest. Grotius, Hobbes and Pufendorf had responded to the scepticism of Carneades, particularly the proposition that nothing can be held to be universally true,

150 *Ibid.*, p. 20. 151 *Ibid.*, p. 6. 152 *Ibid.*, p. 26. 153 *Ibid.*, pp. 12–13. 154 *Ibid.*, p. 14.
155 *Ibid.*, p. 20.

by arguing that self-interest was universal.[156] For Ferguson, their response was Epicurean. But for him, this Epicurean universality of self-interest was untenable and also undesirable on many grounds: 'The epicure, who consults his physician, how he may restore his relish for food, and, by creating an appetite, renew his enjoyment, might at least with an equal regard to himself, consult how he might strengthen his affection to a parent or a child, to his country or to mankind; and it is probable that an appetite of this sort would prove a source of enjoyment not less than the former.'[157] In *Principles of moral and political science*, Ferguson stated even more vehemently that: 'The Epicurean was a deserter from the cause of his fellow-creatures, and might justly be reckoned a traitor to the community of nature, of mankind, and even of his country, to which he owed his protection.'[158] Those who are merely interested, he argued, 'would enter, if not restrained by the laws of civil society, on a scene of violence or meanness, which would exhibit our species, by turns, under an aspect more terrible and odious, or more vile and contemptible, than that of any animal which inherits the earth'.[159] He conceded, however, that the dispositions of self-preservation give rise to 'man's apprehensions on the subject of property, and make him acquainted with that object of care which he calls his interest'.[160] Indeed, the term 'interest', he argued, while often elevated by philosophers to explain all human behaviour, even the love of a parent for a child, 'commonly implies little more than our property'.[161]

For Ferguson, as for many eighteenth-century Whigs, the dangers of interest and property were greatest in commercial society, that is, in what was supposedly the highest stage in the progress of history:

> Let those examples [of sociability and civility in Greece and Rome] be compared with the spirit which reigns in a commercial state, where men may be supposed to have experienced, in its full extent, the interest which individuals have in the preservation of their country. It is here indeed, if ever, that man is sometimes found a detached and a solitary being: he has found an object [namely, property] which sets him in competition with his fellow-creatures, and he deals with them as he does with his cattle and his soil, for the sake of the profits they bring.[162]

156 On Carneades, Epicureanism and the rise of self-interest, see Tuck, 'The "modern" theory of natural law', pp. 108–10; and Brooke, *Philosophic pride*.

157 Ferguson, *Essay*, p. 22.

158 Adam Ferguson, *Principles of moral and political science*, 2 vols. (Edinburgh, 1792), vol. 2, p. 5.

159 Ferguson, *Essay*, p. 20. 160 *Ibid.*, p. 19. 161 *Ibid.*, p. 24. 162 *Ibid.*, p. 31.

Here Ferguson was not only building on Whig concerns about property and corruption that dominated eighteenth-century British politics, he was also building on the Protestant natural law account in which property was closely associated with the Fall of Man or arose from human motivations which prevailed after the fall. Whereas Hutcheson challenged the association between property and sin, Ferguson followed the idea to a scepticism of property.

The implications of Ferguson's theory of sociability for the understanding of property were spelt out in his *Principles of moral and political science*, which as a 'retrospect of lectures' that he had delivered at the University of Edinburgh were not as remote from his earlier writings as the publication date might suggest. His dismissal of the state of nature and his claim that all human societies were civil societies could lead us to contrast him with Hobbes. He had ridiculed Hobbes' idea of equal rights in nature as equivalent to saying that all dead people are equally alive.[163] However, Ferguson did share with Hobbes the argument that property is a creation of civil society. It is evident, moreover, that he attempted to reconcile the various accounts of natural law in his understanding of property. He agreed with the classical theory of occupation insofar as he argued that occupation was the origin of property. The occupier, he claimed, has an 'exclusive right' to whatever he is the first to occupy.[164] But this right is a right of possession; 'it does not amount to property'.[165] Possession becomes property 'when mankind willingly enter into conventions'.[166] Here he seemed to agree with Hobbes and Pufendorf. But then in his chapter on labour, he argued in clear Lockean terms that a right to property is created by labour. He fused this Lockean argument with the claim that whatever is created by labour must be recognised by law.

Ferguson seemed close to re-admitting the state of nature in this discussion, but then hastily insisted that: 'Mankind . . . could not continue to exist without proceeding to occupy and possess the means of subsistence and accommodation.'[167] Civil society was therefore the natural condition: 'the supposition of a state, prior even to the origin of adventitious rights, must have been of so short a duration as to resemble an abstraction of the mind . . . rather than period of history'.[168] What Ferguson made possible, therefore, was that occupation could continue to be perceived as the origin

[163] Ferguson, *Principles*, p. 205.

[164] *Ibid.*, p. 203. The masculine pronoun is important because Ferguson understood property holders, at least historically, to be men, which partly explained the historical subjection of women, see: Pocock, *Barbarism and religion, vol.* 2, pp. 335–9.

[165] Ferguson, *Principles*, p. 204. [166] *Ibid.*, p. 205. [167] *Ibid.*, p. 206. [168] *Ibid.*

of property without any hypothetical apparatus of a state of nature, and in this respect he helped establish premises which enabled occupation to continue to hold a place in the theory of property developed by positivists in the nineteenth century. Clearly also implicit in Ferguson's claim that all human states are civil states was a refusal to accept that some non-European peoples could be described as living in a state of nature distinct from a civil state, and therefore without rights, and he developed this assumption into an explicit critique of colonisation.

It was Ferguson's ambivalence, not to say scepticism, regarding the pursuit of property that inspired his further scepticism regarding the claims of European colonising powers. He attacked the dispossession of non-European peoples, largely inspired by his scepticism regarding the supposed superiority of the commercial societies that sought to dispossess them. In addition, and like many Whig contemporaries, he argued that the continued expansion of civil society led to the weakening of its bonds and he was accordingly sceptical of empire-sized polities.[169] Along with his contemporaries, he adopted a stadial theory, but he did not see movement from one historical stage to another as unambiguous progress. On the move from the 'savage' to the 'barbarous' state, property becomes more common and attachment to interest therefore also becomes more common. Now begins the ambivalence that Ferguson perceives regarding all propertied societies: 'But we may apprehend, that the individual having now found a separate interest, the bands of society must become less firm, and domestic disorders more frequent.'[170] Here we find echoes of Titius' argument that civil society may be more rather than less prone to conflict than the state of nature or, what was for Ferguson primitive civil society. Ferguson had additional cause to be sceptical of European empires because of his claim that all societies should pursue the perfection that is appropriate to their circumstance. As we shall see in Chapter 8, this scepticism of colonisation was particularly strong in his understanding of the law of *res nullius* in *Principles of moral and political science*. Ironically, he was cast in the role of apologist for the British possessions in America when he participated in the Carlisle Commission sent by the Prime Minister, Lord North, in 1778 to negotiate reconciliation with the American revolutionaries. Similarly, in 1776, he had engaged in a polemical exchange with the

169 Gabriel Paquette, 'Colonies and empire in the political thought of Hegel and Marx', in Sankar Muthu (ed.), *Empire and modern political thought* (Cambridge, 2012), pp. 303–5.

170 Ferguson, *Essay*, pp. 163–4. See Hont, *Jealousy of trade*, pp. 296–8; and Garnsey, *Thinking about property*, pp. 139–40 (n. 13) on Ferguson as more sceptical about commercial society than Hume and Smith and also with a stadial theory of society less connected to forms of property.

Welsh radical Whig Richard Price, who supported the independence of the colonies, over the justice of the war in which Ferguson defended the actions of the British government.[171]

While Ferguson was concerned about the impact of empire-sized polities upon the bonds of civil society, his contemporary and friend David Hume (1711–76) was more troubled by imperial over-reach and, in the aftermath of the Seven Years' War, the national debt caused by maintaining empire.[172] In his final years, he rejoiced at the prospect of the colonies' independence in America and was applauded by Richard Price for doing so.[173] Hume split the Roman critique of empire. He agreed with the notion of imperial declension, whereby empires create the conditions for their own downfall, but he argued that wars, taxes, debt, faction and over-reach, rather than commerce, were the causes of that downfall. Amongst writers of the Scottish historical school, it was Hume, and Adam Smith, who went furthest in shedding the scepticism of commerce evident amongst contemporaries such as Ferguson. Hume argued that trade and commerce gave rise to happy subjects and powerful states, rather than being a cause of corruption and decline.

Hume and Smith sought to reconcile moral philosophy with the rapidly developing commercial society found in Britain and in Scotland in particular. Hume considered whether a society should be founded upon the virtues of classical republics, but argued that those values were in conflict with the passions of humankind that valued interest and were driven by 'a spirit of avarice and industry, art and luxury'.[174] A successful society would therefore need to contain those passions not with virtue, but with laws and a good constitution. Property was one of those things that would not only be regulated but also created by law. Occupation was central to his understanding of the law of property, but that understanding was once again established in a new context.[175]

Hume agreed with Hobbes that rights derive from civil society, but unlike Hobbes, he did not perceive civil society to be the creation of self-

[171] Ronald Hamowy, 'Scottish thought and the American Revolution: Adam Ferguson's response to Richard Price', in David Womersley (ed.), *Liberty and American experience in the eighteenth century* (Indianapolis, 2006).

[172] Armitage, *Ideological origins*, pp. 188–92. On Hume and debt, see J. G. A. Pocock, *Virtue, commerce, and history* (Cambridge, 1985), pp. 138–9.

[173] Pocock, *Virtue, commerce, and history*, pp. 137–40.

[174] David Hume, 'Of commerce', in Hume, *Essays Moral, Political, Literary*, edited and with a foreword, notes and glossary by Eugene F. Miller, with an appendix of variant readings from the 1889 edition by T. H. Green and T. H. Grose, revised edn (Indianapolis, 1987), p. 263.

[175] For Hume's understanding of property, see: Garnsey, *Thinking about property*, pp. 155–9; Buckle, *Natural law and the theory of property*, pp. 234–98; Hont, *Jealousy of trade*, pp. 416–19.

interested individuals seeking to leave a natural state. He argued that the state of nature was a myth (although he made fairly frequent recourse to a hypothetical state of nature) and was particularly sceptical of the Hobbesian notion of a war of all against all. For him, the bonds that hold society together are a mixture of self-interest and affection. He agreed, however, that one of the principal aims of society was the creation of property, for clearly property could not exist in a non-civil state where we have no control over 'external' goods.[176] His account of a non-civil condition was reminiscent of Pufendorf's vision of a 'savage and solitary' natural state.[177]

For Hume, the particular rules that govern society are artificial and historical rather than natural.[178] Amongst the artificial rules governing the creation of property, the most important is occupation. Having argued that all property is created by civil society, Hume could have, like Hobbes, simply declared that the rules governing property were to be determined by the contract forming each society. Instead, he sought to reconcile a theory of property as the product of civil society with the law of occupation. In doing so, he placed his theory of sovereignty within the existing reality of laws governing property.[179] In the civil law that applied in many European states, including Hume's own Scotland, the law of occupation was accepted as the origin of property rights and, as we shall see, it applied as positive law codified as the law of *res nullius*. According to Hume, the law of occupation prevailed because, in our haste to leave the misery of the pre-civil condition, we accepted the quickest remedy to the problem of property and that remedy was that each person continued to hold what she or he already had: thus, 'we annex the idea of property to the first possession, or to *occupation*'.[180] Hume maintained, therefore, the seventeenth-century natural law theorists' use of occupation as an explanation for the progress of history and the abandonment of the state of nature.

The question of why occupation dominated the theory of property nevertheless troubled Hume. He conceded its force, but found it difficult to account for that force. He therefore sought a second explanation for the importance of occupation grounded in the passions rather than reason: 'To which we may add, that the first possession always engages the attention most; and did we neglect it, there wou'd be no colour of reason for

176 David Hume, *A treatise of human nature* (Oxford, 1958), p. 505.
177 Garnsey, *Thinking about property*, p. 156.
178 This is not to dismiss the 'natural law interpretation of Hume', for which see Buckle, *Natural law and the theory of property*, p. 236.
179 Garnsey, *Thinking about property*, p. 159.
180 Hume, *A treatise of human nature*, p. 505

assigning property to any succeeding possession.'[181] Declaring that it was most 'expedient' that 'every one continue to enjoy what he is at present possess'd of', Hume added a footnote in which he admitted that no problems in philosophy were more difficult than those which have several plausible explanations and that this empirically observable inclination of people to agree over the origin of property was one such problem.[182] He pointed out that 'there are, no doubt, motives of public interest for most of the rules, which determine property'.[183] But he then concluded, beyond his argument concerning expedience, that 'these rules are principally fix'd by the imagination, or the more frivolous properties of our thought and conception' and it was up to the reader to choose whether expedience or imagination was the better explanation.[184] Here he suggested that we could not account for the resilience of occupation in the philosophy, as well as (as he saw it) the reality, of property rules, through a theory, such as Pufendorf's, that was based upon reason. Property was created through an historical process, guided by imagination and expedience rather than reason. This claim was consistent with his theory that our attachment to justice also comes about through 'the nature of our passions' rather than reason.[185]

Locke had in some ways overcome the metaphysical account of occupation by explaining that it is our property in our labour that underlies the property that arises from occupation. Hume dismissed Locke's argument on this score, declaring: 'Some philosophers account for the right of occupation, by saying, that every one has a property in his own labour; and when he joins that labour to any thing, it gives him the property of the whole.'[186] On the contrary, he argued, there are several ways in which we can occupy something, and so make it our property, and yet without joining our labour with it: 'as when we possess a meadow by grazing our cattle upon it'.[187] If occupation gives rise to possession, Hume continued, this leaves open the question of what constitutes possession. He concluded, like Kant after him, that occupation and possession arise from exercising control over a thing.[188] This understanding of occupation as control over a thing would be far better suited to the idea of the occupation of sovereignty, which was to gain force in the nineteenth century, than were the theories of occupation, such as Locke's, that focused upon labour and the exploitation of nature. Hume did not go as far as Vattel and

[181] *Ibid.* [182] *Ibid*, pp. 503–4. [183] *Ibid*, p. 504. [184] *Ibid.*
[185] Garnsey, *Thinking about property*, p. 157; Buckle, *Natural law and the theory of property*, p. 236.
[186] Hume, *A treatise of human nature*, p. 505. [187] *Ibid.* [188] *Ibid*, p. 506.

Rousseau in discussing the occupation of sovereignty, although his understanding of commerce would later become the focus of that idea.

For Adam Smith (1723–90), as for Hume, commerce was the driving force behind the 'growth of manners and the progress of society'.[189] Smith was a student of Francis Hutcheson at the University of Glasgow and he was a friend of Hume. Like Hume, he strove to reconcile commerce with civil life. He built on Hume's historical understanding of property and occupation,[190] and meshed that account of property with his progressive theory of history. His lecture on property and occupation begins with an outline of the four stages of the history of human societies. He agreed with ancient natural law writers, and with Roman and civil law, that the origin of property was in occupation. The first society was that of the hunters, he argued, and while they had virtually no property except what they kept around them, the game they killed and the apples they pulled from the tree, it was occupation that determined their ownership. In this account, property was prior to civil society as it was for Locke and Pufendorf. Despite his criticisms of Pufendorf, Smith adhered to Pufendorf's understanding of a natural state in which people's needs exceeded their ability to provide for themselves, thus forcing them into sociable and commercial relations with each other.[191]

The principle of occupation remained true for the second stage of society, the age of shepherds. In this age people began to build huts which ceased to be the property of the first occupant if they should temporarily abandon them, so Smith argued that: 'The introduction of the property of houses must have therefore been by the common consent of the severall members of some tribe or society.'[192] Here Smith was arguing that, as human societies progressed, property as occupation in a Lockean sense was abandoned for property based upon compact whereby, as for Pufendorf, occupation was an agreed-upon principle. Such compacts were a form of mutual dependence and so were fundamental to commerce. This need for property arising from agreement became even more pressing, he claimed, as society entered the agricultural and commercial stages of history. Initially, people developed property in land only in cities, while agricultural

[189] Pocock, *Virtue, commerce, and history*, p. 188.

[190] On Hume and Smith on property, see Jeffrey T. Young, 'The Humean foundations of Adam Smith's theory of property', *Journal of the history of economic thought*, 30(1) (2008), 49–64.

[191] Istvan Hont, 'The language of sociability and commerce: Samuel Pufendorf and the theoretical foundations of the "Four Stages" theory', in Hont, *Jealousy of trade*, pp. 159–84.

[192] Adam Smith, *Lectures on jurisprudence*, ed. R. L. Meek, D. D. Raphael and P. G. Stein, vol. V of the Glasgow Edition of the *Works and Correspondence of Adam Smith* (Indianapolis, 1982), p. 21.

land remained common, but it eventually became convenient for people to build their houses near their land and not change their pastures each year: 'In consequence of this design the principall persons of such a community, or state, if you please to denominate a set of men in this condition by that honourable appellation, would divide the common land into separate portions for each individuall or family.'[193] Clearly, therefore, for Smith, property precedes society and private property in land precedes or coincides with the development of the state. Property in a territory, he argued, that is, the property of a 'nation', was also prior to the development of private property: 'It would more easily be conceived that a large body such as a whole nation should have property in land. Accordingly we find that in many nations the different tribes have each their peculiar territory on which the others dare not encroach (as the Tartars and inhabitants of the coast of Guinea).'[194] Here again, Smith appeared more indebted to Hobbes' logic than he was to Locke. For Locke, private property in land preceded the development of a civil society, or 'nation', and its claims to territory, whereas for Hobbes and clearly for Smith, the reverse was true.

The crucial aspect of Smith's analysis was that he historicised occupation and used it to explain progress. He helped transform it into an historical and economic idea rather than a metaphysical entity. He did this in an attempt to explain the evolution of commercial society, with occupation describing the first stages of historical development. A theory of occupation that could explain all four of Smith's historical stages would emerge in analyses of the occupation of sovereignty in the context of discussions of international law and empire in the nineteenth century.

Sir William Blackstone and the common law

The different accounts of occupation and property provided by the Scottish historical school, the Lockeans and the compact theorists attracted the attention of eighteenth-century England's greatest common lawyer: namely, William Blackstone. Writing his monumental account of the common laws of England, Blackstone argued that while God had given the earth in common to all people, it had been made the particular property of individuals through occupation.[195] 'Occupancy' gave 'the original right to the permanent property in the *substance* of the earth

[193] *Ibid.*, p. 22. [194] *Ibid.*

[195] Sir William Blackstone, *The commentaries on the laws of England*, 4 vols. (London, 1765–9), vol. 2, pp. 2–4.

itself'. He then summarised what had been written on this subject over the course of the seventeenth and eighteenth centuries:

> There is indeed some difference among the writers on natural law, concerning the reason why occupancy should convey this right, and invest one with absolute property: Grotius and Pufendorf insisting that this right of occupancy is founded on a tacit and implied assent of all mankind, that the first occupant should become the owner; and Barbeyrac, Titius, Locke, and others, holding, that there is no such implied assent, neither is it necessary that there should be; for that the very act of occupancy, alone, being a degree of bodily labour, is, from a principle of natural justice, without any consent or compact, sufficient of itself to gain a title.

Blackstone drily concluded that this was 'A dispute that savours too much of nice and scholastic refinement', but quickly added: 'However, both sides agree in this, that occupancy is the thing by which the title was in fact originally gained.'[196]

Blackstone assumed the tone of a common law outsider to these disputes in the law of nature and nations, but the very fact that in his work on the common law he was citing continental authorities on natural and civil law, such as Barbeyrac, Titius, Pufendorf and Grotius, reveals the degree to which he was engaged in reconciling the law of nations with the common law. As we shall see in Chapter 8 on *res nullius*, such a move was unnecessary for continental and Scottish writers on occupation because the law of nations drew from the same Roman law codes as the civil law. In England, however, with a weaker civil law tradition (applying only in ecclesiastical courts and Admiralty Courts), there was little foundation for recognising any principles of the law of nations amongst the laws of the land. There was, in consequence, a sharper break between domestic law and domestic politics, on the one hand, and external law and foreign affairs, on the other. Blackstone himself observed in his introduction on the study of the law that whereas on the continent and the 'northern part of our own island', 'imperial' and 'municipal' laws were 'closely interwoven' in the civil law, in England a gentleman could be educated in the municipal law while remaining ignorant of the 'imperial' law.[197]

When earlier generations of English writers had discussed occupation, it had been as a principle of the law of nations and nature. As we have seen, when urging the colonisation of Virginia, John Donne turned to the law of nations, not the common law: 'In the law of Nature and Nations, a land never inhabited, by any, or utterly derelicted and immemorially

[196] *Ibid*, p. 8. [197] *Ibid*, vol. 1, pp. 4–5.

abandoned by the former Inhabitants, becomes theirs that will possesse it.'[198] Similarly, for Locke, occupation was a principle of natural law. Increasingly, however, in the eighteenth century, jurists and parliamentarians sought ways of breaking down the division between domestic and external law, as well as domestic and external politics.[199] In part they were concerned with weakening the hold of the Crown over foreign affairs while, at the same time, a series of momentous political events, including the Glorious Revolution, the Seven Years' War and the American Revolution, revealed the degree to which domestic and international politics were entwined. In 1709, an Act of Parliament for the first time formally adopted the law of nations into statute when it recognised the immunity of ambassadors. According to both Blackstone and the Lord Chief Justice, William Murray, 1st Earl of Mansfield, this act did not alter the law 'from what it was before', but rather simply recognised the principles of the law of nations which had always been part of the laws of the land.[200] By 1794, in parliamentary debate, Edmund Burke could refer to 'the Law of Nature and Nations (always a Part of the Law of England)'.[201]

This engagement with the law of nations explains Blackstone's extensive and seemingly anomalous discussions of the idea of occupation in his account of the common law. In his chapter on occupation in the second book of the *Commentaries*, he repeated the claim that occupation was the 'true ground and foundation of all property' and he acknowledged the Roman law on the matter: 'quod nullius est, id ratione naturali occupant conceditur'. He then conceded that this right of property had been 'confined by the laws of England within a very narrow compass' insofar as it concerned title to land, largely because in the common law the ownership of vacant land reverted to the Crown.[202] In a subsequent chapter, however, on 'Title to things personal, by occupancy', he identified a number of instances in which the principle of occupation gave a right of property, including goods belonging to an enemy, 'unclaimed moveables', the elements such as light, air and water, wild beasts, things which are improved and literary creations. A number of these instances, particularly the latter ones, involved a kind of first taking by labour or use, consistent

[198] John Donne, *A sermon preached to the honourable company of the Virginian plantation* (London, 1622), pp. 25–7.

[199] On the relations between common law and international law in eighteenth-century Britain, see Armitage, *Foundations of modern international thought*, pp. 135–53.

[200] *Ibid.*, pp. 143–4. [201] *Ibid.*, p. 152.

[202] Blackstone, *The commentaries on the laws of England*, vol. 2, p. 258.

with Blackstone's understanding of Locke's theory of labour as a theory of occupation.[203] Here he again acknowledged that occupation 'was the original and only primitive method of acquiring any property at all', but conceded that this right had 'since been restrained and abridged, by the positive laws of society'.[204]

When Blackstone turned, however, from domestic law to 'Countries subject to the laws of England', he recognised a foundational role for occupation in the creation of property and society, and here again he turned to the law of nature and nations. 'Our more distant plantations in America', he observed, are 'in some subject to the English laws', and in this case occupation was both English law and the law of nations: 'Plantations, or colonies in distant countries, are either such where the lands are claimed by right of occupancy only, by finding them desart and uncultivated, and peopling them from the mother-country; or where, when already cultivated, they have been either gained by conquest, or ceded to us by treaties. And both these rights are founded upon the law of nature, or at least upon that of nations.'[205] This is not to say that Blackstone was comfortable with empire. He expressed the concerns about landed empires that we have seen articulated by contemporaries such as Ferguson and Hume. He agreed that the 'cultivation of desert uninhabited countries ... kept strictly within the limits of the law of nature', but he did not see the conquest of the Americas in such terms: 'But how far the seising on countries already peopled, and driving out or massacring the innocent and defenceless natives, merely because they differed from their invaders in language, in religion, in customs, in government, or in colour; how far such a conduct was consonant to nature, to reason, or to christianity, deserved well to be considered by those, who have rendered their names immortal by thus civilizing mankind.'[206] These criticisms were not reserved for rival European imperial powers, nor was he deceived by the rhetorical redescription of conquests as the occupation of unpeopled lands as he referred to: 'Our American plantations ... being obtained in the last century either by right of conquest and driving out the natives (with what natural justice I shall not at present inquire) or by treaties.'[207]

Blackstone's engagement with the law of nations also meant that succeeding generations of common lawyers would cite his *Commentaries* as evidence that occupation, this alien principle of the law of nations, was also in fact part of the law of the land, while others condemned it as a

[203] *Ibid.*, p. 405. [204] *Ibid.*, p. 400. [205] *Ibid.*, vol. 1, pp. 104–5. [206] *Ibid.*, vol. 2, p. 7.
[207] *Ibid.*,vol. 1, p. 105.

principle foreign to common law.[208] His domestication of occupation may also be a reason for his disposition to understanding the law to concern property rather than sovereignty. The crucial tension over occupation in discussions of empire in the eighteenth century was about whether property or sovereignty was in question. The answer to that question had a bearing, in particular, upon the three-way struggle between the British Crown, settlers and Native Americans in North America. As we shall see, a Lockean understanding of the problems was prominent in that struggle, but the prominence of that view would be short-lived. The tensions between property and sovereignty in discussions of occupation continued through the nineteenth century, but sovereignty was central to the understanding of occupation from debates over the Oregon Territory in the first half of the century to the race for Africa in the 1870s and 1880s.

[208] See, for example, *Mabo and Others* v. *State of Queensland* (1992) 107 Australian Law Reports, 22–23 and 31.

CHAPTER 6

The Seven Years' War, land speculation and the American Revolution

The theories of occupation developed in Europe in the eighteenth century were to have a deep impact upon events in North America surrounding the Seven Years' War, the dispossession of Native Americans west of the Appalachians and the American Revolution. At the heart of these conflicts were two views of occupation I have explored in the writings of philosophers and lawyers. The first of these saw property arising from occupation alone, without, as Blackstone put it, 'the assent of mankind'. The second focused upon the theory of property created by compact and even sovereignty, as well as the occupation of sovereignty. In their conflicts with the Crown and Native Americans, the settlers of North America have often been described as having taken a Lockean point of view, but they were not consistently Lockean in their understanding of property.[1] They can be more accurately described as having taken the more general view that the proper object of occupation is property. They were divided on the question of whether occupation and labour gives rise to rights outside the state (the Lockean position) or whether occupation only created property through compacts. The Crown, on the other hand, consistently argued against the occupation of property that belonged to Native Americans and claimed instead that what it occupied in North America was sovereignty. The position of the Crown following the Seven Years' War and the Proclamation of 1763 was analogous with the critiques of landed empire being articulated by contemporaries such as Adam Ferguson and David Hume. The view of the settlers in this conflict would, of course, prevail, although their success may be seen as the high point in the understanding of occupation as an uncoveyanced origin of property. The positions would be reversed in the conflict over the Oregon Territory that followed closely

[1] Tully, *An approach to political philosophy*; Arneil, *John Locke and America*; and Tomlins, *Freedom bound*.

upon the Revolution. In the Oregon conflict, the triumphant revolutionaries would endorse the notion that occupation was a matter for a nation.

In the seventeenth century, the argument of occupation had been used by English colonisers to legitimise their claims to land inhabited by Native Americans. Locke's writings on property gave these arguments greater force by adding a labour theory of value as a justification of why the use of something gives us a right in it over someone else. In the eighteenth century, American colonists developed and strengthened these arguments against the Native Americans, but at the same time they acquired an additional polemical force that was previously absent. From the beginning of the eighteenth century, occupation was employed not only against native peoples but also in order to distinguish the political and legal claims of the colonisers from the claims of the imperial state. Here was the beginning of separate legal and political positions which, when pursued more vigorously later in the century, would develop into one of the main justifications of the Revolution. For the first time, occupation was being used *both* to question the rights of colonised people and to oppose the imperial state, and in this double-sided use it was able to prise open a new political space. As we have seen, throughout the seventeenth and eighteenth centuries, Europeans debated whether subjects possessed rights unilaterally or through conventions, and in this sense the arguments used by American colonists were not new. The change in context, however, made the arguments explosive. In Europe, the claims that rights exist outside the state were employed to resist sovereignty and could, in their most radical form, be used to justify revolution, as, for example, in the case of Locke's justification of the Glorious Revolution. But when exported to colonies, the potential of these arguments was not merely to overthrow a ruler but also to create a new state.

The dispossession of the Native Americans became a necessary, and not just an accidental, condition of political independence. In order to justify the Revolutionary struggle, it was necessary for the colonists to argue that they had created property outside the state and, from it, a new political space. These arguments were driven by, and drove, the appropriation of western territories from the 1750s and 1760s. The arguments rested on the premise that the settlers had rights existing outside state sovereignty arising from their occupation of land – land upon which Native Americans lived. That argument in turn left no space for the rights of Native Americans. America could not become independent of British rule and leave Native Americans in possession of their land. Just as the colonists argued that property rights may be created outside sovereignty, the Crown unsurprisingly responded to their arguments with a claim derived from seventeenth- and eighteenth-century theories of convention: namely, that all rights come from sovereignty.

Critiques and adaptions of Locke: the Mohegan case

In 1725, the Connecticut clergyman John Bulkley made one of the earliest uses of the claim to occupation as a means of questioning the rights of both the imperial state and colonised peoples. Bulkley wrote a powerful treatise on what he described as 'aboriginal rights', although his main purpose was to deny the existence of such rights. The background to his treatise was a dispute over land between the Mohegans and the colony of Connecticut that had endured for decades.[2] From 1703 through to 1705, the Crown and its appointed commissions ruled repeatedly in favour of the Mohegans in this dispute (partly because they sought to weaken and revoke the New England colonies' charters at this time), ordering the colony to respect the rights of the Mohegans over several tracts of land that had been reserved for them. The colony refused to act upon these rulings and although Mohegan power was diminished when Bulkley wrote in 1725, the legal and political dispute had not abated.

Bulkley's treatise appeared as a preface to a volume of poems by Roger Wolcott, the future Governor of the colony. Bulkley declared that his preface had been inspired by his reading of the poems. It is not difficult to see why. Wolcott provided a verse account of the founding of the American colonies, including John Winthrop's winning of the Connecticut Charter. In this account, the Native American nations willingly ceded their territory to the English, claiming to put no value in their lands. The Algonquin 'King Aramamet' met the English leader's request for land with the response: 'What you propose, (quoth he), is Just and Good,/And I shall e're Respect your Neighbourhood;/Land you may have, we Value not the Soil,/Accounting Tillage too severe a Toil.'[3]

Just as the Virginia Company had launched its legal arguments in the early seventeenth century in response to the claims of the Powhatans, Bulkley was provoked into writing about the colonisers' claim to land by the success of the Mohegans' land claims.[4] His treatise has been widely

[2] See Craig Yirush, *Settlers, liberty and empire: the roots of early American political theory* (Cambridge, 2011), pp. 113–57 for an account of the context to this dispute.

[3] Roger Wolcott, *Poetical meditations* (London, 1725), p. 30.

[4] On the English response to claims by the Powhatans, see Andrew Fitzmaurice, 'Powhatan legal claims', in Belmessous (ed.), *Native claims*.

interpreted as a piece of practical Lockean argument applied to the question of Indian rights.[5] It was not, however, straightforwardly Lockean at all. He attempted to prove his argument with the assumptions of the compact theorists of occupation, such as Pufendorf, as well as with Locke, even if the philosophical assumptions of those different positions were in conflict. Bulkley was philosophically eclectic and his eclecticism was driven by the need to persuade the broadest possible audience.

In the Mohegan case, the Crown acted in order to protect the Mohegans, described as dependent allies, from the incursions of its subjects, the colonists. From the perspective of the colonists, it was not they who found themselves seeking political distance from the Crown, but rather the Crown that had failed to extend its protection over the colony. It was therefore necessary for the colonists to establish their rights to property in some degree independent of the Crown. The argument of occupation was ideal for this purpose. Certainly, Bulkley was typically Whiggish in the strength of his arguments against '*Despotick Forms of Government*'.[6] He claimed that the law of nature 'knows no difference or Subordination among Men'. It is not, therefore, possible for any man to grant an 'ARBITRARY Power over himself or any other to Destroy his own or the Life and Property of another'. To this end, he cited 'that Great Man Mr. *Lock*, who well understood the true Origine of al Lawful Authority'.[7] Thus, from the outset, for Bulkley, as for Locke, the question of property was necessarily a question of liberty and of political autonomy. As such, for Bulkley, 'all lawful Authority' is taken from that '*Compact* or Contract that is the true Origine of it'.[8]

Bulkley then turned to the question of '*Native Right* as it is commonly called, or the *Right the Aborigines of this Country* (all or any of them) had or have to *Lands* in it'. He noted that this 'Interest' has 'not wanted many Advocates among us, especially of late years'.[9] These advocates, he claimed, had set 'native right' up 'as our only Valuable Title to whatever lands are in the Country'.[10] Bulkley moved on to a typically Lockean dismissal of native claims to land in which, unsurprisingly, Locke's theory of property

[5] See, for example, Tully, *An approach to political philosophy*, p. 166, who claims that Bulkley's essay is a 'refutation of the Mohegans' claim to political society and property in their traditional lands based in its entirety on Locke's *Two Treatises*' and p. 159, where he argues that in Bulkley's account, 'the only sure and indisputable title was thus occupation and cultivation'; according to Arneil, *John Locke and America*, p. 174, Bulkley was 'basing his claims on Locke's *Two Treatises*'; Dunn, 'The politics of John Locke', p. 72 also describes Bulkley as a Lockean; as does Yirush, *Settlers*, pp. 129 and 138.

[6] John Bulkley, 'Preface', in Wolcott, *Poetical meditations*, p. xii. [7] *Ibid.* [8] *Ibid.*, p. xiii.

[9] *Ibid.*, p. xv. [10] *Ibid.*, p. xvi.

features. He agreed that 'there is such a thing as *Native Right*', but quickly added that this right rests upon the degree to which the land is improved.[11] The argument used by 'many' that native title could 'extend to *all Lands* in the Country, whether Cultivated by them or not; is what I never could, nor yet can see any Sufficient reason for'.[12]

Bulkley did not merely rest on this argument of improvement. He knew that it would face a strong challenge from the claim, based on Hobbes' and Pufendorf's thought, that the Indians may have extensive territorial rights which derived from having established a social compact and a constitution under which it had been agreed to possess land in common. For this reason, it was necessary to determine:

> what *their Condition* was, whether they were a People in the *State of nature*, and so had only what the *Law of Nature* gave them, or had quitted that State, entred into *Communities*, and by *Compact* one with another, and Positive Constitutions of their own (Tacit or Express) had fixed the *Bounds* of each *Community* respectively and Settled or Determin'd the matter of Property in Land within themselves severally.[13]

If this was the case, Bulkley added, it must also be determined what the bounds of those communities were. Yet, on these questions – whether the native people were in a state of nature or not, and what, if they were in civil societies, the bounds of those societies were – such questions remained, he said, to be determined. He resolved to consider all the possibilities so that those who were attached to the 'Extravagant Principle' of extensive native property rights would admit that they had no evidence for the truth of their claims.[14]

He began by saying that he would take it for granted that a '*State of Nature*' did at one time prevail in the world.[15] He then pointed out that '*Josephus Acosta*' had shown that some peoples in the present day continued to live in a state of nature 'without any form of *Civil Polity* among them'.[16] What, then, was this state of nature? It was a state in which men lived without law, and without 'Authorities to decide Controversies between them', and therefore each man was judge and executioner.[17] Bulkley cited from Locke's *Two Treatises* at great length in order to describe this state.[18] It was the difference over the administration of justice that separates the natural state, where 'men have no other Law than that *of Nature*' from civil society, where the right to execute the law is given up by each individual 'into the hands of the *Community*'.[19]

[11] *Ibid.*, p. xvi. [12] *Ibid.*, p. xvii. [13] *Ibid.*, p. xviii. [14] *Ibid.*, p. xix. [15] *Ibid.*
[16] *Ibid.*, p. xxi. [17] *Ibid.* [18] *Ibid.*, pp. xxii–xxiii. [19] *Ibid.*, p. xxiii.

In order to establish what rights the Indians held in land at the time of colonisation, Bulkley argued that it was necessary to clarify whether or not they lived in the state of nature or a civil state. If they lived in a natural state, it may still be possible that they established property in land and so this matter must also be determined. Moreover, if they lived in a civil state, it would be necessary to establish whether the natives had created laws whereby they agreed to keep land in common (as would be permitted by Pufendorf). In order to resolve the issue, Bulkley therefore proceeded through a dialectical series of questions and answers about the rights of the Native Americans. Thus, his treatise takes a form remarkably similar to that employed by Vitoria, although with Bulkley we are never left in doubt about his conclusion.

Bulkley first turned to the 'supposition that the *Aborigines of this Country*, before and at the time of the *First Discovery & Planting of it* by the *English*, were ... not to be considered as having put on any Form of *Civil Policy*'. What then, he asks, would have been 'the *Extent of their Rights to Lands in it*' if the Native Americans had been in a state of nature when the English colonised the continent? He proposed the Lockean argument that it is possible to establish property in a state of nature, including property in land. This can be done, he argued, by a person 'adding to it something which is his own, for Instance his Labour'.[20] 'The law of nature', he continued in Lockean fashion, 'allows the Land a *Man Tills & Subdues* to be his *Peculiar Property*.'[21] He then cited Locke again in the passage in which Locke paraphrased the Roman law of occupation in order to explain the origin of property: this was Locke conceding that wild beasts killed by the Native American are his own, just as is the fish caught in the sea and the ambergris taken on the shore. Indeed, at this point in his argument, Bulkley repeatedly underlined the claim that the 'cause and original of all Property' was the removing of it from the common through labour: 'Labour only seems to be the thing that begins Property.' But, he added, what is not removed from the common in this way 'must remain still in the same *Common State* it was made in'.[22] Moreover, 'as to a Right of *Property in Land particularly*, it can't be of great Extent during mens continuance *in this State*'.[23] The limit on the extent of property arises because people living in this state, having simple needs, are satisfied with the 'Spontaneous productions of Nature' and so are not obliged to till the earth. Arriving at the matter in hand, he declared that this was

[20] *Ibid.*, p. xxiv. [21] *Ibid.*, p. xxv. [22] *Ibid.*, pp. xxvi–xxvii. [23] *Ibid.*, pp. xxvii–xxviii.

certainly the case 'with *the Aborigines of this Country* before the arrival of the *English* to it'.[24]

Bulkley turned to 'the *Moheags* [Mohegans] in particular' and their '*Pretended Claims*' about which there had been 'so much Noise and Strife'.[25] If, he continued, what has been said of the state of nature is true, then it is abundantly clear that the Native Americans fit that description, namely: 'That they were with their Bretheren in *Peru, Florida, Brasil &c* before mentioned from *Acosta*, to be rank't with those in a State of *Nature*.'[26] The repeated use of Acosta is important.[27] Acosta, as we have seen, had developed a progressive theory of anthropology while employing Vitoria's tests of civility, including the possession of technology and law. Bulkley followed suit: he observed that the natives have no 'Utensils, such as *Ploughs, Hoes, Axes*, &c' and they therefore cannot 'Till the Earth'.[28] But he devoted a far greater space to the absence of law. Who can say, he demanded, that the 'Essentials of a state of *Civil Policy* are to be found among them?' Who can find '*Established, Setled, common Law*'? And who amongst them can 'Judge with Authority to determine differences according to this Established Received Law?' Trying to find this rule of law amongst the native peoples was, he declared, 'like a search for the Living among the Dead'. When controversies arose among them, the Native Americans behaved as Hobbes or Locke would have individuals behave in a state of nature: 'every one looks on himself as Vested with the *Rights of the Law of Nature*, and accordingly is *Judge for himself* and *Executioner*!'[29] Anybody who is familiar with '*Our Natives* as we call them' could not disagree with this description. It looks 'very much like *the State of Nature* (if the forementioned Account of it be true)' and it is certainly 'Evidence of such *an Imperfect State of Civil Policy* as borders very near upon it'. The qualification 'if' here allows Bulkley to maintain the form, if not the substance, of dialectic. If all that has been said is true of the current state of the natives, then it can hardly be believed that prior to English colonisation, their ancestors were in a superior condition.[30]

Bulkley then made a sharp turn in the direction of his argument and from this moment he appears to have shaken most modern commentators from his path. He confronted face-on the problem that caused so much confusion and incoherence in the early seventeenth-century English

[24] *Ibid.*, p. xxviii. [25] *Ibid.* [26] *Ibid.*, p. xxix.
[27] *Ibid.*, p. xxxiii cites Acosta again. See Yirush, *Settlers*, p. 129, n. 81 on Locke as Bulkley's probable source for Acosta, although Acosta's text is paraphrased at times in ways that suggest a more detailed knowledge than the passages reproduced by Locke.
[28] Bulkley, 'Preface', p. xxviii. [29] *Ibid.*, p. xxx. [30] *Ibid.*, p. xxxi.

reaction to Native American people; that is, he addressed the fact that, despite all he had said so far, there was strong evidence for native political organisation. 'They Liv'd', he conceded, 'in *some sort of Society* or Neighbourhood and had their *Chiefs* or *Superiors* among them.' In addition to chiefs, they had 'Relations of *Parents & Children, Husband & Wife, Captain & Soldiers*'. But these inequalities, he insisted, were in no way inconsistent with the state of nature: 'The State of *Nature* is a *State of Subjection* to the Dictates and Direction of the *Law of Nature*' and that law is 'so far from Banishing *all Inequality* or *Subordination* among Men, that *it Ordains it in diverse Instances*'.[31] Here Bulkley ingeniously squared the circle by rejecting a Hobbesian understanding of the state of nature as a war of all against all. Yes, it is true that the state of nature, as Locke agreed, is a state in which each takes the law into her or his own hands. But it is nevertheless a sociable state, as both Locke and Titius insisted, and therefore the marks of sociability amongst the Native Americans could be taken as evidence of their being outside the civil state rather than evidence of civility itself. Thus, the apparent sociability which had troubled sixteenth- and seventeenth-century commentators on the Native Americans could be included in the case for their dispossession.

The possibility nevertheless remained that the Native Americans had been in a civil state at the time of colonisation. In this case, Bulkley asked, what standing would the native claims to land have if they had been in a civil state when the English arrived? However defective the natives' societies may be as civil societies, he conceded that it was necessary to examine the possibility that they had left the state of nature, that: 'they had *really quitted it*, entering into *Communities*, and by *Compact* and at least *Tacit Constitutions* of their own, settled the *matter of Property*, both with *their Neighbours* respectively, & *severally among themselves*'. In this case, he conceded, the customs previously presented as evidence that they lived in a state of nature would reveal rather a defect in the proper execution of law rather than 'Evidence that they had none'.[32] Here Bulkley, who has generally been regarded as presenting a straight-up-and-down Lockean case for the absence of native rights, had departed from the Lockean script almost entirely. Rather, he considers the case from the perspective of Grotius, Hobbes or Pufendorf – namely, the assumption here is that property is established by compacts and constitutions and, moreover, that it is, as Pufendorf argued, at the will of each compacting society to hold

[31] *Ibid.*, p. xxxii. [32] *Ibid.*, p. xxxv.

property in whichever form they see fit, even if they should choose to hold it in common.

Bulkley claims that even if Native Americans had created constitutions, this did not mean that they had necessarily resolved the question of property: 'allowing it *to be true* that they *had quitted the state of Nature*, and put on *some Form of civil Policy*, yet it does not from thence necessarily follow that Lands were brought under the Regulation *of Compact*, or any *Positive Constitutions of their own*, (tacit or express)'. Here he reveals that property rather than sovereignty carried the highest priority in his argument. He insisted on this point: 'Certain it is there is no necessary Connexion between those things, the *Former* does not infer the *Latter*; A People may put on some Form of *Policy* without any Determination of the matter of *Property in Lands* whether by *Compact* with Neighbouring *Polities* or any *Positive Constitutions* of their own.'[33] This argument – that by entering into society we do not necessarily create compacts on the distribution of property – was a radical departure from Locke. For Locke, the preservation of property (defined in the largest terms as property over life, goods and liberty) was the driving force in the creation of civil society. The possibility raised by Bulkley was that civil society can be created without individual property relations having been established. With this idea, he departed from Locke's thought and followed Pufendorf.

Bulkley expanded at length upon this un-Lockean idea that it was possible to live in civil society without determining particular property. He did so by imagining an island separated from the rest of the world in which the 'Inhabitants embodied together in *Civil Societies*, yet Living almost entirely on what *Nature prepared to their Hands*'. In such societies where there is great abundance and '*no danger of Want*', it was possible, he argued, to make compacts about laws regulating society without making compacts about property.[34] To support this theory, he cited scripture which showed that in: 'Early Times . . . men did not always immediately upon their *Entring into Society*, set out the Bounds of their *distinct Territories*, and by *Laws* within themselves respectively *Settle the matter of Property*.'[35] For Bulkley, this state, to be found in Abraham's time, was clearly also a possible description of America. Again, by raising this possibility, he had found a way of dealing with the uncomfortable fact that Native Americans had been understood to live in civil society and yet could not be admitted to be in possession of property. Clearly, for Bulkley, if the Native Americans did live in sovereign civil societies, he did not

[33] *Ibid.*, p. xxxvi. [34] *Ibid.*, p. xxxviii. [35] *Ibid.*, p. xxxix.

envisage the settlers coming under the umbrella of that native sovereignty. The sovereignty he envisaged was not territorial sovereignty. Rather, as he believed that it was a possibility that the Native Americans possessed sovereignty without territory, he assumed that native sovereignty was confined to the Native American peoples and their habitations, and did not touch upon the settlers who lived alongside them.

At this point Bulkley realised he had still not exhausted all the possible arguments as to why the Native Americans may possess property. He next turned to the concession that the Native Americans lived in civil society and had also created compacts determining the 'matter of *Property in Lands, each Society* with *its Neighbours*, and among *themselves severally*'.[36] This possibility was the most dangerous for his case. He acknowledged that there were signs that Indians understood the nature of property and value. But this understanding, he argued, was something they had imitated from the English after their arrival. He admitted that the Native Americans made many claims to territories, a fact in itself which revealed a conception of property. Indeed, it was this fact in the Mohegan case before the Privy Council that had motivated him to write. In this case, however, he argued that the various Native American claims were contradictory: 'One *Sachem* or *Community* often Claiming *what another did*.'[37] These overlapping claims cancelled each other out, proving that there were no settled territories and revealing the various interests to be opportunistic. Even if, he added, taking the case even further, property had been settled and these claims were not merely opportunistic, it remained impossible now to establish who had owned what, since 'all their Rights or Properties instantly became so Perplext and in the Dark that nothing can be Known or Determin'd upon them, and consequently *no good Title* possibly founded on them'. He pointed out that 'Gentlemen deputed by this Government' had set out to solve these problems by enquiring into 'the Claim of the *Moheags*', but that they found this claim to be in conflict with 'the *Pequots, Quinebaugs, Nahanticks*', who had 'given another Account'.[38]

Still not having reached the bottom of the matter, Bulkley asked that if it was true that the Native Americans had created civil society *and* established compacts to settle the question of property, what kind of compacts did they create?[39] Did they share the land equally? Moreover, 'in whom did they place the Lands'?[40] Were they, for example, placed in the hands of a single person: namely, the king? This latter conclusion was drawn by 'Our *Bigots*', who declared all the Indian lands to be vested in '*the*

36 *Ibid.*, p. xl. 37 *Ibid.*, p. xli. 38 *Ibid.*, pp. xliii–xliv. 39 *Ibid.*, p. xlv. 40 *Ibid.*, p. xlvi.

Crown'.[41] If that were the case, the settlement of Indian property would not differ greatly from that of England, where all lands that were not held privately belonged to the Crown and were not open to occupation. But if this were so, Bulkley continued, then it was necessary to determine whether the Indian constitutions allowed land held by the Crown to be alienable, as in England, or if it was inalienable.[42] If the land was alienable from the Crown, 'we must be resolved also *whether any Alienations* were made by *their Kings* to *their Subjects*'.[43] It is at this point that Bulkley terminated his dialectic and turned to the conclusion.

It is in the conclusion that we see that establishing a Lockean understanding of Indian property rights had only been one possibility raised by Bulkley. The aim was not to establish a Lockean case, but rather to show that it is possible to develop so many interpretations of the property rights of the Indians and to draw so many contradictory conclusions that the only sure conclusion was that nothing certainly could be said and so there was no sound basis for native title. The question invoked 'so many inextricable Difficulties and renders them all so *Uncertain* Perplex't and in the Dark that *nothing Certain* can be Known or Determined upon them'.[44] Locke served merely to establish one of a number of possibilities in considering whether the Indians possessed property. Bulkley realised that if he based his argument entirely on Locke, an opponent using Pufendorf or another philosopher might easily come and dismiss his claims entirely. Indeed, Bulkley treated the argument that property derives from compact with great seriousness and never dismissed that possibility. One might say that for Locke, property would also be derived from compact once civil society was established. What mattered for Bulkley, however, was the origin of property and whether that was outside contract, as Locke argued, or a product only of compacts. Bulkley certainly did at one point claim that labour in the state of nature is 'the beginning of Property', but in the second half of his essay, he was less clear on this question.[45] When considering the possibility that property could be settled by agreement, he spoke of land being 'brought under the Regulation of *Compact*', implying a Lockean perspective that once property is created in nature, it can be regulated by law. However, later in the essay he raised the possibility, as we have seen, that civil society could precede property and in this case he quite clearly believed that it was society that was the origin of property.[46] What

[41] *Ibid.*, p. xlvii. [42] *Ibid.*, p. xlviii. [43] *Ibid.*, p. l. [44] *Ibid.* [45] *Ibid.*, p. xxvi.

[46] As he put it at one point, it could be through the acts that created '*a State of Society Civil*' that the 'Aborigines' had 'Determined and Regulated *the matter of Property*': *ibid.*, p. xliii.

counted for him was winning the argument that settlers held property in the disputed lands, not establishing the veracity of Locke's theory of property.

Whether or not he won the argument, Bulkley succeeded in separating his position from those taken by sixteenth- and seventeenth-century writers on the rights of colonised peoples. Those previous generations had used theories of property to diminish the rights of colonised peoples and also to critique the power of colonial government (when they defended the rights of colonised peoples). But they had never both diminished the rights of colonised peoples and critiqued the metropolitan power in the same act. Bulkley nevertheless maintained that the settlers' rights to property were derived from the Crown and colonial charters, not from occupation (consistent with his use of occupation as only one possible claim to property).[47] In this respect, his position was similar to that of John Norris, the Carolina assemblyman who wrote to justify the rebellion against the authority of the Lords Proprietor of Carolina. The 1669 Constitution of Carolina, in which John Locke had a hand, had created a system of absentee landlords and high rents that was overthrown by the Carolina Assembly in 1719. The Assembly appealed for direct Crown intervention in the colony. James Tully has argued that Norris cleverly used John Locke's *Two treatises of government* in order to justify the rebellion against the constitution which Locke himself helped write.[48] Certainly Norris' arguments declaring that consent is the foundation of government resemble Locke's. It is striking, however, that Norris did not use Locke's understanding of property – or the theory of occupation more generally – to claim that Carolina colonists were justified in their failure to pay rents. He did not systematically argue that they had tilled the land and taken it for themselves. At one point, Norris did claim that the colonists' lands were 'by hard Labour cleared from the Woods',[49] but this claim was not the seed for a larger argument about the foundation of property. Rather, for Norris, the colonists' title rested upon their purchase of the land from the Lords Proprietors who sold by virtue of their grant from the Crown. The most telling aspect of Norris' treatise for later claims to the autonomy of the American colonies is that the immediate cause of the dissent amongst the colonists was the heavy burden of taxation imposed due to the cost to the Lords Proprietors of defending the colony against the

[47] On this point, compare Tully, *An approach to political philosophy*, p. 159, who argues that Bulkley perceived 'occupation and cultivation' as the 'indisputable title' to land.

[48] *Ibid.* [49] John Norris, *The liberty and property of British subjects asserted* (London, 1726), p. 30.

Native Americans (with whom peace had only recently been concluded), and against the Spanish and the French.

The Seven Years' War

To find the claim to title through occupation used systematically not only to justify colonies against the claims of the Indians but also against the demands of the Crown, it is necessary to turn to the Seven Years' War. In the context of the Seven Years' War, or the French and Indian War, we can see that the argument of occupation began to be used to make a claim to property and to a political space that was at least semi-autonomous from the Crown and Crown charters. The question of the occupation of frontier lands was almost as important as the issues of taxation and representation, and was closely linked to both these issues amongst the causes of the American Revolution. Following the end of the Seven Years' War, the English government sought to pacify the Native American nations who had fought with the French by assuring them that English colonists would not settle further westward of a boundary defined by the waters that flowed into the Atlantic from the Appalachian Mountains. This boundary was set down in the Proclamation of 1763. Victory in the Seven Years' War brought a vastly greater territory over which the Crown claimed sovereignty, a correspondingly greater military burden and, with that, a greater financial burden.[50] The Seven Years' War had already been a drain on the public expenses. In making the Proclamation, the English government sought to limit future costs in garrisoning its American colonies and the territories it had acquired from France. It was also obliged to protect the lucrative fur trade it had inherited. Peace with the Native Americans was cheaper and more prosperous than war. At the same time, the British government began to levy new taxes on the colonies in order to pay for the forts on the frontier: these forts were maintained largely with the intention to impose the post-war peace. The colonists were paying the government to protect the Indians from the colonies as much as they were paying for the protection of the colonies from the Indians. These were the taxes against which the colonies rebelled.

[50] Jack Sosin, *Whitehall and the wilderness: the Middle West in British colonial policy, 1760–1775* (Oklahoma, 1961), p. 35. See also Williams, *The American Indian in Western legal thought*, p. 241 on the cost to the British of maintaining troops in America after the war and policing the new territories (i.e. 500,000 per year).

In order to justify the Proclamation, the Crown invoked the right of sovereignty. The colonists, however, were outraged by what they saw as limits on their right to expand and to occupy land in the manner they had employed since first establishing their colonies. The ensuing dispute between the colonies and the Crown would only be resolved by the Revolution (and it continued in another form after that date). At the heart of this dispute was a conflict between two understandings of occupation which were outlined in the previous chapters – namely, between the notion that occupation of land creates rights of property in nature and the growing concern that the proper object of occupation should be sovereignty rather than property when it was evident that the occupation of property would result in the dispossession of a subject people. Indeed, the Crown not only opposed the occupation of property west of the Appalachians, its officers were also frequently obliged to concede that it did not even exercise sovereignty in those territories.

It is often remarked that sovereignty was the central political problem in the unfolding of the American Revolution. Bernard Bailyn observes that: 'In the last analysis it was over this issue that the Revolution was fought.'[51] According to this interpretation, the crucial issue at stake in the Revolution was the sovereignty of the Crown and the colonists' attempts to limit this sovereignty with Lockean arguments about the limits of the sovereign over a subject's property. Bailyn is sceptical about the revolutionaries' depth of understanding of Locke. As I will seek to show, however, the degree to which critiques of the Crown were Lockean at all is questionable through the period from the Seven Years' War to the Revolution. Broader arguments concerning occupation did have an important role to play in these critiques, but not always in expected ways.

Moreover, relations between the Crown, Native Americans and settlers were not characterised solely by a contest between the Crown's claim to sovereignty, in protection of the Native Americans, and the settlers' claimed rights to occupation in an attempt to limit Crown sovereignty.[52]

[51] Bernard Bailyn, *The ideological origins of the American Revolution*, enlarged edn (Cambridge, MA, 1992), p. 198.

[52] The Proclamation has frequently been understood in these terms. See Williams, *The American Indian in Western legal thought*, p. 238 on the Crown having sovereignty over the territory west of the colonies: 'The proclamation was the legal installation of the Crown's political control over this newly acquired territory earned by the outcome of its war'; and p. 245: 'The proclamation and the imperial plan of 1764 declared in essence that the absolute power of the king's prerogative extended to enclosing the virgin forests of the New World from the colonists' claims and ambitions.' Compare Tully, *An approach to political philosophy*, pp. 172–4, who argues the Proclamation acknowledged Native American sovereignty.

There were other players in the struggle over American sovereignty: namely, the Native Americans. The presence of this third perspective modulated the arguments about sovereignty employed by the other participants. It is not possible to see the conflict in terms of a simple claim and counter-claim regarding the limits of sovereignty and the rights of occupation. The fact was that the Crown did not possess sovereignty in the contested territories, and each of the major players – the settlers, the different and sometimes conflicting nations of Native Americans, the Crown, and the French, while they remained – knew this and acted accordingly. The settlers beyond the Appalachians used the argument of occupation because they knew that they were *outside* the reach of Crown sovereignty. It was precisely in this context that the Lockean argument of rights to property arising from occupation was most appropriate. If the settlers had believed themselves to be making claims within the limits of Crown sovereignty, they would have needed a contract version of the occupation argument – namely, that property came from occupation because it was recognised to do so by the sovereign. However, that was not the case. But rights of occupation arising from nature and outside the reach of sovereignty were recognised in some versions of the law of nations upon which Locke had drawn to develop his own theory. Indeed, the settlers appealed to that broader discourse and only to Locke within that context. The Crown attempted to control the settlers, but not because they thought of the Native Americans as their subjects. Rather, they sought to control them because they did not want the settlers to provoke a war with neighbouring sovereign nations – namely, the Native Americans. The native Amercan nations did not accept the idea that the British Crown was sovereign over them.

Thus, the context for the Proclamation of 1763, and the political debate and political thought contained therein, was not simply a contest between Crown sovereignty and Lockean occupation employed by the settlers, but a far more complex negotiation between the sovereignty of the Native American nations (that those nations claimed and enforced), the sovereignty of the Crown and the Lockean arguments employed by the settlers to claim property rights in nature separate from the sovereignty of both Indians and the Crown.

In the Proclamation of 1763, the Crown's claim to sovereignty over North America was implied to exist as far west as the Pacific coast. This claim was also implicit in the charters of some of the colonies (for example, 'landed' colonies such as Virginia). These were, however, partly rhetorical claims and were understood as such. There were numerous occasions on which British ministers and officers were forced to recognise that the Crown did not exercise sovereignty west of the Appalachians. In 1774, the Secretary of State, the Earl of Dartmouth, wrote to the Governor of Virginia, Lord Dunmore, criticising settlements and saying that Dunmore must have been aware that 'they would be out of the control and protection of the imperial government'.[53] Dartmouth was effectively declaring that the settlers and Native Americans were beyond the reach of the Crown's sovereignty.

Ministers and officers were frequently also obliged to recognise the sovereignty of the Native Americans. Indeed, the Proclamation of 1763 should be understood as a response by the Crown to its absence of sovereignty in these territories. Prior to the Proclamation, in 1761, the new Secretary of State, the Earl of Egremont, made rulings for the Southern colonies, namely Virginia, Maryland and Pennsylvania, 'prohibiting settlement on any soil they [the Indians] claimed'.[54] According to Richard Peters, the Secretary of Pennsylvania, writing to the Superintendant of Indian Affairs, Sir William Johnson, in 1761, the conflict with the Indians was 'a national and not a provincial Cause'; that is, 'the controversy was not between Subject and Subject, but between Indians and Englishmen'.[55] By national and not provincial, Peters meant that the issues were between nations. The relations in question were not between subjects of the same Crown, but between peoples of different nations.[56] Jeffrey Amherst, the Commander in Chief of the British forces in the French and Indian War, agreed with Johnson's judgement in this matter.[57] These attitudes endured through to the Revolution. While trying to enforce the 1763 Proclamation in 1770, General Thomas Gage, who took over as Commander in Chief from Amherst after the war, wrote privately to the Secretary of War, William Barrington, that: 'I wish most sincerely that there was neither Settler nor Soldier in any part of the Indian country.' Agreeing, Barrington responded that the sentiments of the other ministers were 'no different'.[58]

The main concern of the ministers and officers was the cost of becoming engaged in further conflict. They recognised that they were not territorially competent beyond the Appalachians and they constantly cautioned against any acts that would violate Indian territory. The President of the Board of

[53] Sosin, *Whitehall and the wilderness*, p. 234 n. 51. [54] *Ibid.*, pp. 40–3. [55] *Ibid.*, p. 50.
[56] Yirush, *Settlers*, p. 120 notes that the Crown had similarly seen the Mohegans as allies rather than subjects.
[57] Sosin, *Whitehall and the wilderness*, p. 50. [58] *Ibid.*, p. 221.

Trade, the Earl of Halifax, wrote to Virginian Governor Francis Farquier that his failure to respect treaties made with the Indians would involve 'us in a very bloody and dangerous' war. Peace, he argued, could be guaranteed 'solely upon Our having engaged . . . not to Settle upon their hunting grounds'. The 'open Violation of our engagements' was inadmissible.[59] This was the language of the law of nations, not of the internal politics imagined in the Proclamation. In 1759 and 1760, Governor Farquier was again being pressed by his officers in the Seven Years' War, particularly George Washington and George Mercer, to grant land between the mountains and the Ohio to the Virginian veterans of the war. The Board of Trade repeated its warnings to Farquier that any action that 'whatever may in any degree, have a tendency' to alarm the Indians 'cannot fail of being attended with fatal Consequences'.[60] If the Indians regarded settlements as a violation of their rights, 'then it would be imprudent in the highest degree' to allow such settlements.

The Crown's policy of controlling westward expansion applied as much to the northern colonies as to Virginia. Initially the Commissioners of Trade approved the expansion of the colonists in the north 'provided such Settlements do not interfere with the Claims of our Indian Allies' and the 'most solemn Treaties' with Indians. But when the Mohawks protested at the rush of New Yorkers onto their lands, the government immediately reversed its policy. The commissioners now condemned the New Yorkers' expansion as 'a measure of the most dangerous tendency' and on 3 December 1761, the Privy Council instructed all American governors under the King's 'immediate Government and where the property of the Soil is in his Majesty' from allowing settlement on lands where the Indians are 'bordering'.[61] The clear implication of this argument was that the Crown also acknowledged that its sovereignty applied where it had 'property of the Soil' and that the Indians were outside that jurisdiction. They were recognised as 'bordering' nations. Contrary to the language of the Proclamation two years later, it was understood that the Crown had no property of the soil outside its colonies.

What power the Crown was able to exercise beyond the Appalachians was largely derived from its possession of forts, many of which it inherited from the French. Far from extending this power in the years after the Proclamation, the Crown progressively closed these forts, abandoning what little territorial competence it had over the Native Americans and

[59] *Ibid.*, p. 45. [60] *Ibid.*, p. 46. [61] *Ibid.*, p. 48.

over the settlers who were increasingly moving into these regions without licence to do so. In the summer of 1771, Gage decided he had to abandon Fort Chartres, which was rapidly decaying.[62] On 1 December 1771, the Cabinet agreed with Gage's decision and also agreed that he could evacuate Fort Pitt. Gage declared that this decision to abandon 'two such expensive and troublesome Forts' gave him 'great pleasure'. He thus had acted on his declaration a year earlier that he would like to see no soldier west of the Appalachians. The Secretary of State for the colonies, the Earl of Hillsborough, agreed with Gage 'that the cost of the establishment in the Illinois country exceeded any possible benefit'.[63] The policy of withdrawing from this territory was pursued to such an extraordinary degree that Gage abandoned seven of the nine forts that the British held at the end of the Seven Years' War. Richard White observes that the 'declining authority of British chiefs was everywhere apparent' in 1771 in the Pays d'En Haut.[64] We might conclude that in the years between the Proclamation and the Revolution, British sovereignty in North America receded to the east rather than expanding to the west and, as such, it was complementing an increasingly sceptical mood towards landed empire within Britain.

The consequence of this shrinking British sovereignty was the creation of what Richard White has described as a British middle ground, which replaced the middle ground that had previously been maintained between the French and the Algonquian nations in the Pays d'En Haut. The middle ground in which the French had participated had been a restless and dangerous world, but its successor was even more so. While the British imitated the French middle ground, the British system 'was a Frankenstein monster . . . it was only a soulless imitation of the old alliance; the missing soul was mediation', which had been provided by the day-to-day shared lives of the French and the Algonquians in villages.[65] Without a sufficient budget to provide the gifts needed to maintain alliances, Johnson pursued a low-cost policy of pitting the Indian nations against each other instead of reconciling them as the French had tried to do.[66] The British settlers did not share their day-to-day lives with the Indians in the same way as the French. The British middle ground was diplomatic, not quotidian. What emerged was a more independent series of Indian nations and the incursion of British traders and settlers into Indian lands at the same time as the

[62] *Ibid.*, pp. 221–2. [63] *Ibid.*, p. 221.
[64] Richard White, *The middle ground: Indians, empires and republics in the Great Lakes region, 1650–1815* (Cambridge, 1991), p. 322.
[65] *Ibid.*, pp. 313–14. [66] *Ibid.*, p. 315.

British Crown withdrew from the territories and effectively abdicated what little claim to authority it had.

It was in this context that British settlers first used the argument of occupation to make claims against both the Indians and the Crown. But just as the British diplomatic middle ground was a Frankenstein monster, so was the middle ground of property rights that was now created by the settlers. Rather than being based upon negotiation and accommodation, it left no room for the Indians; indeed, it was predicated upon their dispossession and dehumanisation. Even an opponent of slavery such as James Otis was able to describe the North American colonies as 'well settled, not as the common people of *England* foolishly imagine, with a compound mongrel mixture of *English*, *Indian* and *Negro*, but with freeborn *British white* subjects'.[67]

The Proclamation of 1763 was followed by the Sugar Act in 1764 and the Stamp Act of 1765, which imposed taxes that were intended to pay for the jurisdiction of Britain's newly gained territories from the Seven Years' War and for maintaining the peace on the frontier between the colonies and the Indian nations. These attempts to regulate and finance the colonies provoked an outpouring of pamphlets condemning the Crown's measures and asserting the rights of the colonies to regulate their own affairs. One of the more prominent of these pamphlets was Richard Bland's *An inquiry into the rights of British colonies*, which was published in 1766. As a member of Virginia's House of Burgesses, Bland had already fought against the Crown prerogative to impose taxes and laws since the 1650s.[68] Now he fought against the impositions of Parliament.[69] He based his assertion of the colonists' rights upon their occupation of territory. Indicating the basis of his ideas in a theory of natural law that posited the existence of rights outside sovereignty, he observed that as 'we can receive no Light from the Laws of the Kingdom . . . to direct us in our Inquiry, we must have Recourse to the Law of Nature, and those Rights of Mankind which flow from it'.[70]

For Bland, it was the law of nature, and specifically the rights that arise from occupation of territory, which permitted men to leave the sovereignty

[67] James Otis, *The rights of the British colonies asserted and proved* (Boston, 1764), pp. 36–7.

[68] For Bland, see Yirush, *Settlers*, pp. 158–79; and Bernard Bailyn (ed.), *Pamphlets of the American Revolution 1750–1776*, 2 vols. (Cambridge, MA, 1965), vol. 1, pp. 293–9.

[69] See Yirush, *Settlers*, p. 183 on the shift in the control of the Empire between the early years of the eighteenth century to the years after the Seven Years' War. This shift moved authority away from royal bureaucracy, and the use of prerogative, to the ministry and Parliament.

[70] Richard Bland, *An inquiry into the rights of British colonies* (Williamsburg, 1766), reprinted in Merrill Jensen (ed.), *Tracts of the American Revolution 1763–1776* (Indianapolis, 1967), p. 116.

of one country when moving to establish colonies in another. He agreed that each member of society must 'submit to the Laws' of that society to which they belong and by which they 'agree to be governed', but he endorsed the Lockean claim that 'they retain so much of their natural Freedom as to have a Right to retire from the Society, to renounce the Benefits of it, to enter into another Society, and to settle in another Country'. 'This natural right', he added, 'remains with every Man, and he cannot justly be deprived of it by any civil Authority.'[71] He was rejecting the Hobbesian notion that rights are derived almost entirely from civil society. He then took this argument to its radical conclusion – namely, by implying that colonists created a sovereign state which was independent from the state they quitted:

> when Subjects are deprived of their civil Rights, or are dissatisfied with the Place they hold in the Community, they have a natural Right to quit the Society of which they are Members, and to retire into another Country. Now when Men exercise this Right, and withdraw themselves from their Country, they recover their natural Freedom and Independence: The Jurisdiction and Sovereignty of the State they have quitted ceases; and if they unite, and by common Consent take Possession of a new Country, and form themselves into a political Society, they become a sovereign State, independent of the State from which they separated.

Bland then passed from this abstract claim to the concrete situation of the North American colonies. Here the claim regarding occupation became, in the first instance, that the continent was virtually unoccupied (by which he meant uncultivated). 'The colonies of North America', he declared, were 'founded by Englishmen; who, becoming private Adventurers, established themselves, without any Expense to the Nation, in this uncultivated and almost uninhabited Country'.[72]

Much has been made of the importance of Vattel to the eighteenth-century American colonists.[73] Indeed, Vattel's *The law of nations* was more popular in its English editions than in the original. There is no doubt that Vattel's description of 'erratic nations' who fail to cultivate the earth was of great use in the settlers' claims to title, particularly when Vattel described the 'savage tribes of North America' in such terms.[74] However, as we saw in the previous chapter, there is an important point on which Locke and Vattel differed, and it is underlined in Bland's Lockean appeal to the right

[71] Bland, *An inquiry into the rights of British colonies*, p. 113. [72] *Ibid.*, p. 116.
[73] See, for example, Tully, *An approach to political philosophy*, pp. 168–9.
[74] Tuck, *Rights of war and peace*, p. 195.

of 'private Adventurers' to set up new civil societies. For Vattel, individuals and private associations have no power to create civil societies of their own volition; for them to do so would be preposterous against the claims of nation states to the same territories. Bland cited Vattel alongside Locke on the freedom of individuals in the state of nature. But Bland's emphasis upon the rights of private adventurers did not sit comfortably with Vattel's views on this issue and it would appear that to some degree he read Vattel through Locke. As we shall see, where Vattel would be useful for the American colonists was in making claims to territory once the Revolution was successful; that is, once sovereignty was established.

At the same time that it was important for Bland's argument to point out that the Native Americans had not cultivated the land, he was also obliged to claim that they had not been conquered, contrary to the rhetoric of the Proclamation of 1763 (as indeed Crown officials well recognised in their private statements), because if they had been conquered, title to the land would clearly lie with the Crown: 'America was not a Part of the Kingdom of England; it was possessed by a Savage People, scattered through the Country, who were not subject to the English Dominion, nor owed Obedience to its Laws. This independent Country was settled by Englishmen at their own Expense.'[75] Settlement and occupation thus became the basis for the new civil society, for its sovereignty and the rights of its subjects.

Bland stopped short of advocating outright rebellion and for this reason he has been seen as a federalist.[76] He argued that while colonists had an opportunity to break from the states from which they emigrated, the Virginian colonists had entered into a compact with the Crown and that compact ought to be respected. In Lockean fashion, he stated that the colonists could resist tyranny, but he did not argue that this point had been reached. At the time Bland was writing, however, land speculators were pushing westward into areas beyond the Appalachians and beyond the sovereignty of the Crown. For the new colonies in these regions, Bland's thoughts on the right of peoples leaving sovereignty to establish new societies had radical implications. In that broader context, Bland's ideas could be used to revolutionary ends and precisely such ideas would be.

If the colonists' rights were to be derived directly from the occupation of land, Grotius, Hobbes and Pufendorf were likely to be political thinkers who would prove hostile to their interests. The most 'widely known' and 'commented upon' tract published in the context of the Sugar and Stamp

[75] Bland, *An inquiry into the rights of British colonies*, p. 118. [76] Yirush, *Settlers*, p. 158.

Acts was James Otis' *The rights of the British colonies asserted and proved* (1764).[77] Otis was a politically ambitious Boston lawyer who held, at one time, the position of Advocate General to the Vice-Admiralty Court.[78] As Advocate General, he was obliged to be learned not in common law, but in Roman law, natural law and the law of nations, and that learning showed in his writings. In *The rights of the British colonies*, he began his discussion 'Of the natural rights of colonists' with the following dismissal of seventeenth-century compact theory: 'Those who expect to find any thing very satisfactory on this subject in particular, or with regard to the law of nature in general, in the writings of such authors as *Grotius* and *Pufendorf*, will find themselves much mistaken.'[79] With their claim that rights are derived from agreement, he objected that these writers 'establish the matter of right on the matter of *fact*'. Their study of the law of nature was therefore, as Rousseau had declared, nothing but a 'history of ancient abuses'. Otis resolved that his 'sentiments on this subject have therefore been chiefly drawn from the purer foundations of one or two of our *English* writers, particularly from Mr. *Locke*'.[80] In order to maintain that property could exist outside civil society, he argued, like Adam Ferguson writing three years later, that humans are always in all states sociable – 'men came into the world and into society at the same instant' – but he shared Hutcheson's scepticism of the idea of the state of nature as an historical state.[81] For him, as for Bland, the rights of the British colonists rested upon their separation from the mother country and their 'toils of hard labour' in tending their plantations and defending them in 'war with the Savages'.[82]

But Otis was no revolutionary. He was merely claiming the rights and liberties that he believed should be bestowed on all British subjects. While he portrayed the discomfort that seventeenth-century compact theory could cause for American settlers, his understanding of the autonomy that arose from occupation was less extensive than Bland's. Only for one moment did he anticipate the truly extensive rights that could arise from occupation when he worried that all the efforts to reform the colonial government could fail and the colonists would find themselves 'driven and persecuted into a more western wilderness' and so, presumably, at last free from metropolitan control.[83] It was indeed from the 'western wilderness' that the most radical ideas regarding occupation would be generated and these were to find voice with the leaders of the Revolution.

[77] Bailyn, *Pamphlets*, p. 409. [78] *Ibid.*, pp. 410–11.
[79] Otis, *The rights of the British colonies*, p. 38. [80] *Ibid.* [81] *Ibid.*, pp. 42–3. [82] *Ibid.*, p. 51.
[83] *Ibid.*, p. 62.

The Lockean nature of some attacks on the Crown did not go unnoticed. In the same year that Bland wrote, the anonymous tract *Thoughts on the origin and nature of government* was written in London presenting a largely Hobbesian argument that '*Sovereignty* admits of no degrees, it is always *supreme*'.[84] However, the author agreed with critiques of Hobbes' account of the state of nature, arguing that 'some writers have been so senseless' as to describe a state of nature as 'a state of war and confusion'.[85] At the same time, the author claimed that civil society is generated from a desire for self-preservation,[86] arguing that Locke's theory of compacts had been misunderstood and misused in the dispute between the settlers and the Crown.[87] Similarly, the Pennsylvania assemblyman Joseph Galloway argued for loyalty to the Crown. He used Locke (and Pufendorf) to promote obedience as well as the need for representation.[88] Galloway argued that land in America was held either by conquest or by discovery and 'in either case the right of property is in the state'. He therefore dismissed all claims to property based upon occupation, thereby rejecting one of the colonists' principal grievances against the Crown as well as the foundation for their claim to a right of resistance: 'This property being vested in the state, no subject can lawfully enter upon, and appropriate any part of it to his own use, without a commission or grant.'[89] Even while ministers and officers of the Crown were acutely aware of the limits of sovereign authority, and were even seeking to impose those limits, loyalist pamphleteers were taking a more robust view of the extent of sovereign power and of the occupation of sovereignty. The American Tory, Thomas Chandler, similarly made an apology for the supremacy of sovereignty, arguing that even if a sovereign power 'should adopt measures that are wrong or oppressive', its subjects may complain 'in a respectful manner', but they are bound never to behave 'undutifully', much less 'insolently and rebelliously'.[90] Chandler attacked Locke as 'weak and sophistical'.[91] John Adams responded that Chandler was advancing 'the principles of Hobbs and Filmer'.[92]

[84] Anon., *Thoughts on the origin and nature of government. Occasioned by the late disputes between Great Britain and her American Colonies, written in the year 1766* (London, 1769), p. 53.

[85] *Ibid.*, p. 16. [86] *Ibid.*, p. 10. [87] *Ibid.*, p. 53.

[88] Joseph Galloway *Candid examination of the mutual claims of Great Britain and the colonies* (New York, 1775), pp. 18 and 21.

[89] *Ibid.*, p. 10.

[90] Thomas Chandler, *A friendly address to all reasonable Americans* (New York, 1774), pp. 4–5.

[91] *Ibid.*, p. 9.

[92] John Adams and Daniel Leonard, *Massachusettensis and Novanglus*, in Jensen (ed.), *Tracts*, p. 302.

Westward expansion: the Suffering Traders

The fallout from the Seven Years' War also produced the most sophistical use of the argument of occupation applied to the colonisation of North America. This was the campaign by the Suffering Traders, a group of Pennsylvania land speculators led by George Croghan and Samuel Wharton. The Traders claimed to have lost property at the hands of the Six Nations Iroquois in Pontiac's Rebellion at the end of the Seven Years' War and they negotiated a series of land cessions with the Six Nations as compensation after the war. For the Traders, these grants were to be the basis for nothing less than a new colony, initially named Indiana, and later when grants were obtained for a far larger territory, the planned colony was called Vandalia.[93] Sir William Johnson confirmed the Suffering Traders' grants in the Treaty of Fort Stanwix in 1768, but the British government frowned upon Johnson's recognition of the claims, partly because the claims violated the Proclamation of 1763, and it withheld its approval. Wharton then travelled to London and spent the next eight years attempting to influence people who moved in government circles to support the grants. He also enlisted Benjamin Franklin, resident in London at this time, to support his efforts.[94]

Unfortunately for Wharton, as he came closer to his goal, the American Revolution robbed the British government of the power to grant his wish and he was obliged to turn his claims upon the new government of the United States of America. A tenacious man, as late as 1781, he published a treatise outlining his claim that was now pitched against the rival claims of the state of Virginia over the same western territories. It was in this treatise that he made extensive use of the argument of occupation. In doing so, he cited at length from the library of philosophers and jurists who had written on occupation from Roman times to his own day. But whereas most revolutionaries used the idea of occupation to support their claims to autonomy from the British government at the same time as denying the rights of the Native Americans, he used occupation to argue that the right to land in North and South America rested entirely with the Native Americans. In the manner of the theologians of Salamanca, whom he cited on the matter, he declared that all American colonisation had been unjustified.[95] It may have been possible in 'ignorant and superstitious ages . . . to

[93] Sosin, *Whitehall and the wilderness*, p. 147. [94] *Ibid.*, p. 146.

[95] Samuel Wharton, *Plain facts: being an examination into the rights of the Indian nations of America to their respective countries* (Philadelphia, 1781), pp. 3–4 on the School of Salamanca.

believe it justifiable for them to cross the Atlantic, and usurp the possessions of unoffending nations, only because they did not believe in religious doctrines of which they had never heard, yet the pervading liberal influence of philosophy, reason, and truth, has since given us better notions of the rights of mankind'.[96] Echoing Pufendorf and Wolff, Wharton argued that: 'The right of territory in a community is ... founded on the great natural law of self-preservation, and arises neither from the perfection of our religious opinions, nor from our progress in the refinements of civilization; being antecedent to all these adventitious circumstances'.[97] The right of territory, therefore, was not to be determined by the degree of labour expended on it, as Locke would have it, and the progressive theory of history that that theory supported. A people could have a right to territory, as Pufendorf and Wolff concurred, with any degree of civilisation, and that right was based upon their choices about the measures needed for self-preservation.

Pursuing this argument, Wharton explained that at the first discovery of America by Europeans, it was found already to be 'inhabited and possessed by numerous tribes or nations of people, who had divided this Continent between themselves'. The idea that property was originally determined by division was again a reminder of Grotius and Pufendorf. Nobody knew how long these people had occupied their 'respective districts', but it was certain that 'they undoubtedly were the original and first occupants and possessors of the country, and consequently must have best and most unexceptionable title to it; as none else could possibly have a claim prior to their own'. Discovery of these lands by European princes, he added, conferred no title, 'as all civilians, &c. agree'.[98] He then turned to the Roman law of occupation, conceding that property 'without an owner, may be appropriated and possessed by the first finder, who thus renders it his own property by *occupancy*. – "*Quod enim est nullius per occcupationem acquiritur ejus dominium*"'.[99] In other words, if property in America had not been established in the first divisions of the world through which each nation took its own territory, then it would be open to Europeans to settle. He concluded: 'But as the Continent of America was neither *derelict nor uninhabited*, we may safely conclude, that the first European emigrants to America had no right to establish themselves there.'[100] The continent, that is, was not derelict because it had been included in the first division of the world into various territories. It was entirely consistent with Pufendorf's understanding of property for Wharton to see both division and

[96] *Ibid.*, p. 5. [97] *Ibid.*, p. 7. [98] *Ibid.*, p. 10. [99] *Ibid.*, p. 11. [100] *Ibid.*, pp. 11–12.

occupation as origins for property. Occupation, according to this theory, was a law established by agreement and was the way in which property was established over those lands that were not first disposed of by division. Wharton cites Pufendorf on precisely this question, noting: '"Now it was at the same time agreed, that whatever did not come under this grand division, should pass to the first occupant"... These are the words of Puffendorf, who concludes with Grotius, that whereas originary acquisition was at first made by division, "*it can be now made only by occupancy*".'[101]

According to Wharton, all philosophers and jurists acknowledged that occupation has a fundamental role to play in the origin of property. The 'several nations' of America, he asserted, 'must have been independent communities, and as such, must have been capable of acquiring territories, and other kind of property'. Given that this was so, 'The most common and effectual means, by which a nation and people may acquire the property of a country is *original* or *primitive occupancy*'.[102] Wharton turned to Thomas Rutherford's *Institutes of Natural Law* (1754–6) to support this statement. Rutherford was a latitudinarian Professor of Divinity at Cambridge and Wharton's contemporary, for whom 'rights were powers granted for a purpose', and that understanding included his account of property.[103] Wharton cited Rutherford to the effect that: '"Occupancy, (adds he) in the gross, gave the nation, from the first, a right of absolute property in the land where it settled".'[104]

It has been argued that Wharton failed to understand that Locke's theory of property rested upon labour and not 'occupation alone', but his use of Rutherford (as well as Pufendorf) indicates the degree to which he rejected Locke's theory of property rather than misunderstanding it.[105] It was not possible to read Rutherford as Wharton had and fail to notice

[101] *Ibid.*, p. 15. [102] *Ibid.*, p. 14.

[103] The *Institutes* were Rutherford's Cambridge lectures on Grotius' *De jure belli et pacis.* On Rutherford, see Haakonssen, *Natural law and moral philosophy*, pp. 312–15; John Gascoigne, *Cambridge in the age of the Enlightenment* (Cambridge, 1989); Peter Miller, *Defining the common good* (Cambridge, 1994), pp. 142–9; Tuck, *Rights of war and peace*, pp. 183–4; Goldie and Wokler (eds.), *The Cambridge history of eighteenth-century political thought*, p. 771.

[104] Wharton, *Plain facts*, p. 15. See also pp. 27–8 employing Rutherford's concept of 'full property'.

[105] Tully, *An approach to political philosophy*, p. 170 has observed that 'Following Blackstone's interpretation of Locke, Wharton holds that Locke's labour criterion is met by occupation alone; an act of occupation being a degree of bodily labour' and that 'Wharton and Blackstone are incorrect to assume that occupation, or hunting and gathering, meets Locke's criterion of labour or "due use"'. It is not clear that Wharton agrees with Blackstone to such a degree, but I would suggest that Wharton did not misunderstand Locke; rather, he was concerned with a far broader tradition of thinking about occupation than simply with Locke's understanding.

the extensive critique of Locke's theory of labour, and it was therefore impossible to fail to understand that labour was central to Locke's understanding of occupation. Parts seven to nine of Rutherford's chapter on property, detailing the theory of division and occupancy, were closely followed by a tenth part, 'Mr Lock's opinion examined', which was an extensive critique of Locke.[106] According to Rutherford, Locke's theory of the origin of property assumed that consent to the existence of property had already taken place. Locke insisted that we cannot take more from nature than we can use. The exception to this rule is that instance which allows the beginning of commerce. In other words, we may take more acorns than we can eat and then barter those acorns for a piece of metal or anything else we value. But 'the very notion of bartering implies property. Our author therefore must suppose the man to have property in what would spoil before he can use it'.[107] If property already exists in something that is in excess of what the man can use, then it can only have come to exist through a compact. Thus, for Rutherford, as for Wharton and Pufendorf: 'Property therefore could not be introduced, consistently with justice, unless mankind consented to it either expressly, or tacitly.'[108] For Rutherford, the express agreement to create property is called 'division' and 'a tacit agreement is called occupancy'.[109] To say that the origin of property is in labour would be too restrictive of the liberty open to any civil society to make a compact determining the nature of property within the limits of division and occupation.

From Rutherford, Wharton found support for the idea that not only was occupation the means by which title was established over land which had not been divided in the first compact, but it was also the means by which a nation obtained a territory: '"A nation says Dr Rutherford by settling upon any tract of land . . . acquires, in respect of all other nations, an exclusive right of full or absolute property".'[110] Because property cannot be developed in vacant territory without consent, it is impossible for individuals to act in the creation of property in vacant lands. Only a nation can create property in the first instance. Thus, Rutherford, and Wharton, articulated an understanding of the nation in relation to occupation that agreed with Vattel, Rutherford's contemporary, and was derivative of Wolff as well as Pufendorf.

106 Thomas Rutherford, *Institutes of natural law* (Cambridge, 1754–6); part 10 is pp. 50–661 of Rutherford's lectures.
107 Rutherford, *Institutes of natural law*, p. 56.
108 *Ibid.*, p. 47.
109 *Ibid.*, p. 49.
110 Wharton, *Plain facts*, p. 14.

Wharton was ready to acknowledge the divisions amongst philosophers on the question of the rights conferred by occupation. One way to reconcile the different philosophical perspectives was to turn to Blackstone. He cited Blackstone's well-known observation that: '"There is, indeed, (observes he) some difference among writers on natural law, concerning the reason *why* occupancy should convey this right".' For '*Grotius* and *Pufendorf*, a right derived from occupation must be granted by 'a tacit and implied assent of all mankind'. By contrast, for '*Barbeyrac, Titian* [i.e., Titius], Mr. *Locke* ... there is no such implied assent'.[111] Wharton clearly approved of Blackstone's conclusion that while this debate 'savours too much of nice and scholastic refinement', it does indicate, in Wharton's paraphrase of Blackstone, 'that *occupancy* has been universally admitted, as sufficient to vest property of a country, or district, in a nation, a tribe'. Consequently 'the aborigines of America have an absolute exclusive right to the countries they possess'.[112]

Having said that Europeans had no right to establish themselves in America, Wharton added the coda that was fundamental to his own case – namely, '*without the consent of the native proprietors*'.[113] He devoted the greater part of his treatise to making the case for the legitimacy of the cession to the Suffering Traders and the injustice of Virginia's claims to territory west of the Allegheny Mountains. Wharton's use of occupation was, of course, cynical because his purpose was to establish the argument that Native Americans possessed a right to their territories in order to dispossess the same peoples through the bogus treaties of cession (it was not only Europeans who cynically manipulated the treaties; the land which the Six Nations had ceded to the Suffering Traders was the territory of another native nation). His use of occupation was also ironic because he was aware that it was the pillar of settlers' claims against both the Native Americans and the Crown. But his use of occupation, while cynical and ironic, was also realistic. It reflected the reality of the middle ground: that is, he understood that the Crown had not exercised sovereignty in the Western lands and that the United States of America was not territorially competent over those territories. At the same time, it was necessary to deal with Native Americans who did exercise sovereign powers. It is perhaps for this reason that he chose to reject the Lockean understanding of occupation used by many settlers, and according to which Indians could be portrayed as nationless individuals in nature, and instead to emphasise Pufendorf's and Rutherford's understanding of occupation as

111 *Ibid.*, p. 15. 112 *Ibid.*, p. 16. 113 *Ibid.*, p. 11.

a right exercised in the first instance only by nations, in this case the Native-American nations.[114]

Occupation and the Revolution

When the disputes surrounding the Proclamation of 1763 gave way to the Revolutionary struggle in the 1770s, the uses to which occupation could be put changed again. The settlers extended their claims, based upon occupation, to the colonies themselves and not just to the land that had been beyond the reach of the Crown. Now land that was under the sovereignty and the territorial competence of the Crown came to be contested in terms of the arguments settlers had previously used (and were still using) for native territory. The colonists argued that they had rights to the land in the colonies themselves that arose from their occupation and labour, and that the Crown's claim to title, extended through royal charters, had always been an illusion.

Thomas Jefferson was typical of this use of occupation. In his *Summary view of the rights of British America* (1774), he echoed Richard Bland's argument of eight years earlier, but did not stop short as Bland had. He reminded the King that the colonists' Saxon ancestors had exercised their natural right to leave the 'wilds and woods' of Northern Europe to take possession of Britain, that no prince from their mother country in Europe made any claim to their dependence and that, if he had, they would never 'bow down the sovereignty of their state before such visionary pretensions'.[115] The British Americans had similarly, as Bland had argued, exercised their right to quit one civil society and establish another. The British Americans' own labour was spent and their blood spilt in 'acquiring lands for their settlement' and, accordingly, 'for themselves alone they have a right to hold'.[116] The Crown never made any efforts in the foundation of these colonies; all expenses were private. The Crown had only very recently become involved in paying for the defence of the colonies because of their commercial jealousies with the French and yet now claimed authority over them.

[114] It was appropriate in this regard that Wharton's partner, Croghan, was closer to the French in his understanding of the middle ground than any other British settler. Croghan married a Native American woman and participated in the daily life of the Native Americans.

[115] Thomas Jefferson, *Summary view of the rights of British America* (Williamsburg, 1774), reprinted in Saul K. Padover (ed.), *The complete Jefferson* (New York, 1943), pp. 7–8. On ancient Saxon liberties in Jefferson's work, see Williams, *The American Indian in Western legal thought*, pp. 267–8.

[116] Jefferson, *Summary view*, p. 7.

The rights of the British Americans, according to Jefferson, were based upon their occupation of the land. As the President of Yale College, Ezra Stiles, had succinctly put this argument: 'Dominion is founded in property.'[117] Jefferson conceded that, in the past, many settlers had been deceived into believing the legitimacy of the Crown's title: 'The fictitious principle, that all lands belong originally to the King, they [the colonisers] were early persuaded to believe real, and accordingly took their grants from the Crown.' But acceptance of this title was an illusion – real title came from occupation and it was now time to declare to His Majesty 'that he has no right to grant lands of himself'. Jefferson declared that: 'America was not conquered by William the Norman, nor its lands surrendered to him or any of his successors. Possessions there [i.e., in America] are, undoubtedly of the Allodial nature.' To declare all of America as held by allodial title, that is, free of conveyancing by any lord or sovereign, is to declare all possession to arise from occupancy. He drew precisely this conclusion and appealed directly to the Roman law of occupation, which was a pillar of his case: 'each individual of the society, may appropriate to himself such lands as he finds vacant, and occupancy will give him title'.[118] Here the argument that something which belongs to nobody becomes the property of the first taker is understood to apply to 'each individual of the society' and is not reserved to nations. Jefferson maintained this view, as we shall see shortly, not only in relation to the Crown but also, after independence, in relation to the westward movement of settlers into the Oregon Territory.

If the settlers had the right to remove themselves from Britain and to establish a new civil society, and if the legitimacy of that society was based upon its occupation of territory, it necessarily followed that the people who were living in North America prior to their arrival could not possess rights over the same territory. Jefferson's use of occupation was therefore also employed to dispossess the American Indians insofar as it was used to argue that they had not occupied the land. Occupation in this sense was understood in the Lockean sense of employing labour: 'I know of no such thing existing as an Indian monument; for I would not honor with that name arrow points, stone hatchets, stone pipes, and half-shapen images. Of labor on a large scale, I think there is no remain as respectable as would be a common ditch for the draining of lands.'[119] Stiles made the same claim and phrased it in Lockean terms:

[117] Ezra Stiles, *The United States elevated to glory and honour: a sermon* (New Haven, 1783), p. 8.
[118] Jefferson, *Summary view*, p. 17.
[119] Thomas Jefferson, *Notes on the state of Virginia (1781–1785)*, in Padover (ed.), *Complete Jefferson*, p. 633.

> But numerous *population*, as well as *industry*, is necessary towards giving value to land, to judiciously partitioned territory . . . A very inconsiderable value arose from the sparse thin settlement of the American aboriginals . . . The protestant Europeans have generally bought the native right of soil, as far as they have settled, and paid the value ten fold; and are daily increasing the value of the remaining Indian territory a thousand fold.[120]

There is a long tradition of scholarship that portrays Jefferson as a Lockean or, more broadly, as a 'liberal', particularly in regard to his drafting of the Declaration of Independence.[121] He has also been described as Lockean in terms of his analysis of occupation as the basis of the new civil society established in America and his descriptions of Native Americans.[122] But his argument concerning occupation is more complex than that. He was no straightforward Lockean.[123] For him, the rights created by the settlers in their occupation of land did not establish a new civil society that was the historical equal to European societies, as Locke had imagined would be the case. Locke articulated a stadial theory of history, albeit a rudimentary one, and indeed his theory of property was an attempt to explain the improvements that were made in the progress from one historical stage to another. Jefferson was far less convinced about the merits of progress. He shared the scepticism of civil society that had been evident in natural law writers from Titius and Ferguson through to Rousseau, a scepticism that was also strongly expressed in eighteenth-century Whig concerns about corruption. His understanding of the new civil society created by occupation of the wilderness was bent to his ambivalence about civilisation. For him, the occupation of the wilderness created a third space between the Indians and the metropolis. Here he took the argument from occupation further than contemporaries such as Stiles, who argued that the greatness of a nation is

[120] Stiles, *The United States elevated to glory and honour*, pp. 8–9. John Adams later echoed the same argument: 'Shall we say that a few handfuls of scattering tribes of savages have a right of dominion and property over a quarter of this globe capable of nourishing hundreds of millions of happy human beings?' The Indians, he argued, had a right to property, life and happiness like any human being and in their case this meant that they had the right to their few utensils and wigwams and the few crops they planted, but to nothing more and certainly not to a whole continent: Adams, 'Letter to William Tudor, 13 September, 1818', in Charles Francis Adams (ed.), *The Works of John Adams, Second President of the United States*, 10 vols. (Boston, 1856), vol. X, pp. 359–60.

[121] See, for example, Appleby, *Liberalism and republicanism*; Pangle, *The spirit of modern republicanism*; Dworetz, *The unvarnished doctrine*. For critiques of this interpretation, see Bailyn, *The ideological origins of the American Revolution*; Dunn, 'The politics of John Locke in England and America in the eighteenth century'; Pocock, *The Machiavellian moment*.

[122] Barbara Arneil, 'Locke, Jefferson, and the Amerindian', in Arneil, *John Locke and America*, pp. 168–200.

[123] Pocock, *Virtue, commerce, and history*, p. 272.

founded upon the size of its population. Stiles remained within the progressive theory of history. Great multitudes of people, he observed, demand 'civil government'. He then declared that only one nation in history had attempted to establish that civil government upon liberty and that was the United States. Most of the rest, he declared with unintended irony, have established their civil societies 'both as to policy, and to property . . . upon rapacity, usurpation, and injustice'.[124]

For Jefferson, occupation of the wilderness elevated the settlers from the state of nature in which the Indians remained, but brought them to a pastoral ideal that was short of the corruption of the metropolis. In the *Notes on the state of Virginia*, he suggested that it may be:

> made a question, whether no law, as among the savage Americans, or too much law, among the civilized Europeans, submits man to the greatest evil, one who has seen both conditions of existence would pronounce it to be the last; and that the sheep are happier of themselves, than under the care of the wolves. It will be said that great societies cannot exist without government. The savages, therefore, break them into small ones.[125]

Like Ferguson, Jefferson found fault with both commercial society and that of the 'savage Americans'. He used the contrast between the Native Americans and the Europeans to carve out the third space for the new society of the Euro-Americans (whom he clearly did not identify with 'civilized Europeans') and occupation opened the space between the two. This is the space in which there is not too much law and in which government is broken into smaller units.

Similarly, Jefferson seemingly at first adopted a Lockean position when writing of the population density of the Powhatan confederacy at the time of English settlement. He clearly regarded the Powhatans as typical of the nature of all Indian nations as well as symbolic of the moment at which the English began their possession. He concluded: 'The *Powhatan* confederacy, then, would consist of about eight thousand inhabitants, which was one for every square mile; being about the twentieth part of our present population in the same territory, and the hundredth of that of the British islands.'[126] Here we see Locke's point that labour creates far greater wealth from land, and so supports a greater population. But Jefferson adapted Locke's theory in a way that again points to the perception of a third position between that of the European and the Native American, because he pointed out that the Virginian population density, while twenty times

[124] Jefferson, *Summary view*, pp. 14–15. [125] Jefferson, *Notes on the state of Virginia*, p. 632.
[126] *Ibid.*

that of the Indians, was still one-fifth that of the British. The colonies represent a desirable mean, an improvement upon nature, but a pastoral alternative to the corruption of commercial society.[127]

For Jefferson, this third political space, based upon the right of occupation, was formalised into his theory of liberty. This liberty too was different from that enjoyed either by Native Americans or Europeans. Writing to James Madison in 1787, Jefferson argued that there are three forms of government: 1) no government; 2) government with a 'precious degree of liberty', as was partly the case in England and largely the case in the new republic; and 3) government based upon force, 'as is the case in all other monarchies and most of the other republics'.[128] The European monarchies had passed the desirable historical point of equilibrium in the tension between agrarian and commercial society.

While Jefferson's understanding of occupation was important as a justification of the Revolution, it was not hegemonic in eighteenth-century America. John Adams, his friend and rival, writing after the Revolution, subscribed to the idea that property comes from sovereignty, not the other way around. Prior to civil society, argued Adams, property was fragile and 'confined to actual possession', whereas after the social compact, property was 'the creature of convention, of social laws and artificial order'.[129] As we shall see below, while Jefferson's understanding of property was useful for the Revolution, Adams' understanding would prevail for the newly independent and expanding state.

Vattel versus Locke in the Oregon Territory

For the first half of the nineteenth century, the northwest of America, known as the Oregon Territory, was a place perceived to be void of sovereignty. It was the ground upon which one of the most intense nineteenth-century contests for sovereignty was conducted. It was subjected to a contest between competing theories of how sovereignty was established, including discovery and treaty. But occupation trumped all other claims to title in the debates over Oregon. Indeed, much of the debate was between rival theories of occupation, or sought to reveal that

[127] This concern was taken up in the pastoral and anti-industrial sentimentality of American writers in the nineteenth century – see Leo Marx, *The machine in the garden: technology and the pastoral ideal in America* (New York, 1964).

[128] Thomas Jefferson, 'Letter to James Madison, January 30, 1787', in Padover (ed.), *Complete Jefferson*, p. 270.

[129] John Adams, 'Letter to William Tudor, 13 September, 1818', in Adams (ed.), *The Works of John Adams, Second President of the United States*, vol. X, p. 360.

other claims to title were consistent with the theory of occupation, rather than being between occupation and its rivals. Locke and Vattel's contrasting understandings of the origin of sovereignty were at the heart of these tensions. On one side of the debate was a claim, supported by Locke's writings and nourished by the American Revolution, that new nations can be established by individuals in nature. Against this claim, a number of protagonists employed Vattel's argument that only existing nations can establish new sovereign states. Whereas the Lockean view might be said to have dominated debates in the eighteenth century, particularly in the context of the Revolution, in the Oregon debate we see a turn, even amongst former Revolutionaries, to the argument that sovereign rights prevail over those of individuals in the creation of new states.

Spain, Russia, Great Britain and the United States all argued for priority in the right to claim sovereignty, or to impede the sovereignty of rivals, in the contest over the northwest of America. The Russians based their claim upon the activities of the Russian American Company, which established fur trading posts between 60° and 51° latitude. The British had claims and aspirations through the Hudson Bay Company's fur trade in the region. The Spanish based their claim to the whole west coast of the Americas on the Papal Bull of 1493, on the right of discovery since the sixteenth century and upon the foundation of Spanish outposts in the eighteenth century. The United States based its claims upon the increasing number of settlers coming from the East, its growing sense of 'manifest destiny' which in terms of international law was expressed as 'contiguity', and through the Spanish cession of its claims to the west coast of America north of 42° by virtue of the Adams-Onís Treaty of 22 February 1819. By 1846, the principal rivalry was between the British and the United States, but the first phases of the Oregon dispute were ignited by the Nootka conflict in the 1780s and 1790s, and the Russian 'ukase' or edict on 4 September 1821. The Nootka crisis arose from competing Spanish and English attempts to establish outposts in Nootka Sound on the west coast of what is now Vancouver Island. The outcome from this conflict was a series of conventions in which both nations acknowledged that they did not possess sovereignty in the northwest.[130]

The Russian ukase of 1821 claimed property over 'the whole of the north west coast of America', meaning north of 51° and, perhaps more alarmingly, claimed that the sea between the Bering Strait at 65° north and

[130] On the Nootka conventions, see Frederick Merk, *The Oregon question* (Cambridge, MA, 1967), pp. 2–5.

51° north would be closed within 100 'Italian miles' of the coast.[131] In response to the edict, Russia, Britain and the United States engaged in extended negotiations leading to the convention of 1825 whereby the Russians agreed to confine themselves to the region north of 54° 40′ and the British to the south. During the negotiations leading to this convention, both Britain and Russia acknowledged occupation to be a paramount rule.

On 17 October 1822, the Duke of Wellington wrote to Karl Nesselrode, the Russian Foreign Minister:

> We object, first to the claim of sovereignty as set forth in this Ukase; and, secondly, to the mode in which it is exercised. The best writers on the laws of nations do not attribute the exercise of sovereignty, particularly of continents, to those who have first discovered them, and although we might, on good grounds, dispute with Russia the priority of discovery of these continents, we contend that the much more easily proved, more conclusive, and more certain title of occupation and use, ought to decide the claim of sovereignty.[132]

This was a revealing statement of the diplomatic uses to which texts on the law of nations could be put. It was also a resounding endorsement of occupation and use as the basis of title and those principles, moreover, were fully endorsed in the Russian response. The Russian Cabinet replied to Wellington's complaint with the statement that 'Russia is far from failing to recognise that use and occupation constitute the best titles by which a state can lay claims to rights of sovereignty' and that Russian claims were based precisely upon the belief that the Russian American Company had established extensive settlements from the 60th degree parallel to below the 55th.[133]

Occupation was used to test claims at every stage of the negotiations. In the autumn (2 October) of 1823, Pierre de Poletica, Russia's Foreign Minister and former Ambassador to the United States, met the British Ambassador to Russia (and future Governor General of Canada), Sir Charles Bagot, in Poletica's house in St Petersburg. In his report on their

[131] *Rules established for the limits of navigation and order of communication along the coast of eastern Siberia, the north-west coast of America, and the Aleutian, Kurile, and other islands, under Russian ukase of September 4/16, 1821*, in *Proceedings of the Alaskan Boundary Tribunal* (Washington DC, 1904), vol. 3, pt. 2, pp. 19–27.

[132] *Memorandum* from the Duke of Wellington to Count Nesselrode, 17 October 1822, in *Proceedings of the Alaskan Boundary Tribunal*, vol. 3, pt. 2, p. 47. One striking aspect of this British rejection of discovery as a basis of title is that their American opponents in 1846 argued that the British based their case on discovery.

[133] *Confidential memorandum*, Russian Cabinet, 11 November 1822, in *Proceedings of the Alaskan Boundary Tribunal*, vol. 3, pt. 2, p. 49.

discussion of the contested claim over Northwest America, Poletica observed that he and Bagot made overlapping claims:

> Chevalier Bagot, after a moment's reflection, replied that the point of demarcation which I had just designated was very far from being that which his Government would have wished to fix. He then told me ... that the only legitimate title to any territorial possession was, according to the opinion of the English publicists and that of the lawyers who had been consulted, not the first discovery, nor even the taking possession in accordance with the ancient formalities used by navigators, but the actual occupation of the newly discovered territories.[134]

The British government had indeed consulted lawyers and, as was usual in such cases, they consulted the King's Advocate, the government advisor on civil law, which included matters relating to the law of nations. In this instance, the King's Advocate was Christopher Robinson, a civilian lawyer of the Doctors' Commons.[135] The links between the theory and practice of international law were therefore direct and the dominant place that the theory of occupation held in the law of nations was embraced in practice without controversy.[136]

Prior to the Russian ukase, the United States and Britain discussed rights of sovereignty in the northwest as part of peace negotiations in 1818. They were unable to agree to a line separating their interests and, at the same time, aware of competing Spanish and Russian claims, they could agree only to 'shared occupancy' for a period of ten years, after which time negotiations might be restarted. During this period, the United States sought to strengthen its claims over the region. It pressured Spain into ceding its claims to the territory in the Adams-Onís Treaty. Spanish claims were largely based upon so-called 'rights' of discovery and the United States' adoption of the Spanish claim showed some recognition that discovery could at least strengthen claims for title. However, US politicians rapidly acknowledged a principle already adopted by many jurists: namely,

134 'M. Poletica to Count Nesselrode', St Petersburg, 3 November 1823, in *Proceedings of the Alaskan Boundary Tribunal*, vol. 3, pt. 2, p. 81. It should be noted that at the same time the British ambassador was seeking an agreement with the Russians (p. 82). The presence or absence of occupation was a trump card used in reaching that agreement. The negotiators repeatedly returned to the principle of occupation throughout the discussions; see, for example, *ibid.*, pp. 93 and 145.

135 'The King's Advocate to the Marquis of Londonderry', Doctors' Commons, 20 November 1821, in *Proceedings of the Alaskan Boundary Tribunal*, vol. 3, pt. 2, p. 30. On Robinson, see *The annual biography and obituary* (London, 1834), pp. 325–31.

136 The British and Russian governments agreed to guarantee freedom of the seas and the Russians retracted the ukase in the *Convention between Great Britain and Russia, signed at St Petersburg, February 28/16, 1825* in *Proceedings of the Alaskan Boundary Tribunal*, vol. 3, pt. 2, pp. 56–60.

that the right acquired by discovery was a right to occupy and if that right was not exercised in a reasonable time, then the opportunity to claim title would be lost.

President James Monroe responded to British and Russian claims by arguing that no new colonies should be established in the Americas by the nations of the Old World and that they should remain the domain of the people of the New World who had a greater attachment to liberty. He supported the foundation of a colony by the United States on the Pacific coast of the continent, but he took Jefferson's view on the matter – namely, that the new colony, although aided in its foundation by the United States, would in time separate from its parent and pursue its independence, just as the United States had from Britain. Jefferson was convinced that a new republic would be established on the Pacific coast, but he strongly supported the limitation of the United States at the natural boundary of the Rocky Mountains – the Pacific republics would be too distant to be a part of the Union. Beginning in the 1820s, an alternative view of the westward expansion emerged, led by John Quincy Adams, arguing that settlements on the west coast should remain under the sovereignty of the United States.[137]

By the 1840s, with increasing numbers of settlers arriving on the west of the Rockies through the Oregon Trail, pressure was increasing in the United States for a resolution of the question of sovereignty. Expansionists sought title to the entire region up to 54° 40′, the boundary between the British and the Russians. The British steadfastly refused to relinquish their interests in the area. In 1846, at the peak of the crisis, another war between Britain and the United States appeared imminent, but with war also looming between the United States and Mexico, prudence dictated the need for a compromise. Albert Gallatin was one of the voices of moderation, calling for a boundary at 49°. As one of the most senior US diplomats and a minister in Paris, the Swiss-born Gallatin had been responsible for conducting the negotiations with Britain over the Oregon Territory in 1818 and again in 1826.[138] In 1846, as the House of Representatives and the Senate debated the issue, he published a series of essays on the Oregon Territory in which he stated a strongly Jeffersonian, and Lockean, position:

> The essential difference is that migration from the United States to Oregon is the result of purely natural causes, whilst England, in order to colonize

[137] Merk, *The Oregon question*, pp. 117–19. [138] *Ibid.*, pp. 38–43, 53–8, 65–71.

> that country, must resort to artificial means ... Whether more or less prompt, the result is nevertheless indubitable. The snowball sooner or later becomes an avalanche: where the cultivator of the soil has once made a permanent establishment game and hunters disappear; within a few years the fur trade will have died its natural death ... When the whole territory shall have thus fallen in the possession of an agricultural industrious population, the question recurs, by what principle will then the right of sovereignty, all along kept in abeyance, be determined? The answer is obvious. In conformity with natural law, with that right of occupancy for which Great Britain has always contended, the occupiers of the land, the inhabitants of the country, from whatever quarter they may have come, will be of right as well as of fact the sole legitimate sovereigns of Oregon. Whenever sufficiently numerous, they will decide whether it suits them best to be an independent nation or an integral part of our great Republic.[139]

For Gallatin, sovereignty arose from occupation and so occupation would settle the dispute in the Oregon.[140] Crucially, he subscribed to the Lockean view that private individuals, rather than sovereign nations, could create rights of property and sovereignty through their cultivation and industry. This Lockean perspective in turn supported Gallatin's Jeffersonian conclusion that the republics established on the Pacific coast would be independent of all other powers and could choose to join the Union as they wished.

Gallatin's Jeffersonian and Lockean outlook was broadly shared in Congress during the Oregon crisis. Robert Dale Owen, the representative of Indiana and son of the socialist Robert Owen, made a speech on the 'Occupation of Oregon' in 1844. Owen spoke of the 'future Pacific States' and the place they would hold amongst the powers of the earth to 'which the laws of nature and the progress of improvement entitle them'.[141] Similarly, in 1846, Robert Winthrop, of Massachusetts, spoke on the Oregon question, declaring that he had 'the most sincere desire to see that territory in the possession of such of our people as desire to occupy it – whether hereafter as an independent nation, as was originally suggested by a distinguished Senator from Missouri (Mr Benton), and more recently by a no less

139 Albert Gallatin, *The Oregon question* (New York, 1846), pp. 47–8.

140 Gallatin's understanding of occupation was informed by a scholarship that was deeper than Locke alone. He observes, for example, that 'Grotius, however, sustains the right of occupation by a maxim of the Roman Civil Code': *ibid.*, p.15.

141 Robert Owen, *Occupation of Oregon*, delivered in the House of Representatives of the United States, 23 and 24 January 1844 (Washington DC, 1846), p. 8.

distinguished member Senator from Massachusetts, (Mr. Webster), or as a portion of our own wide-spread and glorious Republic'.[142]

This Lockean notion that individuals could venture into a state of nature and establish rights that would eventually lead to sovereignty was against the grain of the law of nations in the nineteenth century. After Grotius, and certainly following Vattel, the law of nations jealously reserved the right to establish sovereignty to sovereign nations. Many British commentators were infuriated by the insistence of the Jeffersonians that private individuals could unilaterally establish sovereignty through their industry in a territory that belonged to no one. One such Briton was the jurist Sir Travers Twiss, Professor of Political Economy at Oxford and Advocate in the Doctors' Commons. Twiss' professional life spanned the century and he shall return in the context of the Berlin Conference in 1884/5. One of the most important treatises on the Oregon conflict was the young Twiss' 1846 *The Oregon territory*, which included a chapter entitled 'On the acquisition of territory by occupation'. For Twiss, occupation at first glance did not differ greatly from Roman law: 'Occupation . . . denotes the taking possession of a territory previously vacant, which has either always been unoccupied, or, if ever occupied, has been since abandoned. It constitutes a perfect title, and its foundation may be referred to an axiom of natural law: "Quod enim ante nullius est, id ratione naturali occupanti conceditur." (Dig.I.3.D.de Acq.Rer.Dom.).'[143] But Twiss' approach to occupation was dominated by Vattel's outlook. Twiss began the chapter with a quote from Vattel on how nations can lay claim to territories over which 'no prior owner can lay claim'. As with Vattel, for Twiss, the only agent who could acquire sovereignty in territory was a sovereign state, so that: 'The acquisition of sovereignty, therefore, attends as a necessary consequence upon the establishment of a nation in a country. But a nation may establish itself in a country, either by immigration in a body, or by sending forth a colony.'[144] Twiss was quite clear on the fact that by a nation he meant a sovereign state: 'every nation that governs itself by its own authority and laws, without dependence on any foreign power, is a sovereign state; and when it acts as a nation, it acts in a sovereign capacity. When a nation therefore occupies a vacant country, it imports its sovereignty with it'.

[142] Robert Charles Winthrop, *Speech of Mr Winthrop of Massachusetts, on the Oregon question*, delivered in the House of Representatives of the United States, 3 January 1846 (Washington DC, 1846), p. 13. For Benton, see Thomas Benton, *Speech of Mr Benton of Missouri on the Oregon question*, delivered in the United States Senate, 22, 25 and 28 May 1846 (Washington DC, 1846).

[143] Travers Twiss, *The Oregon Territory* (London, 1846), pp. 112–13. [144] *Ibid*., p. 111.

This is not to say that individuals could not occupy vacant territory in which they could establish property rights: 'an independent individual may settle in a country which he finds without an owner, and there possess an independent domain (the dominium utile, as distinguished from the dominium eminens), yet he cannot arrogate to himself an exclusive right to the country, or to the empire over it. His occupation of it would be, as against other nations, rash and ridiculous (Vattel, b.ii., §96)'. Twiss underlined the point that if individuals were engaged in establishing colonies, they must carry the authority of their nations:

> A nation, however, may delegate its sovereign authority to one or more of its members for the occupation of a vacant country ... The colonists represent the nation which has sent them forth, and occupy their new country in the name of the mother country. But the colonists must be sent forth *by the public authority of the nation*, otherwise they will possess no national character, but will be considered to be a body of *emigrants*, who have abandoned their country.[145]

He concluded that 'to constitute a valid territorial title by occupation, the territory must be previously vacant (*res nullius*) and the *state* must intend to take and maintain possession'.[146] No stronger statement of Vattel's position could have been made than Twiss' declarations in his work on the Oregon Territory. It was intended to combat the Lockean and Jeffersonian position, and it was entirely consistent with mainstream thought in nineteenth-century international law (with which Locke's theory of property might also be said to be at odds).

There was an American response that satisfied Twiss' critique: namely, Adams' doctrine that the west coast of the continent should be colonised under the sovereign authority of the United States. Adams knew Vattel well and, more importantly, he was well versed in the law of nations. Writing of Edmond Charles Genêt, the French Revolutionary Ambassador to the United States, Adams commented that 'the French Minister "thanks God, that he has forgotten what GROTIUS, PUFUNDORF AND VATTEL have written upon the law of nations," [but] he ought to be told, that his forgetfulness "is not a thing to thank God on"'. Genêt had dismissed these 'hired jurisprudists' as men who 'wrote when they were all enchained', but Adams insisted upon their possession of a 'liberal and enlightened spirit of freedom'.[147] Adams understood as well as anyone the principles involved in the conflict over the Oregon Territory.

145 *Ibid.*, p. 112. 146 *Ibid.*, p. 114.
147 John Quincy Adams, *Writings of John Quincy Adams* (New York, 1913), vol. 1, pp. 165–6.

A number of congressmen shared his expansionist position and its basis in the law of nations. Prominent amongst them was Garrett Davis, of Kentucky, who chaired the Committee on Territories. The Committee had been created in direct response to the Oregon question and the problem of whether and how to extend civil government over new territories. On 7 February 1846, Davis delivered a speech in the House of Representatives, 'On the Oregon question', in which he appealed directly to the principles laid down by Grotius and Vattel as justification for the extension of US sovereignty over the Oregon Territory.

Davis noted that the Americans acquired title to Oregon from the Spanish by the Adams-Onís Treaty of Florida in 1819, but he did not regard that title to be of great value. The Spanish were first discoverers, however: 'Discovery of itself does not give title to a country, but, if followed with certain acts of the discoverers it does.' He then cited Vattel, chapter and verse, to support this claim:

> Vattel, page 99: 'All mankind have an equal right to things that have not yet fallen into the possession of any one; and those things belong to the person who first takes possession of them. When, therefore, a nation finds a country uninhabited, and without an owner, it may lawfully take possession of it . . . But it is questionable whether a nation can, by the bare act of taking possession, appropriate to itself countries which it does not really occupy, and thus engross a much greater extent of territory than it is able to people or cultivate. It is not difficult to determine that such a pretension would be an absolute infringement of the natural rights of man, and repugnant to the view of Nature . . . The laws of nations will, therefore, not acknowledge the property and sovereignty of a nation over any uninhabited countries, except those of which it has really taken actual possession, in which it has formed settlements, or of which it makes actual use.[148]

Crucially, for Davis, and in contrast to Gallatin and the Jeffersonians, sovereignty could only be acquired by a nation and not by individuals acting without the authority of any state.

According to Davis, occupation must be the act that follows discovery in order that sovereignty is acquired. Discovery is an inadequate basis for sovereignty: 'Discovery is the first inception of title, but it lapses unless followed up within a reasonable time by possession. Grotius and some of the earlier writers required cultivation in addition. Occupancy, and the

[148] Garrett Davis, *On the Oregon question*, delivered to the House of Representatives, 7 February 1846 (Washington DC, 1846), pp. 9–10. For a similar endorsement of the extension of US sovereignty over the territory, see John A. Dix, Speech of John A. Dix, of New York, *On the Oregon question*, delivered in the Senate, 18 and 19 February 1846 (Washington DC, 1846).

exercise of dominion, are indispensable.'[149] Davis then pointed to the thousands of Americans moving to the area, compared to the mere hundreds of English, and thus based his argument on the claim to occupation, which had previously been recognised by the English and the Russians as the sound basis of title. He acknowledged the Nootka Sound Convention of 1790 between the Spanish and the British, which agreed that the northwest coast should be open to trade and commerce and settlement. He responded:

> There are the mutual rights which those powers recognised each other to possess in the country of Oregon. They are such rights as are universally incident to all uninhabited vacant countries, where there are neither settlements, nor people, nor laws, nor officers, nor dominion ... these rights belonged not to England and Spain only, but to all nations of the world. The earth is the common heritage of mankind ... It is alike the law of reason and of nations, that such portions of it as are not occupied may be appropriated by any people; and Oregon ... having no people, no government, no laws, no political authority of any kind, but being in a state of unbroken, unsubjugated, primeval solitude ... was open to any race who might seek it.[150]

Again, for Davis, occupation was supreme in deciding sovereignty. The Oregon was a territory open to occupation because it had not previously been taken, or occupied, by anyone. He dismissed Native Americans as part of the primeval solitude. And, again, for him, sovereignty would only be established by the acts of nation states and not by individuals. In this sense, the actions of people who settled outside the authority of any state had no more rights than the Indians. For Vattel, such people were, as Davis well knew, to be thought of as emigrants who had abandoned their country, equivalent to the 'wandering tribes' of Indians, without any status in the law of nations.

Davis' argument that the law of occupation applied equally to all nations in the Oregon, 'to any race who might seek it', did not fit with the Monroe Doctrine, whereby the Americas should be open only to the nations of the New World, and the west to the United States in particular. But this did not mean that apologists for US expansionism could not fit the square peg of the Monroe Doctrine into the round hole that was the law of occupation. A reconciliation of the two perspectives was possible

[149] Davis, *On the Oregon question*, p. 10.

[150] See also *ibid.*, p. 4: 'England claims to have as much right to all Oregon as she concedes to the United States; that it is a vacant unappropriated country, and open to the people of the world.'

and it was articulated in Daniel Dickinson's speech to the Senate on 24 February 1846. Dickinson, Senator for New York, endorsed Monroe's doctrine when he declared that: 'But, sir, this is not a mere struggle for the Oregon ... it is a contest between two great systems – between monarchy and freedom – between the darkness of the Old World and the sunlight of the New – between the mines and manufactories of Europe and the fertile fields of the distant West.'[151]

But Dickinson also supported right of occupation by nations. He cited 'Marten, Professor of Law in the University of Gottingen' (Georg Friedrich von Martens), on the 'right of the first occupier'. This was the right of the first occupier as understood by Vattel, that is, the right of nations: 'From the moment a nation has taken possession of a territory in right of first occupier, and with the design to establish themselves for the future, they become the absolute and sole proprietors of it, and all that it contains; and have a right to exclude all other nations from it, to use it, and dispose of it as they think proper; provided, however, that they do not, in anywise, encroach of the rights of other nations.' Dickinson also acknowledged some role for discovery, but, like most contemporaries, insisted that discovery only led to sovereignty when accompanied by occupation: 'The first discovery ... carries with it all the advantages of a perfect discovery. Though occupation should follow, it need not immediately succeed discovery. But there must be an intent to follow up the discovery by occupation.'[152]

Dickinson was able to link the principle of occupation with the Monroe Doctrine through the concept of 'contiguity'. A claim, he argued, is strengthened not only by occupation but also by a further element: namely, 'contiguity'. 'Contiguity may come in aid of discovery', he argued: 'Even contiguity will carry a title without discovery, if the possession of the territory be necessary to the interest and convenience of the adjacent power.'[153] Contiguity, the claim to adjacent territory, was the legal expression of the Monroe Doctrine and for Dickinson it served occupation in a similar way to discovery; that is, it established the basis for a claim upon which occupation could follow. It was for this reason that Dickinson, like Davis, rejected the rights of individual settlers in the Oregon and argued that the sovereignty of the territory belonged to the United States. He thus argued for sovereignty going to the United States and not to the settlers:

[151] Daniel S. Dickinson, *On the Oregon question*, speech to the Senate, 24 February 1846 (Washington DC, 1846), p. 15.

[152] *Ibid.*, p. 4. [153] *Ibid.*

'The first article of the treaty of Ghent, under which Astoria was restored, unlike the Nootka convention, provided for the restoration to this government; and under this provision, the country was restored, not to individuals, but to the *sovereignty* of the United States.'[154] In the dispute over the Oregon Territory within the United States, it was this Vattellian position that prevailed over the Jeffersonians. The claims of individuals in the law of nations were judged, as Vattel put it, to be preposterous against those of nations. This position, and not the Lockean defence of individual rights to property established in nature, prevailed in discussions of occupation throughout the nineteenth century. The dispute over the Oregon Territory marked a turning point whereby the competing Lockean theorists of property of the eighteenth century gave way to the theory of occupation as compact and a concern with occupation by nations. Crucial to this turning was the new role the United States of America played in the society of nations.

[154] *Ibid.*, p. 8.

CHAPTER 7

Occupation in the nineteenth century

From the medieval period to the Enlightenment, discussions of property in natural law and natural rights theories were a strong source for the prominence of occupation both as an explanation for the origin of property and also in debates over the justice of empire. In the seventeenth and eighteenth centuries, occupation was a key concept in the understandings of human advancement from the state of nature to civility and through the various stages of society. By most accounts, natural law and natural rights theories were eclipsed in the nineteenth century by positivism and historicism as a means of explaining the world in which we live. We might expect, therefore, to find that occupation would be diminished in nineteenth-century discussions of property and empire. However, this was not the case. Occupation persisted into the nineteenth century as an explanation of the origin of property and also, particularly, in discussions of empire, as a means of understanding the principles upon which things that were believed to belong to nobody could be appropriated. Above all, writers on occupation distinguished between the occupation of sovereignty in the process of extending empire, under the view of international public law, and the occupation of property which was innapropriate as the action of a state, or an empire, and was a matter for private law.

There are several reasons for the endurance of occupation into the nineteenth century. First, occupation continued to be central to accounts of property and sovereignty because seventeenth-century natural law theorists had developed a theory of occupation as a kind of positive law; that is, in their theory, occupation was the creation of compact and human law. This rationalisation for occupation was amenable to both historical and positive law accounts of property that flourished in the nineteenth century. Occupation had found a place in David Hume's and Adam Smith's historical explanations of the development of property, and it no longer needed the explanatory apparatus of natural law. Moreover, occupation held an important explanatory role in the progressive theory of history and the notion of economic development which dominated the understanding of history and civilisation.

Occupation also retained its place in the discussion of property in civil law, which continued to be central to the legal systems of most European states. In addition, the natural law tradition was not extinguished in the nineteenth century. It was brought into a synthetic form of social explanation that included positivism and historicism, and in that form remained a vehicle for introducing occupation into discussions of property and empire. This synthetic form of understanding natural law was found to be useful as a means of understanding international law, a domain in which positive law was weak, and occupation thus persisted as an account of property and sovereignty in the natural law foundations of international law. A final reason for the persistence of occupation was that within this law of nations discourse, it continued to be useful for thinking about the justice of empire. As in previous centuries, occupation was used to argue that empire was unjust as much as it was used to argue that it was just.

As a principle of international law, occupation came largely to be understood in terms of sovereignty and, eventually, territorial sovereignty. Nineteenth-century discussions of occupation absorbed the Enlightenment critiques of early modern empires that were based upon the occupation of other peoples' property. The focus of empire, and of the law of nations, shifted away from the appropriation of land and towards commerce that required the control of subject populations, rather than their elimination, and their use in the creation of goods for trade. This policy meant that large colonising European populations were no longer necessary, so that subject peoples could be left in possession of property, even if in modified forms. What was important, however, was the control of their sovereignty and it was to that aim that theorists of occupation in international law came to direct their attention. At the same time, many discussions of occupation and property in the context of empire were directed, in the spirit of the Enlightenment critique, at rejecting the idea that the property or sovereignty of non-European peoples could be occupied.

This chapter will first examine occupation in German civil law and the law of nations in the early nineteenth century. It will then examine occupation in British civil law and international law. Finally, it will move on to the discussions of occupation in the treatises produced by the members of the *Institut de droit international* in the second half of the century.

German civil law and the law of nations

We have become accustomed to the notion that natural law peaked in the seventeenth century in the writings of Hugo Grotius, Thomas Hobbes, Samuel Pufendorf and John Locke. In the Enlightenment, the emphasis shifted from natural law to natural rights as writers such as Francis Hutcheson and Adam Ferguson questioned the usefulness of basing theories of human behaviour on an original state of nature, and argued that everything that could be learnt from this hypothetical state could more easily be gained from history. The Enlightenment natural rights theorists were superseded in the late eighteenth century and the nineteenth century by the positivists, led by Jeremy Bentham and John Austin, and by the historicists and evolutionary legal theorists, particularly Freidrich Carl von Savigny, Henry Sumner Maine and, later, John Westlake.[1] The rise of positivism in the nineteenth century was tied to the rise of nationalism as the positive description of rights was disposed to their understanding in the context of positive law and therefore within the boundaries of the nation state. Positivism did not lend itself to speculation on the existence and nature of universal rights. Having been buried by positivism, the concern with universal rights would only re-emerge in the twentieth-century reaction to the horrors of the two World Wars and the Holocaust, expressed in the 1948 Universal Declaration of Human Rights.

Some cracks are now starting to appear in this account insofar as it concerns the nineteenth century and the decline of both natural law and natural rights.[2] Natural law and theories of universal rights (as opposed to

[1] A wide spectrum of historians and philosophers have assumed the demise of natural law and natural rights theories in the face of hostile nineteenth-century positivism. See, for example: Anthony Pagden, 'Human rights, natural rights, and Europe's imperial legacy', *Political Theory*, 31(2) (2003), 171–99; J. B. Schneewind, *The invention of autonomy: a history of modern moral philosophy* (Cambridge, 1998); Jeremy Waldron (ed.), *Nonsense upon stilts: Bentham, Burke and Marx on the rights of man* (London, 1987), pp. 151–6; Jeremy Waldron, 'The decline of natural right', in Allen W. Wood and Songsuk Susan Hahn (eds.), *The Cambridge history of philosophy in the nineteenth century* (Cambridge, 2012), pp. 623–50; Muthu, *Enlightenment against empire*; Hochstrasser, *Natural law theories in the early Enlightenment*; Moyn, *The last utopia*, 31. Some early twentieth-century histories of natural law, while also pointing to the decline in natural law in the nineteenth century, remained aware of the continuity of the tradition throughout that century; see, for example, Heinrich Rommen, *The natural law: a study in legal and social history and philosophy*, trans. Thomas R. Hanley (Indianapolis, 1998 [1936]).

[2] Martti Koskenniemi has tried to 'do away' with the image of nineteenth-century lawyers as positivists with a passion for sovereignty (although Koskenniemi is sceptical about the persistence of a nineteenth-century natural law tradition): Koskenniemi, *The gentle civilizer of nations*, pp. 4 and 48. Jennifer Pitts has argued that there were one or two natural law exceptions to the positivist rule: Jennifer Pitts, 'Boundaries of Victorian international law', in Duncan Bell (ed.), *Victorian visions of global order* (Cambridge, 2007), p. 69. Casper Sylvest has recognised that the 'succession of an

narrower theories of national rights) remained strong throughout the nineteenth century. It was partly in the context of that continuing tradition that theories of occupation also continued to have an important role to play in the understanding of property. Because the idea of occupation had been a civil and natural law understanding for the origin of property, the persistence of natural and civil law in the nineteenth century provided a fertile field for the continued endurance of occupation.

Nineteenth-century jurists and philosophers looked to eighteenth-century models in order to help them forge an eclectic theory of natural and positive law. Georg Friedrich von Martens (1756–1821) was one of the most important of those models. Martti Koskenniemi has argued that there was a clear break between Martens' generation, which included the jurist Johann Ludwig Klüber (1762–1837), and the liberal jurists who formed the *Institut de droit international* in the 1860s.[3] To the later generation, Martens' and Klüber's listing of treaties and 'naturalist deduction' seemed 'devoid of political direction'.[4] The jurists of the *Institut* were reformers. They were concerned with pressing matters of the day, including the internal constitutions of states, which the earlier generation had ignored in their emphasis upon the balance of power, war, dynasties, kings and diplomats.[5]

This contrast between the two generations of jurists is somewhat overdrawn. Certainly, there were important differences of tone and substance between the jurists of the early nineteenth century and those of the later period, but there were also important continuities. Martens and Klüber were not entirely indifferent to internal questions of reform, nor, more importantly, were their systems of law entirely rule-bound and static. Moreover, one of the most important reforms pursued by these late Enlightenment jurists concerned the behaviour of European imperial powers. Their observations on the law of occupation revealed a strong sense of political consciousness and of political direction expressed as a

outmoded naturalism by a confident positivism' is 'too simplistic', while conceding that natural law nevertheless had a 'rough ride': Casper Sylvest, 'The foundations of Victorian international law', in Bell (ed.), *Victorian visions*, p. 59. See also Sandra den Otter, '"A legislating empire": Victorian political theorists, codes of law, and empire', in Bell (ed.), *Victorian visions*, pp. 95–6. I have discussed the persistence of natural rights theories in the nineteenth century in Andrew Fitzmaurice, 'The resilience of natural law in the writings of Sir Travers Twiss', in Ian Hall and Lisa Hill (eds.), *British international thinkers from Hobbes to Namier* (New York, 2009).

3 Koskenniemi, *The gentle civilizer of nations*, p. 19. On Martens, see also Martti Koskenniemi, 'Into positivism: Georg Friedrich von Martens (1756–1821) and modern international law', *Constellations*, 15 (2008), 189–207.

4 Koskenniemi, *The gentle civilizer of nations*, p. 24.

5 *Ibid.*, pp. 22–3.

critique of empire. As citizens of German states that had little interest in extra-European imperial expansion, they were perhaps able to view the actions of European imperial powers more dispassionately than many of their French or English colleagues, although their views had much in common with critics such as Diderot and Hume at the heart of imperial states.

More recently, it has been argued that late eighteenth-century natural law had served its purpose in legitimating the modern state, but was 'rather empty in terms of practical directives for government'.[6] According to this view, it was the positive understanding of law that performed the reforming role in the state. However, this reforming role for positive law was necessarily weaker in the case of law between nations where positive law consisted of treaties lacking the sanctions of sovereignty. While natural law was on the wane in the understanding of national law, the very weakness of the positive law of nations provided a space in which natural law continued to possess a strong explanatory power. Nowhere was that power more evident than in the discussions of property and occupation. What role could treaties play where land fell outside the sovereignty of all nations and was perceived to have had no previous owner? Here was a field in which natural law could continue to flourish. Moreover, discussions of occupation increasingly focused upon territories where property and even 'personal' sovereignty was acknowledged to exist but territorial sovereignty was said to be void. In these territories, treaties ceding personal sovereignty only made sense in conjunction with claims to occupy territorial sovereignty.

Koskenniemi is careful to point out that there was one important aspect of international law in which the reforming spirit of the *Institut* generation failed them – namely, in their discussions of empire and colonisation. When it came to discussions of empire, these jurists turned from their role as critics of sovereignty to apologists for the projection of European sovereignty outside of Europe and America. In fact, this is only half true. There were certainly plenty of apologists for empire amongst international jurists throughout the nineteenth century. But there was also a strong tradition of imperial critique that linked the jurists of the second half of the century, the jurists of the *Institut*, with Martens' and Klüber's generation and which self-consciously thought in terms of a tradition that stretched back as far as the sixteenth century and the writings of the Salamanca

[6] Martti Koskenniemi, 'The advantages of treaties: international law in the Enlightenment', *Edinburgh Law Journal*, 13(1) (2009), 27–67, at 58.

School. Some of these critics agreed with Enlightenment scepticism of landed empires and it was from this basis that they developed a theory of occupation appropriate to commercial, or 'informal', empires. Others criticised both landed empires and the new arguments for commercial empire and for the occupation of territorial sovereignty.

Martens was a civil lawyer and diplomat. He was a professor of jurisprudence at the University of Göttingen and a councillor of state in Hanover, dedicating his 1788 *Précis du droit des gens moderne de l'Europe* to the three Hanoverian 'princes' of Great Britain. His importance for the nineteenth-century jurists lay partly in his massive compilations of treaties in the law of nations, his eleven-volume *Recueil des traités* (1791–1801) – monuments to the positive understanding of law – which he placed in a natural law framework. His enduring importance also lay in his understanding of the law of nations as a hybrid between positive and natural law.

Martens has been described as a proponent of a system of neutral and rational rules which govern the behaviour of the state and which proved to be static and 'distant' when confronted with the great reforming impulses that spread across nineteenth-century Europe.[7] But this description does not do justice to the philosophical underpinning of his theory of the law of nations. His understanding of natural law was based upon the pursuit of perfection. The obligation to pursue perfection is imposed on each person in a state of nature, in which 'chacun suit ses propres lumières'.[8] Wolff, Vattel and Kant's understandings of perfection were Martens' guides. The pursuit of perfection was carried into society that, consistent with Hobbes and Pufendorf, is created by mutual fear. Societies created out of mutual fear stood in relation to each other like individuals in the state of nature. Each society, which constitutes a moral person, thus had the right, like an individual in a state of nature, to pursue its own understanding of enlightenment.[9] Needless to say, this was a highly relativistic stance on the moral position of each nation or people and this understanding was carried over into later nineteenth-century scepticism of empire. Moreover, this idea of self-perfection was not simply rationalistic and static insofar as the internal constitutions of states were concerned. Martens seriously canvassed the possibility that European states might federate and, citing

[7] Koskenniemi, *The gentle civilizer of nations*, pp. 19–20.
[8] Georg Friedrich von Martens, *Précis du droit des gens moderne de l'Europe*, 2 vols. (Paris, 1831), vol. 1, p. 36.
[9] *Ibid.*, vol. 1, p. 37.

Kant, he conceded that all peoples on the globe might one day share a 'jus cosmopoliticum', a common society built on positive law.[10]

Martens' relativism was articulated in his understanding of property and occupation. According to him, there are two ways to acquire a right over something – that is, to create property: either by making treaties in positive law or by occupation. Both titles, he claimed, are based upon 'la loi naturelle'.[11] However, when it came to taking a position on whether natural law allows a person 'unilaterally' to establish property in 'a state of nature', he noted merely that this question was not 'without difficulty' and, citing Grotius, Locke, Pufendorf and Kant, had been resolved differently by various writers on natural law.[12] Like Blackstone, he was reluctant to get involved in the disputes over occupation, but, also like Blackstone, despite those disputes, he accepted that occupation was one of two fundamental means of creating title.

Martens was more forthright when it came to describing the conditions in which it was possible to acquire property through occupation. For occupation to lead to title, the object must become the exclusive possession of a person or nation, it must have a real utility for it to be removed from the common and it must be *res nullius*, which, for Martens, meant that it must belong to no one.[13] He insisted on the universality of these principles. He declared that: 'The right of property is the same for all men, natural law does not authorise Christian people to claim territory already effectively occupied by savages against their will, even if practice offers too many examples of seeming usurpations.'[14] On these usurpations, he cited Abbé Raynal, whose collaborative work (with Diderot amongst others), the *Histoire philosophique des établissements des Européens aux Indes*, was one of the Enlightenment's most ferocious critiques of European empire.[15] The spirit of his thoughts on occupation would seem, therefore, to have been shaped by anything but a static attachment to the status quo. He articulated the Enlightenment rejection of the European landed empires and his understanding of occupation was central to that critique.

Martens' fusion of natural and positive law was carried through into the practice of the German civil lawyers of the early nineteenth century and into writings on the law of nations more generally. In 1819 Johann Ludwig Klüber (1762–1837) made the by now standard division of the law of nations into natural and positive laws in his *Droit des gens*. Klüber was Professor of Public Law at the University of Heidelberg, but was also a

[10] *Ibid.*, p. 50. [11] *Ibid.*, p. 115. [12] *Ibid.*, p. 116. [13] *Ibid.*, p. 117. [14] *Ibid.*

[15] See Muthu, *Enlightenment against empire.*

counsellor to the Grand Duke of Baden and a diplomat who attended the Congress of Vienna in 1814–15, establishing a new European order after Napoleon's demise, upon which he wrote a nine-volume account.[16] Like Martens, he was prepared to countenance the possibility that a universal world state could come into existence, but pointed out that, until that time arrived, a community of rights nevertheless existed in the form of the law of nations. For him, the purpose of the law of nations was not to reinforce the existing order, the balance of great powers or the political settlements made in the Congress of Vienna. Rather, he argued that universal rights existed in order to combat arbitrary power and he condemned jurists who presented practices, and 'subversive maxims' of the powers, as rights or principles.[17] Importantly, he also understood, even more than Martens, that the law of nations was historical (as well as positive and natural) and so was not static. He portrayed the *ius gentium* as evolutionary, adapting to historical circumstances.

Klüber brought a reforming spirit to the understanding of occupation. His discussion of occupation made the familiar observation that: 'A state can acquire things that belong to no one (res nullius) by occupation.' He then repeated that if the occupation was to be legitimate, the 'thing' must belong to nobody and must be capable of becoming the 'exclusive property' of the occupant; that is, the thing could not be employed by others in any capacity whatsoever. To explain his meaning, he added a note to this sentence referring to the first volume of K. G. Günther's *Europäisches Völkerrecht in Eriedenszeilen*, published in 1787. Günther was, with Martens, one of the first compilers of manuals of the positive law of nations in the late Enlightenment.[18] Citing Günther, Klüber explained that when speaking of 'exclusive property', he had the practices of European colonising powers in mind: 'Property is acquired as a right by an occupation without compromise; it is conserved by continuous possession. In consequence, no nation is authorised by its qualities, whatever they may be, notably not by a higher form of culture of whatever kind, to ravish another nation of its property, not even that of savages or nomads.'[19] Klüber's understanding of occupation rejected the early modern landed empires that had been the focus of Enlightenment critiques.

[16] On Klüber, see Koskenniemi, *The gentle civilizer of nations*, p. 21.
[17] Jean-Louis Klüber, *Droit des gens moderne de l'Europe*, 2 vols. (Paris, 1834), vol. 1, pp. vi–viii.
[18] On Günther, see Koskenniemi, 'The advantages of treaties', p. 47.
[19] Klüber, *Droit des gens moderne de l'Europe*, vol. 1, pp. 209–10.

This rejection was also evident in the work of Klüber's younger contemporary, Auguste-Wilhelm Heffter (1796–1880). Heffter was born in Saxe and later became Professor of Law at the Universities of Bonn, Halle and Berlin.[20] He was almost as influential a jurist as Klüber within the German Vormärz School of public law spanning 1815–48 and he remained an important authority throughout the nineteenth century. As late as 1873, he became a founding member of the *Institut de droit international.*[21] For him, a constitutional state, which was an expression of the popular will, was the highest form of political development.[22] He regarded the 'absolute state' as belonging to the 'ancien régime'. He published these views in successive editions of *Das europäische Völkerrecht* in 1844 and 1848 at a time when Prussia was torn between supporters of the monarch's divine right to rule and the revolutionaries who, in 1848, sought constitutional government. He wrote, moreover, when imperial designs beyond Europe were remote from German political life. His text was republished in 1873, the year in which the *Institut* was founded.

Heffter moved away from the eclectic mix of natural law and positivism found in Martens' and Klüber's work. He argued that the arbiter of international law was not the positive law of treaties and custom, nor was it natural law.[23] Rather, in a manner not unlike the reformers of the second half of the century, he declared that public opinion was the arbiter of international law.[24] The arbitration of opinion was based upon recognition of the need to live together in peace and to escape a permanent state of war.[25] History, he argued, would act as judge and Nemesis.[26] He revealed a greater debt to the natural law tradition when he had to identify the source of right in international law. Right, he argued, is based either upon maintaining the liberty of the person (or state) or upon that person's 'outside interests' – 'ses interest du dehors' – which his contemporary, the American diplomat Henry Wheaton, translated as 'self protection'.[27]

[20] Ernest Nys, *Le droit international: les principes, les théories, les faits*, 3 vols., 2nd edn (Brussels, 1904), vol. 1, pp. 289–90.

[21] See 'Liste des membres effectifs de l'institut de droit international, Octobre 1873', *Revue de Droit International et de Législation Comparée*, 5 (1873), 711–12, at 711.

[22] Auguste-Guillaume Heffter, *Le droit international public de l'Europe* (Paris, 1873), p. 39.

[23] *Ibid.*, p. 4.

[24] *Ibid.*, p. 3. On the rise of public opinion as the arbiter of international law, see Koskenniemi, *The gentle civilizer of nations*, p. 28.

[25] Heffter, *Le droit international public*, p. 5. [26] *Ibid.*, p. 3.

[27] See Henry Wheaton, *Elements of international law*, 6th edn (Boston, 1855), p. 15; Heffter, *Le droit international public*, p.2.

In other words, Heffter articulated the basis of right in terms of the principles established by seventeenth-century natural law theory.

When Heffter turned to the discussion of occupation, he employed the language of nature as well as public conscience. This emphasis again indicated the persistence of natural law thinking in the law of nations and discussions of occupation in particular. His discussion of occupation was continuous with Martens and Klüber in its rejection of contemporary colonising practice. Indeed, he went further than his predecessors with his scepticism of colonial propaganda and of the civilising mission in particular. In a discussion of occupation that was widely noted amongst the *Institut de droit international* generation of jurists later in the nineteenth century, he agreed with the principle originally stated by Vitoria that European subjects 'can try to establish commercial relations with' non-European subjects and can 'stay with them in case of necessity, ask them for necessary objects and food, and even negotiate with them the voluntary cession of a piece of land which would be colonized'.[28] But he declared:

> occupation could only be applied to goods that, though susceptible to ownership, have no master. [Occupation] can't be extended to people who could only be subjected [in a way that is] ... either voluntary or forced. Occupation is notably applied to areas or islands that are not inhabited or not entirely occupied, but no power on earth has the right to impose its laws upon wandering or even savage peoples.[29]

And he added:

> Nature, it is true, does not forbid nations to extend their empire on earth. But nature does not give the right to only one of them to establish its domination everywhere it suits that nation. Propaganda about civilization, the development of commercial and industrial interests ... do not justify it either.[30]

Here Heffter rejected not only the immense European landed empires, like Klüber and Martens before him, but also the emerging imperial justifications cast in terms of commerce and the civilising mission.

Discussions of occupation in continental Europe were not confined to German civil lawyers. Debates over the occupation of territory were common in writing upon the law of nations. The French jurist Eugène Ortolan published an account of occupation in his *Des moyens d'acquérir le*

[28] Heffter, *Le droit international public*, p. 142: 'Ses sujets peuvent chercher à nouer des relations commerciales avec ces derniers, séjourner chez eux en cas de nécessité, leur demander les objets et vivres indispensables, et même négocier avec eux la cession volontaire d'une portion de territoire destinée à être colonisée.'

[29] *Ibid.* [30] *Ibid.*

domaine international in 1849.[31] Ortolan worked as a diplomat in the Ministry of Foreign Affairs, holding posts in Belgium, Russia and, eventually, as Consul General in Australia. He identified occupation with labour in the same manner as Locke. He insisted that the 'premier cause for the acquisition of property' was 'labour' and that we call this labour occupation: 'We believe that there exists, in reality, a sole and true means of original acquisition, that which the jurists call *occupation*.'[32] He stressed that occupation could only create property when the condition was strictly applied that it must concern things which belonged to no one. 'No one', he observed, did not include Native Americans when Europeans arrived.

Ortolan conceded Vattel's point that, if a nation did not fully occupy a territory but only inhabited a few isolated points, the territory would be open to appropriation by others. As an example, however, of the justice of this argument, he cited not the case of the American Indians, but the claim Britain made to Oregon over the United States. The British had not backed up their claim by occupation (of course, in this argument the claims of the Native Americans to the northwest of the continent were ignored).[33] Ortolan then proceeded directly to confront the question of whether Native Americans were nomadic peoples and whether, therefore, they had justly been dispossessed: 'Should the American Indians be compared to nomadic peoples, should their right to the countries they inhabit be respected?'[34] This question, he declared, had been dissected at great profit to the Europeans. He concluded: 'As for science, which should not distinguish between men, the truths of justice exist for all.'[35] With his Lockean understanding that labour was the basis of property, Ortolan could not attribute rights of property to nomadic peoples. In this sense he agreed with Vattel, but he refused Vattel's description of Native Americans as nomads and aligned himself with contemporary critics of empire.

It was not every natural rights theorist who was prepared to accept occupation as a theory of property. Heinrich Ahrens, Professor of Natural Rights at the University of Brussels, argued in 1838 that Bentham's theory of utility was immoral as well as impossibly relativistic as a means whereby we can understand the true good of all humankind. The complete and

[31] Eugène Ortolan should not be confused with his uncle Jean-Félicité-Théodore Ortolan, who wrote two volumes on maritime law in 1844/5 (see Nys, *Le droit international*, vol. 1, p. 290), or with his father Joseph Louis Elzéar Ortolan (1802–73), who made his name with a series of works on Roman law which can be seen to be part of a larger enterprise, led by Niebhur, in which Roman law was being placed in its historical context.

[32] Eugène Ortolan, *Des moyens d'acquérir le domaine international* (Paris, 1849), pp. 35–6.

[33] *Ibid.*, p. 48. [34] *Ibid.*, p. 49. [35] *Ibid.*

harmonious knowledge of human nature was the only way we could measure the 'true good'.[36] An understanding of natural law was the means to the complete knowledge of human nature. But when it came to the origin of property, Ahrens rejected the natural law theory of occupation.[37] He agreed that occupation was historically the origin of property in fact but not in right. Occupation had to be supported by force, and force should not be confused with right. He then pointed out that certain philosophers (clearly meaning Pufendorf) had sensed that the material fact of occupation created no obligation to respect a right of property and they therefore created the notion that a convention recognised occupation as the origin of property. He acknowledged that such conventions had indeed been recognised by 'advanced' and 'cultivated' societies. However, in the first societies, such a principle was never agreed upon in either an explicit or a tacit form. He added, moreover, that in contemporary times, all things that might be occupied had been occupied and, according to the law of most states, the few that had not been occupied belonged to the states under which they fell.[38] For Ahrens, therefore, the theory of occupation held very little explanatory power for the reality of property in his own time. He also rejected Locke's theory of labour and Montesquieu and Bentham's theories of law as possible origins for property. He endorsed instead Kant's theory of convention as the basis for property.[39]

Ahrens was not the only writer to reject occupation as a theory of property. In *What is property?* (1840), the socialist Pierre-Joseph Proudhon included a chapter entitled 'Property considered as a natural right – occupation and civil law as efficient bases of property'.[40] In this chapter Proudhon did not reject the idea of natural rights, but he did reject the notion of property as one of those rights and he argued, therefore, that occupation could not be the origin of property. Occupation, he observed, was given in the Civil Code as well as Roman law and the writings of jurists and philosophers as the origin of the right of property. But it was, he argued, merely the origin of possession, not of a right of property. Turning to Cicero's comparison of the earth to a theatre, Proudhon pointed out that we possess the seat that we take in the theatre for the time which we continue to possess it. But when the occupation ceases, so does the possession, and at no time do we establish a right to that seat. Proudhon's discussion of occupation was reminiscent of Vázquez de Menchaca's

[36] Heinrich Ahrens, *Cours de droit naturel ou de philosophie du droit* (Brussels, 1858), pp. 25–6.
[37] *Ibid.*, pp. 174–7. [38] *Ibid.* [39] *Ibid.*, pp. 185–98.
[40] Pierre-Joseph Proudhon, *What is property?*, ed. and trans. Donald R. Kelley and Bonnie G. Smith (Cambridge, 1994), pp. 35–66.

understanding of property in terms of prescription – that is, as something mutable. Cicero's doctrine would, Proudhon argued, lead to perfect equality. Yet this equality was abandoned when possession was taken for property.

Proudhon's rejection of occupation as a right and origin of property did not, as we might assume, lead to the rejection of occupation itself. Rather, the doctrine of occupation found a new life in his writings as it became the basis for just possession and true equality, and the rejection of property: 'Not only does occupation lead to equality, it PREVENTS property.'[41] Occupation provides us with the material for cultivation that ensures our survival. Its temporary nature allows the possession of those materials by other people and other generations as their needs arise and ours decline – it creates a right of usufruct, but not property over the goods of the earth.

Proudhon's arguments about occupation, as we shall see, would be an important reference point at the time of the Franco-Prussian War and after. Further echoes of his arguments can be found in the twenty-first-century 'Occupy' movement, which similarly sees occupation as a basis for equality and as an alternative to capitalistic understandings of property.

The British account of occupation

Just as there were natural rights theorists in the nineteenth century, such as Ahrens, who rejected the theory of occupation, so there were philosophers hostile to natural rights theory who, following Scottish Enlightenment historicists, employed the concept of occupation as part of an historical explanation of the progressive theory of history and economic development. While John Stuart Mill rejected natural rights theories, like Hume and Smith, he provided an historical account of the evolution of property in which occupation held an important role.

In his essay 'On the use and abuse of the word *right*', Jeremy Bentham argued that 'asserting *rights* of any kind' was 'in the times of Grotius [and] Pufendorf' little more 'than improprieties in language, prejudicial to the interests of knowledge', but since the French Revolution such language had become a '*moral* crime, and not undeserving of being constituted a legal crime, hostile to the public peace'.[42] For Bentham, rights were the child of law – they could not be 'natural'.

[41] *Ibid.*, p. 65.

[42] Jeremy Bentham, *Rights, representation and reform: nonsense upon stilts and other writings upon the French Revolution*, eds. Philip Schofield, Catherine Pease-Watkin and Cyprian Blamires (Oxford, 2002), p. 401.

John Stuart Mill, while regretting Bentham's passion on this subject, largely agreed. Writing in the 1850s, in his essay 'Nature', he complained that: 'No word is more commonly associated with the word Nature, than Law.'[43] He distinguished two kinds of natural laws: those that concerned the natural world, such as the law of gravitation, and described 'observed uniformities' in natural phenomena; and those that concerned the moral world, such as the 'laws of the land, the law of nations'. He argued that the problems that arose in the understanding of the moral world derived from confounding the two senses of natural law. The first writers on the natural law of the moral world were the ancients and the idea of such natural laws accordingly found its way into the Roman jurists. Mill then observed that 'as the modern systematic writers not only on law but on moral philosophy, have generally taken the Roman jurists for their models, treatises on the so-called Law of Nature have abounded; and references to this Law as a supreme rule and ultimate standard have pervaded literature'.[44] He noted that it had been writers on international law and the law of nations who had done more than any other moral philosophers to promote the idea of a law of nature for the reason that they wrote about a domain which had no sovereign and thus no positive law:

> The writers on International Law have done more than any other to give currency to this style of ethical speculation; inasmuch as having no positive law to write about, and yet being anxious to invest the most approved opinions respecting international morality with as much as they could of the authority of law, they endeavoured to find such an authority in Nature's imaginary code.[45]

Indeed, in the nineteenth century, it was in the domain of international law, as Mill perceived, more than in any other field of moral speculation that natural law would persist, and it would do so for precisely the reasons Mill gave.

While Mill refused to acknowledge natural law as a branch of moral philosophy, when he turned to the question of the origin of property, he provided an historical rather than a utilitarian account. 'Private property', he argued, 'as an institution, did not owe its origin to any of those considerations of utility, which plead for the maintenance of it when

[43] John Stuart Mill, *Three essays on religion*, in *Collected works of John Stuart Mill. Volume X Essays on ethics, religion and society* (Indianapolis, 2006; reprint of the Toronto University Press 1969 edn), p. 378.

[44] *Ibid.*, p. 376. [45] *Ibid.*

established.'[46] Rather, in order to account for the origin of property, he furnished an account of occupation that was indebted to the Scottish historical school. He observed:

> Enough is known of rude ages, both from history and from analogous states of society in our own time, to show, that tribunals ... were originally established, not to determine rights, but to repress violence ... With this object chiefly in view, they naturally enough gave legal effect to first occupancy, by treating as the aggressor the person who first commenced violence, by turning, or attempting to turn, another out of possession.[47]

In this account, occupation only gave rise to property subsequent to the creation of tribunals and laws. This understanding of occupation as following law, rather than giving rise to law, would dominate nineteenth-century accounts of property.

The civil law in England

Within Britain, civil law was not confined to Scotland. Two of the eminent figures of nineteenth-century English civil law were Robert Joseph Phillimore (1810–85) and Sir Travers Twiss. Phillimore, along with colleagues such as Twiss, was not a professional international lawyer but a professional civil lawyer. One of the main contexts for discussions of occupation in England was in civil law. Civil law is often said to have been buried by the English common law, but it was practised within two institutions – namely, in the ecclesiastical courts and in the Admiralty Court, for which Phillimore rose to become a judge. These two institutions were served by a college of civilian lawyers, the Doctors' Commons, and by posts in civil law in both Oxford and Cambridge. Although these university posts were supposedly moribund by the nineteenth century, one of the chairs, Travers Twiss, made great and persistent efforts to revive both the chairs and the role of civil law in the law curriculum of the universities. In 1855, Twiss followed Phillimore as Regius Professor of Civil Law at Oxford. Immediately following his appointment, he petitioned the university to reinvigorate the discipline of civil law, pointing to its links with all fields of the law, and he saw his own tenure of the chair as an opportunity to that end.[48]

46 John Stuart Mill, *Of property*, in Mill, *Collected works of John Stuart Mill. Volume II Principles of political economy* (Indianapolis, 2006; reprint of the Toronto University Press 1965 edn), p. 201.
47 *Ibid.*
48 See Travers Twiss, *A letter to the Vice Chancellor of the University of Oxford* (London, 1856).

Both Twiss and Phillimore were prominent members of the Doctors' Commons, the college of civilian lawyers.[49] The Doctors' Commons was dissolved in the 1860s, prior to which time it was notoriously described by Charles Dickens as 'a cosey, dosey, old-fashioned, time-forgotten, sleepy-headed little family party'.[50] Before its demise, however, the civilian lawyers of the Doctors' Commons exercised real power through serving the ecclesiastical courts and the Admiralty Courts. While marriage law was the focus of the ecclesiastical courts, the Admiralty Courts dealt with maritime laws – crucial for a maritime empire – and thus with numerous issues in international relations. The role of Queen's (or King's) Advocate General, a position held by Phillimore and later Twiss, was drawn from the Doctors' Commons and was parallel to that of Attorney General in the common law. The Queen's Advocate General was consulted by the government on Admiralty matters in particular. Roundell Palmer, who was Solicitor General from 1861 to 1863 in Lord Palmerston's government, remarked that when, for example, a British ship, *The Prince of Wales*, was wrecked and plundered on the Brazilian coast, 'reprisals were taken on the advice of Sir Robert Phillimore only' (Phillimore being at that time the Queen's Advocate General), while Palmer was completely bypassed.[51]

Far from being dozy and cozy, the Doctors' Commons was a busy and tempestuous college in its last century. The Minute Book for the period 12 July 1828–10 July 1865 reveals that Twiss, for example, was present at college meetings several times a year for thirty-seven years.[52] The Court of Probate Act of 1857 sounded the death knell for the College, transferring authority in ecclesiastical matters to the common law courts. The meeting of the College held on Friday 15 January 1858 with 20 of 26 members present revealed that a small majority of the College members were in favour of dissolving the Doctors' Commons and profiting from the sale of its property (worth a tantalising £4,000 per member).[53] Dr John Lee led a spirited but ultimately futile resistance against this movement and, despite 'most stormed' debates, the college gradually wound down.[54]

[49] The best account of the Doctors' Commons is G. D. Squibb, *Doctors' Commons: a history of the College of Advocates and Doctors of Law* (Oxford, 1977).

[50] Charles Dickens, *David Copperfield* (New York, 2000), pp. 326–7.

[51] Roundell Palmer, Earl of Selborne, *Memorials: family and personal 1766–1865*, 2 vols. (London, 1896), vol. 2, pp. 377–81.

[52] 'The Minute Book', Lambeth Palace Library MS. DC2.

[53] LPL, MS DC2 ff. 217–20.

[54] See the correspondence between Twiss and Lee in the Lee Papers, Lambeth Palace Library MS 2876, particularly MS 2876 ff. 148–9, 153, 156. The reference to 'most stormed discussions' is in MS 2876 ff. 156, Twiss to Lee, 10 November 1857. Writing to Lee, who was absent from most meetings, Twiss

Just as the formal functions of civil law began to become redundant, the rise of international law provided a new need for civil law and civil lawyers as it inherited from the law of nations a deep debt to the Roman law *jus gentium* and modern civil law. This was the time at which Phillimore produced his four-volume *Commentaries upon international law*.[55] Far from being moribund, civil law gained a new lease on life. Indeed, Twiss' own life was divided by the changing role of the civil law. In his early career, from the 1830s to the 1860s, his time was largely consumed by his thriving practice in the ecclesiastical courts.[56] In this period he also held university lectureships, practised in the Admiralty Courts and published on a variety of subjects, including international law. By the 1850s and 1860s, with the gradual demise of the ecclesiastical courts, he was increasingly occupied with international law, including his role as Queen's Advocate General. By the 1870s and 1880s, international law was very much Twiss' focus, just as it had by that time become the main concern of civil law in England. His career mirrors the development and professionalisation of international law over the course of the century.

This shifting role for civil law was evident in *Commentaries on the Modern Civil Law* (1851) written by George Bowyer (1811–83). Bowyer, a Reader at the Middle Temple, argued that Roman law, the foundation of civil law, was the 'most important source of equitable rules to determine questions in the Law of Nations'.[57] Twenty-three years later, he argued that the civil law had flourished even more since the publication of his *Commentaries* because of the growing importance of international law.[58] Like many of his contemporaries, he placed international law in a natural law framework. He argued that the ancients had misunderstood the character of natural law. For a correct understanding, it was necessary to turn to the 'moderns', including Grotius and Pufendorf.[59] He saw his book

declared 'I voted in our meetings in the negative about our property and the dissolution of the College': MS 2876 ff. 148–9, Twiss to Lee, 17 March 1854.

55 Robert Joseph Phillimore, *Commentaries upon international law*, 4 vols. (Philadelphia, 1854–61), vol. 1, p. v.

56 See 'Travers Twiss', *Oxford dictionary of national biography*.

57 George Bowyer, *Commentaries on the modern civil law* (London, 1851), p. iv. See also George Bowyer, *Readings delivered before the Honourable Society of the Middle Temple in the year 1850* (London, 1851), in which Bowyer explored the common law debt to civil law at a time when the Inns of Court was still responsible for the training of common lawyers (this function would cease in 1852).

58 George Bowyer, *Introduction to the study and use of the civil law* (London, 1874), p. 1.

59 Bowyer's use of such terminology and the distinctions made between the different epochs of natural law thinking should lead us to question Richard Tuck's claim, in his seminal essay on the subject, that the distinction between the 'modern' and 'ancient' natural law traditions had been swept away

as 'an introduction to Grotius, Pufendorf and Vattel', who, he observed, could not be understood without a 'competent knowledge of the Civil Law'.[60] This view was shared by many international lawyers. William Oke Manning commented in 1839 that the reason why 'the systematic writers on the Law of Nations' had 'been all foreigners' was chiefly due to 'the similarity of the method of studying the Law of Nations, and that adopted in the study of the Roman Law'.[61]

A genealogy of the law of nations

There were a large number of writers on the law of nations in the nineteenth century who would not have recognised the claim that they worked in a field dominated by positivism and historicism that had followed the naturalism and historicism of the Enlightenment. These writers provided a very different description of the development of their discipline. Travers Twiss provided an instructive genealogy for the history of the law of nations and international thought in his numerous works including *Two introductory lectures on the science of international law* (published in 1856) and *The law of nations* (published in 1861). According to Twiss, the law of nations was initiated in its first period by Grotius, who depended largely upon natural law for his general conclusions about relations between states.[62] Twiss argued that, following the Thirty Years' War, an increasing number of treaties were made between states and that this enabled for the first time the study of the theory of the law of nations along with the positive study of their relations. Grotius had instituted this distinction, Twiss said, in his division between natural and customary law. But it was the Oxford Professor of Civil Law, Richard Zouch, he argued, who in 1650 developed the distinction between natural law-based theory and the positive description of relations between states.[63]

The second period in the history of the law of nations was dominated by Pufendorf, who, as far as Twiss was concerned, obstructed rather than advanced the study of natural law.[64] The third period, from 1740 to 1785, was characterised by the writing of Christian Wolff, who perfected

after 1800 with the rewriting of the history of moral philosophy during the Enlightenment, with Kant's work in particular, as the pivot. See Richard Tuck, 'The "modern" theory of natural law', in Anthony Pagden (ed.), *The languages of political theory in early modern Europe*, pp. 100–1.

60 Bowyer, *Commentaries on the modern civil law*, p. v.

61 William Oke Manning, *Commentaries on the law of nations* (London, 1839), p.vi.

62 Travers Twiss, *Two introductory lectures on the science of international law* (London, 1856), p. 31.

63 *Ibid.*, p. 30. 64 *Ibid.*, pp. 31–2.

the natural law approach to the law of nations. This period was also characterised by a great advance in positivism led by Gottfried Wilhelm Leibnitz and Johann Jacob Moser.[65] Leibnitz, according to Twiss, was the first to begin the positivist work of collecting conventions concluded between independent states. But Twiss' positivist hero was Moser, the German constitutionalist. Moser appealed to experience over reason as a weapon against absolutism and compiled a history of judicial artefacts that Dale van Kley describes as a 'sprawling formless museum'.[66] According to Twiss, Moser had 'constructed a science, hitherto unknown, of the positive law of nations'.[67]

At the end of the eighteenth century, therefore, Twiss saw the law of nations divided between two great branches: the natural law approach and the positivists. He then went on to explain the final and most important development in the understanding of law of nations that began with the work of Georg Friedrich von Martens. This fourth period, which Twiss believed continued through to his own time of writing, was, he declared, 'characterised by the combined cultivation of the two branches as a whole'.[68] For Twiss, therefore, the dominant understanding of international law in the nineteenth century came not from positivism, but, rather, was a *fusion* of natural and positive law. According to him, Martens, followed by Theodore Schmalz, Johann Ludwig Klüber and Henry Wheaton, brought these two branches of international law together into one system in which the practical application of law followed the general principles distilled by the great natural law theorists.

Importantly, Twiss did not believe himself to be promoting his preferred system of international law in this history. What he understood himself to be doing was simply describing the development of theories of international law up to the present day. Historians have focused upon Bentham and Austin in describing a nineteenth century dominated by positivism and, in particular, a positivism hostile to natural law.[69] In

[65] *Ibid.*, p. 40.

[66] Dale K. van Kley, 'Piety and politics in the century of lights', in Goldie and Wokler (eds.), *The Cambridge history of eighteenth-century political thought*, p. 136.

[67] Twiss, *Lectures*, p. 49. [68] *Ibid.*

[69] The exception is Koskenniemi, who argues that our image of nineteenth-century international law is 'focused on a deviation': Koskenniemi, *The gentle civilizer of nations*, p. 48. David Ritchie, Professor of Logic and Metaphysics at the University of St Andrews, writing at the end of the century, said he initially hesitated to write his attack on natural rights theories because he might be viewed as engaged in 'slaying the already slain'; see David G. Ritchie, *Natural rights: a criticism of some political and ethical conceptions* (London, 1895), p. ix. However, Ritchie hastened to add, he discovered that natural law theory had been thriving in political discourse ever since the attack by

contrast, Twiss saw natural law maintaining a central role in the understanding of international law and, importantly, he understood natural law and the positive study of law to be complementary. Indeed, according to him, natural law had only just reached its peak in his own time because it had developed a mature relationship with positivism. Thus, there could hardly be a greater contrast between Twiss' perception of the natural law tradition and the notion that natural law was in decline in this period. He completely dismissed what he regarded as two extremes of the late eighteenth century: first, he dismissed Kant and his followers as Utopians and, notably, he ignored Bentham and dismissed Austin amongst the positivists.[70] In the final pages of his *Two introductory lectures on the science of international law*, Twiss turned to Austin, who he noted 'seems disposed to banish the term "international law" from the vocabulary of jurisprudence, and to substitute "international morality"'.[71] Twiss responded that there was indeed no international sovereign, no lawgiver or supreme judge. But he insisted on maintaining the notion of a law by returning to the central tenet of the seventeenth-century natural law theorists – namely, 'self-protection', or self-preservation. Self-protection was sufficiently powerful to merit the title of law, he argued, because like the laws of a sovereign, it is compelling. A state, he said, 'cannot violate this law without exposing itself to the hazard of suspending its own international life'.[72]

Twiss was sceptical about the notion of a state of nature. 'Man is sometimes spoken of', he observed, 'as living in a state of Nature when he is living under the rudest forms of physical life, and the law of his existence under such forms is by certain writers laid down to be the Law of Nature applicable to human beings.'[73] He argued, however, in the fashion of Adam Ferguson, that all human states are natural, although he cited the Scottish lawyer James Reddie on the application of that principle to the law of nations: 'Whether we regard man in a rude state of what is termed savage life, or in a refined state of what is called civilised society, the one condition being equally *natural* with the other, the law which Reason suggests to him in either case will be equally the Law of Nature.'[74] For Twiss, this was the law of nature, 'the law which Natural Reason teaches all mankind'.[75] It has been argued that as the natural law tradition

Bentham and that it maintained 'enormous influence', and he then devoted an entire treatise to it in an attempt to put it down once and for all.

70 Twiss, *Lectures*, p. 49. 71 *Ibid.*, p. 58. 72 *Ibid.*

73 Travers Twiss, *The law of nations considered as independent communities: On the right and duties of nations in time of peace* (Oxford, 1861), pp. 118–19.

74 *Ibid.*, pp. 119–20. 75 *Ibid.*, p. 119.

increasingly emphasised natural rights during the eighteenth century, there was a corresponding shift away from thinking about duties.[76] Importantly, however, Twiss emphasised that the first role of natural law was that it imposed 'obligations', or duties, upon states. The test of the 'Independence' of a political community was 'their aptitude or capacity to discharge the obligations of Natural Society towards other political communities'.[77] 'It is obvious', he argued, 'that Nations are under a *natural* obligation to refrain from all acts which tend to destroy their Natural Society.'[78] The purpose of the natural society of political communities is to allow the preservation of its members so that the failure of a state to act according to its natural duties would lead to it ceasing to exist: 'The sanction of the Natural Law of Nations is found in the fact that its violation terminates the existence of an Independent State.'[79] Indeed, Twiss presented the strikingly contemporary argument that self-preservation among the states was enforced all the better by the threat of war in the context of the 'Balance of Power amongst the Greater States'.[80]

Just as Britons shared the civil and natural law heritage so central to their continental European colleagues, they also shared many views on occupation. The hostility of many German and French jurists to the occupation of the lands of non-European peoples could also be found in Britain. Some of this concern was expressed as a consequence of the controversy over free trade, and other opponents of empire were socialists.[81] But some liberal jurists also agreed with their European counterparts. Edward Creasy (1812–78), who became Chief Justice of Ceylon in 1860, expressed grave doubts about the legal arguments used to justify European empire. Creasy was Professor of Jurisprudence at the Inns of Court. His *First platform of international law* was written to 'prove the value of the rules of Utilitarianism'.[82] He argued that: 'There are International Moral

[76] See, for example, Hochstrasser, *Natural law*, p. 6. [77] Twiss, *Law of nations* (1861), p. 110.

[78] *Ibid.*, p. 114. [79] *Ibid.*, p. 111. Compare Pitts, 'Boundaries of Victorian international law', p. 70.

[80] Twiss, *Law of nations* (1861), p. viii; see also pp. 110–11.

[81] On contemporary socialist opposition to the British Empire, see: Gregory Claeys, 'The "left" and the critique of empire c.1865–1900: three roots of humanitarian foreign policy', in Bell (ed.), *Victorian visions*, pp. 239–66; Gregory Claeys, *Imperial sceptics: British critics of empire 1850–1920* (Cambridge, 2010). On Spencer's critique of empire, see Duncan Bell and Caspar Sylvest, 'International society and Victorian political thought: Herbert Spencer, T. H. Green and Henry Sidgwick', *Modern Intellectual History*, 3(2) (2006), 207–38. For the free trade opponents to 'formal' empire, see: Gallagher and Robinson, 'The imperialism of free trade'; Oliver MacDonagh, 'The anti-imperialism of free trade', *Economic History Review*, 14 (1962), 489–501; R. J. Moore, 'Imperialism and "free trade" policy in India, 1853–1854', *Economic History Review*, 17 (1964), 135–45; Anthony Howe, 'Free trade and global order: the rise and fall of a Victorian vision', in Bell (ed.), *Victorian visions*, pp. 26–46.

[82] Edward Creasy, *First platform of international law* (London, 1876), p. viii.

Laws and there are International Positive Laws.'[83] Although he was mainly concerned by the latter, he did not regard positive law to be mutually exclusive with moral law and he claimed that moral law is 'equivalent to the *Naturalis Ratio*, the *Lex Naturae*, and the *Jus Naturale*, as generally meant by the Stoic philosophers and the Roman Jurists'.[84] He commented that Ortolan had best summarised the difference between natural law and positive law in the observation that the former is based upon reason and the latter on power.[85]

Creasy, like Mill, agreed that occupation was the original mode of acquisition, but he stipulated that this rule 'applies in strictness to the taking possession of uninhabited or desert places only'.[86] He then proceeded to build upon the long-standing critique whereby occupation was employed to defend the rights of colonised peoples rather than to justify colonisation. 'The cases', he caustically observed, 'in which the territories beyond Europe, now held by Europeans, were quite "desert and uninhabited" when first visited by Europeans, are rare and exceptional.'[87] 'In the vast majority of instances', he continued, 'the European "occupants" found native tribes already existing in the countries which were new to Europeans, but not new to human beings.'[88] It might be thought, he added, that in many instances the native peoples were roving over large territories and so could not be considered as having occupied such territory so that 'the European newcomers gained a new title by occupancy'.[89] However, he dismissed this Vattel-like argument, claiming that 'in many cases the natives were in considerable numbers: they were often more or less agricultural; in some cases they had attained a high degree of peculiar civilization'.[90] The problem, he declared, was that the 'interpretation of the Law of Nations, as between European new comers and old-natives, was always pronounced by the European – that is, by the stronger party'. In other words, while native peoples held just titles by occupation, Europeans supplanted them through force, that is, through conquest, not through occupation. Creasy cited Chief Justice Marshall at length to this effect and concluded that 'Altogether the processes by which civilized Christians have supplanted heathen savages ... reflect little credit on our creed or on our culture' such that the 'mode' whereby such 'territories were originally taken is generally indefensible'.[91]

Despite this opposition, most British jurists were enthusiasts for empire, particularly commercial empire, and they worked towards an

[83] *Ibid.*, p. 11. [84] *Ibid.*, p. 12. [85] *Ibid.*, p. 14. [86] *Ibid.*, p. 207. [87] *Ibid.*, p. 208.
[88] *Ibid.* [89] *Ibid.* [90] *Ibid.* [91] *Ibid.*, p. 211.

understanding of occupation that would emphasise the taking of territory, or sovereignty, while respecting the property of the native inhabitants. In this way they accommodated the Enlightenment critique of the large landed empires and produced a justification of empire that would focus upon control of subject peoples rather than settlement. Bowyer, Phillimore and Twiss, all colleagues in the Doctors' Commons, agreed that occupation was the original form of acquisition. They also concurred that this right of occupation was, as Bowyer put it, 'subject to an important qualification' – namely, 'though it is indeed founded on natural law', the right of occupation is subject to the will of the community; that is, it flows from sovereignty or adventitious states.[92] Phillimore, too, recognised occupation as the original form of acquisition and he debated whether this right derived from 'the natural law of nations' or whether Grotius and Pufendorf were right to 'consider it as proceeding only from civil institutions'.[93] Similarly, for Twiss, 'Primitive Acquisition is termed *Occupation*'.[94] He agreed that the law of nature was the foundation of this right: 'Such being the Law of Nature in regard to primitive acquisition on the part of individuals, the Law of Nations is in perfect accord with it.'[95] These writers also agreed that: 'Use and Settlement, or in other words, *continuous use*, are indispensable elements of occupation properly so called.'[96] The corollary of that argument was that 'the mere erection of crosses, landmarks and inscriptions' is a frivolous means through which to claim possession in the law of nations.[97] For Twiss, the right of occupation was 'established by usage', 'Discovery is only an inchoate title'.[98]

In placing this right of occupation in the law of nations, these authors concurred with Vattel's argument that the claims to occupation by nations are superior to those of individuals. For these jurists, the sovereign nation state was supreme in international law – there was little or no consideration of tribes or 'savages', or, for that matter, for any individuals. Phillimore pointed out that occupation by a discoverer must be 'fortified by the public authority and by a commission from the State of which he is a member' and the discovery must be 'subsequently adopted by that State, otherwise it does not fall, with respect to the protection of the individual, under the cognizance of International Law'.[99] The supremacy of

92 Bowyer, *Commentaries on the modern civil law*, pp. 72–3.
93 Phillimore, *Commentaries upon international law*, vol. I, p. 199.
94 Twiss, *Law of nations* (1861), p. 160. 95 *Ibid.*
96 Phillimore, *Commentaries upon international law*, vol. I, p. 201.
97 *Ibid.*; see also Bowyer, *Commentaries on the modern civil law*, p. 73.
98 Twiss, *Law of nations* (1861), p. 162.
99 Phillimore, *Commentaries upon international law* vol. I, p. 198.

sovereignty in Twiss' thought was nowhere more apparent than in his discussion of occupation, for example, in the chapter 'The acquisition of territory by occupation' in his 1846 treatise *The Oregon Territory.*[100] In this work, he had argued that the right of occupation rests upon what he described as an 'axiom of natural law', namely 'quod enim ante nullius est, id ratione naturali occupanti condeditur'. As we have seen in the debate over the Oregon Territory, Twiss followed Vattel in arguing that occupation was reserved to sovereign bodies only, not to private individuals.[101] He agreed that, of course, an individual may occupy a vacant country and thereby exercise rights of *dominium*, or property, but he or she cannot claim 'empire' or sovereignty. To do so, he argued (paraphrasing Vattel), would be 'rash and ridiculous . . . as against other nations'.[102]

Phillimore stated his regret that even Britain 'is not without her share of the guilt in forcibly dispossessing and exterminating unoffending inhabitants of countries with whom she had no just cause of war'.[103] But at the same time, he was in no doubt that 'the cultivation of the soil is an obligation imposed upon man'.[104] In contrast to Heffter's scepticism of civilisation, he added that the 'practice of nations in both hemispheres . . . is in favour of any civilized nation making settlement of an uncivilized country'.[105] Phillimore's Scottish contemporary, James Lorimer, was strongly in agreement on this question. Lorimer held the Regius Professorship of Public Law and the Law of Nature and Nations at the University of Edinburgh. He was a keen advocate of the civilising mission and he too understood the argument of occupation as an instrument of that mission.[106] He was in no doubt that certain races suffered from either 'nonage', that is, childishness, or imbecility. This disqualified them, of course, from membership in the family of nations and therefore put them outside the law of nations except insofar as the laws of guardianship were concerned: 'the right of undeveloped individuals, is a right not to recognition as what they are not, but to guardianship'.[107] He commented that: 'The recognition of the equality of the negro with the white races in America is a case in which law has outrun fact, and for the present, at least, it furnishes no precedent of which international law can take cognisance'.[108] As far as he was concerned, the only question that remained to be settled in cases of imbecility was whether it was congenital or not.[109]

[100] Twiss, *The Oregon Territory*, pp. 111–14. [101] *Ibid.*, p. 112. [102] *Ibid.*
[103] Phillimore, *Commentaries upon international law*, vol. 1, p. 210. [104] *Ibid.*, p. 209. [105] *Ibid.*
[106] On Lorimer, see Pitts, 'Boundaries of Victorian international law'.
[107] James Lorimer, *The institutes of the law of nations*, 2 vols. (Edinburgh, 1884), vol. 1 p. 157.
[108] *Ibid.*, p. 158. [109] *Ibid.*

While these jurists believed the right of occupation to be derived from sovereignty, they also focused upon the occupation *of* sovereignty. As we shall see in the following chapters, Travers Twiss shared his colleagues' enthusiasm for the civilising mission. Indeed, he went so far as to place his services at the disposition of King Leopold II in his occupation of the Congo. It was Twiss, more than any of his contemporaries, who furnished the justification for the Congo Free State. He also wrote the constitution for that state. He was acutely conscious that the law of occupation could work as much against the justification of conquest as it could work for it. He accordingly addressed this problem by arguing that it was only the absence of territorial sovereignty that could justify the intrusion of Europeans into the Congo. Although, he conceded, a form of sovereignty existed in central Africa, it was personal sovereignty, as had prevailed in medieval Europe, and it was therefore possible for Europeans to fill the vacuum in territorial sovereignty. What they would occupy would not be the land of other peoples, but the void where territorial sovereignty remained unrealised.

Henry Sumner Maine

Before concluding the examination of British accounts of occupation, I will examine the writings of Henry Sumner Maine.[110] Maine was the chief exponent of the British historical school in international law and contemporary to the generation of Phillimore, Twiss, Lorimer and Bowyer, although it should be stressed that the naturalism of these writers was only part of a synthetic approach to international law that included positivism and a strong historical consciousness of law. Maine's thought was shaped to a large degree by the German historical school led by Friedrich Carl von Savigny. Savigny's work had a wide impact in Britain. James Reddie, too, believed himself to be continuing the work of German legal scholarship, notably Savigny. For Reddie, the presiding judge in the Glasgow Town Court, Savigny's work was a continuation of the historical ideals of the Scottish Enlightenment.[111] Savigny had many British admirers. John Westlake, who, along with Maine, was a leader of the British historical school of international law, had devoted an 1859 treatise

[110] On Maine, see Karuna Mantena, *Alibis of empire: Henry Maine and the end of liberal imperialism* (Princeton, 2010).

[111] See, for example, James Reddie, *Inquiries in international law, public and private*, 2nd edn (Edinburgh, 1851), pp. 6 and 88.

to explaining Savigny to British audiences.[112] Lorimer studied in Geneva and Italy. He then studied law in Berlin and there met Savigny. Savigny had identified and edited Gaius' *Institutes* that, as Travers Twiss recounted in his *Epitome* of Barthold Georg Niebuhr's *History of Rome*, had been discovered by Niebuhr as a palimpsest in the Chapter Library of Verona in 1816.[113] Gaius' work was one of the principal sources of Roman law, including the law of occupation, but had previously only been known through references in other texts. Whereas Justinian's *Institutes* treated laws abstractly, Gaius added historical context to laws in a way that complemented Savigny's development of the German historical school of jurisprudence. But while Savigny was an historicist and was hostile to what he perceived to be the arrogance of natural law, he remained deeply committed to the Roman law (unlike some of his colleagues) and he was accordingly greatly admired by contemporary natural and civil lawyers who, at the same time, usually saw no conflict between their universalist principles and an historical approach to their subject.[114]

Maine was far more sceptical about Roman law than Savigny, particularly when it came to the question of the law of occupation. According to him, the Roman *ius gentium* was simply a codification of the customs that had been 'observed to prevail among the various tribes surrounding Rome' in early antiquity.[115] Later lawyers then mistook this *ius gentium*, on account of its simplicity, for a law of nature, and as the law of nature, it then became the model for the law of nations.[116] For Maine, the law of occupation was emblematic of this process. The laws governing the acquisition of territory in international law had been 'merely transcribed' from the Roman law of occupation.[117] The dignity with which those laws had been invested was 'quite out of proportion to their original importance'.[118] In some astonishment, he conceded that: 'The Roman principle of Occupancy, and the rules into which the jurisconsults expanded it, are the source of all modern International Law on the subject of Capture in War and of the acquisition of sovereign rights in newly discovered countries.'[119] He also lamented that occupation had become a 'theory of the Origin of Property, which is at once the popular theory, and the theory which, in one form or another, is acquiesced in by the great majority of speculative

[112] Koskenniemi, *The gentle civilizer of nations*, pp. 45–6.
[113] Travers Twiss, *An epitome of Niebuhr's history of Rome* (Oxford, 1836), p. xv.
[114] On Savigny's refusal to abandon Roman law, see Koskenniemi, *The gentle civilizer of nations*, pp. 43–5.
[115] Henry Sumner Maine, *Ancient law* (Tuscon, 1986), p. 97. [116] *Ibid.*, p. 98. [117] *Ibid.*, p. 97.
[118] *Ibid.*, p. 238. [119] *Ibid.*, p. 239.

theorists'.[120] The use of occupation to determine the acquisition of territory was, as far as Maine was concerned, almost as arbitrary and absurd as the public law of occupation that had granted continents to various monarchs.[121]

Maine was more interested in the use of occupancy to understand the origin of property. Even Savigny, he noted, appeared to have been seduced by this theory in making the observation that the origin of property was 'founded on Adverse Possession ripened by Prescription' – that is, property could be created by taking possession of what belongs to everyone (what belonged to everybody belonged to nobody in particular) and holding on to it for a long time.[122] Far, however, from being a primitive law, Maine concluded that occupation was a law of property that could only be maintained by settled and sophisticated societies. The first societies, he argued, were characterised by too much instability for occupation to become law.

Despite Maine's strong scepticism of the Roman and natural law origins of the law of occupation, when he came to write a treatise on international law, he was obliged not only by historical but also positivist principles to acknowledge that occupation dominated 'the acquisition by a State of unappropriated territory'.[123] 'What takes place' in the practice of international law and the practice of states 'may still be described by the Roman phrase *occupatio*'.[124] It seemed that the law of occupation, even for those who detested its Roman and natural law principles, was a fact that could not be avoided. For Maine, the law of occupation was not a natural law, but an empirical fact based upon an absurd attachment to a primitive understanding of law. His concession to the reality of the law in the face of his own hostility once more revealed the extraordinary resilience of the concept.

Like many of his contemporary British colleagues, Maine then discoursed at length on whether the land of a 'savage or barbarous tribe' could be justly occupied by a civilised power.[125] His historical approach to law committed him to a belief in the law's organic development and he was therefore uncomfortable with the imposition of a foreign body of law upon a colonial population. In 1862, the year after *Ancient law* was published, he accepted an offer to become a legal member of the Governor General's Council of India.[126] He remained there until 1869, and during those seven

[120] *Ibid.* [121] *Ibid.*, p. 242. [122] *Ibid.*, p. 247.
[123] Henry Sumner Maine, *International law* (New York, 1888), p. 69. [124] *Ibid.*
[125] *Ibid.*, pp. 72–5. [126] Maine, *Ancient law*, p. xv.

years, he struggled to establish native small claims courts following local customs. When he later delivered his Whewell lectures on international law in 1887, he echoed the Enlightenment critique of landed empires shared by his contemporary British colleagues. He agreed that the justice of colonial dispossession, including that in North America, had been questionable.[127] For him, as for contemporaries such as Twiss, sovereignty and not property should be the proper objects of occupation. While he found himself able to accept the occupation of *imperium*, or sovereignty, he insisted that native populations 'retain whatever rights they possessed before'.[128] When we turn, however, to Maine's contemporaries in the *Institut de droit international*, we find that the *imperium* of European colonisers was sometimes brought into question.

The Franco-Prussian War: occupation in Europe

We have seen that from the writings of Grotius onward, occupation was as much a concern regarding the laws of war – that is, regarding problems of occupation following conquest – as it was a means of taking possession of things which were 'sans maître' or belonging to nobody. These two concerns, with conquest on the one hand and colonisation on the other, were linked. They were linked superficially because they were governed by the same principle in Roman and civil law. At issue in the law of war was the degree to which the property of an enemy could be treated as belonging to no one, and so the same issues regarding the occupation of things with no owner were applied. As we have seen, much of the critique of the law of occupation as it was used to justify colonisation was made on the basis of fears about the sovereign's repatriation of abuses of property in the colonies to the metropolis. Here there is a deeper link. With the law of war, this critique also ran in the other direction; that is, fears regarding occupation during war, particularly European wars, led European jurists to expand their critique to concerns about the principles of occupation as they were applied in the colonies. One of the principal conflicts to generate this anxiety in the nineteenth century was the Franco-Prussian War in 1870–1. This saw the occupation of large areas of France, including Paris, by German armies and an armistice in which France paid the price of peace by handing over Alsace-Lorraine to the newly unified German state.

One of the consequences of this bloody war, and the American Civil War in the 1860s, was pressure for an international organisation of jurists

[127] Maine, *International law*, pp. 73–5. [128] *Ibid.*, p. 5.

who would codify international law, including the laws of war, in such a way that future conflict could be avoided or, at least, civilised. That organisation would become the *Institut de droit international* and it became the premier forum for debate over international law in the nineteenth century. One of the principal concerns for this generation of jurists, particularly for French jurists, was the law of occupation. If occupation in conquest was treated in the same manner as the occupation of things which have no master, as it had been employed in colonisation for over 300 years, then all property that fell under the jurisdiction of the conqueror could be treated as having no owner and so as booty. This problem had occupied jurists since the time of Grotius, but it acquired a new urgency when the Prussian armies were in France. There was a long-standing critique in the law of nations on the occupation of territory outside Europe whereby it was stated that the laws of the first taker could not apply where property relations already existed. This critique tended to be sceptical of the excessive claims of sovereign powers.

One of the treatises that were most revealing of these tensions arising from the Franco-Prussian War was Edouard Tartarin's *Traité de l'occupation*, published the year after the armistice in 1872. Tartarin was a jurist in Poitiers who was equally fearful of the potential violation of property by the socialists and anarchists as he was of the Germans. Socialist and anarchist forces had established the Paris Commune in 1871 in the power vacuum created by the war, and liberals such as Tartarin feared their Proudhon-inspired attack on property, particularly property in land. Tartarin engaged in a delicate balancing act. He wished, first, to justify property in land against socialist critiques and so he based the right to land upon the principle of occupation, and, second, he sought to defend property against the claims of the conqueror.

Tartarin opened his treatise by claiming that occupation was the 'philosophical foundation and justification' of the right to property.[129] Occupation, he continued, takes us to the very origin of property, to the first relations between humans and things – there we find a primitive fact and that fact is occupation. Such simple and legitimate occupation was recognised by natural law.[130] Occupation provided the means of existence and existence was the first duty of man.[131] Without occupation, we would be forced to admit that the things that can serve our existence would remain without owners, which would be 'absurd'.[132] Occupation was

[129] Edouard Tartarin, *Traité de l'occupation* (Paris, 1873), p. 5. [130] *Ibid.*, p. 8. [131] *Ibid.*, p. 5.
[132] *Ibid.*, p. 6.

therefore 'one of the sacred rights and, far from becoming weaker, it has a tendency to be exaggerated'.[133] It is exaggerated because 'just as the right of self-defence, when misunderstood, could be used to justify torture, the right of occupation has legitimised conquest amongst nations and theft in society'.[134] In reaction to these abuses, certain writers, and here he cited Rousseau and Proudhon, had attacked property in the name of equality. He responded by defending the thesis that occupation is the foundation of property.[135] He acknowledged Bentham's claim that law is the foundation of property, but, as we shall see, he believed that occupation must be sanctioned by agreement, so he was not greatly troubled by Bentham's proposition.[136] He also examined the theory of labour.[137] He understood Locke to have argued that we 'labour and occupy at the same time', but replied that we must first occupy in order to labour.

What most troubled Tartarin in the theory of property was the notion that 'if occupation was illegitimate, then property would be so too, and those [such as the anarchists of the Commune] who say that it is theft would be right'.[138] He turned to Cicero's example of the seat in the theatre employed by Proudhon. According to Proudhon, the occupant of the seat has no more right to it than the next person who will sit there. Tartarin responded that if we assume the occupant has no right, then the aspirant to the seat has no more right to it than the occupant. Why, he asks, would the occupant cede the seat to another person if a conflict should arise about who should sit there? Without a title, the only possible resolution of a conflict between occupant of the seat and aspirant would be 'the law of the strongest or, rather, the negation of all right'.[139] God, he declared, 'gave the earth to men's children but in giving to everybody he gave it to nobody. Unoccupied land is *res nullius*. To take from that negative community parts that fall in individual domain, there must be occupation and that occupation, because it is anterior to all other possession, to all other title, makes man proprietor'.[140] In conclusion, he argued that to agree to Proudhon's rejection of property was 'to legitimise the theories of Rousseau and Mably [Gabriel Bonno de Mably, 1709–85, who had proposed the abolition of private property], all the exigencies of the sovereign, sole proprietor of all domains . . . the fiscal measures, the confiscations, the taille [a land tax of the Ancien Régime], and all the socialist accessories of feudalism and absolute monarchy'.[141] Socialism was thus a return to the absolutist past.

[133] *Ibid.*, p. 8. [134] *Ibid.* [135] *Ibid.*, pp. 8–9. [136] *Ibid.*, p. 10. [137] *Ibid.*, p. 11.
[138] *Ibid.*, p. 12. [139] *Ibid.*, p. 14. [140] *Ibid.*, p. 16. [141] *Ibid.*, p. 18.

Turning to the Prussian occupation, Tartarin declared that conquest confers only a right of sovereignty;[142] it does not confer property. The law of nations does not confer a right to spoil a people of their property. It is against the law of nations, he argued, for a conqueror to hand out territory and goods of a conquered people to his soldiers and generals, as Napoleon had.[143] All rights, according to Tartarin, are based upon agreement. This includes occupation, which 'outside of contract is just a provisory fact'.[144] In this sense, Tartarin's thoughts on occupation were consistent with Grotius' and Pufendorf's treatment of the subject (which he cited). The right of a conqueror, he added, was also based upon a tacit agreement. All nations of the globe, he declared, recognise the right of conquest and therefore a tacit agreement on that right exists in the law of nations. Conquest, however, confers absolutely no rights of occupation of property.[145] Occupation of property can only follow conquest if a further treaty is made between the conqueror and the vanquished that agrees with the terms of occupation, or to a provisory fact of occupation. Historians have justifiably been sceptical of European jurists' discussions of the conditions of treaties of occupation as a legal means for sanitising conquest. But the context for Tartarin's discussion reminds us that those discussions could be entirely earnest.

Tartarin insisted that the principles he had laid out must be respected in the Prussian occupation of France, as had been largely agreed in the treaty of 26 February 1871.[146] He insisted again that even where treaties of conquest and occupation applied, they applied only to the goods of the nation, not to those of private individuals, and they could only be exercised by the conquering nation and not by individual soldiers. Outside of these limits, all taking of property was mere 'rapine, theft and against the law of nations'. But against such actions, he conceded that 'sadly, the violated nation is always impotent'.[147] At the same time, occupation was for Tartarin always a right subordinate to sovereignty and to agreement and it was this right which conferred some protection to private individuals in France from German occupation. It was also this right from agreement which he believed protected private property from the claims of the anarchists who had also been roused by the Prussian conquest. Importantly, he agreed with contemporaries, such as Twiss, that occupation should not exceed taking control of sovereignty. In making these arguments, these late nineteenth-century jurists were developing a new understanding of occupation.

142 *Ibid.*, p. 215. 143 *Ibid.*, pp. 215–16. 144 *Ibid.*, p. 216. 145 *Ibid.* 146 *Ibid.*, p. 219.
147 *Ibid.*, p. 223.

The *Institut de droit international*

This new understanding of occupation was forged by the jurists of the *Institut de droit international.* Most late nineteenth-century international lawyers were members or associate members of the *Institut,* which was the first organisation of international lawyers. It established the idea of international law as a profession, rather than a sideline pursued by diplomats and civil lawyers, and it rapidly deepened debate on the issues that concerned this community.[148] It was founded in 1873, partly as a reaction to the failure to respect the Geneva Convention during the Franco-Prussian War, but its members were moved by a broader liberal and reforming spirit. It was established by prominent liberals; men such as the Belgian politician and lawyer Gustave Rolin-Jaequemyns (1835–1902), the jurist and political theorist Johann Kaspar Bluntschli (1808–81) and Gustave Moynier (1826–1910), co-founder and President of the International Committee of the Red Cross. Membership embraced all the major European and American powers, and this group met every two years.[149] These self-described liberals aimed not only to establish a system of rules that would govern the behaviour of states, but also to reform states and combat authoritarian rule. It has been argued that the exception to their reforming spirit was their attitude to empire.[150] They are said to have endorsed the projection of European sovereignty abroad as enthusiastically as they pursued reform at home. In fact, they were divided in their views regarding empire and also civilisation. Many were indeed enthusiasts for European civilisation, some were ambivalent, some were relativists and yet others were damning of the 'pretensions' of civilisation.

Occupation and the *Institut de droit international*

For members of the *Institut,* the defining moment in the history of occupation was in their own time, surrounding the events leading up to and following the conference called by Otto von Bismarck at Berlin in 1884/5 to create rules for the carving-up of Africa (and the Pacific) and in so doing to agree on just terms for occupation. From a distance, the

[148] Koskenniemi, *The gentle civilizer of nations* contains the most comprehensive history of the *Institut de droit international.*

[149] For the constitution and objectives of the *Institut,* see 'Communications relatives à l'Institut de Droit International' and 'Documents relatifs à l'Institut de Droit Internatinal', in *Revue de Droit International et de Législation Comparée,* 5 (1873), 667–712.

[150] Koskenniemi, *The gentle civilizer of nations,* pp. 4–5.

agreements made in the Act of the Berlin Conference do not appear remarkably different from many of the principles of effective occupation agreed amongst jurists for centuries. But what excited the *Institut* jurists was that the principles that had stood for so long in the theory of the law of nations had at last been recognised through treaty in positive international law. Moreover, the Conference, or more particularly the forums on international law that followed it, recognised the idea of *territorium nullius*, a new doctrine of occupation which focused upon the occupation of sovereignty. A full analysis of this doctrine will be given in the following chapters.

Francis Lieber (1800–72) helped create momentum for founding the *Institut*, although he died in the year that formal discussions for its creation began. Lieber was German born and educated (he spent time in Italy as a young man where he befriended Niebuhr), but he left Europe for the more liberal environment of the United States in 1827, where he gained employment first in South Carolina College and then in Columbia College as Professor of History and Political Science. He is best known now for his work on the laws of war during the American Civil War, particularly the so-called 'Lieber Code', which subsequently influenced the Hague and Geneva Conventions on war. In his *Essays on labour and property*, he provided a classic account of property arising from occupation. He rejected the Hobbesian idea of a state of nature as 'a state of war, everyone warring with everyone', and so he also rejected the notion that property was a 'later invention of man'.[151] He followed the Scottish historical school with his scepticism that a state of nature was anything more than a hypothetical tool. He insisted on the natural sociability of humans: 'love is before hatred, and in its nature lasts longer'.[152] 'Civilization', he declared, 'is man's real state of nature.'[153]

Accordingly, for Lieber: 'Property, like government, shows itself from the earliest periods.'[154] The basis of property was occupation: 'The primary origin of all individual property must be occupation.'[155] Expanding on this claim, he observed that: 'The act of taking possession of things unowned, or of seizing them and making them subject to ourselves, with the intention of holding them as property, is called occupying them. Occupation leads to appropriation.'[156] The striking aspect of Lieber's Lockean account of occupation was that it concerned property

[151] Francis Lieber, *Essays on property and labour as connected with natural law and the constitution of society* (New York, 1842), p. 35.
[152] *Ibid.*, p. 36. [153] *Ibid.*, p. 34. [154] *Ibid.* [155] *Ibid.*, p. 44. [156] *Ibid.*, p. 33.

rather than sovereignty. One reason for that focus was that his *Essays on property and labour* was concerned with national more than international questions. When writing of international society, however, his contemporaries increasingly focused upon sovereignty as the subject of occupation.

Paul Pradier-Fodéré (1827–1904) discussed occupation in the context of both property and sovereignty. He was born in Strasbourg and practised as a jurist in Paris as well as holding a professorship in public law at the Armenian College in Paris.[157] In 1874 he was charged by the Peruvian government with establishing a faculty of political science at Lima. He was an influential editor of Vattel and Grotius as well as being a theorist of law in his own right. He was a prominent member of the *Institut de droit international*.[158] Noting the objections of the utilitarians to the idea of natural law, he argued that one of the great achievements of the nineteenth century had been the application of experimental method to the claims of natural law so that only those principles of natural law which survived this test remained as part of the system of law.[159] Citing Bentham, he noted that it had been objected that there are no rights where there is no legislator. But this, he objected, was a 'false and dangerous' doctrine. To claim that there were no rights anterior to the creation of civil society was to confound rights with the guarantee of rights. Such confusion would legitimise all the acts of the legislator, which would not only be absurd but would also lead to the 'most monstrous despotism'.[160] This fear of despotism was common amongst members of the *Institut* and it animated their discussions of occupation.

Like Lieber, Pradier-Fodéré closely identified occupation with labour. There is a right, he argued, that arises from the 'application of moral and physical force . . . to a territory which belongs to nobody' and the 'source of this right we name occupation'.[161] He acknowledged Proudhon's objection to occupation as a basis of property.[162] He responded that occupation was not a right inherent in humanity, but a fact of circumstance. According to Pradier-Fodéré, 'man did not have a right to occupy by his mere existence'. The first occupant of a field could became the owner, however, when that field belonged to nobody previously and so no other right had been violated.[163] For him, the means of acquiring title were the

[157] For Pradier-Fodéré's life, see Nys, *Le droit international*, vol. 1, p. 302.

[158] 'Noms et adresses des membres honoraires, membres et associés de l'institut de droit international', *Annuaire de l'institut de droit international*, 10 (1888–9), xvi.

[159] Paul Pradier-Fodéré, *Principes généraux de droit, de politique et de législation* (Paris, 1869), p. 24.

[160] *Ibid.* [161] *Ibid.*, p. 138. [162] *Ibid.*, p. 140. [163] *Ibid.*, p. 141.

same for nations as for individuals; that is, they were governed by 'occupation and by convention'.[164] According to him, occupation applied only to 'unoccupied' territory. The crucial question, as always, was what constituted unoccupied.

Having dismissed natural law thinking from international law, Frantz Despagnet, like Henry Sumner Maine before him, sought to treat occupation as an historical and contemporary fact. Despagnet (1857–1906), Professor of Law at Bordeaux, was one of those jurists who rejected natural law as a part of his understanding of international law. According to him, the 'idealism' of Hobbes and Pufendorf had been entirely abandoned by his age and replaced with a tradition of thinking about international law that rested upon practice and could thus be traced through Vattel and Wolff back to Grotius.[165] Theories of international law, he argued, could only be based upon close analysis of experience and facts and the observation of their historical evolution, and upon this point he cited Henry Sumner Maine. Moreover, he argued, the revolutions of 1848 had brought a new democratic spirit to Europe, and one of the consequences of this new reality was that the international relations of states became less secretive and more the concern of the 'mass of the population'. This meant that international affairs were submitted to 'the control of public opinion which tends to direct as much as it is directed by domestic politics in almost all countries'.[166] International law was thus directed by a melange of experience, history and public opinion.

Despagnet accordingly devoted considerable attention to the history of the occupation.[167] He divided his analysis of that history into three periods. The first centred upon the great discoveries of the Spanish and Portuguese, while the second turned to the English, French and Dutch in the seventeenth and eighteenth centuries. Both of these epochs were largely regulated by the Roman and natural law of occupation.[168] The third period climaxed, according to Despagnet, in his own time with the Berlin Conference on the occupation of Africa. For him, the significance of the Conference was that it transformed the natural law of occupation in the law of nations into a law of treaty recognised by the Act of the Berlin Conference. There was no escaping the natural law foundations of the Berlin Act, but the consecration of the principles of occupation as an act of positive law at least obviated the necessity, prior to the time of the

[164] *Ibid.*, p. 525.
[165] Frantz Despagnet, *Cours de droit international public*, 2nd edn (Paris, 1899), p. 46.
[166] *Ibid.*, p. 23. [167] *Ibid.*, pp. 425–9. [168] *Ibid.*, pp. 425–7.

Conference, to appeal to natural law in order to explain the acquisition of territory.

Most importantly, for Despagnet, occupation of property was no longer a matter for discussion in international law – it was a matter for private law. The principle of occupation in international law differed from private law because it concerned the taking of possession of sovereignty rather than property. The 'modern' definition of occupation, according to Despagnet, was 'taking possession, with the intention to submit to sovereignty, of a territory presently with no owner from the point of view of international law'.[169] From this definition, he argued, it was evident that occupation in international law had elements similar to occupation in private law, but we must, he added, 'clearly distinguish between the two, because occupation in international law takes for its object the acquisition of sovereignty and not property'. As we shall see, other jurists agreeing with this distinction argued that *res nullius* was the doctrine concerning the occupation of property in private law, while *territorium nullius* was the doctrine for the occupation of sovereignty in international public law.

In Despagnet's work, the law of occupation was yet again transformed into an entirely new intellectual framework. In the light of defeat in the Franco-Prussian War, he sought a place for France in the international order whereby it could recover its grandeur and yet pursue progress, justice and peace.[170] He agreed with the broad nineteenth-century consensus upon Vattel's dictum that the right to occupy territory 'incontestably' belonged only to states.[171] Occupation must be effective and could only be applied to territories that were not already under sovereignty. According to these principles, occupation was not only performed by sovereign states, but also took sovereignty as its object.

The focus upon sovereignty was common. When Johann Caspar Bluntschli turned to the rules governing the acquisition of territory, he imported his concern with sovereignty into the matter, posing the question of how to acquire 'territorial sovereignty' and not simply territory.[172] Bluntschli (1808–81) was typical of the liberal apologists for empire and was in tune with the developing interest, within Germany, in overseas expansion in the 1870s.[173] Amongst his many offices, he was a professor of constitutional law at Heidelberg, Counsellor to the Grand Duke Frederick

[169] *Ibid.*, p. 425. [170] Frantz Despagnet, *La diplomatie de la Troisième République* (Paris, 1904), viii.

[171] Despagnet, *Cours de droit international public*, p. 429.

[172] Johann Caspar Bluntschli, *Le droit international codifié*, 4th edn (Paris, 1886), p. 174.

[173] On Bluntschli 'parmi les modérés ou *libéraux*', see Alphonse Rivier, 'Notice sur M. Bluntschli', in *ibid.* p. viii; and Koskenniemi, *The gentle civilizer of nations*, pp. 42–7.

I of Baden and a member of the Baden Parliament. He devoted his life to theorising and valorising the state, and strongly supported Prussian hegemony and Bismarck's policy of unification.[174] He was one of the founders of the *Institut* and was one of the most prominent political scientists of his generation.[175] He was also a moderate liberal and a reformer. He had been a student of Savigny, Frederic-Louis Keller and Niebuhr in 1827, but moved beyond historicism and positivism to an organic understanding of law that reflected social change.[176] Like many of his contemporaries, his dynamic understanding of law was eclectic, open to historicism, positivism and natural law. As Ferguson had concluded before him, Bluntschli argued that it is pointless to speculate about a pre-civil state because humans have always lived in various forms of civil society.[177] This did not mean that all civil societies were equal. For him, the state was the highest expression of human sociability and, as an expression of the greatest common will, it had the greatest rights accorded to it.

In adopting the focus upon territorial sovereignty as the object of occupation, Bluntschli agreed with contemporaries. They warned that property could not be acquired by imperial powers. To admit such a possibility would be to confuse sovereignty and property, whereas the purpose of the modern revolutions had been precisely to prevent that confusion. Continuing this theme, Bluntschli did not argue that 'territory which belongs to no-one becomes the property of the first taker', but rather that 'the sovereignty of territory which does not form a part of any state, can be acquired'.[178] Acquisition had to conform to the principles of effective occupation and not mere discovery.

Similarly, for Henry Bonfils (1835–97), occupation was principal amongst the original modes by which states acquire territory; that is, he placed occupation in the context of actions by states, not individuals concerned with property.[179] A number of jurists articulated the Enlightenment ideal of perfectibility. Bonfils claimed that 'international law has its roots in the nature of man, in the instincts and needs of sociability and in perfectibility'.[180] He was Professor of Law at the University of Toulouse and wrote one of the most

[174] Johann Kaspar Bluntschli, *The theory of the state* (Oxford, 1895); and 'Nécrologie. M. Bluntschli', *Revue de Droit International et de Législation Comparée*, 13 (1881), 626.

[175] Koskenniemi, *The gentle civilizer of nations*, pp. 42–7.

[176] Rivier, 'Notice sur M. Bluntschli', p. viii. [177] Bluntschli, *The theory of the state*, pp. 300–2.

[178] Bluntschli, *Le droit international codifié*, p. 175.

[179] Henry Bonfils, *Manuel de droit international public*, third edn revised by Paul Fauchille (Paris, 1901), pp. 300–17.

[180] *Ibid.*, p. 3. Note that this work was substantially revised by Paul Fauchille after Bonfils' death following the publication of the first edition.

popular textbooks of international law in the late nineteenth century. Like many liberals inspired by the notion of human perfectibility, he saw international law as the means to creating a vast association, an international community, but he rejected the Kantian notion that that community could become a universal state.[181] He stressed that occupation applied only to 'uninhabited' territory. However, he also noted that occupation, as a mode of acquiring territory, had attained a special importance in the 'feverish precipitation' of the great powers of Europe upon non-European lands and he conducted the entirety of his discussion of the principle in that context.[182]

Spectrum of imperial critique

While the members of the *Institut* were liberals, they have been represented as having abandoned their liberal values when they discussed the projection of European sovereignty onto non-European peoples. It is true that their discussions of occupation focused upon sovereignty, but that focus was used as much to critique the projection of European sovereignty as it was to promote it. Where their discussions of occupation concerned property, they generally agreed that the property of non-European peoples could not be occupied. Where they differed was on the question of sovereignty. There was a spectrum of imperial critique. Some members of the *Institut* were indeed fervent promoters of European empire and the civilising mission. Others accepted the reality of empire and endorsed the occupation of sovereignty, but questioned what had been done in the name of the civilising mission and argued that the property of indigenous peoples should be respected. A third group rejected the civilising mission and even put the question of sovereignty into serious debate.[183]

As a promoter of the awakening German imperial ambitions in the 1870s, Bluntschli can be placed in the first group – the liberal promoters of empire. His enthusiasm for European sovereignty as the highest expression of the freedom of human beings was again evident in his discussion of the occupation of the territory of 'barbarian tribes'.[184] He questioned whether civilised peoples had the right to dispossess savages who were ignorant not only of sovereignty but also of property and who spent their time hunting.

[181] *Ibid.*, p. 6. [182] *Ibid.*, p. 300.

[183] Historians of the civilising mission have paid little attention to opposition to the project of civilisation. See, for example, Schmitt, *The nomos of the earth*; Gerrit Gong, *The standard of 'civilization' in international society* (Oxford, 1984); Grewe, *The epochs of international law*, pp. 445–82; Bowden, *The empire of civilization*.

[184] Bluntschli, *Le droit international codifié*, p. 176.

He argued that 'natural law recognises in the first instance the right to all human beings to existence' and therefore requires respect for natives' legitimate practices pursued for their own survival.[185] These tribes, he argued, could not be expelled, they must be allowed to 'emigrate' in peace.[186] At the same time, the colonising state had a right to 'extend its sovereignty on territory occupied by savage tribes in order to promote civilisation and the extension of culture'.[187] Quoting Vattel, he pointed out that the 'surface of the earth is destined to be cultivated by man'.[188]

Through his focus on property, Pradier-Fodéré also endorsed Vattel's views on the rights of nomadic peoples. 'Property in territory', Pradier-Fodéré argued, 'attaches to peoples as it does to nations; nomadic peoples, as we have already recognised [in this treatise], constitute nations only when they are seated on the soil. The right of property is therefore a right of international natural law [Droit natural international].'[189] It is not entirely clear which nomadic peoples would be judged, according to Pradier-Fodéré's criteria, as constituting nations and which would not. It may seem that he was rejecting Vattel's claim that nomadic people possessed no rights to the soil, but Vattel too had distinguished between nomadic peoples in America, who had no rights, and those in north Africa, who did.

Despagnet played a role justifying the expanding French empire in Africa, although he can be placed amongst those who critiqued empire at the same time as they excused it. He claimed that nobody can occupy the territory of barbarian peoples and lamented that 'the true end of the occupation of territories is the enrichment of the strong to the detriment of the weak'.[190] The 'pretended right to spread civilisation' had been used to 'despoil savage peoples of their sovereignty'.[191] 'We know', he said, 'with what casualness the powers have treated ... the rights of indigenous peoples: neither their institutions, their property, their goods, nor, most of all, has their sovereignty as states been respected.'[192] He continued: 'publicists, in favour of respect for their right of sovereignty, such as Francisco de Vitoria, Domingo de Soto, Diego Covarrubias and

[185] *Ibid.*, p. 177.
[186] *Ibid.*, pp. 176–7. On the use of this argument in practice to dispossess Native Americans, see Michael Paul Rogin, *Fathers and children: Andrew Jackson and the subjugation of the American Indian* (New York, 1975).
[187] Bluntschli, *Le droit international codifié*, p. 177. [188] *Ibid.*
[189] Pradier-Fodéré, *Principes généraux de droit, de politique et de législation*, p. 525.
[190] Despagnet, *Cours de droit international public*, p. 433. [191] *Ibid.*
[192] Frantz Despagnet, *Essai sur les protectorats* (Paris, 1896), p. 241.

Francisco Suarez were without effect in stopping the monstrous abuses of force against the weakest races'.[193] This 'lamentable history' was well known, he observed, and it would seem 'that the series of horrors observed in the past have not completely ended'.[194] He concluded, therefore, that the 'propaganda of civilisation' could only justify the nourishment of pacific relations with barbarian countries, including the right of communication and trade.[195] 'An absolute respect', he declared, 'was due to all sovereignty, even barbarian.'[196]

Despagnet's absolute respect for sovereignty meant that any peoples who were not perceived to live in sovereign political systems could have the sovereignty of their territory occupied, while their property remained intact. We can, he argued, 'consider as susceptible to occupation a land inhabited by groups without appreciable political organisation, who don't even have a conception of sovereignty and who cannot, as a consequence, make a claim to that right. We can, in the same manner, recognise a right of property or at least an anterior possession, but of sovereignty there is no question'.[197] It was on these principles that in his later work on the diplomacy of the Third Republic, he argued forcefully to justify French occupations, or 'protectorates', in Africa, including Tunisia and Brazza's civilising mission in the Congo.[198]

Bonfils too can be placed amongst those who rejected the civilising mission and the wave of empire that followed in its wake, but at the same time admitted the possibility whereby European powers could expand through the cession of sovereignty. When Bonfils turned to the acquisition of territory, he commented that it was a 'controversial question amongst publicists' whether a 'territory occupied by savage and barbarian tribes can be considered as *res nullius* and susceptible to occupation'.[199] He observed that three 'theses' propose themselves on this question. The first, which was adopted from the fifteenth to the seventeenth centuries, was that savage and barbarian peoples 'have no right to the earth that they occupy, no right of property and certainly no right of sovereignty'.[200] This argument, he noted, was rejected by Vitoria and Bartolomé de Las Casas. Amongst the jurists of the *Institut de droit international*, Vitoria became a ubiquitous authority for sceptics of colonisation and humanitarian apologists for colonisation alike. Many devoted large sections of their treatises to

[193] *Ibid.*, p. 242. [194] *Ibid.* [195] Despagnet, *Cours de droit international public*, p. 434.
[196] *Ibid.* [197] *Ibid.*
[198] Koskenniemi, *The gentle civilizer of nations*, pp. 272–3; Despagnet, *La diplomatie de la Troisième République*.
[199] Bonfils, *Manuel de droit international public*, p. 305. [200] *Ibid.*

exegeses of his arguments. Ernest Nys made Vitoria a central figure in his many histories of international law, arguing that Vitoria's pages 'breathed with the love of humanity'.[201] In 1917, he published Vitoria's works for the Carnegie Foundation.

A more substantive critique of empire was launched in response to the new imperialism of the 1880s, particularly in the work of two French jurists, Charles Salomon and Gaston Jèze, but also in debates within the *Institut* in the years immediately after the Berlin Conference. We will return to this critique after first considering in more detail the context to which it responded – namely, the debates surrounding the Berlin Conference over the justice of the projection of European sovereignty and the invention of a new legal instrument in those debates, *territorium nullius*, for examining that question.

[201] Ernest Nys, *Les origines du droit international* (Brussels, 1894), p. 129 (see also pp. 126–9); and Ernest Nys, *Etudes de droit international et de droit politique* (Brussels, 1896), pp. 126–7.

CHAPTER 8

Res nullius and sovereignty

As we saw in Chapter 2, the term 'res nullius' was absent in Roman law discussions of occupation. It was established through medieval jurists' attempts to bring order to Roman law. It did not become a common concept in the law of nations before the eighteenth century. Historians' accounts of *res nullius* have paid little or no attention to the different meanings of the term depending on whether it was employed by the writers who assumed that rights over property could exist independently of agreement or community, or by those who argued that property rights were the creation of compact. Well into the eighteenth century, *res nullius* was only partially concerned with questions of land ownership, even if those questions are what have most attracted recent historians' interest. Moreover, historians have used *res nullius* to articulate the doctrine that the first person to take something becomes the owner, but it was also frequently used to describe things that could not be occupied.[1] Finally, the historical understanding of the concept takes little account of the fact that many accounts of *res nullius* were more concerned with private property in civil law than public questions in the law of nations, nor do they take account of the complex relationship between those private civil law discussions of *res nullius* and its broader use in the law of nations.

The increasing use of *res nullius* in the eighteenth century was linked to discussions of the occupation of property in empire. In the nineteenth century, attempts were made to distinguish *res nullius* as a theory of private law concerning property from matters concerning the occupation of sovereignty, or *territorium nullius*, in the public international law of nations. These nineteenth-century jurists acknowledged that public international law was more than the positive law of treaty and drew upon

[1] A point made in Fitzmaurice, 'A genealogy of *terra nullius*'; and Benton and Straumann, 'Acquiring empire by law'.

private Roman law for many of its principles.[2] They accordingly attempted to restrict *res nullius* to its private Roman law origins while developing a new theory of occupation in public international law.

Each of these problems underlies a larger point: namely, that *res nullius* was not a transhistorical concept. Having been established by medieval jurists, *res nullius* was adopted in the law of nations in the seventeenth century, and by the eighteenth century it was employed as part of an effort to codify the rules governing the behaviour of modern states. It was thus part of a vocabulary that sought to define and limit the modern state itself. As part of this process, *res nullius*, like many political concepts, was a tool rather than simply a doctrine. Whereas it has been represented as a doctrine of territorial appropriation, it was an instrument used both to legitimise colonisation and also to critique it. Indeed, an examination of *res nullius* reveals some of the deep tensions between state and empire.

Grotius appears to have been one of the first theorists of the *ius gentium* to employ *res nullius*, although the issue is confused and complicated by the fact that his modern translators inserted the term into the Anglophone editions of his works more frequently than he actually employed it.[3] It was the translater Gwladys L. Williams who inserted *res nullius* into Grotius' account of the origin of property in the Carnegie Endowment edition of *De jure praedae*.[4] Significantly, however, for later discussions of prizes at sea, Grotius employed *res nullius* in his analysis of the right of acquiring things taken in war. Here he declared: 'we say that the nations have decided that the property of enemies should stand to enemies in the same relation as

[2] For the argument that nineteenth-century public international law drew upon private Roman law principles and was thus more than a body of positive law, see Lauterpacht, *Private law sources and analogies in international law*; and Lesaffer, 'Argument from Roman Law in current international law'.

[3] Christopher Tomlins argues that the references to *res nullius* in Grotius' *Mare liberum* and *De jure belli ac pacis* were inserted by his modern translators. This claim is also true for Grotius' *De jure praedae*, but, as we shall see below, some references to *res nullius* in *De jure belli ac pacis* are to be found in the 1645 edition of the work. The term '*res nullius*' is absent from Alberico Gentili, *De Legationibus libri tres*, vol. 1, a photographic reproduction of the edition of 1594 with an introduction by Ernest Nys (New York, 1924). Compare Straumann, 'The Corpus iuris as a source of law between sovereigns', pp. 113–15. *Res nullius* is also absent from the discussion of occupation in Francisco Suárez, *Selections from three works*, 2 vols. (Oxford, 1944).

[4] Hugo Grotius, *De jure praedae commentarius*, vol. 1, a translation by Gwladys L. Williams of the 1604 manuscript (Oxford, 1950), p. 232. Williams' translation is in turn the basis for the text of the Liberty Fund edition; see Hugo Grotius, *Commentary on the law of prize and booty*, ed. Martine Julia van Ittersum (Indianapolis, 2006), p. xxiii on the text. Compare Hugo Grotius, *De jure praedae commentarius*, vol. 2, the collotype reproduction of the original 1604 manuscript in the handwriting of Grotius (Oxford, 1950), 102 recto and verso.

ownerless property [*res nullius*]'.[5] As we saw in Chapter 4, for Grotius, property was a creation of agreement, or compacts, rather than an uncoveyanced product of natural law. It just so happened that after dividing the earth amongst themselves, the various peoples of the planet decided that those things in which property had not already been determined by division would become the property of the first taker. It is for this reason that Grotius says that the peoples of the earth 'decided' that the property of enemies could be treated as 'res nullius'. *Res nullius* therefore became the creation of agreement and human law rather than a direct form of natural law.

Perhaps the most serious problem in accounts of *res nullius* has been a failure to recognise that, insofar as the *ius gentium*, the law of nations or international law were concerned, it was largely a creation of the natural law argument that property is a product of compact. Because *res nullius* has been identified as a principle of Roman law, which presents occupation as a principle of the law of nature, it has been thought to concern the possibility of creating property outside law or without any form of conveyance (or it has simply not been placed in the context of distinctions between different natural law understandings of property).[6] In terms of seventeenth-century natural law, such an understanding could be consistent with Locke's theory of property (although Locke did not use the term). Many discussions of *res nullius* in the law of nations assumed, however, that *res nullius* was a human law which post-dates the first division of property by humankind. For seventeenth-century compact theorists (particularly Grotius and Pufendorf), that which was nobody's was in such a state not simply because it had not been used or exploited, but because it had been *agreed* in the first division of things that such things would belong to no one.

According to the natural law argument that property could be created by taking something in nature without human compact, to say something was not *res nullius* would be to say that property exists, but it was not necessarily to declare the existence or immanence of sovereignty. For seventeenth-century compact theorists, to say that something was not *res nullius* was an indicator of a progression towards or of the presence of sovereignty as well as property. This presence or immanence of sovereignty in the assumptions of seventeenth-century natural law made *res nullius* a

[5] Hugo Grotius, *De jure belli ac pacis*, 2 vols. (Washington DC, 1913, a reproduction of the edition of 1646), vol. 1, p. 476: 'dicimus gentibus placuisse ut res hostium hostibus essent non alio loco quam quo sunt *res nullius*'.

[6] The most recent discussion of this type is Benton and Straumann, 'Acquiring empire by law'. As I will argue, *res nullius* was precisely the creation of a 'conveyanced' understanding of property

more powerful tool in the defence of non-European peoples than the understanding of the term that implied no conveyance of property.

Although *res nullius* was being established as a term in the law of nations, that process was taking place slowly and it received little systematic treatment throughout the seventeenth century. While Pufendorf made extensive use of the Roman law of the first taker, he did not use the term 'res nullius' in his discussions of occupation. There is no mention of *res nullius* in his *De officio hominis et civis* in the editions published in 1701, 1708, 1715 or 1724. *Res nullius* finally made an appearance in a 1735 edition of Pufendorf's *Duty of man*, but only in the notes of the Cambridge-based editor Thomas Johnson. This use of *res nullius* is where we would expect to find it: namely, in Book 1, Chapter 12 on the origin of property. In Pufendorf's longer work, *De Jure naturae et gentium*, upon which *De officio* was based, there was again no discussion of *res nullius* (although the term does appear in the introduction to the Carnegie Endowment edition of that work).

Textbooks of Roman law cited *res nullius* in an increasingly reified way in the eighteenth century. Thus, in his textbook *Summary of the Roman law*, published in 1772, John Taylor, Rector of Lawford in Essex, included the large subheading '*RES NULLIUS*', which he defined as: 'Things that lie in common; parts of the world not yet discovered, animals not claimed.'[7] Taylor claimed to be describing Roman law as it was codified and yet he introduced not only 'res nullius' as a category, but also emphasised 'parts of the world not yet discovered'. We find the same emphasis in another textbook from the second half of the eighteenth century, this time in Alexander Adam's *Roman antiquities; or, an account of the manners and customs of the Romans*, published in Edinburgh in 1791. Adam was the Rector of Edinburgh High School. He declared that: 'Things which properly belonged to no body, were called *RES NULLIUS*; as, parts of the world not yet discovered, animals not claimed.'[8] It is less noteworthy that Adam repeats Taylor's formulation of *res nullius* verbatim than that, like Taylor, he was claiming to report a principle in Roman law and culture. This reification of occupation as *res nullius* in eighteenth-century textbooks shaped modern accounts of Roman law, notably William Buckland's classic *A textbook of Roman law from Augustus to Justinian*, thereby contributing to recent scholars' sense of *res nullius* as a transhistorical concept.[9]

[7] John Taylor, *Summary of the Roman law* (London, 1772), p. 244.

[8] Alexander Adam, *Roman antiquities; or, an account of the manners and customs of the Romans* (Edinburgh, 1791), p. 50.

[9] William Warwick Buckland, *A textbook of Roman law from Augustus to Justinian* (Cambridge, 1921), pp. 184–5. For the discussion of *occupatio* in Roman law in terms of *res nullius*, see also Alan Watson, *The law of property in the later Roman republic* (Oxford, 1968), pp. 62–74.

Res nullius and civil law

Many of the eighteenth-century discussions of *res nullius* were drawn from examples of civil law rather than the law of nations. The law of nations acquired the notion of *res nullius* from its great debt to Roman and civil law. Roman law principles of occupancy, including the law of the first taker, were adopted in the civil law codes of a number of European states and principalities. After the middle of the eighteenth century, Prussia became one exception to this rule. In his codification of the civil law, Frederick II (or Frederick the Great) of Prussia, or rather his First Minister, Samuel von Cocceji, who compiled the code, abolished many supposedly confusing doctrines.[10] The first thing Cocceji abolished was *res nullius.* Consistent with Frederick's absolutist pretensions, Cocceji declared that anything that belonged to nobody was the sovereign's property and that *res nullius* did not therefore exist in Prussia. For Cocceji, as for Grotius, *res nullius* was a creation of human law rather than the law of nature and so he could endorse that law or refuse it at his will. As the English translation of the Frederician Code put it in 1761: 'it has been shown to be unnecessary to bring into this division [of things] things which belong to nobody (*res nullius*), because, according to the constitution of the empire, they belong to the royalties'.[11]

In England it is often said that the civil law had little or no application because of the primacy of the common law, but the independence of the common law from civil law has been greatly over-stated. English common lawyers from Bracton to Blackstone acknowledged debts to the civil law. There were chairs in civil law at Oxford and Cambridge and ecclesiastical law, including marriage law, was conducted in civil law through to the mid-nineteenth century, while Admiralty law still is. The Doctors' Commons, the college of civil lawyers, held a role, albeit a secondary one, alongside the common law Inns of Court. The civilians from the Doctors' Commons were charged with advising the government on matters concerning the law of nations.[12] The debt to civil law was evident in treatises such as Samuel Hallifax's *An analysis of the Roman civil law, compared with the laws of England*, published in 1774. Hallifax, the Cambridge Professor

[10] For Cocceji, see Haakonssen, *Natural law and moral philosophy*, pp. 135–45.

[11] *The Frederician Code*, 2 vols. (Edinburgh 1761), vol. 1, p. 351. On the translation of the Code as part of the British debates over law reform in the 1750s and early 60s, see Haakonssen, *Natural law and moral philosophy*, p. 138.

[12] Squibb, *Doctors' Commons*. See also Fitzmaurice, 'The resilience of natural law in the writings of Sir Travers Twiss'.

of Civil Law, included a discussion of *res nullius* under 'the natural modes of acquiring property', which in its use of upper case letters reflected the increasingly reified nature of the term: 'Things as had been possessed by no one before called RES NULLIUS.'[13]

Scotland, in contrast to England, maintained civil law as the foundation of its legal system and Scottish treatises on the civil law consistently dealt with *res nullius* throughout the eighteenth century. Lord John Maclaurin Dreghorn wrote in *Observations on some points of law* published in Edinburgh in 1759 under 'Observation XXIII' entitled '*Res nullius*': 'By the laws of Scotland, things which never had an owner, e.g. pearls found on the shore of the sea, &c. *cedunt occupanti.*'[14] It comes as no surprise, therefore, to find that the idea of *res nullius* played a role in the *Decisions* of the Scottish Court of Sessions in the eighteenth century. Robert Carmichael, for example, brought a case on 20 November 1787 against the landowner Sir James Colquhoun in which he demanded access to Colquhoun's estate in order to fish for trout. Colquhoun declared that 'Trout-fishings are not more *res nullius*, or less capable of appropriation, than salmon-fishings' and salmon were explicitly a part of Colquhoun's title deeds. However, the court decided that 'trouts were *res nullius* in ... that any person standing on a high-road, or other public ground contiguous to the stream, might lawfully catch them'.[15] Similarly, the Earl of Breadalbane brought proceedings against a gentleman, Thomas Livingston, who had hunted game on his estate without permission. Livingston responded that 'in Scotland, the animals that come under that denomination [namely, game] being *res nullius*, they according to the principles of Roman law, *cedunt occupanti*'.[16]

Roman law had been the basis of the medieval *jus gentium*, or the law of peoples. By the seventeenth century, the *jus gentium* was being described as the law of nations or the *droit des gens*. Thus, the foundations of the law of nations were in the Roman or civil law. There was, therefore, sometimes a

13 Samuel Hallifax, *An analysis of the Roman civil law, compared with the laws of England* (London, 1774), pp. 22–3. See also Thomas Wood's *Institute of the imperial or civil law* (London, 1704), which also according to the title page showed how 'the Laws of England' 'differ from it [civil law]'; or John Ayliffe's *A new pandect of Roman civil law* (London, 1734), which, as its title page stated, showed how 'Law differs from the Municipal Laws of Great-Britain'.

14 John Maclaurin Dreghorn, *Observations on some points of law* (Edinburgh, 1759), p. 78. See also Lord Andrew MacDowall Bankton, *Institute of the laws of Scotland in civil rights* (Edinburgh, 1751), pp. 85 and 89.

15 *Decisions of the Court of Sessions from November 1787 to August 1788*, collected by William Steuart and Robert Craigie (Edinburgh, 1789), pp. 10–11.

16 *Ibid.*, p. 276.

fine line between European civil law that we see, for example, operating in the Scottish Court of Sessions, and the law of nations. This fine line was evident in the case of the ship called the *Joanna Catherina*, previously known as the *John and Robert of Newcastle*. The *Joanna Catherina* was seized in Aberdeen when it was under control of the Danish master John Matthias Brink. In 1757, at the height of the Seven Years' War, the *John and Robert of Newcastle* was captured by French pirates off the coast of Denmark. It was taken to the town of Christiansands in Denmark (which remained neutral during the war), where it was judged by the law of nations, specifically by the law of prizes in war, to be the property of the captor. The ship was sold at public auction to a merchant in Christiansands, Christian Severine Balle, who gave her the new name of *Joanna Catherina* and placed her under the command of John Mathias Brink. When Brink arrived in Aberdeen, Robert Benton, a Newcastle merchant and former owner of the *John and Robert*, had the ship seized by the Admiralty Court and commenced proceedings to regain ownership or, as he saw it, possession. The case reached the Court of Sessions, where John Mathias Brink argued that in a state of war, the goods of an enemy are treated as *res nullius*. Brink, or his counsel, declared that: 'This matter is treated by the doctors of the civil law . . . where they are considered to be in the same state with the *res nullius quae sunt primo occupantium*. And the doctrine is established by numberless texts of the law itself.' Brink continued on to cite the *Institutes* of Roman law, Grotius and Pufendorf in order to establish this principle of *res nullius*. In appealing to Grotius and Pufendorf, Brink underlined an understanding of *res nullius* which he assumed in his own discussion – namely, that *res nullius* was accepted as law by virtue of the agreement of the society of nations and not because the law of the first taker was believed to apply in nature. Indeed, Scottish civil law recognised the principle of *res nullius* and the ship was returned to Brink.

It was not always necessary, however, to recognise *res nullius* in civil law in order to employ it in the law of nations. After having banished the *res nullius* law from his kingdom, Frederick II championed the same idea as it applied to the law of nations. He was greatly concerned by the fact that Prussian ships were being taken as prizes by English pirates in the years preceding the Seven Years' War. The injury was all the worse given that England and Prussia were allies against France. Frederick was sufficiently concerned to have published a pamphlet in Berlin and London in 1752 arguing the cause of his subjects whose ships had been taken as prizes. In this pamphlet, Abraham Louis Michell argued on Frederick's behalf, employing the very term Frederick had removed from Prussian civil law – namely, *res nullius*. This was the same principle Frederick had abolished in domestic law because all things that belonged to no one belonged to him. He was obliged to engage with this idea in the law of nations in order to defend the property of his subjects in international space. There was, however, a difference. The principle 'res nullius' banished by Frederick was that whereby things belonging to no one become the property of the first taker. The interpretation of *res nullius* employed on his behalf in the law of nations is equivalent to Grotius' doctrine of freedom of the sea and refers to those things which belong to all or are *res communis*. According to Michell, 'eighteen Prussian ships have been stopped by English privateers' in a manner that was 'equally unjustifiable and illegal'. 'This procedure', Michell continued, 'is visibly contrary to the Law of Nature and Nations; according to which, it stands a principle universally acknowledged by all reasonable Countries, that the sea is in the Number of those Things called *res nullius*, or of which Man cannot make himself Master.'[17] Michell understood *res nullius* to be a law that arises from universal agreement, a human law, rather than a law that arises directly from nature. Moreover, it was a law established by countries rather than individuals.

Disputes arising from the law of prizes in war in the conflicts preceding and during the Seven Years' War stimulated what was by now the established idea of *res nullius* in the law of nations. A measure of just how important this term had become in the law of nations can be seen from its employment in the mid-eighteenth-century treatises on the relatively new commerce in insurance, particularly shipping insurance. The German merchant Nicholas Magens, writing in *An essay on insurances* in Hamburg in 1755, attacked the English pirating of Prussian vessels and cited Michell's treatise on the subject from three years earlier, again repeating the argument that the sea is amongst those things which are *res nullius* and cannot therefore be a place of which anyone is master.[18] The significant aspect of these discussions of *res nullius* is that they arose not in the struggle between England and France over the vast territories of North America, but in the context of the law of war-prizes. It was not possible even at this advanced stage of the eighteenth century to say that the term

[17] Abraham Louis Michell, *Exposition of the motives founded upon the universally received law of nations, which have determined the King (of Prussia) upon the repeated instances of his subjects trading by sea, to lay an attachment upon the capital funds, which his majesty had promised to reimburse to the subjects of Great-Britain, in virtue of the peace-treaties of Breslau and Dresden* (London, 1752), p. 25.

[18] Nicholas Magens, *An essay on insurances* (London, 1755), p. 448.

'res nullius' had yet become focused on the question of land even if land had become part of its jurisdiction.

Res nullius and common property

It is evident from a number of cases above that not all uses of *res nullius* concerned questions of whether a thing had been subject to occupation or not. Many discussions of *res nullius* sought to show that certain things could not be subject to occupation. Building on Grotius' use of the Roman law of occupation to show that the sea cannot be occupied, numerous discussions of *res nullius* employed the term to describe things which were *not* subject to occupation. Thomas Wood, the Rector of Hardwick in Buckinghamshire, argued in 1704 in *A new institute of the imperial or civil law* that '*Res nullius* (or Things which are not the Goods of any Person or Number of Men) are those that are of a Divine Right'. 'Things therefore of a Divine Right', he continues, 'are those that are exempted from the promiscuous Use of Men, and are in a Manner the Property of God only; of which there are three sorts, Res Sacrae, Res Religiosae, Res Sanctae.' Under these headings, he included churches, graveyards and ambassadors. Surprisingly, Wood explicitly excludes from *res nullius* precisely those things in Roman law which were described as the property of the first occupant: 'Wild Beasts, Birds, Fishes and Pearl found in the Sea are not to be reckoned under this Head, being of a private Nature, and capable of a Proprietor.'[19] Wood's discussion alerts us to the care that must be exercised when we attend to the meaning that an historical agent employs when he or she describes something as *res nullius*. Wood's understanding of *res nullius* as things which cannot be occupied is not exceptional. The lawyer George Wallace in his *A system of the principle of the law of Scotland*, published in 1760, wrote that: 'Things, which belong to nobody, *res nullius*, are such as either want an owner or are not the property of private persons.' In this class he included things which were 'appropriable', that is, things susceptible to occupation and ownership, things which were derelict (that is, things which had had an owner but no longer did so) and, finally, things in the sense discussed by Grotius as incapable of ownership and described in Roman law as *res communis*: 'Such, for instance, is the air, the sea, and every thing which . . . is common.'[20] Francis Hutcheson similarly

[19] Thomas Wood, *A new institute of the imperial or civil law* (London, 1704), pp. 67–8; and Thomas Wood, *A new institute of the imperial or civil law*, 4th edition (London, 1730), p. 142.

[20] George Wallace, *A system of the principle of the law of Scotland* (Edinburgh, 1760), p. 102.

argued that: 'The goods called by the Civilians *res nullius*, which as they say, are not in property, and yet not exposed to occupation, such as temples, the fortifications of cities, and burial places, are truly the property either of larger societies, or of families.'[21] Here *res nullius* was, once again, indicative of the presence rather than the absence of society. In this sense it shares the Grotian assumption that *res nullius* is a law concerning property that is established by agreement rather than existing in nature.

Res nullius as a critique of colonisation

When *res nullius* was used in discussions of colonisation, it was used as often to assert and defend the rights of people being colonised as it was to justify dispossession.[22] This scepticism of colonisation was evident in Adam Ferguson's understanding of the law of *res nullius* in *Principles of moral and political science* (1792), in which he stated that 'in the history of rights, the first question relates to things which, prior to the origin of the right in question had not become matter of right to any one [and in the margin he notes that these things are "*res nullius*"]'. 'The object of science', he argued, 'is to ascertain by what means a thing till then open to the first occupier, may have become a matter of exclusive right to some particular person.'[23] To this question, he responded that 'we may answer in general, that things belonging to no one may become matter of right to some one, either by mere occupancy, or in consequence of labour employed to improve or accommodate the subject to use'.[24] He moves on at length to forms of colonial occupation and concedes that if nations have agreed to the principles amongst themselves, various kinds of symbols and so-called rights of discovery may be treated as a form of occupation in the short term when claiming new territories. He added, however, that no such agreement is sufficient to 'exclude' the rights of 'any stranger who is not a party' to the convention, 'much less a plea sufficient to deprive the native, however rude or barbarous, of the inheritance of possession to which he is born'.[25] He argued that such symbolic acts and discoveries cannot, therefore, 'be derived, either from the principle of occupancy, or the principle of labour'. 'Such', he concluded, 'are the ways in which a subject,

[21] Francis Hutcheson, *A short introduction to moral philosophy in three books*, 2nd edn (Glasgow 1753), bk. 2, p. 150.

[22] Anthony Pagden is one of the few contemporary historians to have appreciated this point in his discussions of *ferae bestiae*. It has also been emphasised by Fitzmaurice, 'A genealogy of *terra nullius*'; and Benton and Straumann, 'Acquiring empire by law'.

[23] Ferguson, *Principles of moral and political science*, p. 201. [24] *Ibid.*, p. 202. [25] *Ibid.*, p. 212.

the right of no one ["*res nullius*" is again the marginal subtitle] may become the right of some one; either while he occupies it, or in consequence of the effect he has produced in it by his labour.'[26]

In a fashion reminiscent of Vitoria's use of *ferae bestiae*, Ferguson thus employed *res nullius* to show that the lands in which even the most supposedly primitive peoples lived could not be understood as unoccupied, or as having not been taken, and could not therefore be considered to be *res nullius*. Indeed, for Ferguson, these people were merely pursuing the perfection of which they are capable and which is appropriate to their circumstances. Here we see *res nullius* used not to describe things held in common, but closer to the more commonly understood sense employed by historians in the twenty-first century as meaning things which were not appropriated by anyone. But the salient aspect of this discussion is that *res nullius* was used not, as is commonly assumed, to legitimise dispossession, but to oppose it.

While Ferguson echoed Vitoria's defence of the rights of non-European peoples, he placed his theory of occupation in the context of a very different understanding of property from both that assumed by Vitoria on the one hand and the seventeenth-century natural law theorists on the other. The occupier, he claimed, has an 'exclusive right' to whatever he is the first to occupy, but this right of possession 'does not amount to property'.[27] Possession becomes property 'when mankind willingly enter into conventions'.[28] For Ferguson, as for Grotius, the *res nullius* law was a product of one such convention. He concluded that the territory of non-European peoples, 'however rude or barbarous', was not *res nullius* because he believed they had already entered into conventions. Yet he rejected much of the apparatus of seventeenth-century natural law. Like Hutcheson before him, and others in the Scottish historical school, he dismissed the notion of a state of nature as hypothetical speculation.[29] Without the state of nature to provide the motives and, in some accounts, the conditions for the development of property, it would become necessary for philosophers such as Ferguson, Hume and Smith to substitute the seventeenth-century natural law theorists' abstract and hypothetical basis to property with an account of the development property in historical time. What these theorists took, however, from seventeenth-century natural law was an understanding of property, and laws regarding property such as *res nullius*, as a product of compact. In this respect they shared an understanding of *res*

[26] *Ibid.*, p. 213. [27] *Ibid.*, pp. 203 and 204. [28] *Ibid.*, p. 205.
[29] Adam Ferguson, *Essay on the history of civil society* (London, 1767), pp. 3–20.

nullius as a matter of convention and it was this understanding of *res nullius* as a human convention, rather than a natural law, that made it palatable for nineteenth-century positivism.

Res nullius and international law

It was in the context of the development of international law in the nineteenth century that *res nullius* attracted greatest attention. As discussed in the previous chapter, in nineteenth-century international law, positivism did not entirely eclipse natural law and nor were positivists always hostile to natural law thinking. Commonly, positivism, natural law, historicism and public opinion became part of one synthetic and eclectic way of understanding law in a space where there was an absence of property or sovereignty.

In the nineteenth century, *res nullius* came to refer more often than not to things which could be occupied (as opposed to those which could not). German public lawyers writing on the law of nations in the early nineteenth century typified this tendency. Thus, the German jurist Johann Ludwig Klüber declared: 'A state can acquire things which belong to nobody (*res nullius*) by occupation.'[30] *Res nullius* was also far more frequently employed in discussions of empire than had previously been the case. A salient aspect of this international law scholarship on *res nullius* was that it maintained the polemical force of Vitoria's discussion of occupation in order to raise questions about the justice of colonisation.

As we have seen in the previous chapter, the authors in the new discipline of international law were a cosmopolitan community. These jurists and diplomats spoke, corresponded and, with the creation of the *Institut de droit international* in 1873, met as one society. Their aim was to establish a set of rules which would govern the behaviour of states and could, accordingly, minimise conflicts between states. One of their main concerns within this aim was to establish the principles by which territory could be occupied. The occupation of territory through colonisation became increasingly feared as a source of tension in the delicate balance between the great powers of the nineteenth century. Many of the international jurists can be regarded as apologists for contemporary colonising

[30] Jean-Louis Klüber, *Droit des gens* (Paris, 1831), p. 209. See also Martens, *Précis du droit des gens moderne de l'Europe*, vol. 1, p. 117. *Res nullius* did continue, however, to be used in reference to common property; see, for example, Heffter, *Le droit international public de l'Europe*, p. 134, who used *res nullius* to encompass both categories – that is, those things that were nobody's because they could not be appropriated and those things which simply had not been appropriated.

practices because, while they rejected the dispossession of 'civilised' peoples, they were prepared to regard the territories of 'savage' or nomadic peoples as 'res nullius'. A further group of these writers, however, were strongly sceptical not only of the civilising mission but also of civilisation itself and they used the idea of *res nullius* in order to defend the rights of colonised peoples.[31]

For many of these authors, Vitoria was also the source for the theory of *res nullius*. This attribution of the theory to Vitoria would appear to be one source of recent historical confusions about *res nullius*. Importantly, these jurists, even the apologists for colonisation amongst them, generally used the term to state a negative thesis – namely, that the goods and land of non-European peoples *cannot* be considered as 'belonging to no one' and therefore *are not res nullius*. Both the link with Vitoria and the negative character of the term are evident in the French jurist Charles Salomon's observations on the legal apology for the Spanish conquest: 'If that point of view [the idea of natural slavery] is correct, the Spanish had the right to occupy that land, because all the territory discovered was *res nullius*, was unappropriated. Vitoria rejected without trouble this reasoning.'[32] Similarly, Henry Bonfils, Professor of Law at the University of Toulouse, demanded: 'Can territory occupied by barbarous and savage tribes be susceptible to acquisition by occupation?'[33] And he replied: 'This was the doctrine generally adopted by the authors of the fifteenth, sixteenth and seventeenth centuries but rejected by Vitoria.'[34] It was into this context that Franz Despagnet brought his understanding of *res nullius*: 'territory ruled even by a barbarian sovereignty and organised in a rudimentary manner must not be regarded as *res nullius*'.[35]

The distinction between a natural law which argued for rights which exist outside positive law and one which saw rights as the creation of states was not always clearly made by the nineteenth-century international jurists.[36] Vitoria was valued for his scepticism of empire. He gave weight

[31] Compare Koskenniemi, *The gentle civilizer of nations*. Koskenniemi portrays nineteenth-century international lawyers as liberal critics of state sovereignty. Following Antony Anghie (*Imperialism, sovereignty and the making of international law*), he argues that the exception to this liberal critique was the jurists' apology for the imperial projection of sovereignty.

[32] Charles Salomon, *L'occupation des territoires sans maître* (Paris, 1887), p. 44.

[33] Bonfils, *Manuel de droit international public*, p. 305. [34] *Ibid.*

[35] Despagnet, *Cours de droit international public*, p. 598. See also Despagnet, *Essai sur les protectorats*, p. 243; Gaston Jèze, *Étude théorique et pratique sur l'occupation* (Paris, 1896), pp. 121–4; Ernest Nys, *Droit international. Les principes, les théories, les faits*, 3 vols. (Brussels, 1904), vol. 2, pp. 79–80; Édouard Engelhardt, 'Étude sur la déclaration de la conférence de Berlin relative aux occupations', *Revue de droit international et de législation comparée*, 18 (1886), 573–86, at 577.

[36] See Tuck, 'Modern natural law'. Tuck perhaps over-states the degree of misunderstanding.

to the Enlightenment critique of the occupation of property, while remaining ambivalent on the occupation of sovereignty that had become the focus of nineteenth-century European expansion.[37] Certainly, these nineteenth-century jurists often shared the assumption, common to seventeenth-century natural law theory and the historical school, that *res nullius* was a law that had been created by compacts and therefore was a human rather than a natural law as such. They could also read Vitoria in those terms. When they said that a particular non-European territory was not *res nullius*, they could mean not only that there was property in that place (whether particular or common property), but also that there must be some kind of sovereignty, or immanent sovereignty, no matter how barbarous the inhabitants may be.

For colonial apologists, the idea of *res nullius* could thus represent a serious impediment to their aims. It could remove the ambiguity between property and sovereignty that had been present in discussions of the rights of non-Europeans since Vitoria brought *ferae bestiae* into the question. The idea of *res nullius* as the creation of positive law could be employed in such a way as to leave little doubt that non-European peoples possessed sovereignty. Colonial apologists sought to overcome this obstacle by representing the principle of *res nullius* as a matter of private law rather than public international law (as it had indeed been in early modern civil law and as it remains in European civil law to this day) and by raising the bar on the political status needed to qualify for membership in the law of nations – namely, from 'personal sovereignty', which was believed to prevail in pre-modern societies, to 'territorial sovereignty'. This understanding of *res nullius* focused, as we shall see in the following chapter, on its replacement with a cognate term, *territorium nullius*, which would measure *territorial* sovereignty rather than mere sovereignty.

Despite these efforts, *res nullius* continued to flourish as a term in public international law throughout the twentieth century. Jurists and diplomats found the concept to be particularly useful in discussions of occupation of the polar regions and the Space Race.[38] Their analyses revived the sense of

[37] Koksenniemi argues that Vitoria was valued by late nineteenth-century jurists for his 'universally applicable legal vocabulary'. See Martti Koskenniemi, 'Colonization of the "Indies": the origin of international law?', unpublished manuscript, 2009, available at: www.helsinki.fi/eci/Publications/Koskenniemi/Zaragoza-10final.pdf, pp. 1–2.

[38] For the polar regions, see, for example, René Waultrin, 'La question de la souveraineté des terres arctiques', *Revue générale de droit international public*, XV (1908), 78–125. And for space, see Philip C. Jessup and Howard J. Taubenfeld, *Controls for outer space and the Antarctic analogy* (New York, 1959), pp. 18, 34–9, 181, 257–8. See also Philip C. Jessup, *The use of international law* (Ann Arbor, 1959), pp. 148–9.

res nullius as common property, so that both space and the poles were described as things that were held in common and therefore were not open to occupation. It was not until the late twentieth century that a concept of *res nullius* emerged which isolated two aspects of earlier discussions – namely, the idea that *res nullius* are things that are open to occupation and also the claim that this idea was used to justify empire and colonisation. Clearly, both meanings of the term were present from the eighteenth century. But such characterisations have largely tended to ignore the diverse and contradictory ways in which the idea of *res nullius* has been employed over the past 500 years, as well as ignoring the different natural law and historical assumptions within which it has been employed. Perhaps most importantly, this understanding has ignored the role that the concept of *res nullius* played in scepticism of colonisation.

On the face of it, the statement that that which belongs to nobody becomes the property of the first taker would appear to be fairly transparent, whether it is found in the *Digest of Justinian* or Pufendorf's *De jure naturae et gentium*. But the context radically alters the meaning of those statements. When such a claim is said to be true in 'nature', its meaning is different from when it is true only because it is a rule agreed by civil society. This Wittgensteinian point is equally true of the history of *res nullius*. For most seventeenth-century natural lawyers, civil society, or a pre-civil adventitious state, would be found wherever there is property. This convention-bound understanding of property remained true for most theorists in the Scottish historical school and for many of the eclectic international jurists of the nineteenth century. According to this view, saying that a place (to use the example of one kind of thing) was not *res nullius* – that is, that property existed in that place – also meant that civil society existed in that place or was in the process of being established. Locke and Lockeans, as well as many medieval jurists, held that rights, including property rights, could exist outside of human agreement. According to this view, the observation that property existed in a certain place, such as in America, could be highly ambiguous in terms of its implications for whether civil society existed in the same place. The natural law understanding of *res nullius* as the creation of human convention provided a potentially far more powerful defence of indigenous rights than what could be achieved with unconveyanced understanding of the law of occupation.

CHAPTER 9

Territorium nullius *and Africa*

Over the past thirty years, historians have exposed liberalism's complicity in empire.[1] Many figures in the liberal canon had close ties with colonial enterprises. More importantly, they developed central aspects of their philosophies through reflection on the relative status of European and non-European peoples, and consideration of the political and economic problems of empire and global commerce. The progressive or stadial theory of history, which was central to the liberal outlook, was developed through the experience of empire. Stadial theory described a hierarchical system in which the European state sat at the top with a cascade of lesser political societies below. It was a view of the world that allowed Europeans to justify empire through the projection of their understanding of sovereignty onto societies which they judged to be inferior.

This account of liberal thought and empire has become so historiographically dominant that it has obscured the depth of liberal opposition to empire. It is true that liberalism acted as an engine of empire, but the liberal tradition also generated debates over the justice of empire. As we saw in the previous chapter, self-described 'liberal' thinkers opposed and

[1] B. Parekh, 'Liberalism and colonialism: a critique of Locke and Mill', in J. N. Pieterse and B. Parekh (eds.), *The decolonization of imagination: culture, knowledge and power* (London, 1995); James Tully, *Strange multiplicity: constitutionalism in the age of diversity* (Cambridge, 1995); Singh Mehta, *Liberalism and empire*; Tuck, *Rights of war and peace*. John Locke has been a focal point of these studies, not because he was a liberal but because he became a rallying point for liberals: Arneil, *John Locke and America*; Tully, *An approach to political philosophy*; Armitage, 'John Locke, Carolina, and the two treatises of government'. Recent studies point to a more supple liberalism, but one still largely beholden to empire – see, for example: Duncan Bell, *The idea of Greater Britain: empire and the future of world order, 1860–1900* (Princeton, 2007); Karuna Mantena, 'The crisis of liberal imperialism', in Bell (ed.), *Victorian visions*; Pitts, *A turn to empire*; Jeanne Morefield, *'Covenants without swords': idealist liberalism and the spirit of empire* (Princeton, 2005); Caspar Sylvest, *British liberal internationalism, 1880–1930: making progress?* (Manchester, 2009); Jane Burbank and Frederick Cooper, *Empires in world history: power and the politics of difference* (Princeton, 2010). For a comprehensive review of the literature on empire and liberalism, see Pitts, 'Political theory of empire and imperialism'.

critiqued empire from a variety of motives. Many of these critiques came from international law. The law of nations and international law have in recent years been shown to have made a key contribution to the liberal apology for empire.[2] Liberals turned to international law when they sought to establish the legitimacy of empire. It was, however, within international law that a vigorous debate was conducted about the civilising mission, the hierarchy of nations and the degree to which peoples at different levels of that hierarchy possessed rights. International law created a forum for discussion about which peoples should be regarded as legitimate members of the society of nations and which would be open to the projection of European sovereignty. It was also a forum for debate about whether the European understanding of sovereignty could be used as an objective standard. In light of these debates, the emerging discipline of international law needs to be understood as something more than a liberal instrument created for the domination of global political society.

The debate over sovereignty amongst international jurists covered a spectrum of views. On the one hand, there were those who sought to impose European sovereignty on the non-European world. On the other hand, a number of jurists insisted that each society should determine the kind of sovereignty that was appropriate to it. To different degrees, this latter group expressed scepticism about both the projection of European imperial power and the civilising mission. They insisted that European sovereignty could not be used as a model for non-European societies. These sceptics of empire were not motivated by philanthropy or humanitarianism; indeed, most philanthropists and humanitarians have been correctly portrayed as apologists for empire.[3] The jurists who critiqued European empire were motivated by concern over liberty rather than with sovereignty. Freedom was as important in the liberal tradition as sovereignty, and the pursuit of freedom was frequently in tension with the demands of the state. For these jurists, empire posed a threat to the fragile freedoms that had been secured by the modern revolutions. Although those revolutions had, they argued, overthrown absolutism, empire created a space in which arbitrary rule and absolutism could return and could then be repatriated to Europe.

[2] Anghie, *Imperialism, sovereignty and the making of international law*; Koskenniemi, *The gentle civilizer of nations*.

[3] See Koskenniemi, *The gentle civilizer of nations* on humanitarian international law as an apology for empire.

These liberals were not the only nineteenth-century opponents of empire.[4] The Whiggish concern with luxury and empire continued to flourish.[5] Moreover, a third, socialist mode of opposition to empire developed over the course of the nineteenth century.[6] Finally, nineteenth-century liberals, such as the Manchester-based manufacturer Richard Cobden, launched a powerful critique of empire on the basis that it was a hazard to free trade, although these critics were happy, on the same grounds, to see the extension of what has been described as 'informal' empire.[7] In the second half of the nineteenth century, opposition to empire was nothing new, although it found new material. What was remarkable about this rights-based critique of empire, however, was that it found a place at the heart of liberalism at a time, according to recent scholarship, when it had reached the high-water mark of pro-imperial sentiment.

My intention in this chapter is to present the liberal divisions over empire through the lens of the Congo. The Congo was a focus of the great expansion of European imperial enterprise in the 1870s and 1880s. The debates about empire within international law became most heated leading up to and following the carve-up of Africa. In the 1870s, European colonial powers were increasingly drawn into conflict in their competition to seize territory in Africa. Otto von Bismarck, the Chancellor of the newly established German Empire, called a meeting of those powers who were recognised as members of the community of nations in Berlin in 1884. His intention was to establish the principles upon which European sovereignty could be extended over Africa in a manner that contained rivalries. It was expected that international law could furnish those principles. These efforts provoked innovation in the legal apparatus used to justify the extension of sovereignty over non-European peoples. But the same efforts to justify European empire also stimulated and intensified opposition which drew upon the long-standing critiques of empire. A number of the actors in this debate used the conference and its instruments to implement their particular visions of a just international legal order. The

[4] Jennifer Pitts, 'Liberalism and empire in a nineteenth-century Algerian mirror', *Modern Intellectual History*, 6(2) (2009), 287–313; Andrew Sartori, 'The British Empire and its liberal mission', *Journal of Modern History*, 78 (2006), 623–42.

[5] Miles Taylor, 'Imperium et libertas? Rethinking the radical critique of imperialism during the nineteenth century', *Journal of Imperial and Commonwealth History*, XIX (1991), 1–23.

[6] Claeys, 'The "left" and the critique of empire c.1865–1900'; Claeys, *Imperial sceptics*.

[7] For the free trade opponents to 'formal' empire, see: Gallagher and Robinson, 'The imperialism of free trade'; MacDonagh, 'The anti-imperialism of free trade'; R. J. Moore, 'Imperialism and free trade policy in India, 1853–1854', *Economic History Review*, 17 (1964), 135–45; Howe, 'Free trade and global order'.

debates between the jurists bore directly on decisions about Africa's destiny, as well as the broader world order, and they were realised through such tools as a constitution for the Congo and the creation of the concept of *territorium nullius*. The critics of these instruments would lose their struggle against the occupation of Africa, but at the same time they underlined the fact that liberalism contained resources with which it was possible to oppose empire.

The thesis that liberalism drove empire is sustained partly by the notion that concepts of universal rights were eclipsed in the nineteenth century by nationalism and positivism.[8] According to this view, rights were defined by national boundaries. The positivists scorned the idea that rights could be natural and could therefore exist outside civil authority. Rights were only guaranteed by positive law and so by the state. Positivism thus encouraged the notion that peoples outside the nation could only possess rights by virtue of possessing sovereignty. If they had no sovereignty, then they could only benefit from the rights that would come from the projection of European sovereignty. There could be no *ius gentium*, no law of peoples whereby people possessed rights as people rather than as citizens or subjects. In this way, positivism, combining powerfully with a stadial theory of sovereignty, has been seen as the epistemology of the liberal apology for empire. According to this view, if it can be shown that rights were used in the nineteenth century to justify empire, then it can reasonably be concluded that liberalism was inherently disposed to empire. A self-described liberal tradition did not emerge until the nineteenth century, so it would certainly appear to be more than a coincidence if the universal understanding of rights, which reached its peak in the Enlightenment, was buried at the historical moment liberalism was born.[9]

As we have seen in the previous chapters, however, there are problems with the representation of positivism and nationalism as hegemonic nineteenth-century discourses.[10] Positivism, public opinion, historicism and natural law combined to form a synthetic understanding of rights in the writings of many international lawyers. It was the notion of rights

8 Waldron (ed.), *Nonsense upon stilts*, pp. 151–6; Schneewind, *The invention of autonomy*; Pagden, 'Human rights, natural rights, and Europe's imperial legacy'; Moyn, *The last utopia*, p. 31.

9 Many historians and political theorists have sought the origins of liberalism in the writings of early modern authors such as Thomas Hobbes, John Locke and even John Milton. On the early modern origins of liberalism, see, for example: Macpherson, *The political theory of possessive individualism*; Annabel Patterson, *Early modern liberalism* (Cambridge, 1998).

10 For recent awareness of the limits of positivism in the nineteenth century, see: Pitts, 'Boundaries'; Sylvest, 'The foundations of Victorian international law', p. 59. See also den Otter, '"A legislating empire"', pp. 95–6; Fitzmaurice, 'The resilience of natural law in the writings of Sir Travers Twiss'.

having universal moral force, and not just as the creation of the legal regimes of states, that fed much of the liberal critique of empire during the course of the century. It may seem contradictory that jurists, who were sceptical of empire, argued both that civilisation was relative and that rights were universal. They may seem to have replaced one Eurocentric universal standard with another, but their conception of right was negative; it was a space in which different civilisations would be able to define their own understanding of the best way of life.

The different traditions of understanding rights in the history of Western political thought point to the fact that liberalism, within which rights held a central place, was itself divided. Nineteenth-century liberalism was a loose consensus on the desirability of liberty, rights and duties, freedom of commerce, the rule of law and the sanctity of property. One of the central divisions within liberalism, and in political thought prior to the existence of a self-conscious liberal tradition, was precisely over the question of whether rights were the creation of states or whether certain fundamental rights belonged to humans in nature. Both sides of this debate, which underlines what Jürgen Habermas has called the Janus-faced nature of liberalism, have produced assumptions which could be used to justify and to critique empire.[11]

The new race for empire in the 1870s and 1880s was stimulated by improvements in military and transport technologies, including rail and the steam ship (which made fast-flowing West African rivers navigable to Europeans for the first time), as well as progress in tropical medicine. Renewed French and British empires, and a new German empire, were also driven by ideologies, by national Darwinism, by capitalism and by a passionate rhetoric of the civilising mission. Jules Ferry, the French Prime Minister at the time of the Berlin Conference in 1884/5, was a champion of the new imperialism, famously declaring in July 1885: 'the superior races have a right vis-à-vis the inferior races'. This statement was not, however, made as part of a calm hegemonic discourse. Ferry was speaking during

11 Habermas, *Between facts and norms*, Chapter 3. In *The last utopia*, Samuel Moyn has recently questioned whether there existed, prior to the second half of the twentieth century, a concept of rights that was attached to persons independently of their membership of states. Moyn's thesis is built on the historical account of modern rights as bound by positive law and upon the modern natural law theorists, such as Hobbes. He is right to draw attention to the rise of a discourse of 'human rights' in the 1970s – certainly, rights meant something different to that generation than any other previously. However, he minimises the fact that theorists such as Hobbes and Pufendorf were reacting against the universalism of scholastic rights theories and he similarly under-estimates the debates that raged over the course of the eighteenth and nineteenth centuries over whether or not, and to what degree, rights could exist outside the state.

uproar in the French Parliament. He was immediately interrupted by Jules Maigne, the Left deputy from Haute-Loire, who cried: 'Oh! You dare to say that in the country where the rights of man were proclaimed.' Ferry responded by asking whether the Declaration of the Rights of Man had been written for 'black people in Equatorial Africa' and then repeated 'the superior races have a right because they have a duty. They have a duty to civilise the inferior races'. Yet again, however, he was interrupted, this time by the republican deputy Joseph Fabre, who protested: 'This is excessive! You thus succeed in the abdication of the principles of 1789 [the Revolution] and 1848 [the July Revolution] . . . and consecrate the replacement of the law of justice with prerogative law [*la loi de grâce*]'.[12] The responses to Ferry express what was at stake for the liberal critics of empire: namely, the possibility that empire would encourage the return of arbitrary rule, thus threatening the freedoms that had been won by the modern revolutions. This sentiment was strong in France, but was to be found amongst critics of empire across Europe. The opposition included strident criticism of the civilising mission, which was perceived as a direct threat to European freedom.[13]

In this context, those jurists and politicians who defended empire took a robust view of the state as the creator of rights, while those who critiqued empire employed the argument that rights exist outside the state or that non-European peoples possessed sovereignty. In this chapter, I will show how one jurist, Sir Travers Twiss, stood at one end of that spectrum in his justification of the Congo enterprise launched by King Leopold II of Belgium in the 1880s. I then turn to the increasingly polarised debates within the community of international lawyers following the Berlin Conference. Finally, I show how a rights-based anti-imperial critique developed out of those debates.

Sir Travers Twiss and the Berlin Conference

As we have seen in the previous chapters, there was a broad spectrum of views regarding empire amongst late nineteenth-century international lawyers, most of whom were members or associate members of the *Institut de droit international.* They were also divided in their views regarding

[12] Jules Ferry, speech given before the House of Representatives, 28 July 1885, in Paul Robiquet (ed.), *Discours et Opinions de Jules Ferry*, 7 vols. (Paris, 1897), vol. 5, pp. 210–11.

[13] Compare Alice L. Conklin, *A mission to civilize* (Stanford, 1997), p. 13: 'Although Ferry's policies did not go uncontested – both conservatives and the radical left criticized them – neither group questioned Ferry's claim that France had a unique civilizing mission.'

civilisation. Importantly, the divisions between these jurists deepened from the 1870s, when the *Institut* was founded, through to the 1890s. The principal cause of this polarisation of views was the scramble for Africa, which raised the stakes in the discussion of the justice of empire. Travers Twiss expressed a robust view of the rights of European nations to colonise and he developed that view further in justifying the occupation of the Congo. He wrote for much of his career in support of British interests, as we have seen, for example, in the dispute over the sovereignty of the Northwest region of North America, the Oregon Territory.[14] Apologists for empire did not always promote narrowly defined national interests and, when writing on the Congo, Twiss served another sovereign.

In 1873 Twiss was obliged to resign his offices in service of the Crown as the consequence of a marriage scandal – his wife had unsuccessfully defended herself against the accusation of having been a prostitute before her marriage to Twiss.[15] Prior to this rupture, Twiss had risen to the position of Advocate General, the government's advisor on civil law. We have seen that like most international lawyers of his generation, Twiss was first and foremost a civil lawyer. In England, this meant that he practised ecclesiastical law, specifically marriage law, and Admiralty law, both of which were conducted in terms of civil law until the middle of the century. Prior to the 1870s, he earned his living primarily through the ecclesiastical courts and international law was a secondary professional concern. After that date, international law was his central concern, in part because he had resigned his public offices but also because ecclesiastical and Admiralty law ceased to be conducted in terms of civil law after the 1850s.[16] He then spent much of his energy promoting King Leopold II's claims over the Congo. As such, he was not even engaged in the service of another nation, but of a private individual and a private association, the International African Association. Leopold's Congo venture was the most extreme statement of the new imperialism insofar as it was launched by a private association

[14] Travers Twiss, *The Oregon Territory: its history and discovery* (New York, 1836). Twiss' role in nineteenth-century international law has attracted attention in recent years. See Koskenniemi, *The gentle civilizer of nations*, pp. 132–3 for Twiss on the rights of Oriental nations in international law and p. 143 on Twiss and the Congo; Pitts, 'Boundaries of Victorian international law', pp. 71–2; and Caspar Sylvest, '"Our passion for legality": international law and imperialism in late nineteenth century Britain', *Review of International Studies*, 34 (2008), 403–23; Fitzmaurice, 'The resilience of natural law in the writings of Sir Travers Twiss'; Andrew Fitzmaurice, 'The justification of King Leopold II's Congo enterprise by Sir Travers Twiss', in Ian Hunter and Shaunnagh Dorsett (eds.), *Law and politics in British colonial thought* (New York, 2010).

[15] On the marriage scandal, see Fitzmaurice, 'The justification of King Leopold II's Congo enterprise by Sir Travers Twiss'.

[16] On the decline of civil law in England, see Squibb, *Doctors' Commons*.

and not by a state. In this instance, the ideological and technological instruments of empire can be seen to be an end in themselves. Twiss' justification of the Congo enterprise extended beyond his numerous publications through to an involvement in the various international institutions which attempted to regulate African colonisation, notably the Berlin Conference of 1884/5. His support for the occupation of the Congo was not only textual but also institutional. He showed that publishing and institutional activism were most effectively employed in concert.[17]

Twiss represented the most confident expression of the projection of European sovereignty upon non-European peoples. Drawing on his knowledge of ecclesiastical law, he deployed the canon law concept of *territorium nullius* in international law, a concept which would soon play a central role in the debates that revolved around the Berlin Conference. Reflecting his role as an Admiralty Court lawyer, he published a series of works through the 1860s and 1870s in which he stated his theory of sovereignty relative to the laws of the sea. To this end, he repeatedly employed the term 'nullius territorium' to explain that the sea could not be subject to the sovereignty of any state.[18] Indeed, he appears to be one of the few, or perhaps the only, international lawyer in the nineteenth century to employ the concept of *nullius territorium*, or *territorium nullius*, prior to 1880.[19] His increasing

[17] On the need to go beyond textual analysis in the study of empire, see Frederick Cooper, 'Postcolonial studies and the study of history', in Ania Loomba (ed.), *Postcolonial studies and beyond* (Durham, NC, 2005); and Pitts, 'Political theory of empire and imperialism', 217.

[18] Twiss, *The law of nations considered as independent political communities*, p. 141; Travers Twiss, 'Applicability of the European law of nations to African slave states', *Law Magazine and Review* (May 1876), 436; Travers Twiss, 'On the international jurisdiction of the Admiralty Court in civil matters', *Law Magazine and Review* (May 1877), 304; and Travers Twiss, 'The criminal jurisdiction of the Admiralty of England in the case of the *Franconia*', *Law Magazine and Review* (February 1877), 147; Travers Twiss, 'Collisions at sea. A scheme of international tribunals', *Law Magazine and Review* (November 1878), 4; Travers Twiss, 'Collisions on the high seas', *Albany Law Journal* (12 October 1878), 288. The term *nullius territorium* was also used in 1880 in the meeting of the Association for the Reform and Codification of the Law of Nations at Berne. See *Association for the Reform and Codification of the Law of Nations. Report of the eighth annual conference held at Berne, August 24th—27th, 1880* (London, 1881), p. 104. In this discussion, in which Twiss participated, *nullius territorium* was employed concerning the protection of telegraph cables at sea at times of war.

[19] The one exception was Edward Creasy, who in 1876 used *nullius territorium* in his *First platform of international law* and cited Twiss as the authority on the idea. 'Dr Travers Twiss in another place says that the High Seas are said in a certain sense to be *nullius territorium*, as not being subject to the exclusive possession or empire of any Nation': Creasy, *First platform of international law*, p. 232. But Twiss was certainly not the originator of the term. *Territorium nullius* and *nullius territorium* were relatively frequently employed in European canon law, at least as early as the 1830s and probably well before. In general the term was used by Catholic canonists to describe sacred land, church land which could not be occupied and was not subject to sovereignty. See Johann Friedrich Schulte, *Das katholische Kirchenrecht* (Giessen, 1856), p. 745; Lucius Ferraris, *Prompta bibliotheca, canonica, juridica, moralis, theological*, ed. Jacques-Paul Migne (Paris, 1863), p. 33. For 'nullius territorium' in canon law, see Giovanni Fortunato Zamboni, *Collectio declarationum sacræ congregationis*

use of the term 'nullius territorium' in the late 1870s corresponded to the intensifying interest shown by European colonial powers in west Central Africa, but there was as yet no apparent connection made with that colonial ambition.

In the 1870s, King Leopold II of Belgium failed to interest the Belgian government in his ambition to establish a colony in the Congo. Undeterred, he held a geographical conference in 1876 on the need to civilise Africa, to which he invited representatives of all the major occidental nations.[20] At the same time, he created the *International African Association* for furthering the civilisation of central Africa.[21] He eventually succeeded in converting this humanitarian organisation into a state which would be responsible for the death of millions of Congolese people in one of the most brutal and violent episodes in the already-brutal history of European empire.[22] At the outset, however, Leopold faced significant political and legal obstacles to his ambitions, particularly insofar as the acceptance of the international community was concerned. To overcome these obstacles, he enlisted Sir Travers Twiss. In Twiss, he found an eminent international lawyer who was desperate for a return to public life following his public humiliation and ostracism from Britain in 1873.[23] From 1878, Gustave Moynier, European President of the International Red Cross, put the question of the legal status of the Congo to the members of the *Institut de droit international* as requiring urgent attention.[24] In the absence of a legal framework, he feared that the increasing competition between the various European interests acting in the Congo could quickly lead to conflict. He was also concerned about the legal status of the African peoples and warned against the exploitative behaviour of the

cardinalium sacri Concilii tridentini interpretum (Rome, 1868), p. 5. See also Johann Adam von Ickstatt, *Elementa juris gentium* (Wirceburgi, 1740), pp. 173 and 132.

20 G. Rolin-Jaequemyns, 'Œuvre de l'exploration et de la civilisation de l'Afrique centrale', *Revue de droit international*, 9 (1877), 288–91, at 291.

21 The best accounts of the negotiations leading up to and during the Berlin Conference are: William Roger Louis, *Ends of British imperialism: the scramble for empire, Suez and decolonization* (London, 2006); S. E. Crowe, *The Berlin West African Conference, 1884–85* (London, 1942).

22 Adam Hochschild, *King Leopold's ghost* (Boston, 1998) provides a vivid account of the terror in the Congo Free State.

23 Lambeth Palace Library, Tait MSS 184, fols. 92–3, Letter from Twiss to Archbishop Tait, addressed Basle [1872]: 'in giving up my offices I have given up the income which has been the support of my family and of many who depended upon me, and I am anxious that no additional mark of the Queen's displeasure should be inflicted upon me . . . and destroy my future chances of usefulness in some humbler department of life'.

24 'Proposition de M. Moynier concernant le Congo', *Annuaire de l'institut de droit international*, 7 (1885), 237–8.

'whites' on the Congo.[25] Travers Twiss responded to Moynier's challenge with four essays published in 1883.[26]

For Twiss, the necessary condition for peace in the Congo would be territorial sovereignty. Contemporaries were raising concerns about the property and sovereignty of the native Congo peoples. Twiss acknowledged that some form of law already existed in the lower Congo, but he declared that: 'The organisation of the native races on the banks of the Congo is still *tribal*, and *territorial* Sovereignty in the sense in which it has superseded *personal* Sovereignty in Europe, is still unknown.'[27] He claimed that in the upper Congo it was not clear at all to whom European merchants owed obedience.[28] In both cases, so far as Twiss was concerned, the presence of even personal sovereignty exercised by native peoples meant that there was a void of territorial sovereignty.

Twiss was not only concerned about the native peoples of the Congo when he spoke about the vacuum of territorial sovereignty; he was also referring to the empty pretensions of certain European powers to possess sovereignty over the region and, in particular, he devoted much of his argument to dismissing the claims of the Portuguese, who were one of the main rivals to Leopold. The Portuguese claims were not to be taken lightly. At the time that Twiss was writing in 1883, they were in the process of being recognised through the negotiation of a treaty with the British government, which, in desperation, promoted Portugal over the growing influence of the French in the Congo.[29] The Portuguese claimed sovereignty over the Congo by right of discovery since the fifteenth century and had a continued presence there in terms of trading factories. But Twiss pointed out that the measure of sovereign claims should be effective occupation. The Portuguese exercised nothing like effective occupation over most of the lower Congo and did not occupy the upper Congo at all.

It is sometimes argued that, prior to the Berlin Conference, nobody suspected Leopold's intention to turn the International Association of the

[25] Gustave Moynier, 'Lettre-circulaire de M. Moynier à messieurs les membres et associés de l'Institut de droit international', Geneva, 1 July 1883, *Annuaire de l'institut de droit international*, 7 (1885), 239.

[26] Travers Twiss, 'La libre navigation du Congo', *Revue de droit international*, 15 (1883), 437–42 (dated 24 July 1883); Travers Twiss, 'La libre navigation du Congo. Deuxième article', *Revue de droit international*, 15 (1883), 547–63 (dated 21 November 1883); Travers Twiss, 'An international protectorate of the Congo River', *Law Magazine and Review* (November 1883), 1–20; Travers Twiss, *An international protectorate of the Congo River* (London, 1883). The 24 July 1883 essay was also presented to the *Institut de droit international* the following year and was then reprinted in its *Annuaire* in 1885. See Travers Twiss, 'La libre navigation du Congo', *Annuaire de l'institut de droit international*, 7 (1885), 242–9.

[27] Twiss, *International protectorate*, p. 17.

[28] *Ibid.*, pp. 16–19.

[29] Louis, *Ends of British imperialism*, p. 90.

Congo into a colonial state.[30] There was, however, strong opposition to Leopold within the British Foreign Office, including scepticism of his humanitarian intentions and a damning assessment of his cynicism. The Portuguese government also brought attention to numerous abuses by Leopold's agents in the Congo, even in the years leading up to the Berlin Conference. In the months prior to the Conference, a tract was published anonymously in Brussels which made it clear that Leopold's intentions were no secret and that Twiss' efforts were not at all disinterested.[31] The author accused Leopold of seeking a colonial empire for Belgium. 'Who would believe', the author stormed, that anybody would wish to spend millions civilising Central Africa out of a 'simple love of humanity'. In any case, the author argued, a neutral but colonial Belgium was a contradiction and was politically imprudent, not to say dangerous.[32] The title of this tract was *Sir Travers Twiss et le Congo* and it devoted its forty-four pages to a point-by-point refutation of Twiss' legal pronouncements on the question. The author argued that 'to demand today the recognition of absolute rights, without them even being exercised in fact, as is the case in the Congo, would seem to us to leave the path of serious juridical debate'.[33] This linking of empire with absolutism was a common fear amongst late nineteenth-century jurists.[34]

Leopold's ambitions in Africa were not, however, the main concern of the European powers. Germany and France feared that Britain and

[30] Most recently Caspar Sylvest and Martti Koskenniemi. See Sylvest, 'Our passion for legality', pp. 411 and 415; and Koskenniemi, *The gentle civilizer of nations*, pp. 157–65. This also seems to be the position of earlier scholarship. See, for example, Jesse Siddall Reeves, *The international beginnings of the Congo Free State* (Baltimore, 1894), p. 71 and also to some degree Crowe's *The Berlin West African Conference*. William Roger Louis, 'The Berlin Conference and the (non-)partition of Africa', in Louis, *Ends of British imperialism* presents a complex view of the lead-up to the Conference, with some parties prepared to be believe Leopold's assurances while others were cynical.

[31] Anon. *Sir Travers Twiss et le Congo. Réponse à la Revue de Droit International et de Législation comparée et au Law Magazine and Review, par un membre de la Societé Royale de Géographie d'Anvers* (Brussels, 1884).

[32] *Ibid.*, pp. 5–6, my translation. [33] *Ibid.*, p. 40.

[34] In May 1884, Twiss responded to his attacker with a third article on the Congo in the *Revue de droit international*: Travers Twiss, 'La libre navigation du Congo. Troisième article', *Revue de droit international*, 16 (1884), 237–46 (dated 8 May 1884). It is a moot point whether Joseph Conrad's *Heart of darkness*, which condemned the brutality of Leopold's rule in the Congo, was truly anti-imperialist or expressed typical humanitarian ambivalence concerning empire. For this debate, see the contributions to Gail Fincham and Myrtle Hooper (eds.), *Under post-colonial eyes: Joseph Conrad after empire* (Rondebosch, 1996). Edward Said's argument that Conrad's conscience was noble but that it was only possible for him to think imperially is based upon a Foucaultian assumption about the hegemony of imperial discourse, an assumption shared by many historians: see Edward Said, *Culture and imperialism* (New York, 1993), pp. 19–31. At the time that Conrad was writing, and even prior to the foundation of the Congo Free State, there was substantial opposition to empire and, in particular, to the expansion of empire into the Congo.

Portugal were contriving to gain control over the Congo, and the fears were mutual. In June 1884, Bismarck refused to recognise the Anglo-Portuguese treaty and shortly after he called for a conference of the community of nations in Berlin so as to establish rules that would govern the carve-up of Africa and the international order more generally, with the specific aim of restraining Britain. The British reluctantly agreed to the conference, to which they sent five delegates.[35] They were led by Sir Edward Malet, the British Ambassador at Berlin, and included senior diplomats from the Foreign and Colonial Office. The five also included Travers Twiss as an unofficial delegate.[36] Twiss was thus able to return to public service simultaneously for Britain and Leopold, albeit that their interests at the conference were not identical. During the conference, Bismarck came to the conclusion that Britain, like Germany, did not seek power in the Congo, but sought to deny it to any of the other great powers. He seized upon Leopold's desire to turn the International African Association into a state which guaranteed free trade as the best possible solution to the negotiations. Twiss presented Leopold's case to the British delegation and they reluctantly acquiesced. Lord Granville, the British Secretary of State, agreed to 'negotiate a treaty with the Association to recognise its flag as that of a friendly government'.[37] Travers Twiss was given the task of drafting this treaty.[38]

The Congo Free State was now born in all but name. In anticipation of this outcome, Leopold had already commissioned a draft of its constitution. For this task, he turned once again to Twiss. In the draft, the new state was to be called 'L'Afrique Equatoriale'. In November 1884, while the Berlin Conference was under way, Twiss provided Sir Julian Pauncefote, the Permanent Under-Secretary of State for Foreign Affairs, with an advance view of the draft constitution.[39] In a memo written two weeks after Pauncefote had received the constitution, Thomas Lister, the Assistant Under-Secretary of State for Foreign Affairs, commented that 'The constitution is I believe the work of Sir T. Twiss', adding that: 'It is a

[35] Crowe, *The Berlin West African Conference*, p. 99.

[36] It was Lord Granville, the Foreign Secretary, who wrote Twiss' letter of introduction to Malet. Granville to Malet, National Archives, Foreign Office 14 November 1884, FO 84/1814, 348. Telegram, Malet to Lord Granville, Berlin, 12 November 1884, FO 84/1814, 310. Granville noted that 'Sir T. Twiss' should not 'be put on the Official List of Delegates', FO 84/1814, 309v.

[37] Crowe, *The Berlin West African Conference*, p. 147. [38] *Ibid.*

[39] Julian Pauncefote, 'Memo, 6/11/84', National Archives, FO 84/1814, 222: 'Sir Travers Twiss has handed me for Lord Granville's information this copy of the Draft Constitution of the new state to be founded by the King of the Belgians under the name of L'Afrique Equatoriale. JP. 6/11/84.'

highly coloured sketch of a Bureaucratic Utopia.'[40] But the extraordinary aspect of this constitution was that, in an age of colonial administrative reform, it granted the King of the Congo state prerogative power. In this regard, it confirmed all the fears that had been expressed by Twiss' anonymous attacker. According to the constitution, Leopold could suspend laws and officers of the state 'à sa discrétion'.[41]

Twiss' efforts are an indication of the degree to which the jurists who belonged to the *Institut* were concerned that real-world consequences follow from textual debates. Most members of the *Institut* held diplomatic and political positions, as well as being practising jurists, and in these roles they sought to bring their visions of global order to reality. Twiss, for example, played a key role in transforming the private association that was the International Association of the Congo into a new state and he did this by taking his published ideas into an international organisation, by winning the argument in that forum and then by helping to create the institutional instruments that would establish that new state.

Twiss' projection of his vision of European sovereignty upon Africa did not end with his drafting of the constitution to Equatorial Africa. In recognition of his eminence in international law, he was appointed to chair the commission at the Berlin Conference which would determine the rules of effective occupation.[42] The Conference had been called to resolve three issues: the question of free commerce in the Congo, the problem of free navigation on the Congo and Niger Rivers, and the nature of effective occupation.[43] The discussion of effective occupation brought the question of what it means to occupy to the forefront of international attention. Jurists had agreed for centuries that occupation was the original form for the acquisition of territory (as opposed to the derivative forms of conquest and cession), but nineteenth-century jurists and diplomats asked what legal forms and institutions needed to be established for a territory to be

[40] T.V. Lister, 'Memo', 23 November 1884, FO 84/1815, 214. Sylvest, 'Our passion for legality', p. 414 notes that Twiss is 'reported to have drafted the constitution of the Congo Free State', adding that it could not be traced. A copy, provided by Twiss, is available in the Foreign Office documents. Louis, *Ends of British imperialism*, p. 105, mentions that Twiss 'actually drafted the Congo State's constitution', but does not provide a source.

[41] 'West African Conference. Confidential. Projet. – La Constitution de l'Etat. – L'Afrique Equatoriale', National Archives, FO 84/1815, 80–1.

[42] Telegram, Edward Malet to Granville, Berlin, 19 January 1885, National Archives, FO 84/1820, 58: 'On Saturday a restricted Committee with Sir Travers Twiss in the chair met to agree upon the ultimate wording of the 3rd Basis.'

[43] 'Rapport de la Commission chargée d'examiner le projet de Déclaration relative aux occupations nouvelles sur les côtes d'Afrique', National Archives FO 84/1820, 233–8.

truly occupied. Occupation was now something that required much more than the 'taking with the hands' that earlier jurists spoke of, nor was Locke's plough enough. Moreover, for some participants in Berlin, different kinds of occupation could be possible.

Negotiations over the third issue broke down, largely over whether protectorates would be bound by the obligations attached to effective occupation. Twiss' commission was charged with resolving the deadlock from which the British got their desired outcome. Whereas most participants in the Conference wanted effective occupation to apply to protectorates, the British argued that the kind of sovereignty exercised in a protectorate did not bring the obligations which apply to a colony.[44] They insisted upon the distinction between protectorates and colonies. In a protectorate, 'native' law and even some degree of sovereignty could remain after occupation, whereas in a colony, any laws from a previous regime would be extinguished. By the early twentieth century, the distinction between protectorates and colonies became blurred as European powers began to encroach upon the internal affairs of the territories over which they initially claimed only a protecting power – that is, a power particularly over external sovereignty.[45] The invention of the 'colonial protectorate' with far greater meddling in internal affairs effectively nullified the distinctions.[46] In the 1880s, however, the distinction between protectorate and colony was still very much alive, although even then jurists such as Twiss began to speak of the occupation of protectorates. The concern with how to justify the occupation of a society that possessed some degree of law, and even sovereignty, became the focus of jurists' discussions after the Berlin Conference.

The debate after Berlin

Indeed, the distillation of exactly what principles regarding occupation had been established at the Berlin Conference consumed discussions at the meetings of the *Institut de droit international* as well as the jurists'

[44] Twiss did not even like the term 'protectorate', although this did not stop him from chairing the commission on the third basis. On Twiss and protectorates, see Louis, *Ends of British imperialism*, p. 114.

[45] Jörg Fisch, 'Africa as *terra nullius*: the Berlin Conference and international law', in Stig Forster, Wolfgang J. Mommsen and Ronald Robinson (eds.), *Bismarck, Europe, and Africa: The Berlin Africa Conference 1884–1885 and the onset of partition* (Oxford, 1988), pp. 364–9.

[46] Alexandrowicz, *The European-African confrontation*, pp. 80–1.

publications for the next two or three years.[47] Shortly after the Conference, in September 1885, the *Institut de droit international* met, appropriately, in Brussels. At this meeting, the members decided that it was necessary to establish a commission to study the question of effective occupation and to declare what were the fundamental principles of that doctrine. This commission was chaired by a relatively young German professor of ecclesiastical and international law, Ferdinand Martitz.[48] Two years later, Martitz presented the report of that commission to the meeting of the *Institut* in Heidelberg. In Martitz's report it became clear that a new understanding of effective occupation was being articulated, albeit that his recommendations were not adopted. According to Martitz, the measure of whether colonial occupation was possible was not property but sovereignty, and not merely sovereignty but territorial sovereignty, not *dominium* but territorial *imperium*. To this end, he applied the term 'territorium nullius' to the question of colonisation. Apart from Travers Twiss' works in which *nullius territorium* had been used, the term was fresh in international law and it had not been used to discuss colonisation prior to this point. The seven members of the Brussels committee were Tobias Asser, Edouard Engelhardt, Friedrich Geffcken, Emile de Laveleye, Georg Friedrich von Martens, Martitz and, almost inevitably, Twiss. Each member of the committee was eminent in international life. For example, Asser, who would later win the Nobel Peace Prize, and de Laveleye were amongst the founders of the *Institut*. The Belgian de Laveleye had written on the economics of colonisation since the 1860s and was a close advisor to Leopold on the creation of the International African Association and its successor, the International Association of the Congo.[49]

The members of the committee were, however, divided and could not reach a common position. Their division reflects the polarisation of pro- and anti-imperial views amongst jurists over the scramble for Africa in the 1880s. Martitz's report reflected only one side of that debate. According to Martitz: 'All regions are considered to be *territorium nullius* which do not find themselves effectively under sovereignty ... no matter whether the

[47] Twiss, as always, was at the forefront of this effort; see, for example, Travers Twiss, 'Le congrès de Vienne et la conférence de Berlin', *Revue de droit international*, 17 (1885), 201–17.

[48] *Annuaire de l'Institut de droit international*, 6 (1883), 327.

[49] Laveleye's role in promoting Leopold's colonial ambitions is discussed in Jan Vandersmissen, *Koningen van de wereld. Leopold II en de aardrijkskundige beweging* (Leuven, 2009). On Leopold's deliberate confusion of the distinction between the International African Association and the International Association of the Congo, see Hochschild, *Leopold's ghost*, p. 65.

region is inhabited or not.'[50] 'It is an exaggeration', he declared, 'to speak of the sovereignty of savage or semi-barbarian peoples.' Moreover, 'international law does not recognise rights of independent tribes'. For this reason, he concluded, '*territorium nullius* is not the same thing as *res nullius*'.[51] He accepted that African tribes had rights under the law of *res nullius*; in other words, for him, *res nullius* was a rule of property or *dominium*. The African peoples could possess property rights but that did not give them any rights of sovereignty and, in this sense, the *imperium* of their regions remained unrealised. All of Martitz's arguments regarding *territorium nullius* in relation to the Congo were consistent with Twiss' pronouncements on the same subject. Indeed, the test that Martitz applied to whether colonial intervention was justified was one of territorial sovereignty. *Territorium nullius* was a measure of territorial sovereignty which, according to Twiss, was precisely the form of political organisation absent in the Congo.[52] Indeed, *territorium nullius* was both the legal complement to treaty making and the legal expression of the protectorate. It is fairly clear, therefore, that Twiss would have been at least one member of the committee on occupation who would have agreed with the report of its chairman.

Just as there was a distinction in the minds of these jurists between *res nullius* and *territorium nullius*, it is also important to distinguish between *territorium nullius* and the now more commonly known term 'terra nullius'. Jörg Fisch has argued that there was a contradiction between the application of the doctrine of *terra nullius* to African peoples, denying them any rights, and the common claim to title through purchase and cession from those same tribes.[53] One problem with this argument is that the term 'terra nullius' was not applied to Africa in the late nineteenth century. Although sometimes previously employed in canon law, the term became popular in international law in early twentieth-century debates over the polar regions and in that context it signified a complete absence of

[50] Ferdinand Martitz, 'Occupation des territoires: Rapport et projet de résolutions présentés à l'Institut de droit international', *Revue de droit international*, 19 (1887), 371–6, at 373. Martitz's report was also published in the *Annuaire de l'Institut de droit international*, 9 (1888), 243–51.

[51] Martitz, 'Occupation des territoires', 374.

[52] For Achille Mbembe, one of the key elements in the 'European imaginary' necessary to late nineteenth and early twentieth-century colonisation was the 'territorialisation of the sovereign state'. It was precisely that idea that the concept of *territorium nullius* articulated. According to Mbembe, the people who were to be colonised were also perceived as not being 'sovereign subject', although it is striking that the concept of *territorium nullius* was developed in order to justify even the colonisation of a people who could be perceived in that way. See Achille Mbembe, 'Necropolitics', trans. Libby Meintjes, *Public Culture*, 15(1) (2003), 11–40, at 23–4.

[53] Fisch, 'Africa as *terra nullius*'. See also Sylvest, '"Our passion for legality"', p. 415.

rights.[54] Fisch's point, however, is broader than the term – namely, he argues that there was a contradiction between European powers' conclusion of treaties in Africa at the time of the Berlin Conference and their simultaneous claim to occupy territories that had no owner.[55] The theories of cession and occupation, he rightly points out, historically contained contradictory assumptions: one assuming that there were subjects who could cede sovereign power and the other assuming that there were no such subjects. I have discussed precisely such contradictory arguments made by English colonisers in seventeenth-century North America and it is unsurprising that efforts to rationalise empire often strained ideological coherence. The arguments justifying the colonisation of Africa were certainly not free of similar problems of ideological stress and incoherence. At the same time, however, it is important to recognise that diplomats and jurists in the second half of the nineteenth century, and Twiss in particular, were attempting to reconcile the theory of occupation with that of the protectorate by legally parsing what could be occupied.[56] The doctrine of *territorium nullius* denied rights only of territorial sovereignty. According to the doctrine, indigenous peoples could still have rights of property and, as Twiss observed, rights of personal sovereignty, without possessing territorial sovereignty. Those peoples could therefore cede through treaties those rights they were believed to have without there being any implication that they were territorially sovereign and so exempt from the laws applying to effective occupation.

Twiss had argued for the need for treaties in order to occupy *territorium nullius* in his submission to the United States Congressional Committee on Foreign Relations. According to the report of this Committee, the 'exhaustive statements of Sir Travers Twiss' had demonstrated that the United States should recognise the International Association of the Congo as a state because 'the native chiefs have the right to make these treaties' ceding 'any powers' which belonged to them.[57] The effort to occupy the Congo had been accompanied by a race to make treaties with local rulers. Leopold's agents acting for the International Association, on the one hand, and Pierre Savorgnan de Brazza, acting for France on the other, gathered

[54] Fitzmaurice, 'A genealogy of *terra nullius*'. See also the following chapter.

[55] Jörg Fisch, *Die europäische Expansion und das Völkerrecht* (Stuttgart, 1984).

[56] Alexandrowicz, *The European-African confrontation*, p. 4 argues that at this time, occupation was understood in a broad way to include any kind of acquisition of title. It would be preferable to say that different kinds of occupations were imagined, including the protectorate.

[57] *Report of the Committee on Foreign Relations*, 26 March 1884, printed in Henry Wellington Wack, *The story of the Congo Free State* (New York, 1905), p. 498.

hundreds of signed treaties through the 1880s which purported to cede sovereignty. Henry Stanley, Leopold's agent in the Congo, came to the Berlin Conference with 'treaties made with over 450 independent African chiefs'.[58] The Conference then determined the destinies of those peoples without any signatories of the treaties present – a fact upon which even the British Ambassador, Sir Edward Malet, felt obliged to comment: 'I must remind myself that the indigenous people are not represented in our meeting', albeit that 'the decisions of the Conference have for them an extreme gravity'.[59]

As the French plenipotentiary minister at the Berlin Conference and a member of the *Institut*'s subsequent commission on effective occupation, Édouard Engelhardt (1828–1916) might have been expected to toe Jules Ferry's line. He presented a report, however, to the Heidelberg meeting dissenting from Martitz's conclusions.[60] His report reflects the hardening of scepticism amongst many jurists about imperial propaganda. In this report, he addressed the classic theory of occupation – namely, that what is taken by nobody becomes the property of the first taker – and he then completely rejected that doctrine as belonging to the 'période des grandes acquisitions coloniales'.[61] He insisted, moreover, that at no point did the

[58] Henry Stanley, *The Congo*, 2 vols. (London, 1885), vol. 2, p. 379. Examples of the treaties as well as a list of treaties made through to 1883 are reprinted in Wack, *The story of the Congo Free State*, pp. 487–91. The Treaty of Vivi typically claimed that the chiefs 'abandoned' 'all sovereign rights' (p. 487). There is every reason to be as dubious about these treaties as most other treaties made throughout European colonial history, although Franz Ansprenger has argued that in some agreements the chiefs understood the nature of sovereignty and willingly abandoned it in favour of improved trading prospects: Franz Ansprenger, 'African perception of the new European policies in Africa during the 1880s', in Forster, Mommsen and Robinson (eds.), *Bismarck, Europe, and Africa*, p. 516. Kristin Mann shows that the property and sovereignty claims in treaties were put in question during the colonial history that followed their making; see Kristin Mann, 'African and European initiatives in the transformation of land tenure in colonial Lagos (West Africa), 1840–1920', in Belmessous (ed.), *Native claims*.

[59] Cited in Ansprenger, 'African perception', p. 507.

[60] Édouard Engelhardt, *Etude sur la déclaration de la conférence de Berlin relative aux occupations africaines suivie d'un projet de déclaration générale sur les occupations en pays sauvages* (Brussels, 1887), reprinted from *Revue de droit international*, 18 (1886), 433–41 and 573–86. See also Édouard Englehardt, 'Projet de déclaration internationale, proposé par M. Engelhardt, en vue de déterminer les règles à suivre dans les occupations de territoires', *Revue de droit international*, 19 (1887), 175–9; Édouard Engelhardt, 'Conférence de Berlin', *Revue de droit international*, 18 (1886), 96–8.

[61] Édouard Engelhardt, *Étude sur la déclaration de la conférence de Berlin relative aux occupations africaines suivie d'un projet de déclaration générale sur les occupations en pays sauvages* (Brussels, 1887), pp. 15–16. Wilhelm Grewe notes a similar concern on the part of the American plenipotentiary, Mr Kasson, which, according to Grewe, sheds 'light on the ambiguity of the general intellectual and political prerequisites of the classical law of occupation in this century': Grewe, *The epochs of international law*, p. 550. On the conflict between Martitz and Engelhardt, see also Marco Moretti, *International law and nomadic people* (Milton Keynes, 2012), pp. 114–16.

Berlin Conference describe the indigenous peoples of Africa as outside the law of nations as Martitz had argued; indeed, 'as I have tried to establish in the official report which I have made, at each vote or each proposition which has questioned the interests of the African indigenes, the Berlin assembly has demonstrated that it did not regard those associations or individuals as being outside of the community of the law of nations'.[62]

In the 1888 meeting of the *Institut de droit international* at Lausanne, the subject of occupation was again on the table and Martitz's report was again placed under examination.[63] At this meeting, the meaning and scope of *territorium nullius* became the centre of attention. Guido Fusinato (1860–1914) supported Martitz. Fusinato was Professor of Law at the University of Turin and Under-Secretary of State for Foreign Affairs. He explained that 'the idea of *territorium nullius* in public law corresponds with that of *res nullius* in private law'. He expanded: 'As *res nullius* in private law concerns things which are not objects of property, *territorium nullius* in public law is not an object of sovereignty.' He insisted, moreover, that just as *res nullius* had been regulated by the private law, so 'in public law, the acquisition of *territorium nullius* must be regulated'.[64]

At the same meeting of the *Institut* in Lausanne, sceptics of colonisation, including Engelhardt, were disturbed by the understanding of occupation that jurists such as Martitz, Twiss and Fusinato derived from the agreements made at the Berlin Conference. The polarisation of the community of international lawyers was increasingly evident in the debates. The sceptics were particularly concerned about the idea of *territorium nullius* as it was being applied to colonisation. Engelhardt accordingly demanded that the meeting of the *Institut* 'renounce' the first article of Martitz's report – namely, the article demanding that 'all regions, whether or not they are inhabited, be regarded as *territorium nullius* which do not find themselves under effective sovereignty or under the protection of a state which forms part of the community of the law of nations'.[65] Engelhardt objected that it was dangerous to apply this rule to inhabited regions.[66] Under what conditions, he asked, would a state be regarded as part of the

[62] Engelhardt, *Étude*, pp. 16–17.

[63] 'Sixième commission – Examen de la théorie de la conférence de Berlin sur l'occupation des territoires', *Annuaire de l'Institut de droit international*, 10 (1889), 173–204.

[64] 'Sixième commission', 183.

[65] For Martitz's first article, see *Revue de droit international*, 19 (1887), 373. For Engelhardt's opposition, see 'Sixième commission', 179. On private law sources for the law of nations, see Lauterpacht, *Private law sources and analogies in international law*; and Randall Lesaffer, 'Argument from Roman Law in current international law'.

[66] 'Sixième commission', 177.

community of nations? What was the situation of a state, such as Morocco, that recognised some of the rules of the law of nations and not others? Other societies, he insisted, were outside the law of nations and yet still deserved respect. He argued that there were even savage peoples, who were completely outside the law of nations, for whom it would nevertheless be 'exorbitant to consider their territory as *territorium nullius*'.[67] He prevailed after intensive debate and the first article, the concept of *territorium nullius*, was suppressed. The opponents of treating Africa as *territorium nullius* were concerned about the potential for European sovereigns having arbitrary power over private property. That potential would arise if those sovereigns were able to seize power over peoples who clearly possessed both *dominium* and *imperium*. This concern was particularly strong in relation to the Congo because Leopold's state, based upon a private company, was ruled by prerogative rather than by law. Prerogative power, as we have seen, had been legitimised by Twiss in his constitution for the new state.

Development of the anti-imperial critique

The projection of European sovereignty, and the principles discussed in the aftermath of the Berlin Conference, became the topic of a number of treatises in the last years of the nineteenth century. Some of these subjected the Berlin agreements and the *Institut* debates to highly sceptical scrutiny. A number of French jurists and politicians had become sceptical of empire following the Franco-Prussian War in 1870–1. The effort required to maintain the French empire was partly blamed for domestic military weakness. Sceptics of empire responding to the Berlin Conference in the 1880s were mindful of this recent debate upon the causes of French humiliation. They focused, however, not upon the possibility that empire may weaken a state in relation to its neighbours, but upon a different concern – namely, the potential that abuses of rights in the empire could endanger liberty at home.[68] In other words, they focused less upon the

[67] *Ibid.*, 178. See also Engelhardt, *Étude*.

[68] Edouard Tartarin's *Traité de l'occupation* was one of the treatises arising from the Franco-Prussian War and was published the year after the armistice in 1872. Tartarin was concerned about the confusion of sovereignty and property, as were critics of empire after the Berlin Conference. His motivations, however, were different. He argued that the German conquerors must respect property, but he was even more worried by the socialist and anarchist forces which had established the Paris Commune in 1871 with their Proudhon-like attack on property, particularly property in land.

problems raised directly by the Franco-Prussian War and instead upon arguments used by neo-imperialists, such as Jules Ferry, who were themselves emerging from the shadow of the 1870–1 War. Their concerns were different from the generation that had founded the *Institut*, partly in response to the war, because they were responding to a new and increasingly strident imperialism. Prominent amongst these critics were Charles Salomon and Gaston Jèze.

Salomon, a jurist at Bordeaux, wrote *L'occupation des territoires sans maître* (1889) in response to the Berlin Conference. The Conference, according to Salomon, had recognised some of the limits in which occupation can be applied. For example, it recognised that 'indigenous peoples, as indigenous peoples, are not incapable of having rights of sovereignty. Their rights of private property must [also] be respected'. But, Salomon objected, the principles agreed at Berlin had not been respected by imperial governments and 'we could not say that the history of colonisation these last five years presented a tableau more moral than the rest of the century'.[69] Indeed, in the two decades after he wrote, the assurances made at Berlin regarding the property rights of native peoples were ignored by most colonial states in Africa, which deprived the native farmers and pastoralists of their land. For Salomon, however, the principles established at Berlin concerning occupation were themselves 'incomplete and insufficient'.[70] He thus used much of the rest of his treatise to explain what limits should be placed on the theory of occupation, partly through an analysis of the debate over occupation that followed the conference, and demonstrating the ways in which those principles continued to be abused by colonial governments.

Having discussed many unjust examples of occupation, Salomon turned to the conditions under which occupation could be just. In Roman law, he argued, for property in something to be acquired, it must belong to no one. In international law, it is sovereignty rather than property that is acquired. In that case, the same rule applied – namely, the object of occupation must belong to no one – but the difference was that it must not be under any form of sovereignty; it must be a 'territorium nullius'. Thus, he agreed that *territorium nullius* was the equivalent in international public law of *res nullius* in private Roman law.[71] However, for him, a *territorium nullius* was where there was no form of political organisation at all in the territory in question, whereas Twiss and other apologists for the

[69] Salomon, *L'occupation des territoires*, pp. 83–4. [70] *Ibid.*, p. 96. [71] *Ibid.*, p. 191.

occupation of Africa had attempted to base the concept upon a distinction between different levels of sovereignty.

In the sixteenth and seventeenth centuries, according to Salomon, all territories not inhabited by Christians were taken to be *res nullius*. In his own day, he said, an even more odious doctrine prevailed – namely, that all territories that were not civilised were treated as *res nullius*:

> the argument used nowadays by civilized peoples to justify and disguise the spoliation of the weaker races is no longer religious interest, it is the interest of civilization: modern peoples have a civilizing mission to fulfill from which they cannot escape. One can sustain without paradox that the point of view of the sixteenth-century popes and princes was, in short, more legitimate than the position of nineteenth-century governments, that there was more sincerity and less hypocrisy in the former when they spoke about the mission that falls to them.

He continued by pointing out that, while the use of religion to justify conquest at least appealed to a form of moral absolute, 'the idea of civilization, on the contrary, is variable and relative: nobody seriously argues that there is a sole civilization and that it is necessary that all men participate in its benefits'. 'No word', he declared, 'is more vague and has been used to commit greater iniquities than the word civilization.' Revealing the motivation for his scepticism, he warned: 'Take guard! The pretended right of civilization could serve to legitimize the most grave attacks, even in Europe ... Is there not a German civilization, a Slavic civilization, a Latin civilization? Have we not often supported the incontestable superiority of one over the other?'[72]

While Salomon was at one end of a spectrum that became polarised after the 1880s, his views were by no means radical in the 1890s. As we saw in the previous chapter, authors who were ambivalent about empire, such as Henry Bonfils and Frantz Despagnet, nevertheless expressed deep scepticism about the civilising mission. Salomon, by contrast, took his concerns about the imperial mission further. His understanding of what kind of societies possess sovereignty was extensive and included 'half civilized or savage small tribes, tribes or hordes': 'If we suppose that a territory is the residence of a half civilized or savage small tribe, tribe or horde, making a beginning, however rudimentary or imperfect it may be, of political organization, we say that the territory is not a *territorium nullius*, that it cannot be the object of an occupation pure and simple.'

[72] *Ibid*., pp. 192–6.

He added that the only way occupation could proceed in such circumstances – which were the only realistic circumstances, as he had already observed – was by means of a treaty. And such a treaty had, as Kant had insisted, to observe the rules of justice, the first of which was the genuine consent of the indigenous people.[73] Salomon devoted a large part of the remainder of his treatise to the theory and practice of treaties. He concluded that the vast majority of treaties with non-European peoples had not been just. But, like most contemporary critics of empire, he nevertheless left some room for treaties which meet all the conditions of justice (even if none for the civilising mission). Indeed, he had little choice. Treaties were central to the law of nations, including treaties for the cession of land, and they were employed extensively between European nations as well as being a means of extending empire. The problem was not whether treaties were legitimate, but how their abuse could be prevented.

Salomon used the introduction to his treatise to explain why the legality of occupation in colonial contexts troubled him. Here we do not find an author with a deeply humanitarian or philanthropic conscience. Indeed, he seems almost to be untouched by contemporary philanthropic movements, many of which pursued the civilising mission of which he was so contemptuous. Rather, he was motivated less by concern about what happened to colonised peoples than he was about the possibility that legal abuses in the colonies could be repatriated to Europe.

Foremost amongst his concerns was that the occupation of non-European people's territory confused sovereignty with property. *Imperium*, or sovereignty, and *dominum*, or property, had, he argued, been confused in civil law prior to the French Revolution. After the Revolution, the distinction had been clarified. It was a fundamental principle preventing the arbitrary appropriation of property by the sovereign. According to Salomon, however, while *dominium* and *imperium* had been separated in 'public internal law', the confusion found a last refuge in public international law and in the behaviour of imperial states. For him, the threat posed by illegal occupation in empire was a threat to the Revolution itself.[74]

Gaston Jèze (1869–1953) was in many ways typical of jurists who were sceptical of the claims attached to occupation. A professor of law at the Sorbonne, Jèze opened his *Étude théorique et pratique sur l'occupation* (1896) with a candid examination of the economics and politics of colonisation.

[73] *Ibid.*, pp. 199–200. [74] *Ibid.*, pp. 7–11.

He observed that European powers were effectively dependent upon colonisation for their greatness and that those powers that neglected to pursue colonial interests were led to regret it. Colonisation was vital to the strategic interests of the powers. Many colonies were created as military outposts. Colonies provided markets for European goods and also provided agricultural goods for European populations which were growing rapidly as birth rates outstripped death rates. Excess population could be sent to the colonies, as could prisoners. For all of these reasons, Jèze argued, occupation as a mode of acquiring 'sovereignty' had taken on a new importance.[75]

Having furnished an account of the political economy of colonisation and empire that bordered on realpolitik, Jèze then turned to address the justice of occupation in a way that called into question the very foundations of the 'politique coloniale'. The race for empire presented two dangers. The first arose from the conflicts over competition for territory. Laws of occupation would restrain those conflicts. The second danger was the violation of the rights of colonised peoples: 'In the forward march of the civilized world, we must account for the inhabitants of the invaded countries. Barbarian peoples are not without rights. Under the pretext of civilization, we cannot deliver them to the calculations of an immeasurable ambition and to the most shameful speculative manoeuvres. Ideas of humanity and of social progress too often hide a spirit of scandalous plunder.'[76] Philanthropy was a veneer.

Jèze proposed to establish the principles of occupation in such a way that abuses and conflict could no longer be possible if those principles were followed. He briefly surveyed the history of the idea of occupation from Roman law through the natural law writers from the sixteenth to the nineteenth centuries and he also surveyed the history of occupation in European colonial practice.[77] However, for him, the most important acts and documents concerning occupation were those arising from the Act of the Berlin Conference on 26 February 1885 and the *Project* on occupation adopted by the *Institut de droit international* at Lausanne in 1888. He therefore applied himself to clarifying the rules of *territorium nullius* which had been established through those two forums.

Jèze acknowledged the criticism of the Berlin Conference: 'However, we would say, the Powers had in 1884, during the Berlin Conference, a good opportunity to show, in the highest way, their generous intentions and to proclaim in the face of the world their absolute respect for the sovereign

[75] Jèze, *Étude théorique et pratique sur l'occupation*, p. 10. [76] *Ibid.* [77] *Ibid.*, pp. 11–20.

rights of barbarian peoples. And yet, the Declaration does not contain, neither explicitly nor implicitly, anything of that kind.'[78] Yet he disagreed with this judgment. He argued that the Berlin Act contained enough substance to protect the sovereignty and property of Africans, and that the subsequent abuses of those rights had arisen from states and companies acting without regard to the agreement.[79] Reviewing the anti-imperial tradition, he observed:

> As Vitoria already said in the sixteenth century, civilized powers have no more right to seize the territories of savages than savages have to occupy the European continent. The law of nations does not admit any distinction between the barbarians and the so-called civilized: men of all races, white or black, yellow or red, however unequal they are in fact have to be considered equal in the law.[80]

He then turned to Kant:

> The theory is not new, but it is not before the end of the eighteenth century that it started recruiting numerous followers. One of the first, the philosopher Kant, exposed it in excellent terms in his *Metaphysical elements of the doctrine of law* ... we do not 'without a specific contract' have the right to colonize the land of another people.[81]

Delivering his own view, Jèze summarised: 'we decide in favor of the absolute right of the indigenous peoples. We believe the opposite theory does nothing but establish, on the pretext of civilization, the maxim "might is right" and violates, under the appearance of legality, the fundamental rule of racial equality'.[82]

Jèze undertook to examine under what conditions a territory could be said to be a *territorium nullius* and could therefore by justly occupied. He complained that the occasion of the Berlin Conference and the Lausanne meeting of the *Institut* had not led to a rigorous definition of *territorium nullius* in international law. He accepted that it was not for the 'Powers' at Berlin to make a 'declaration of principle' on the question; they did not establish the 'rules of absolute and natural law'. But he could not accept that his colleagues in the *Institut* missed the opportunity to settle exactly what was *territorium nullius*. They could at least, he argued, have accepted Fusinato's formulation that *territorium nullius* regulates in public international law what *res nullius* regulates in civil law – namely, things that are owned by nobody. The object in question in the case of *territorium nullius*

[78] *Ibid.*, p. 131. [79] *Ibid.*, pp. 131–56. [80] *Ibid.*, p. 103. [81] *Ibid.*, pp. 104–5.
[82] *Ibid.*, p. 112.

would be sovereignty and this test would apply whether the land was inhabited or not.[83]

By accepting whether indigenous sovereignty was present as a test of whether there could be colonial occupation, it may seem that Jèze had succumbed precisely to the intention of those jurists who had developed the concept of *territorium nullius.* He then insisted, however, that 'savage' and 'barbarian' peoples held sovereignty. If, therefore, occupation was to be permitted in the territory of barbarian people, it could only be with the consent of those peoples. As for Salomon, Kant provided the terms for what constituted a legitimate treaty. Applying Kant's rigorous test for consent, Jèze observed that: '1. it must be free; 2. it must be intelligent; and 3. it must be conducted according to the customs of the country'. 'If the people refuse', he noted, 'we cannot pass by another route.'[84] He observed that proponents of colonial occupation had argued that it was not possible to make treaties with peoples who are not sovereign, but responded: 'We refuse absolutely to admit such a doctrine. In the first instance, we have recognised a right of sovereignty for indigenous peoples. We can, therefore, speak legitimately of treaties.'[85]

In the conclusion to his long treatise on occupation, Jèze proposed a number of articles for adoption. Article 2 contained a clause stating that: 'We cannot account for the degree of civilisation of the inhabitants for a country we wish to occupy. Savage peoples forming a political organisation have the right to absolute respect for their country. The acquisition of sovereignty in their territory can only result from a free treaty consenting to cession or a protectorate. There cannot be, in that case, occupation properly speaking.' Here Jèze was rejecting the notion of the occupation of sovereignty, and thus the reconciliation of the idea of occupation with the protectorate, that jurists such as Twiss had attempted to develop. Article 3 declared that: 'All states have the right to occupy a sovereign title in territories without owner.' The first clause of Article 3 was that this law applied equally to 'civilised and uncivilised states'. The second clause was that: 'States alone have the right to occupy.'[86] At first sight, this clause may

83 *Ibid.*, pp. 122–3.

84 *Ibid.*, pp. 115–16. Immanuel Kant had demanded that 'settlement may not take place by force but only by contract, and indeed by a contract that does not take advantage of the ignorance of those inhabitants with respect to ceding their lands'. See Kant, *The metaphysics of morals*, p. 490. On Kant's scepticism of empire, see Muthu, *Enlightenment against empire.*

85 Jèze, *Étude*, pp. 118–19. Compare Koskenniemi, *The gentle civilizer of nations*, p. 107: 'Salomon, Jèze and Engelhardt each advocated the formal extension of European sovereignty into colonial territory as the only means to check the excesses of purely commercial colonization.'

86 Jèze, *Étude*, p. 382.

seem intended to restrict action in international law to the club of European states, but his target was Leopold's venture in the Congo. He rejected the recognition at the Berlin Conference of the International Association of the Congo as a sovereign state.

Jèze's opposition to the legal recognition of the Congo Free State was matched by his cynicism for the civilising mission more generally. He bitterly observed:

> Without doubt, we would say, it is nice in theory to declare that we must bring barbarians to civilisation through commercial relations and the good example of Europeans. But do not everyday facts demonstrate the utopian character of these considerations? We know the influence of commerce in Africa and the good results obtained by the great companies. They do not recognise in the slightest degree a civilising mission. They strongly declare – and their conduct does not refute it – that they have as their sole aim their own benefit and the distribution to their shareholders the highest possible dividends.[87]

Jèze, like Salomon, did not turn to humanitarian sentiment to motivate his opposition to colonial expropriation. He too was motivated by the danger that colonial abuses would be repatriated to the metropolis: 'Otherwise, the argument turns against those who propose it. Isn't the right of civilisation invoked even in Europe? Do we not hear certain chauvinistic spirits repeat that the civilisation of this or that European country is superior to a neighbouring state? Must we not admit, under that pretext, that the strongest will crush the weakest?'[88]

A generation later, when Mussolini's army invaded Ethiopia, Jèze agreed to represent the King of Ethiopia, Haile Selassie, in bringing Ethiopia's challenge to the Italian conquest in the League of Nations.[89] The French monarchist and nationalist right mounted 'virulent' demonstrations against Jèze in late 1935 and 1936. The demonstrators' picket, which included the young François Mitterrand, prevented Jèze from delivering his lectures at the Sorbonne that winter. When the League Council, led by Soviet Foreign Minister Litvinoff, agreed that Italy, France and Britain would negotiate the

[87] *Ibid.*, p. 114. Jèze's opposition to the Congo venture, and his scepticism of occupation more generally, did not prevent the Belgian jurist Ernest Nys from citing him to legitimise the occupation of the Congo: see Nys, *Droit international*, vol. 1, pp. 100–1. Nys cited Jèze on the three conditions that treaties must fulfil in order to be valid. He then gave Henry Stanley's treaties concluded in the Congo Basin as an example of this form of ideal practice.

[88] Jèze, *Étude*, p. 115.

[89] Marc Milet, *La Faculté de droit de Paris face à la vie politique, de l'Affaire Scelle à l'Affaire Jèze, 1925–1936* (Paris, 1996); Pierre Péan, *Une jeunesse française. François Mitterrand, 1934–1947* (Paris, 1994), pp. 45–61.

destiny of Ethiopia outside of the Council deliberations, Jèze reportedly 'glared at President Litvinoff and hissed: "You offer us the choice between suicide and assassination. Well, we prefer assassination!"'.[90] Again, during the Second World War, Jèze challenged the powers of the occupying German army over the French Jewish community. The two cases were connected – as Jèze well understood, the laws of occupation applied in colonies and in European wars. As jurists such as Jèze and Salomon had foretold, the practices that had been employed in empire were being repatriated to the occupation of Europe during war.[91] This critique was later taken up in the twentieth century by figures such as Raphaël Lemkin and Hannah Arendt.[92]

Jèze's legal representation of Haile Selassie raises the question of whether the critiques of the liberal anti-imperialists of the late nineteenth century ever had any impact upon the international political life that they tried to shape. Clearly, in the context of the Berlin Conference, figures such as Twiss won the debate insofar as they justified a new wave of empire (even if they lost the battle over the adoption of *territorium nullius*). As the imperialism of the 1880s and 1890s gathered momentum, the opposition became stronger, but still had little impact. It is true that by the 1890s, Leopold was revealed to have conducted a reign of terror in the Congo, but opposition in this instance was galvanised by humanitarian sentiment, not by liberal fears about liberty in the metropolis, so that the territory of the Congo Free State was annexed by Belgium in 1908. If we are to look for a lasting legacy from the anti-imperial critiques of the international jurists, it is more likely to be found in the anti-imperialism of the first fifty years of the twentieth century. They may have achieved little in the 1880s and 1890s, but they were writing on the eve of the break-up of an international order that was based upon empires, and the creation of a new system in which empires persisted, yet self-determining nation states became increasingly prominent. This process was led by anti-imperial nationalism in the colonies, but it was also complemented by liberal anti-imperialists in the metropolis such as Jèze.[93]

90 'The league: assassination preferred', *Time Magazine*, 12 August 1935.

91 There is a growing body of historical scholarship which examines the German occupation of Europe, particularly Eastern Europe, during the war in terms of imperial precedents. See, for example, Wendy Lower, *Nazi empire-building and the Holocaust in Ukraine* (Chapel Hill, 2005).

92 See Raphaël Lemkin, *Axis rule in occupied Europe: laws of occupation, analysis of government, proposals for redress* (Washington DC, 1944); and Hannah Arendt, *The origins of totalitarianism* (New York, 1962).

93 Erez Manela, *The Wilsonian moment* (Oxford, 2007), p. 8.

Self-interest as a basis for imperial critique might be thought to collapse back into a national and positivist understanding of rights. I have pointed out that the juristic critics of empire were partly motivated by the natural rights tradition and so frequently appealed to universals rather than to positive law. If, however, these jurists were merely opposing empire from a sense of national self-interest, or the liberties of subjects in their own states, then it may seem that their interest in rights was not universal but national after all. It is true that their motivations were primarily national. The reason, however, that they often used a universal idea of rights rather than one based upon positive law was because they did not trust sovereignty or positive law as sufficient guarantees of their rights as citizens of their states – that is, they were critiquing sovereignty. Universal laws, laws that were autonomous from the state, were thus employed to argue for the rights of the subjects of nation states. For these jurists, the advantage of natural and universal theories of rights was that they were not subject to sovereignty; in other words, for many liberals, the strength of natural law was what positivists saw as its weakness.

Liberal scepticism of empire was generally not, then, motivated by humanitarian sentiment, but by self-interested concern about the endurance of the European revolutions. The same sceptics frequently identified philanthropy as the apology for empire that it was. This domestic motivation for concern about liberty abroad underlines one of the weaknesses of some of the influential studies produced in international history over the past ten years. In these accounts the human rights wave of the twentieth century has been presented as an international agenda pursued by the major powers in order to satisfy strategic goals.[94] This cynicism has been partly justified, but it diminishes the national rather than international goals of those who pursued rights. Rights theories and rights claims, it must be remembered, were developed by jurists and politicians, many of whom, whether or not they held that rights could be autonomous of states, believed that they placed a limit on state power. In the nineteenth century, these same figures frequently pursued rights in international contexts in order to secure what they believed to be fragile national freedoms.

It remains, therefore, to reconsider the relationship of liberalism to empire and the role that international law played in this relationship. International law certainly was at the forefront of the projection of

[94] Mark Mazower, 'The strange triumph of human rights, 1933–1950', *Historical Journal*, 47(2) (2004), 379–98; Mark Mazower, *No enchanted palace: the end of empire and the ideological origins of the United Nations* (Princeton, 2009); Moyn, *Last utopia*.

sovereignty onto the non-European world and there is no better example of that than Twiss' involvement with Leopold (although it is not a case driven by national interests insofar as Twiss or Belgium was concerned). But international law was also one of the domains in which opposition to empire was most strongly articulated. The liberal reformers from the generation that established the *Institut de droit international* were internationalists. Some were internationalists because they thought international cooperation was the only means by which the expansion of empire could be organised in such a way that would preserve peace, and they placed those ambitions upon the Berlin Conference. The internationalism of the sceptics of empire was motivated by a belief that only international agreements could restrain Europe from plunging into a new imperial epoch which would imperil the new-found liberty of European states. Internationalism, then, was an intellectual tool, as was international law.

These tools could be turned to different, and conflicting, ends. The liberal toolbox offered many such examples. Rights, too, were a tool that could be used to conflicting ends. Rights were used to support the projection of European sovereignty. The concept of *territorium nullius* was a species of rights argument. It was a concept that conceded that Africans did have property and even limited sovereignty, but insisted that their land could still be open to the imposition of territorial sovereignty – that is, open to the creation of protectorates. But even this weapon, which seemed to point in only one direction, could be turned upon its creators. Sceptics appropriated the term and replied that Africa was not *territorium nullius*.

The tool of rights was used in other ways. Amongst the European jurists, diplomats and politicians whom I have examined, many of those who were most sceptical of empire claimed that rights exist outside the system of state sovereignty, while those who believed rights to be the creation of states were often least troubled by empire. By contrast, American expansionists insisted on the rights of property independent of the state (indeed, this was the ideology that had nourished the land speculators after the Proclamation of 1763).

The instability of these arguments underlines a larger point about the nature of international law and liberalism. While it is true that both international law and liberalism emerged in an imperial context, this context must be understood to include both pro- and anti-imperial voices. Liberalism may have been constituted by a consensus about the desirability of liberty, rights and duties, freedom of commerce, the rule of law and the sanctity of property. However, it was also characterised by a dialogue upon how to achieve these objectives and by divisions over fundamental issues such as whether the origin of rights was inside or outside the state. This dialogue was not accidental, it was an engagement between adversaries. As is clear in the case of the debate over Africa, participants in the dialogue were directly responding to each other's arguments and their disagreement was pursued through institutions as well as texts. This dialogue and conflict, rather than doctrine, defined liberalism.

CHAPTER 10

Terra nullius and the polar regions

Terra nullius is a term used widely by historians, social scientists and lawyers to refer to land that belongs to nobody. More precisely, the term has been used to refer to cases where land which did belong to particular peoples was perceived by European colonisers to belong to nobody. The term has thus been used to describe a doctrine whereby the occupation of those lands was justified by the idea that the Europeans were the first takers. *Terra nullius* has become shorthand for the doctrine of occupation as it was deployed in the justification of empire. When, however, one examines most instances in which the so-called doctrine of *terra nullius* is said to have been employed, there is no evidence in the historical record of that being used, although there is usually evidence of the conventions and language of occupation being employed. In recent years, a number of historians have expressed scepticism about the historical presence of *terra nullius* as a justification of colonisation.[1] But the term nevertheless persists in historical analysis, partly as an explanatory tool but also as a claim of historical fact.[2]

[1] Australian scholarship has generated scepticism about the historical accuracy of *terra nullius* as a concept employed to justify colonisation. See: David Ritter, 'The "rejection of *terra nullius*" in *Mabo*. A critical analysis', *Sydney Law Review*, 18(1) (1996), 5–34; Merete Borch, 'Rethinking the origin of *terra nullius*', *Australian Historical Studies*, 32(117) (2001), 222–39, at 222, n. 1; Bain Attwood, '*The law of the land* or the law of the land? History, law and narrative in a settler society', *History Compass*, 2 (2004), 1–30; Michael Connor, *The invention of terra nullius: Historical and legal fictions on the foundation of Australia* (Sydney, 2005); Fitzmaurice, 'A genealogy of *terra nullius*'. This critique is now showing signs of broader acceptance; see, for example: Vicki Hsueh, *Hybrid constitutions: challenging legacies of law, privilege and culture in colonial America* (Durham, NC, 2010), pp. 127–8; Benton and Straumann, 'Acquiring empire by law'.

[2] Anthony Pagden concedes that the term 'terra nullius' was not employed in the law of nations prior to the nineteenth century, but nevertheless identifies the doctrine as having been at work from at least the seventeenth century: Pagden, 'Law, colonization, legitimation, and the European background', pp. 19–22; Carole Pateman, 'The settler contract', in Carole Pateman and Charles Mills, *Contract and domination* (Cambridge, 2007), pp. 35–46 is aware that *terra nullius* is largely absent from the colonial record, but argues that the concept nevertheless usefully summarises the

This disjunction between described historical facts and terminology may seem little more than a semantic problem, as also in the cases of *res nullius* or *territorium nullius*. That semantic problem, however, reveals more important issues. First, it obscures the history of the idea of *terra nullius* as it was used to discuss European expansion. That history is complex, albeit relatively recent, and yet it is disguised by the perception that *terra nullius* could be found all through the historical record, even in Roman law. *Terra nullius* did not begin to be used in any systematic way to discuss European expansion until the second half of the nineteenth century and, even then, it did not take off as a concept in international law until the 1890s and 1900s. That moment becomes invisible if it is obscured by a perception that discussions of *terra nullius* date back to Vitoria and Roman law. The second problem with the disjunction between historical facts and terminology is that it obscures the long and complex history of ways in

doctrine of occupation. David Boucher makes a similar concession in 'The law of nations and the doctrine of *terra nullius*', in Olaf Asbach and Peter Schröder (eds.), *War, the state and international law in seventeenth century Europe* (Farnham, 2010), pp. 69–73. While acknowledging that the term 'terra nullius' is absent from the historical record in the seventeenth century, Boucher argues that the law of nations was not a body of positive law, so we cannot expect to find its doctrines stated in a positive way. This argument would appear to grant considerable licence to the historian in search of a doctrine. *Terra nullius* thus persists as a central term of historical analysis; see also, for example: Stuart Banner, 'Why *terra nullius*? Anthropology and property law in early Australia', *Law and History Review*, 23(1) (2005), 95–132; Banner, *How the Indians lost their land*; Stuart Banner, *Possessing the Pacific: land settlers and indigenous people from Australia to Alaska* (Cambridge, MA, 2007). See also Benton, *Law and colonial cultures*, pp. 168–9: 'English theorists ... countered Spanish claims of conquest in the Americas by asserting that English settlers had not conquered New World territories but had merely occupied them. In doing so they relied on the Roman legal principle of *terra nullius*'. See too Sven Lindqvist, *Terra nullius. A journey through no one's land*, trans. Sarah Death (London, 2007); Laura Westra, *Environmental justice and the rights of indigenous peoples* (London, 2008), Chapter 2; S. James Anaya, *Indigenous people in international law* (Oxford, 1996), p. 29; Moretti, *International law and nomadic people*, pp. 117–19; Robert J. Miller, Jacinta Ruru, Larissa Behrendt and Tracey Lindberg, *Discovering indigenous lands: the doctrine of discovery in the English colonies* (Oxford, 2010), pp. 260–2. See also Alan Daniel McMillan and Eldon Yellowhorn, *First peoples in Canada* (Vancouver, 2004), p. 26: 'Although *terra nullius* now seems a curious intellectual artefact, this legal fiction was once a powerful instrument that legitimated the European claim to land already held by Aboriginal people.' In Canada, the term 'terra nullius' was also used to describe the state of the land in which the first indigenous peoples found themselves; see *Dorothy Marie Van der Peet* v. *Her Majesty The Queen* [1996] 2 SCR 507. The term 'territorium nullius' remained moribund in the second half of the twentieth century, with few exceptions. Brian Slattery tested whether the concept of *territorium nullius* had been used to justify French colonisation in New France, but he rejected this proposition, just as Australian historians were rejecting the idea that Australia had been *terra nullius* at the time of colonisation (although they claimed that it was perceived as such): Slattery, *French claims to North America*, p. 2. Paul Keal, *European conquest and the rights of indigenous peoples* (Cambridge, 2003), pp. 50–2 strikes a more sceptical note on the historical use of *terra nullius*, although he elides the difference between *terra* and *territorium nullius*. *Terra nullius* continues to be a term widely employed by historians of international law: see, for example, the essays in Malcolm Shaw (ed.), *Title to territory* (Aldershot, 2005).

which ideas of occupation have been used to explore the justice of empire. In the case of Australia, for example, to say that colonisation was justified by a doctrine of *terra nullius* is to obscure the complex and often conflicting justifications that were used with one coherent, and mythical, doctrine. Certainly, the doctrine of occupation was employed extensively in justifying Australian colonisation.[3] It was used in subtle ways and adapted to new circumstances, and that complexity is only beginning to be revealed by historians.[4]

Terra nullius prior to the 1890s

While *terra nullius* was not a term employed systematically in the law of nations prior to the late nineteenth century, it was nevertheless occasionally employed in that context, and also in civil and canon law, in the seventeenth and eighteenth centuries. It was employed, moreover, to describe the Roman and civil law of occupation. Samuel von Cocceji, for example, used the term 'terra nullius' more than once in his 1751 commentary on his father's Latin edition of Grotius' *On the law of war and peace*, and he used it to discuss Roman colonisation: 'If part of the people, by their own private authority, fix their seats in the lands of no one [*terris nullius*], they will establish the highest authority of government; whence Rome, a colony of Alba, was founded in a place belonging to no one as a free state by certain private individuals having been thrown out and exiled by the unanimous law of the state.'[5] Cocceji, as we have seen, was First Minister to Frederick the Great.[6] He compiled the Frederician Code, which he completed in 1755, and in which he declared all things that belonged to nobody were to be the property of Frederick. Clearly, however, in the commentary on Grotius, which concerned land that fell

[3] For ample evidence on this point, see Reynolds, *The law of the land*.

[4] For an analysis of the complexities of the law of nature and nations transported to Australia, see Ian Hunter, 'Natural law, historiography, and Aboriginal sovereignty', *Legal History*, 11 (2007), 137–67.

[5] Samuel Cocceius, *Introductio ad Henrici L. B. Coccei Grotium Illustratum* (1751), p. 547: 'Si pars populi, private auctoritate migrantis, sedes figat in terris nullius, ipsi fiunt summa potestas; unde Roma, colonia Albanorum, a privatis quibusdam expositis, & ab omni jure civitatis exclusis, in loco nullius condita, libera fuit civitas.' See also p. 394 for a further example: 'Posito principio, res terra nullius esse, necessario sequitur, cuique hominum jus esse res illas occupandi. & suas faciendi [With the principle having been assumed, that land belongs to no one, necessarily it follows that any person has a right to occupy those things and make them their own].' See also Samuel Cocceius, *Introductio ad Henrici L. B. de Cocceii Grotium Illustratum* (1759), p. 137: 'Omnes res terrae nullius, i.e. in nullius bonis esse [All things of the land belong to no one, that is, they are amongst the possessions of no one.]'

[6] For Cocceji, see Haakonssen, *Natural law and moral philosophy*, pp. 135–45.

outside the law of the state, the principle of the first taker applied, even though Cocceji spurned it in the Code. As we have seen, the Prussians took a similar view of the law of sea as it related to prizes. *Res nullius* and *terra nullius* were principles that could only apply outside the reach of the state.

There are a number of other relatively isolated uses of 'terra nullius' in discussions of occupation over the seventeenth and eighteenth centuries.[7] When, however, we turn to the major sources for the law of nations, the law of nature and civil law, it is absent. There is not a word of *terra nullius* in Pufendorf, Locke, Wolff, Vattel, Ferguson, Hume, Kant or Smith, nor is there any mention in the texts of civil law discussed in Chapter 8, although, as we have seen, it was in those texts that we discover systematic and reified treatment of *res nullius.*

In the mid-nineteenth century, *terra nullius* began to be used for the first time in a reified, doctrinal way and for the first time to describe a theory of occupation in international law. One of the earliest such uses was in relation to the Oregon question. There was no mention of *terra nullius* in the debates over the Oregon Territory up to 1846 (including nothing from Sir Travers Twiss, who would later write of *nullius territorium*). But in 1866 an anonymous author, reviewing a new edition of Henry Wheaton's *Elements of international law* in the *North American Review*, used the term *terra nullius* in relation to the law of nations in a doctrinal way.[8] According to the author, Great Britain and Russia claimed that Oregon was *terra nullius*, although it was plain from the Monroe Doctrine that no part of the American continent remained untouched by the sovereignty of 'civilized nations' and, in this particular instance, the United States. British and Russian treatises and diplomatic correspondence at the time of the Oregon dispute contain no mention of *terra nullius.* It was indicative, however, of future usage that the author used the term to describe an area,

[7] For canon law, see Luke Joseph Hooke, *Religionis naturalis et revelatae principia* (Paris, 1774) p. 359 'Hujus facultatis exercitum ita gratum esse docent, ut res maxime indifferentes, sola electione, fratae efficiantur; sicuti enim terra nullius est natura, cedit vero in jus occupantis, atque ex ipsa occupatione jus oritur [In such a way they teach an army/disciplined mind to be grateful for this opportunity/resource, that the matters are very much neither good nor bad, with only one choice, the spoken of things are brought about; for just as the land, by nature, belongs to no one, it falls truly into the law of occupying, and so the law arises from the occupation itself].' For civil law, see J. P. F. Vander Graef, *Syntagma Juris Publici* (1644), p. 394, who uses the term 'terra nullius' for a chapter on occupation and prescription, but does not otherwise use the term: 'CAP. LV. DE TERRA NULLIUS, DERELICTA, ET PRAESCRIPTIONE LIBERTATIS.'

[8] Anon., 'The present aspect of international law', *North American Review*, 103 (1866), 466–98, at 472. There is no mention of *terra nullius* in the edition of Wheaton this author was reviewing, although there was an extensive discussion of occupation.

the northern part of what is now Alaska, which was believed at the time to be largely uninhabited, with the indigenous Inupiat people not even registering in most accounts.

The eminent German-American historian, Hermann Eduard von Holst, made a similar reference to *terra nullius* in 1885 in relation to the conflict between Spain and the United States over Contoy Island, off the coast of Yucatan, in 1850.[9] Holst claimed that 'Barringer, the American ambassador at Madrid, was unquestionably right when he said that Contoy was not, in an international sense, a desert, that is an abandoned island and hence *terra nullius*'. Barringer's 1850 correspondence reveals his use of the Roman law doctrine of the first taker, but it does not contain the term 'terra nullius'.[10] Importantly, however, Holst's reference to *terra nullius* was to an uninhabited island and this absence of people would be important in later understandings of the concept.

Terra nullius and Venezuela

In 1803 the British seized the three Dutch colonies in Guiana. The Dutch ceded those territories to Britain in 1814. In 1831 the administration of the three colonies was combined into British Guiana. The boundary between this British possession and neighbouring Venezuela became contentious immediately after Venezuela gained full autonomy in 1830. An extensive territory lying between the Orinoco and Cuyini Rivers, greater than the territory of England itself, had remained largely unoccupied by Spanish, Dutch and English colonisers over the previous 300 years. The English pressed their claims harder after the discovery of gold in the Orinoco Basin in the 1880s.[11]

As this crisis deepened, the Venezuelan government employed the American diplomat William Scruggs to lobby the US government to support its cause. Scruggs cast the conflict in terms of the Monroe Doctrine.[12] He argued that British intervention in Guiana was against Monroe's dictate that Old World states should not engage in new

[9] Hermann Eduard von Holst, *The constitutional and political history of the United States*, trans. J. Lalor from the German edn of 1877–92 (Chicago, 1885), vol. 4, p. 51.

[10] 'Barringer to Pidal', Madrid, 19 September 1850, in *Diplomatic correspondence of the United States: inter-American affairs* (Washington DC, 1939), vol. XI, *Spain*, p. 557. I would like to thank David Armitage for assistance with this reference.

[11] *Further documents relating to the question of the boundary between British Guiana and Venezuela. Dispatch from Her Majesty's Ambassador at Washington, inclosing the first part of the brief for Venezuela* (London, August 1896), p. 2.

[12] William Scruggs, *British aggressions in Venezuela: the Monroe Doctrine on trial* (Atlanta, 1895).

colonising ventures in the New World. The Monroe Doctrine implied that the United States should be an interested party in the liberties of any state in its sphere of influence when they did come into conflict with Old World colonisers. Persuaded by Scruggs, President Grover Cleveland pressed for US arbitration of the dispute between Britain and Venezuela.

Julian Pauncefote was now British Ambassador to the United States. He had been Permanent Under-Secretary of State and managed the Foreign Office response to the Berlin Conference in 1884/5. He and the British Prime Minister, Lord Salisbury, reluctantly accepted the American arbitration. This capitulation has been understood as a triumph for the Monroe Doctrine in its first real test.[13] The British, however, manipulated the dispute in such a way as to secure their own victory. The judgment by the arbitration commission was a triumph for Britain; the vast majority of the contested territory was awarded to the British.

Julian Pauncefote negotiated the treaty establishing the rules for the commission of arbitration with the President of Venezuela.[14] The Venezuelan case rested upon a spectrum of claims, including prior discovery and even the Donation of Alexander. Pauncefote succeeded in having the dispute considered almost entirely in terms of the question of occupation. Having been deeply involved in the Berlin negotiations and as a lawyer himself by training (he had been an Attorney General and Chief Justice in the colonies), Pauncefote was familiar with the law of occupation and with its dominance in international law. The first 'rule' established in the treaty was that: 'Adverse holding or prescription during a period of fifty years shall make a good title.' Adverse holding, or adverse possession, was mere occupation in the face of any other legal claims, while prescription constituted a title by occupation to what had previously been occupied by others. The only other rule agreed was that the arbitrators could employ any principles of international law so long as they did not conflict with the first rule of occupation. These rules favoured the British case, albeit that the British did not really occupy the territory any more than the Venezuelans – the true occupants were the native people who the British claimed had recognised Dutch and, by the rules of cession, then British sovereignty. Also in favour of the British was the fact that they could nominate two of the five jurists, while two others would be nominated by

[13] George C. Herring, *From colony to superpower: U.S. foreign relations since 1776* (New York, 2008) pp. 307–8. See also Paul Gibb, 'Unmasterly inactivity? Sir Julian Pauncefote, Lord Salisbury, and the Venezuela boundary dispute', *Diplomacy and Statecraft*, 16(1) (2005), 23–55.

[14] *Treaty between Great Britain and the United States of Venezuela respecting settlement of the boundary between the colony of British Guiana and the United States of Venezuela* (London, 1887), pp. 2–3.

the United States, with the fifth, the president, chosen by the four. The eminent international lawyer, the Russian Frédéric de Martens, was nominated President of the Tribunal of Arbitration. Martens persuaded the American jurors, who favoured the Venezuelan case, to support a compromise that favoured the British. His support for the British has been portrayed as a deal between Russia and Britain, but it also reflected the bias in favour of occupation in the conventions of international law and that bias was reflected in the 1887 treaty agreeing to the rules by which the conflict would be settled.[15]

It was in the understanding of occupation that the term 'terra nullius' was introduced to the Guiana case. It is striking that, only ten years after the Berlin Conference, the term 'territorium nullius' was not employed by either the British or the Venezuelan side in the conflict, or by any of the jurors, or in the cases presented to the Tribunal of Arbitration. This was in spite of the fact that a number of participants, such as Pauncefote, had been prominent in the Berlin negotiations, and Martens had himself been part of the *Institut de droit international* commission, chaired by Ferdinand Martitz, which had examined the rules of occupation established in Berlin and adopted the term 'territorium nullius' to describe territory partly civilised but not under territorial sovereignty. Both the British and the Venezuelans claimed to possess sovereignty over the disputed territory, and both claimed to have established their sovereignty through occupation. The Venezuelans introduced the term 'terra nullius' into the debate in a negative sense – that is, to argue that the disputed territory was not *terra nullius* and that it was occupied by the Spanish when the Dutch arrived in the first half of the seventeenth century: 'The Dutch not having come as occupants of *terra nullius*, but as mere trespassers on territory belonging to Spain.'[16] The British did not respond that the territory had been *terra nullius* when the Dutch arrived. They sidestepped this question, merely arguing that: 'The Dutch were in no sense trespassers on territory belonging to Spain.'[17]

[15] On Martens making a deal between Britain and Russia, see Otto Schoenrich, 'The Venezuela-British Guiana boundary dispute', *American Journal of International Law*, 43(3) (1949), 523–50, at 523.

[16] *The case of the United States of Venezuela before the tribunal of arbitration*, Venezuela-British Guiana boundary arbitration, Venezuela No. 1 (1899), vol. 1, p. 231. This passage was then cited in *Counter-case presented on the part of the government of Her Britannic Majesty to the Tribunal of Arbitration*, boundary between British Guiana and Venezuela, Venezuela No. 2 (1899), p. 138.

[17] *Counter-case presented on the part of the government of Her Britannic Majesty to the Tribunal of Arbitration*, p. 138.

When the case was heard before the tribunal in Paris in 1899, both sides used the term 'terra nullius', which had been employed in the written cases. Benjamin Harrison, the former US President, argued the case for Venezuela, supported by the Venezuelan lawyer Severo Mallet-Provost, and two former members of Harrison's administration, Benjamin F. Tracey and the jurist James R. Soley (1850–1911). Richard Webster, the British Attorney General, argued the British case. On 25 August 1899, Soley, arguing for Venezuela, employed the term 'terra nullius', but he introduced a different context for the term than that which had been used in the written case for Venezuela. Referring to an informal agreement between Venezuela and Britain in 1850 that neither side would encroach on the disputed territory, Soley claimed that an effect of this agreement was to 'negative any possible suggestion of a *terra nullius* between the two parties. The agreement was between coterminous States, and there was certainly no room for a *terra nullius*'.[18] In this instance, Soley was using *terra nullius* to refer to a territory that was unoccupied and common, such as the sea, and he rejected the notion that the disputed territory could be treated in that sense. He accepted that 'no jurisdiction in any real sense had been exercised in those parts even before 1850', but he also assumed that occupation was inevitable. He clearly dismissed the indigenous people as occupants in a legal sense and that dismissal was explicit in the Venezuelan case, which stated that 'by the law of nations and the universal practice of all European states the American tribes having distinct territorial bounds had only a possessory right to the lands occupied, and this right they were incapable to transfer'. A discoverer, having undertaken the 'acts necessary to the appropriation of wild lands', would have 'an exclusive right to extinguish the possessory right of the tribes'. Importantly, the tribes could not cede their lands by 'deed or treaty of cession, much less could they do by any submission or alliance'.[19] This was an anthropology that cast the native inhabitants in far more primitive terms than had recently been the case in Africa.

On 19 September, Harrison took up the case for Venezuela and again made extensive use of the idea of *terra nullius*. According to him, *terra nullius* was a concept used by the British to describe the disputed territory. It was, he argued, highly dubious whether such a territory, void of jurisdiction, existed in fact. *The Times* reported that Harrison 'complained

[18] 'The Venezuela arbitration', *The Times*, 28 August 1899, p. 5.

[19] *The counter-case of the United States of Venezuela before the Tribunal of Arbitration*, Venezuela-British Guiana boundary arbitration, Venezuela No. 5 (1899), pp. 96–7.

that it was difficult to deal with so shadowy a proposition as this of *terra nullius* . . . no Dutch authority and no Spanish authority had ever held any such theory . . . no British authority had ever done so until the present case'.[20] In fact, the British did not use the term 'terra nullius', although they had proposed that the disputed territory was void of jurisdiction. It was clear that the Venezuelan lawyers were using the term 'terra nullius' in more than one sense, although in each case it was employed to refer to an absence of law and so to an absence of occupation, and in this respect it differed from the use of *territorium nullius* and was also consistent with the understanding of *terra nullius* that would soon develop in discussion of the polar regions.

The polar regions debate

While there are a few scattered references to *terra nullius* in international law prior to 1900, the term had not gained much traction in the understanding of occupation. From early on in the new century, however, there was an explosion in the use of *terra nullius* in international law. Moreover, the term began to be employed with a systematic signification, referring to territory which had no law or property and little or no population. The reason for this development of the term was the debate over the polar regions in which the perceived absence of law, property and people required some systematic legal theorisation, particularly insofar as it contrasted with the debates, twenty years before, over the densely populated territories of Africa.

Following the 'carve-up' of Africa in the 1870s and 1880s, European and North American states turned their attention to the only remaining parts of the globe which had not been subject to the competition for sovereignty. These were the Poles. After concerted exploration of the polar regions in the first half of the nineteenth century, it was not until the 1890s that serious efforts were again made to reach and explore the North and South Poles. Expeditions between 1898 and 1917 provoked a prolonged discussion of the Poles' legal status (this discussion is now being reignited by the shrinking of the polar ice cap over the North Pole). The legal arguments concerning the North Pole became unsettled by the realisation as late as 1895 that there was no land under the ice. Could it be possible, the jurists wondered, to establish sovereignty over floating ice? Does the law of the sea apply to frozen water?[21]

[20] 'The Venezuela arbitration', *The Times* (21 September 1899), p. 4.

[21] For these debates, see the *Revue générale de droit international public* from the 1890s to the 1910s.

The arguments found firmer ground when the jurists turned their attention to islands that lay within the Arctic Circle and over which no sovereignty had been established. The most important of these was Spitsbergen between 76 degrees and 80 degrees latitude north and approximately 800 km north of the northernmost point of Norway. Spitsbergen should have been uninhabitable, but it is located at the northeastern end of the Gulf Stream, which moderated its climate and kept its southern and western shores free of ice for half the year.

From at least the sixteenth century, European fishermen travelled north into the Arctic seas each summer. But from the seventeenth century, these visitors came in large numbers – up to 20,000 a year according to some accounts – and established habitation on the island of Spitsbergen. In addition to the fish and whales, fur hunting was established on the island. An international community of nomads, including Dutch, English, Norwegians and Russians, came each summer and most left each winter. The island had no Inuit inhabitants. Finally, in 1906 permanent habitation was established along with a new industry – coal. For the European states, these people formed an anarchic community; that is, they did not live under any formal sovereignty even if they had houses, flourishing commerce, a graveyard, a hotel and a bakery. By the late nineteenth century, polar exploration increased the pressure to resolve this situation and both Norway and Russia made strong claims to the island, although the treaty granting Norway sovereignty over the archipelago of Svalbard, of which Spitsbergen was the principal island, was not signed until 1925.[22]

Between 1908 and 1911, the *Revue générale de droit international public* devoted many pages to the problems of the polar regions, including a series of seminal studies on them by the French jurist René Waultrin.[23] But it was in 1909, while trying to resolve the question of the sovereignty of Spitsbergen, that the Italian international jurist Camille Piccioni described the island as 'terra nullius'. Piccioni declared that: 'The issue would have been simpler if Spitsbergen, until now *terra nullius*, could have been attributed to a single state, for reasons of neighbouring or earlier occupation. But this is not the case and several powers can, for different reasons, make their claims to this territory which still has no master.'[24] By this he

[22] For the pre-twentieth-century history of Spitsbergen, see René Waultrin, 'La question de la souveraineté des terres arctiques', *Revue générale de droit international public*, XV (1908), 78–125 and 185–209.

[23] *Ibid.*

[24] Camille Piccioni, 'L'organisation du Spitzberg', *Revue générale de droit international public*, XVI (1909), 117–34, at 118, my translation. Geir Ulfstein, *The Svalbard Treaty: from terra nullius to*

meant not that the island was uninhabited – he knew well that it was inhabited – but that it was inhabited in such a way that sovereignty had not been established and property had not been secured; that is, it was inhabited sparsely with a low level of exploitation of natural resources.[25] Piccioni was unsatisfied with the status of *terra nullius*. The problem was that Spitsbergen was capable of occupation, yet the powers concerned had 'promised' 'to leave it in the situation of *terra nullius*'.[26] Thus, *terra nullius* was being used to describe territory that it had been agreed would remain common.[27]

This understanding of *terra nullius* as territory that should be left common prevailed throughout the discussions of the problem of polar sovereignty in these early years of the twentieth century. James Brown Scott, the eminent jurist and President of the American Institute of International Law, wrote in the same year as Piccioni on Arctic exploration and international law, and he too concluded that Spitsbergen should remain *terra nullius*, although he was less critical of that status than Piccioni had been. What interested Scott was that, by virtue of international agreements, Arctic territory could remain *terra nullius* even after its discovery. He conceded that in international law discovery vested no title, or only an inchoate title, and that this convention had been confirmed by 'a solemn agreement of the powers interested in Africa'. But he also noted that discovery was usually a first step towards occupation from which title would be established. It was this widely accepted process that would not be followed in the Arctic. The reason for this exception to international law, and thus for the Arctic remaining *terra nullius*, was because the discovery and occupation of the Arctic was conducted with a different 'intent' than was customary – namely, it was conducted for the purposes of scientific exploration and not the appropriation of territory.

Norwegian sovereignty (Oslo, 1995) pp. 36–7 cites 1871 diplomatic correspondence between Sweden and Russia over Spitsbergen as a statement of *terra nullius*. But while that 1871 correspondence contains a statement of the law of the first taker applied to the island, it does not contain the term 'terra nullius'; see *ШПИЦБЕРГЕНЪ 1871–1912* [*Diplomatic Correspondence Spitsbergen 1871–1912*] (St Petersburg, 1912), '17/29 Марта 1871 года', p. 3.

25 Piccioni certainly helped popularise the idea of *terra nullius* in international law. Ernest Nys in the 1904 edition of his *Droit international* and Franz Despagnet in his 1896 *Essai sur les protectorats* made no mention of *terra nullius*. But in the 1912 edition of *Droit international*, Nys adopted the term, citing Piccioni, and in 1910, just one year after Piccioni's article was published, Despagnet employed the term in his *Cours de droit international public*, again citing Piccioni.

26 Piccioni, 'L'organisation du Spitzberg', p.119.

27 *Ibid.*, p. 128. See also Frances Bowes Sayre, *Experiments in international administration* (New York, 1919), p. 92, in which Sayre, a Harvard law professor, declared that Spitsbergen 'has for centuries existed as a *terra nullius*, too far north for human occupation'.

'There is', he observed, 'great difficulty in applying the present theory and practice of discovery and occupation to the Arctic regions . . . for Arctic expeditions are usually voyages of discovery in which there is no present or future intent to annex the territory actually discovered.'[28] Notwithstanding, he argued, the fact that Spitsbergen had been discovered *and* occupied over the past two centuries, it continued to be considered 'no man's land' 'by reason of the fact that the voyages of discovery and the explorations made in islands in the past two centuries were scientific'.

Given, however, that Spitsbergen was occupied, there remained the problem of how to secure property, life and to administer justice. For this purpose, Scott noted, a conference had been called in Christiania (later Oslo) in the following year. This conference would establish 'a system of administration, without, however, appropriating the islands to any one of the participating powers or changing the status as *terra nullius*'.[29] According to this understanding, *terra nullius* was a doctrine that created an exception to the conventions on the occupation of land that had been established in the law of nations and international law over centuries. But it was also an extension of the principles established by Grotius on the law of the sea, only in this case applied to land, namely a territory that would remain in common because it had a value for all, which, in Scott's understanding, was its value for science. As Lage F. W. von Staël-Holstein would later write, Spitsbergen could be 'a great free museum for the display of Arctic nature'.[30]

The 1910 conference in Christiania of the powers concerned with Spitsbergen produced a protocol signed by Sweden, Norway and Russia in 1912. This protocol confirmed the understanding of *terra nullius* as land without owners and that would remain without owners. 'Article 1' of the protocol stated that: 'Spitsbergen will stay *terra nullius*. It cannot, either in whole or part, be annexed by any state, nor can it be submitted, under any form whatsoever, to the sovereignty of any power.'[31] In 1914 a large conference assembled again in Christiania to determine the administration and status of Spitsbergen. All parties were reported to agree that the archipelago should remain *terra nullius* in the sense of remaining common, but before a formal treaty could be established, war broke out and the conference dissolved.

[28] James Brown Scott, 'Arctic exploration and international law', *American Journal of International Law*, 3(4) (1909), 928–41, at 940.

[29] *Ibid.*, 941. [30] Lage F. W. von Staël-Holstein, *Norway in arcticum* (Copenhagen, 1932), p. 8.

[31] *Ibid.*, p. 36, my translation.

In the years prior to the war, a broad range of studies consented to the status of the polar regions, and particularly Spitsbergen, as regions that were and should remain common and open to scientific study, and they employed the term 'terra nullius' to describe this status. Even during the war, Robert Lansing, the US Secretary of State, argued that 'all the world recognises' Spitsbergen 'as *terra nullius*' and he wished it to remain that way.[32] However, he too was concerned with the fact that the island needed a form of government over the people who frequented it, while remaining *terra nullius*. He argued that a form of sovereignty over people, or 'political sovereignty', could be introduced into Spitsbergen without introducing 'territorial sovereignty' 'in order to preserve the doctrine of *terra nullius*': 'Ownership in the case of land in Spitsbergen could not, therefore, exist.' He added that: 'Exclusive use and occupancy is lacking, and so land in Spitsbergen cannot, in the true sense, be owned.'[33] The scientist Robert Neal Rudmose-Brown, writing at the end of the First World War, also acknowledged that some form of government had to be introduced to Spitsbergen in order to regulate the 'anarchy' that prevailed and in order to protect the environment which had been rapidly and greatly degraded by hunters. According to him, the status of Spitsbergen needed to be resolved by the Versailles negotiations after the war.[34] David Miller, who was a legal advisor to the American Commission at the Peace Conference in 1918 and drew up the final draft of the League of Nations Covenant, was similarly dissatisfied with the understanding of the polar regions as *terra nullius*. He commented that the Arctic regions were rapidly becoming occupied and subsumed under sovereignty or claims to sovereignty. In this context, he argued that 'terra nullius' was 'an unsatisfactory ownership by everybody'.[35]

Taking up Lansing's problem of how to administer law in a *terra nullius*, J. E. G. de Montmorency, Professor of Comparative Law at the University of London, wrote in 1918 that: 'An Englishman in a *Terra Nullius* such as

[32] Robert Lansing, 'A unique international problem', *American Journal of International Law*, 11(4) (1917), 763–71, at 767. This article was written, according to J. E. G. de Montmorency, prior to Lansing becoming Secretary of State and so prior to 1915, when he was an editor of the *American Journal of International Law*. See J. E. G. de Montmorency, 'The international position of Spitsbergen', *Journal of Comparative Legislation and International Law* 18(1) (1918), 11–15, at 111.

[33] Lansing, 'A unique international problem', 770.

[34] R. N. Rudmose-Brown, 'Spitsbergen: *terra nullius*', *Geographical Review*, 7(5) (1919), 311–21, at 320.

[35] David Miller, 'Political rights in the polar regions', in *Problems of polar research* (New York, 1928), p. 240. This was first published as 'Political rights in the Arctic', in *Foreign Affairs*, 4 (1925–6), 47–60.

Spitsbergen keeps out the cold with the English common law.'[36] With such extraterritorial powers, it would not really be necessary, therefore, to establish an international government over the island. Far more worrying for Montmorency, and an indication of a new turn in the debate, was the possibility that the people who lived in Spitsbergen could declare that they constituted a sovereign state or, worse, could declare themselves to be under the sovereignty of one state in particular, such as Germany. This 'process of development' seemed 'not improbable' and would create 'new perils for Northern Europe'.[37] Montmorency's and Rudmose-Brown's fears were addressed at the Versailles negotiations. The great powers signed a 'Treaty concerning the archipelago of Spitsbergen' on 9 February 1920.[38] The treaty granted sovereign power over Spitsbergen to Norway while guaranteeing rights of commerce and fishing to all interested parties. It thus ended the state of anarchy while permitting the continuation of the existing mining interests. It also addressed Rudmose-Brown's concern about the environment: 'Norway shall be free to maintain, take or decree suitable measures to ensure the preservation and, if necessary, the re-constitution of the fauna and flora of the said regions.'

Although the status of Spitsbergen was rapidly resolved, Montmorency's fears soon proved to be well founded more generally. In the 1920s and 1930s, the polar regions became the focus of irredentist competition between Northern European powers. They progressively ceased to be perceived as regions of largely scientific interest that should be held in common, like the sea, and began to be the subject of territorial claims. *Terra nullius* continued to be employed to describe the lands subject to this competition, but the meaning of the term was now changed from land that could not be occupied, because it was common, to land that was not occupied but was open to the first taker. This shift in meaning was apparent even as a retrospective description of Spitsbergen. It had been generally agreed that prior to the war, Spitsbergen had been *terra nullius* in the sense of being common, but when the geologist Adolf Hoel wrote about Spitsbergen as *terra nullius* prior to Norwegian sovereignty, his meaning referred to a state of potential exploitation rather than common property. Hoel was a pioneering explorer in Spitsbergen, the founder of *Norges Svalbard-og Ishavsundersøkelser*, which in 1948 became the Norwegian Polar Institute. He was one of the Norwegians most responsible for

36 Montmorency, 'The international position of Spitsbergen', 113. 37 *Ibid.*, 115.

38 'Treaty concerning the archipelago of Spitsbergen' on 9 February 1920, www.austlii.edu.au/au/other/dfat/treaties/1925/10.html.

the grant of sovereignty over Spitsbergen to Norway in 1920.[39] 'Svalbard', he argued, 'was "*terra nullius*"; law and order were not established, and consequently no rules were in place about the claiming of land.'[40] For Hoel, the story of Spitsbergen was the triumph of the coming of industrialisation and Norwegian sovereignty.

Greenland was the main focus of competition in the northern polar regions in 1920s and 1930s, with both Norway and Denmark arguing that they had superior claims. In 1919, Denmark and Norway agreed that if Denmark did not oppose the Norwegian claims to Spitsbergen, Norway would recognise the Danish claim to sovereignty over Greenland. In 1921, however, Denmark sought to exclude all foreigners from Greenland, despite the fact there were a number of Norwegian enterprises located there. Throughout the 1920s and 1930s, Hoel and Gustav Smedal, a Norwegian jurist, urged the Norwegian government to occupy East Greenland and declare sovereignty. It was Smedal and Hoel who 'masterminded' the Norwegian expeditions in the 1930s to occupy part of East Greenland.[41] Norway claimed that East Greenland was *terra nullius* and it claimed sovereignty over the region. The rivals agreed to settle the dispute in the Permanent Court of International Justice (PCIJ) in 1933.[42] The Court's judgment declared that: 'On the Norwegian side it was gradually made clear that, in the opinion of the Norwegian Government, the uncolonized part of the East coast of Greenland was a *terra nullius*.' By *terra nullius*, the Court meant something that could be appropriated in a land that was unpeopled rather than something that was in common.[43] This understanding of *terra nullius* was employed repeatedly throughout the judgment.

The understanding of *terra nullius* as land that was open to the first taker was employed by the Norwegian publicists who wrote at the time of this dispute. John Skeie, Professor of Law at the University of Oslo and Deputy Judge of the Supreme Court, wrote in defence of the Norwegian claims at the time they were under consideration in the PCIJ. He argued that in accordance with international law, title in Greenland should be

[39] Frode Skarstein, '"A cursed affair" – how a Norwegian expedition to Greenland became the USA's first maritime capture in World War II', *Polar Research*, 26 (2007), 181–94.

[40] Adolf Hoel, 'Coal-mining in Svalbard', *Polar Record*, 2(16) (1938), 74–85, at 77.

[41] Skarstein, '"A cursed affair"', 183; and Frode Skarstein, 'Erik the Red's land: the land that never was', *Polar Research*, 29(2) (2006), 173–9.

[42] *Legal Status of Eastern Greenland, Denmark* v. *Norway Judgment*, Permanent Court of International Justice, www.worldcourts.com/pcij/eng/decisions/1933.04.05_greenland.htm.

[43] *Ibid.*, p. 64.

based upon effective occupation and not upon declarations of recognition of sovereignty by third parties (Denmark's title to Greenland had been recognised by Italy, Sweden and the UK). Skeie argued that while Danes had not occupied East Greenland, Norwegian trappers and hunters had effectively occupied the territory for many years and that the foundation of a colony there was recognition of that existing occupation. 'No single foreign state', he declared, 'can prohibit Norway from safeguarding her industrial interests in a *terra nullius*, where her subjects for long periods have pursued lawful occupations.'[44] *Terra nullius* was land open to occupation: 'The position in East Greenland is indisputable that the country until 1921 was a *terra nullius*.'[45] Whether *terra nullius* could be densely populated, or not, was evident from Skeie's observations on the 'Eskimos', or Inuit, who inhabited Greenland prior to the Danish and Norwegian colonies. The Danes had objected to the Norwegian colonisation of East Greenland partly on the basis of their claim to protect the Inuit. Skeie responded that 'there is not a single Eskimo in East Greenland beyond the little colony at Angmagssalik'.[46] *Terra nullius*, it seemed, was a place with very few or no people. Indeed, it was so important to Skeie that *terra nullius* should be a place of no people that he proceeded to argue at length that the Inuit people living in Greenland more generally were fast disappearing as a result of racial mixing. 'Race purity', as Skeie put it, was barely to be found anywhere in Greenland.[47]

It was Smedal and Hoel who did most to put the Norwegian case. Smedal published the most comprehensive consideration of the dispute over East Greenland from the point of view of international law. He published this treatise in the journal on the polar regions edited by Hoel, *Skrifter om Svalbard og Ishavet*. Smedal was an ardent nationalist and, later, a National Socialist and member of the Nasjonal Samling Party, and he collaborated with the National Socialist regime during the war. He was not the only promoter of Norwegian interests in the polar regions to become closely linked with fascist politics. Hoel too joined the Nasjonal Samling Party, largely in response to his anger over the East Greenland decision in 1933.[48] The close identification between expansionist politics and fascism was hardly surprising and it helps to explain the transformation of the idea of *terra nullius*, in the early polar debates, from being a description of land

[44] John Skeie, *Greenland: the dispute between Norway and Denmark* (London, 1932), pp. 74–5.
[45] *Ibid.*, p. 81. [46] *Ibid.*, p. 62. [47] *Ibid.*, p. 63.
[48] On Smedal and Hoel joining the National Socialists, see Skarstein, '"A cursed affair"', 183–4; and Skarstein, 'Erik the Red's land'; and 'Adolf Hoel: Obituary', *Polar Record*, 12(80) (1965), 631.

that was common, and so could not be appropriated, to land that was open to the first taker. As Smedal observed in the introduction to his treatise *Acquisition of sovereignty over polar areas*: 'A third independent cause of the increasing interest in Polar regions may be mentioned. Here we find the only large land areas which are still No-man's-land (*terra nullius*). The desire which exists in all strong political communities to extend their territories can be satisfied here.'[49]

In 1932 the Swedish aristocrat Lage von Staël-Holstein, who had interests in Spitsbergen, argued against the nationalistic tide, declaring that the Poles should remain a domain of scientific cooperation. He condemned Hoel, as well as 'the imperialistic spirit' that 'burns in the Norwegian heart' and the 'imperialistic ambitions' opposed to the 'idea of mutual understanding of common interests'.[50] 'The Norwegians', he observed, 'have recently put up a new conception on behalf of the relations between sovereignty and the right of occupation, which they try to illustrate in their dispute over East Greenland.'[51] But the Norwegians were preaching these theories 'without realising the danger of their application to Spitsbergen'. At least two-thirds of Spitsbergen was 'entirely free from occupation – a unique situation for the present claims of sovereignty'.[52] Where the island was occupied, it was the Soviet Union rather than the Norwegians who had the greater claim.

Smedal, apparently oblivious to these dangers, devoted his treatise to an extensive analysis of the role of occupation in the acquisition of title. He only used the last third of the treatise to examine the East Greenland case, although it was his intention throughout to demonstrate that only occupation can create a true title in *terra nullius*. Whereas the Norwegians had occupied East Greenland, the Danes, he claimed, had failed to do so. His argument that occupation was central to establishing title in international law was certainly justified. In 1909 the French jurist René Waultrin had argued that effective occupation was too stringent a test for title in the polar regions: 'arctic lands cannot be placed', he argued, 'under rules that are as strict as those which apply to tropical lands'. It was not possible, Waultrin argued, to occupy the polar regions in any numbers and therefore a lower bar should be set, with discovery sufficing as the basis for title. Effective occupation should only be a test of title when there is a conflict between parties.[53] Smedal

49 Gustav Smedel, *Acquisition of sovereignty over polar areas* (Oslo, 1931), p. 8.

50 Staël-Holstein, *Norway in arcticum*, pp. 30, 51 and 77. 51 *Ibid.*, p. 67. 52 *Ibid.*, p. 69.

53 René Waultrin, 'Le problème de la souveraineté des pôles', *Revue générale de droit international public*, 16 (1909), 657–8.

strongly disagreed with Waultrin that 'effective occupation' was not necessary in the Poles. 'There is every reason', he argued, 'to dissociate oneself altogether from this opinion, which lacks foundation in international law'.[54] However, he conceded that there was a crucial difference between the occupation of the polar regions and those territories that had been the focus of European colonisation in the past. The difference was in regard to the native population. 'As a rule', he observed, 'more is required for exercising control in densely peopled territories than in territories sparsely peopled or uninhabited. The African Conference in 1884–85, and the *Institut de Droit International* in 1888, had more particularly in view territories with a great native population.'[55] Here Smedal identified the key difference between the theory of *territorium nullius*, which had been produced out of the African Conference in 1884–5 and in the *Institut* debates through to 1888, and the theory of *terra nullius* which he and his contemporaries applied to the Poles. *Territorium nullius* applied to territory rather than simply to land – that is, it applied to inhabited land, even to land where there was sovereignty but no territorial sovereignty. It thus applied to the absence only of territorial sovereignty. *Terra nullius* was a 'no-man's land' which had little or no population (almost all these commentators counted the Inuit for little or nothing). As Smedal put it: 'From a legal point of view it is significant that the Polar areas are, to a great extent, still *terra nullius*, and that they are either uninhabited or have only a scanty population.'[56] *Terra nullius* was thus land where there was not only an absence of territorial sovereignty, but an absence of sovereignty and law altogether.

The Columbia Joint Seminar in International Law

While Norwegian national socialists were discovering in *terra nullius* a doctrine that could justify expansionism, the prominence that had been given to the term by the heat surrounding the polar debate brought it to the attention of a group of international jurists at Columbia University in New York. This group was led by Charles Cheney Hyde and Philip C. Jessup. Hyde came to Columbia in 1925 from the US Department of State to take the Chair in International Law, and Jessup, who had been Hyde's assistant at the Department of State, came with him to an assistant professorship.[57] Along with Joseph P. Chamberlain, who joined the Law School two years earlier, Hyde and Jessup established the Columbia Joint

[54] Smedel, *Acquisition of sovereignty over polar areas*, p. 33. [55] *Ibid.* [56] *Ibid.*, p. 6.
[57] See www.law.columbia.edu/center_program/intl_progs/History.

Seminar in International Law. Students in the seminar included James Simsarian, Oliver Lissitzyn, Arthur Keller and Frederick Mann. This group was concerned with the doctrine of occupation and would remain so for many years. Jessup wrote on the Palmas Island arbitration in 1928 and would publish *Controls for outer space and the Antarctic analogy* in 1959. Their interest in *terra nullius* was stimulated by the debate over the East Greenland case before the PCIJ. Jessup had advised the State Department in 1926 on whether to join the PCIJ. He was an internationalist and would remain so through to the 1960s and 1970s, when he became a judge on the PCIJ's post-Second World War successor, the International Court of Justice (ICJ). He accordingly argued strongly and successfully for US membership of the court which would judge the East Greenland case.[58]

In 1933 Hyde published an article on the East Greenland case.[59] He made no mention of *terra nullius* and concentrated instead on whether the judgment established principles that could be employed more broadly in discussions of occupation, particularly when the circumstances of polar sovereignty were markedly different, as he noted, from other parts of the globe.[60] Hyde would, however, have encountered numerous references to *terra nullius* in reading the East Greenland judgment, and shortly after the publication of this article, the joint seminar was considering whether the concept could be extended beyond the context of the Poles. How useful, they asked, could *terra nullius* be as an explanation of the expansionism of the previous centuries of colonisation? The students in the group published books and articles in which they argued that *terra nullius* could be used to understand the justifications of empire over the previous 400 years. In 1938 James Simsarian published 'The acquisition to legal title in *terra nullius*' in the Columbia-based journal *Political Science Quarterly*, in which he thanked Professors Chamberlain, Hyde and Jessup for having directed his research. In this article he considered all empires from the fifteenth century to the twentieth century. He posed the question of how all the great European empires justified taking possession of *terra nullius*, whether by discovery or occupation. In other words, he assumed that all the territories that had been subject to those imperial designs had in fact been

[58] Philip C. Jessup, *The United States and the world court* (Boston, 1929).

[59] Charles Cheney Hyde, 'The case concerning the legal status of Eastern Greenland', *American Journal of International Law*, 27 (1933), 732–8.

[60] Hyde's earlier two-volume treatise of international law also made no mention of *terra nullius*; see Charles Cheney Hyde, *International law chiefly as interpreted and applied by the United States*, 2 vols. (Boston, 1922).

terra nullius.[61] According to him, discovery and symbolic acts had been sufficient to establish title prior to 1700. He argued that it was only since the competition between England, the United States and Russia over the American Northwest that occupation had become necessary in order to claim title to *terra nullius.* The implication of the changing conditions required for the acquisition of sovereignty meant that different criteria could apply in the one case, depending upon the dates. In the East Greenland judgment, for example, claims made prior to 1700 required a 'less rigid test' to 'legal title to *terra nullius*' than those made after that date.[62]

In the same year that Simsarian published this article, the other students from the seminar, Arthur Keller, Oliver Lissitzyn and Frederick Mann, published a book in which they took their subject to be 'a study of the endeavours of the leading European maritime states, in the period 1400–1800, to acquire dominion over *terra nullius*'.[63] They acknowledged that their subject was 'first brought under our scrutiny' in the Joint Seminar in International Law and they too thanked Professors Chamberlain, Hyde and Jessup. Keller, Lissitzyn and Mann stated that: 'By the term *terra nullius* is meant land not under any sovereignty.' They accordingly confirmed the understanding of the term that developed out of the polar regions debate. This understanding could again be contrasted with the understanding of *territorium nullius* employed in the debate over Africa. While *territorium nullius* was an absence of territorial sovereignty only, but allowed for the possibility of other forms of sovereignty such as 'personal sovereignty', *terra nullius,* as the Columbia professors stressed, was an absence of *any* sovereignty. They then extrapolated: 'The presence of a savage population, of aborigines, or of nomadic tribes engaged in hunting and fishing, was generally disregarded by Europeans. For the purposes of this volume, therefore, insofar as any status of sovereignty is concerned, the existence of such a population will not exclude these lands from our definition of *terra nullius.*'[64]

What is striking about this discussion is that it includes in *terra nullius* many of the peoples, for example, a 'savage population', who had been expressly acknowledged to possess some kind of sovereignty in the debate

[61] James Simsarian, 'The acquisition to legal title in *terra nullius*', *Political Science Quarterly,* 53(1) (1938), 111–28.

[62] *Ibid.*, 128.

[63] Arthur Keller, Oliver Lissitzyn and Frederick Mann, *Creation of rights of sovereignty through symbolic acts 1400–1800* (Columbia, 1938), p. v.

[64] *Ibid.*, p. 4.

over Africa. The expansion of the understanding of occupation in the polar regions to a consideration of the whole history of colonisation, and the territories of many peoples on the globe, was thus a step towards diminishing the recognition of the territorial claims of those peoples. The understanding of polar occupation that was being expanded was not the idea of common land that prevailed prior to the First World War, but rather the notion from the 1920s and 1930s in which those regions were understood as able to be possessed. Importantly, the void in which Spitsbergen and Antarctica were understood to be was extended to lands which were not void of people or sovereignty.

The Columbia Seminar's examination of *terra nullius* was not restricted to its publications. Jessup also wrote to professors of history and law in settler societies asking them about their knowledge of the degree to which *terra nullius* was employed in the understanding of their colonial contexts. In this way the Columbia interpretation of the concept was loaded into its questions and it accordingly facilitated the adoption of its particular understanding of *terra nullius*. The question of whether Australia had been *terra nullius* at the time of colonial occupation was first posed in 1939 when Phillip C. Jessup wrote to the eminent Australian historian Sir Ernest Scott, asking if Australia had been described as *terra nullius* at the time of occupation. In a 'Presidential Address' to the Australian and New Zealand Association for the Advancement of Science in January 1939, Scott recounted the uses of the recently published *Historical records of Australia*, declaring: 'Only last year I received a letter from the Professor of International Law [i.e., Jessup] in one of the greatest of American universities, asking for information on a subject he was working on with advanced students, namely, the assertion of sovereignty over *terra nullius*.'[65] Here Scott gives an insight into the collaborative work of the Columbia group as well as how its ideas were disseminated.

For Scott, it was evident that Australia was *terra nullius* when the Europeans arrived. Indeed, it would be hard to conclude otherwise while employing the Columbia definition, which excluded indigenous peoples as possessors of sovereignty. According to Scott, the volumes of the historical records to which he referred Jessup were enough to establish the fact that

[65] For the delivery of Scott's paper on Australia as *terra nullius* to the Australian and New Zealand Association for the Advancement of Science, see *Report of the twenty-fourth meeting of the Australian and New Zealand Association for the Advancement of Science. Canberra meeting, January 1939* (Sydney, 1939), p. 144. For the delivery of the paper to the Australian Historical Society in October, 1939, see Sir Ernest Scott, 'Taking possession of Australia – the doctrine of *terra nullius* (no-man's land)', *Journal and Proceedings. Royal Australian Historical Society*, XXVI(1) (1940), 1–19, at 1.

Australia had been *terra nullius*. He was sufficiently stimulated by Jessup's inquiry that he twice presented papers on the subject of Australia as *terra nullius*: first, following his Presidential Address, to the Association for the Advancement of Science in January 1939 and again to the Australian Historical Society in October of that year. He died two months later in December, but the paper was published the following year. He claimed that he was 'induced' to write after receiving 'inquiries from Professor Philip C. Jessup'.[66] He shared the Columbia group's understanding that the presence of indigenous people did not prevent the land from being understood to be *terra nullius*, although he noted that as European colonisation proceeded: 'Little regard was paid to the rights of original inhabitants by any of the colonizing peoples.' It was necessary only to consider whether the ceremonies of possession performed by the English gave them sovereignty over that land and, unsurprisingly, Scott concluded that, contrary to the claims of those who performed symbolic acts, they conferred no sovereign rights.[67]

Scott speculated that Jessup's interest in *terra nullius* was provoked by growing competition over the Antarctic. A German expedition was sent to Antarctica in 1938/9 with the partial aim of establishing a German whaling station and naval base as well as sovereignty over a portion of Queen Maud Land, and Nazi flags were duly erected along the coast of that Antarctic territory. The US government sent Rear Admiral Richard E. Byrd on his third expedition to the Antarctic in 1939 in order to establish American bases and limit the German claims. Jessup did not state that the Antarctic expeditions were the immediate cause of his interest in *terra nullius* and, indeed, his seminar had focused upon broadening the scope of *terra nullius* beyond the polar debates. Scott, however, was perceptive in his speculation that Jessup's interest in *terra nullius* was stimulated by American ambitions in the Antarctic.[68] The debate over the polar regions had been an important context for the popularisation of the idea of *terra nullius*. Moreover, the context of competition over the polar regions in the 1930s may explain a seemingly idiosyncratic dimension to Keller, Lissitzyn and Mann's contribution to the debate, *Creation of rights of sovereignty through symbolic acts 1400–1800*. According to the Columbia group, discovery had never been regarded as sufficient grounds for claiming title, but symbolic acts had been. They were speaking about the period prior to 1800 and they focused,

[66] Scott, 'Taking possession of Australia', 1. He also cited Keller, Lissitzyn and Mann's *Creation of rights of sovereignty through symbolic acts*.

[67] Scott, 'Taking possession of Australia', 9.

[68] See *ibid.*, 1–19.

as they said, on state practice rather than publicists (who dismissed claims made on the basis of symbolic acts). Any such claims generally were contested and remained uncertain until secured by conquest (or 'occupation'), but the authors may have had American claims to Antarctica in mind where occupation was impossible.

Jessup retrospectively proved correct Scott's speculations about the motive for his interest in *terra nullius*. Twenty years later, he published (with Howard J. Taubenfeld) *Controls for outer space and the Antarctic analogy*, which discussed the German and American Antarctic expeditions and claims in some detail.[69] As the title suggests, Jessup and Taubenfeld examined similarities in the legal conflicts over the Antarctic and space, and they employed the tools of 'terra nullius' and 'res nullius' to assist the comparison.[70] This legal continuity points to the endurance of European expansion, which passed into the new frontier of space at precisely the historical moment that decolonisation was gaining momentum. As European expansion moved to this new frontier, it carried its library of political and legal arguments with it. The arguments that had been used to debate the justice of colonisation were now turned to space exploration. This should hardly come as a surprise because the ideas of the use and exploitation of nature that underpinned the understanding of property were at the heart of the motivation for European expansion.

With the Space Race heating up in the context of the Cold War, the legal issues were urgent and the rules of effective occupation were re-examined in this new context. Both sides worried about whether it could be possible to claim sovereignty, for example, over the moon simply by sticking a flag into its surface – after all, this had been a ceremony that colonial powers had considered many times before to be sufficient to claim sovereignty over various regions of the globe. It is perhaps hardly surprising in this atmosphere that the idea of *terra nullius* resurfaced in Jessup's discussion of space. One idea of *terra nullius*, generated by the assumption that the origin of property lies in use, could be employed to demonstrate that neither property nor sovereignty could be established by flag-waving ceremonies and other such symbolic gestures. Keller, Lissitzyn and Mann had argued strongly for the importance of symbolic acts in establishing sovereignty. Jessup and Taubenfeld observed that the US Department of

69 Philip C. Jessup and Howard J. Taubenfeld, *Controls for outer space and the Antarctic analogy* (New York, 1959), pp. 151–6.

70 See, for example, *ibid.*, pp. 18, 34–9, 181, 257–8. See also Philip C. Jessup, *The use of international law* (Ann Arbor, 1959), pp. 148–9.

State was deliberately ambiguous about the possibility of making claims to sovereignty in space, as it was for Antarctica. In both cases it denied that 'any other state has established a valid claim to sovereignty'. And in neither case did the United States 'make such a claim for itself'. The Department of State Legal Advisor hedged his bets, however, by asserting that 'if anyone has a right to claim, the position of the United States is as favorable if not more favorable than that of any other contender'. The bases for such potential claims were the 'activities' which gave 'certain rights as distinguished from those states which have not engaged in such activities'.[71] In the case of space, these claims could, Jessup and Taubenfeld argued, lead to the Soviet Union and the United States dividing sovereignty between them. Thus, an understanding of *terra nullius* that allowed a role for symbolic acts was employed to support the division of the political sphere between them.

The Western Sahara and Australia

In the 1970s and 1980s, historians and jurists began to use the term 'terra nullius' with increasing frequency in order to describe the doctrine of occupation as it had been employed to justify colonisation over a number of centuries and in a variety of contexts. This interest in *terra nullius* was not, however, purely historical. The question of the historical status of *terra nullius* was posed primarily as a means of establishing the sovereignty and property over territory in the present and the future, particularly in the context of decolonisation, for example, in the Western Sahara, or ongoing colonisation, in the case of Australia, Canada or the United States.

Probably the most celebrated of these cases concerned the status of the Western Sahara. In 1973 Spain remained the colonial ruler of the Western Sahara, which it had controlled since 1886 following the Berlin Conference, but it was under increasing pressure to relinquish the territory. It proposed that the matter be settled by a referendum whereby the Western Saharan people could choose between an autonomous state and Spanish sovereignty. Morocco reacted furiously to this proposal because they and Mauritania made their own claims to sovereignty over parts of the region. The matter was raised in the United Nations General Assembly, which in turn referred it to the ICJ for an Advisory Opinion – that is, an unbinding ruling. The General Assembly asked the ICJ to resolve two questions, the first being: 'Was Western Sahara . . . at the time of colonization by Spain, a

[71] Jessup and Taubenfeld, *Controls for outer space and the Antarctic analogy*, pp. 215–16.

territory belonging to no-one (*terra nullius*)?'[72] The second question asked the Court to determine the legal ties between the Western Sahara and Morocco and Mauritania. The question concerning *terra nullius* was a response to the Spanish proposition for a referendum to determine the fate of the Western Sahara. A referendum that could lead only to continued Spanish sovereignty or a new autonomous state assumed that no other state could have a claim on the Western Sahara. This assumption was based upon the Spanish claim that the territory was *terra nullius* when it was colonised in 1886. The question concerning legal ties with Morocco and Mauritania was intended to establish the depth of those states' claims to sovereignty over the Western Sahara.

Eight of the fifteen judges in the Western Sahara case had been Jessup's colleagues when he had sat as a judge from 1961 to 1970 on the ICJ, although the concept was in broad currency in international law by 1975. The term 'terra nullius' was, as the judges said, 'a legal term of art employed in connection with "occupation"' and was an 'accepted legal means of acquiring sovereignty over territory'.[73] It was a 'cardinal condition' of a valid occupation that it should be *terra nullius* and this meant that it should belong to no one. On this definition, the judges cited the decision on East Greenland by their predecessors in the PCIJ. The Court then took this understanding of *terra nullius*, established in the polar regions debate of the 1920s and 1930s, examined whether it conformed to the understandings of 'state practice' in the 1880s and concluded, correctly albeit unsurprisingly, that 'tribes or peoples having a social and political organization were not regarded as *terrae nullius*'.[74] On the contrary, the judges argued, acquisition of sovereignty was effected through 'agreements concluded with local rulers'. These understandings and conventions held for Spain in the acquisition of the Western Sahara as they did for other European colonisers of the time. The judges had been asked a legal question – namely, whether the Western Sahara was legally *terra nullius* in 1886. They provided an historical answer to that question – that is, they sought to establish as a matter of historical fact whether the concept had been employed to justify colonisation. They apparently believed that the concept and the term 'terra nullius' were one and the same thing because they noted that while some discussion of occupation

72 *Resolutions adopted by the General Assembly during its twenty ninth session*, p. 104, available at: www.un.org/en/ga/search/view_doc.asp?symbol=A/RES/3292%28XXIX%29&Lang=E&Area=RESOLUTION.

73 *Western Sahara, Advisory Opinion*, ICJ Reports, 1975, p. 39.

74 *Ibid.*

had accompanied the colonisation of Africa, there had been no mention of *terra nullius*.

The Vice President of the Court, Fouad Ammoun from Lebanon, provided a separate opinion in the case in which he expanded upon the question of *terra nullius*, seemingly not satisfied with the depth of his colleagues' views. Ammoun cited Judge Beyona-Ba-Meya of the Supreme Court of Zaire, who 'dismissed the materialistic concept of *terra nullius*, which led to the dismemberment of Africa following the Berlin Conference of 1885'.[75] For Ammoun's colleagues in the case, the Western Sahara had not been *terra nullius* because the term had not been employed to justify colonisation and, rather, treaties had been used. For Ammoun, the territory had not been *terra nullius* even though, he argued, the concept had been employed to justify colonisation. The problem was not the absence of the term, but erroneous assumptions regarding the presence of property and sovereignty in Africa. Beyona-Ba-Meya had argued that the ownership, and sovereignty, over land arose from a spiritual tie, not from an act of appropriation which may be performed by a person who is not born in that land. According to this view, Ammoun argued, *terra nullius* should be a land entirely empty of inhabitants. This was the reply, he said, which might be given to 'the participants in the Berlin Conference in 1885' who 'regarded Sub-Saharan Africa as an immense *terra nullius* available for the first occupier'. He concluded that 'the concept of terra nullius, employed at all periods, to the brink of the twentieth century, to justify conquest and colonization, stands condemned'.[76]

In Ammoun's hands the concept of *terra nullius* had become a substitute for the entire history of occupation and in this sense his analysis was consistent with the Columbia Joint Seminar in International Law. His claim regarding the late nineteenth-century colonisation of Africa may be true of the practices of the European colonisers, but it was not true of the legal perceptions, nor was it an accurate description of the Berlin Conference and the debates surrounding it. In the 1880s, Africa had been perceived as *territorium nullius*, and thus possessed by peoples with property and sovereignty, and this is why treaties had been used to such a great extent. By conflating *terra* and *territorium nullius*, Ammoun was rejecting an historical perception that had not existed in the context that he claimed it existed. To some degree, he was denouncing his own legal fiction.

[75] 'Separate opinion of Vice-President Ammoun', *Western Sahara, Advisory Opinion*, ICJ Reports, 1975, p. 85.

[76] *Ibid.*, p. 86.

In 1977, Paul Coe, an Aboriginal Australian lawyer, brought a case against the Commonwealth of Australia in the High Court in which he argued for the continuing sovereignty of the Aboriginal peoples of Australia. Coe, from the Wiradjuri people in central New South Wales, claimed that Captain Cook in 1770 and Captain Philip in 1788 wrongly claimed British sovereignty over eastern Australia. They 'wrongfully treated the continent now known as Australia as *terra nullius* whereas it was occupied by the sovereign aboriginal nation'.[77] Coe sought to derive support for the specific claim that 'Australia was not *terra nullius*' from the decision of the ICJ on the Western Sahara. His arguments were emphatically rejected by the High Court, which, amongst other objections, refused to recognise the relevance of the ICJ for domestic law.

Five years later, in 1982, Edward Koiki Mabo (known as Eddie Mabo) brought a case to the same court on behalf of the Meriam people of the Murray Islands in the Torres Strait, between the northern tip of Queensland in Australia and New Guinea. In their 1992 judgment, the judges in that case recognised that 'native title' to the Islands remained with the Meriam people. The judges stated that this title, which survived annexation to the colony of Queensland in 1879, was protected by common law where Aboriginal and Torres Strait peoples could demonstrate a continuous relationship to the land, although the judges re-affirmed Australian sovereignty.[78] In contrast to *Coe* v. *The Commonwealth*, the *Mabo* judges made extensive reference to international law. They employed the concept of *terra nullius* throughout their judgment. Two of the seven judges declared: 'The lands of the continent were not *terra nullius* or "practically unoccupied" in 1788.'[79] Three others concurred that: 'The common law of Australia does not embrace the enlarged notion of *terra nullius* or persist in characterising the indigenous inhabitants as people too low in the scale of social organisation to be acknowledged as possessing rights and interests in land.'[80] The judges repeatedly referred to an 'enlarged' concept of *terra nullius*.[81] Indeed, they even asserted that sovereignty over Australia had been acquired through deployment of the 'enlarged' notion of *terra nullius*: 'the Crown's sovereignty over a territory which had been acquired under the enlarged notion of *terra nullius*'.[82] Finally, they rejected this notion, arguing that: 'The common law of this country would perpetuate injustice if it were to continue to embrace the enlarged notion of *terra nullius*.'[83]

[77] *Coe* v. *The Commonwealth and Another* (1978) 18 Australian Law Reports 592, 2–3.
[78] *Mabo and Others* v. *State of Queensland* (1992) 107 ALR 1, at 7. [79] *Ibid.*, 4. [80] *Ibid.*, 2.
[81] *Ibid.*, 2, 18. [82] *Ibid.*, 20. [83] *Ibid.*, 30.

It is essential to establish what the judges understood by an 'enlarged' concept of *terra nullius*. They cited many authorities in the law of nations and international law on the concept of occupation, including Vitoria, Grotius, Wolff and Vattel. They also discussed the Western Sahara decision and Judge Ammoun's separate opinion.[84] They perceived that in some cases discussions of occupation referred to entirely uninhabited land, land with no people in it, and this is what they appear to have understood by a strict meaning of *terra nullius*. Such an interpretation was certainly consistent with the early discussions of the polar regions, although the judges made no reference to those debates (albeit that the Western Sahara decision, which they cited, does). By contrast, an 'enlarged' understanding of *terra nullius*, according to the judges, was one which included indigenous peoples in the territories concerned. For this enlarged understanding of *terra nullius*, the judges followed the discussion in the Western Sahara case and so conflated in the same way the discussion of Africa in 1885, in terms of *territorium nullius*, and the discussions of *terra nullius* that came from the polar debates. The inclusion of inhabited land in *terra nullius* had first been used by the Norwegian National Socialists to describe East Greenland. Indeed, there were striking parallels between the National Socialists' use of *terra nullius* and the discussion in Australia. It was in the National Socialist discussions that the indigenous people of East Greenland were counted as nothing and, moreover, as a dying race being absorbed into the European population. Precisely the same assumptions had been made regarding Aboriginal Australians through much of the nineteenth and twentieth centuries. Australia was frequently represented as being sparsely inhabited at the time of colonisation, and the Aboriginal people were portrayed as more primitive than other colonised peoples in the Americas and Africa.[85] Government policies pursued the absorption of the Aboriginal people into the European population.

While the parallels with the East Greenland case were not made explicit in the *Mabo* judgment, the common assumptions in both cases facilitated the adoption of the National Socialists' understanding of *terra nullius*. Importantly, however, the *Mabo* judges, again like the Western Sahara Advisory Opinion judges, denied that inhabited lands could be *terra nullius* – that is, they opposed themselves to what they called the

[84] *Ibid.*, 20–1.

[85] See, for example, Lindley, *The acquisition and government of backward territory in international* law, pp. 40–1: 'As the facts presented themselves at the time, there appeared to be no political society to be dealt with . . . Occupation was the appropriate method of acquisition.'

enlarged understanding of the term. In this sense, their arguments were consistent with the long history of the negative use of the doctrine of occupation to defend the rights of indigenous peoples; in other words, the claim that land could not be taken because it was already occupied. The judges were not rejecting *terra nullius* so much as reviving it for a long-standing critique of colonisation. Similarly, recent discussions of *terra nullius* added a chapter to a very long tradition of legal scepticism concerning the arbitrary claims of European colonisers.

Between the *Coe* and *Mabo* judgments, and in subsequent years, a number of historians in Australia began to employ the term to describe the doctrine of occupation as it had been used to justify Australian colonisation.[86] *Terra nullius* had not been employed to discuss Australian colonisation prior to Scott, nor had *territorium nullius* (prior to M. F. Lindley). The theory of occupation had, however, been used extensively to justify (and to contest) the colonisation of Australia, as it had throughout all European colonial ventures, and those Australian examples of the doctrine of occupation were employed as evidence for the concept of *terra nullius*. *Terra nullius* was thus used as shorthand for occupation, and sometimes even for conquest. Indeed, the great complexity of justifications for European empire was often reduced to a generalised claim that non-European lands and people were simply treated as *terra nullius*. Similarly, the term began to be taken up by scholars internationally and to be used to describe both the law of occupation and its history.[87]

Over centuries, empires developed complex and nuanced understandings of the occupation of territory which reached their peak in the Africa debate and the discussion of the Poles prior to the First World War. With the decline of empire, the need for these complex justifications for the appropriation of territory no longer existed. *Terra nullius* could be expanded in its meaning to describe the context for all cases of occupation. Writing in 1945, Norman Hill adopted the Columbia understanding of occupation, claiming that for territory to be acquired: 'The occupied territory must have been *terra nullius*, and the occupation must have been

[86] Henry Reynolds, whose work influenced the *Mabo* judgment, was the leading historian in Australia to use the term. See in particular Reynolds, *The law of the land*. See also Tim Rowse, 'Terra nullius', in Graeme Davison, John Hirst and Stuart Macintyre (eds.), *The Oxford Companion to Australian History* (Melbourne, 2001); Bruce Kercher, 'Native title in the shadows: the origins of the myth of *terra nullius* in early New South Wales courts', in Gregory Blue, Martin Bunton and Ralph Crozier (eds.), *Colonialism and the modern world* (New York, 2002), pp. 100–2; Banner, 'Why *terra nullius*?'.

[87] The literature using *terra nullius* to describe the history of occupation is vast and diverse, extending well beyond scholarly studies. See notes 1–4 of this chapter for some examples.

real or effective.'[88] Hill cited both the East Greenland judgment and the collaborative work produced by the Columbia seminar.[89] Through this process, whereby *terra nullius* came to signify all cases of occupation, the concept also greatly simplified the complexity of the history of occupation, including, for example, the recognition of non-European sovereignty that had been at the heart of many discussions of occupation, particularly in the discussions of *territorium nullius*.

[88] Norman Hill, *Claims to territory in international law and relations* (New York, 1945), p. 146.
[89] *Ibid.*, pp. 146–9.

CHAPTER 11

Conclusion

The idea of occupation is one of the most powerful tools employed in Western political thought to explain the origin of property and political society itself. Occupation has proved to be remarkably resilient, finding a central position in Roman law, canon law, medieval and early modern natural law, Enlightenment historicism and nineteenth-century positivism as well as modern international law. The fact that the idea has been adapted to the radically different theoretical structures of these various philosophies and practices over thousands of years tells us that it possesses the power to explain something important in Western political thought. In all of these various manifestations, occupation remained a theory of appropriation. Even when it was used to explain common property, for example, in discussions of freedom of the sea, it was in order to indicate the limits upon appropriation, which would themselves provide the optimum conditions for the growth of commerce (freedom of the sea was fundamental to the expansion of commerce). The history of occupation therefore tells us much about the possessiveness of Western political thought. If occupation was the beginning of political societies, then that beginning was in possession. This foundation story of Western political thought posits a relationship between humans and their environment that is exploitative. As such, occupation also provides an important link between the possessiveness of Western political thought and several centuries of a European drive for empire. It shows also that the objects of possession in Western political thought could change according to circumstances. While occupation was a legal concept in medieval treatises, for early modern authors it provided an explanation for progress through historical stages. While early modern discussions of occupation in empire were concerned with whether it was possible to occupy property in lands already inhabited by indigenous peoples, eighteenth- and nineteenth-century discussions turned increasingly to the question of whether sovereignty could be occupied, taking for granted that property must be left intact.

If the future of political thought remains indebted to its past, as it surely must, then occupation, which can be discovered in almost all past currents of Western political thought, will continue to be a powerful tool for understanding property, sovereignty and appropriation. Moreover, the fact that the law of occupation has been adapted to most major changes in Western political thought (it found an important place even as Proudhon's alternative to property) suggests that it will continue to be adapted to discussions of property and sovereignty in the future. There is also every reason to believe, therefore, that occupation will continue to inspire and justify various imperial dispositions, and to underlie an exploitative and possessive attitude to our environment. Studies of empire and the environment have focused upon the impacts that imperial practices have had on the environment, for example, in the destruction of forests for rubber plantations, or the creation of grazing lands and irrigation, but these links are empirical.[1] The history of occupation points to a deeper link between empire and the environment, one whereby both were driven by the same understanding of nature.[2] These would seem to be grounds for suggesting a revision of the tools of political thought and, in particular, for deep scepticism of liberalism.

In focusing, however, upon the history of occupation as a justification for empire, historians and jurists have often ignored the role of occupation as a critique of empire and, more importantly, have shown little interest in the reasons behind that critique. The motivations for this opposition to empire can help us to engage with the continuing salience of empire as a form of political organisation. The resurgence of interest in empire amongst historians has been stimulated by a perceived return of empire in the twenty-first century.[3] Historians are divided between those who argue that empire is an inevitability and a reality that must be responsibly managed, and those who use the past to reveal the abuses of empire.[4] The argument that empire must be managed diminishes and even ignores the abuses of empire.[5] The focus on the abuses of empire, if one is to use history as a judge, has never been sufficient to curb those abuses.

1 See, for example, William Beinart and Lotte Hughes, *Environment and empire* (New York, 2007).

2 James Beattie, 'Recent themes in the environmental history of the British Empire', *History Compass*, 10(2) (2012), 129–39.

3 Not all historians are convinced that 'empire' is the appropriate term for the twentieth-century projection of power beyond the state; see, for example, Cooper, 'Empire multiplied'. For a contrasting view, see Pitts, 'Political theory of empire and imperialism'.

4 On the necessity of empire, see Ferguson, *Empire*; Ignatieff, *Empire lite.*

5 Pitts, 'Political theory of empire and imperialism', 220; Jeanne Morefield, 'Empire, tragedy, and the liberal state in the writings of Niall Ferguson and Michael Ignatieff', *Theory and Event*, 11(3) (2008).

Indeed, humanitarian sentiment too often collapsed back into an apology for empire. George Steinmetz asks what a critical anti-imperialism might look like today.[6] The tradition of anti-imperial critique in the history of occupation offers some insights. It is possible to reflect on that tradition, not in search of moral lessons from history, but in order to understand the complex heritage of Western political thought with which we live today and to discover what possibilities lie within that tradition.[7] The critiques of empire that were least prone to collapsing into imperial apology were those based not so much on a sense of common humanity, but upon self-interest – that is, upon the problem of liberty at home. This form of rights-based but self-interested critique has been apparent in our own time. Imprisonment in Guantanamo Bay, for example, has been criticised from the perspective of empathy with the human rights of the prisoners, but it has also been opposed by the argument that if such abuses of rights are possible in territory outside US jurisdiction, it will be only a matter of time before the same extrajudicial practices are employed in the United States.[8] Today's most potent anti-imperial critiques may thus be said to owe much to enduring debates within Western political thought, just as, equally, the understanding of rights and freedom in Western political thought owes much to the tradition of imperial critique.

[6] George Steinmetz, 'Imperialism or colonialism? From Windhoek to Washington, by way of Basra', in Calhoun, Cooper and Moore (eds.), *Lessons of empire*, p. 156; Pitts, 'Political theory of empire and imperialism', 221.

[7] See Cooper, 'Empire multiplied', 272 on not using past empire for policy recommendations.

[8] Jeremy Waldron, 'Torture and positive law: jurisprudence for the White House', *Columbia Law Review*, 105(6) (2005), 1681–1750, at 1740–1.

Bibliography

PRIMARY SOURCES

Manuscripts

Catalogus librorum bibliotecæ Johanensis, St John's College Library, Cambridge, MS U.4
Foreign Office Papers, National Archives, 84/1814, 1815, 1820
Lee Papers, Lambeth Palace Library, MS 2876
'The Minute Book', Lambeth Palace Library MS. DC2
Tait Papers, Lambeth Palace Library, Tait MSS 184

Printed primary sources

Abbay, T. and Symonds, William (eds.), *The proceedings of the English colonie in Virginia* (Oxford, 1612)
Acosta, José de, *De procuranda Indorum salute*, trans. G. Stewart McIntosh, 2 vols. (Tayport, 1995–6)
The natuall and morall historie of the east and west Indies (London, 1604)
Adam, Alexander, *Roman antiquities; or, an account of the manners and customs of the romans* (Edinburgh, 1791)
Adams, John, *The works of John Adams Second President of the United States*, ed. Charles Francis Adams (Boston, 1856), vol. X
Adams, John and Leonard, Daniel, *Massachusettensis and Novanglus*, reprinted in Merrill Jensen (ed.), *Tracts of the American Revolution 1763–1776* (Indianapolis, 1967)
Adams, John Quincy, *Writings of John Quincy Adams* (New York, 1913)
Ahrens, Heinrich, *The annual biography and obituary* (London, 1834)
Cours de droit naturel ou de philosophie du droit (Brussels, 1858)
Anon., 'Adolf Hoel: Obituary', *Polar Record*, 12(80) (1965)
'Communications relatives à l'Institut de Droit International', *Revue de droit international et de législation comparée*, 5 (1873), 667–702
'Documents relatifs à l'Institut de Droit Internatinal', *Revue de droit international et de législation comparée* 5 (1873), 703–12

'The league: assassination prefered', *TIME*, 12 August 1935

'Liste des members effectifs de l'institut de droit international, Octobre 1873', *Revue de Droit International et de Législation Comparée*, 1873

'The present aspect of international law', *North American Review*, 103 (October 1866), 466–98

Proceedings of the Alaskan Boundary Tribunal (Washington DC, 1904), vol. 3

'Proposition de M. Moynier concernant le Congo', *Annuaire de l'institut de droit international*, 7 (1885), 237–8

Sir Travers Twiss et le Congo. Réponse à la Revue de droit international et de législation comparée et au Law Magazine and Review, par un membre de la Société Royale de Géographie d'Anvers (Brussels, 1884)

Thoughts on the origin and nature of government. Occasioned by the late disputes between Great Britain and her American colonies, written in the year 1766 (London, 1769)

A true declaration of the estate of the colonie in Virginia (London, 1610)

Aquinas, Thomas, *Political writings*, ed. and trans. R. W. Dyson (Cambridge, 2002)

Arendt, Hannah, *Origins of totalitarianism* (New York, 1962)

Association of the Reform and Codification of the Law of Nations, *Report of the eighth annual conference held at Berne, August 24th–27th, 1880* (London, 1881)

Ayliffe, John, *A new pandect of Roman civil law* (London, 1734)

Azo, *Summa Azonis* (Lyon, 1530)

Summa super codice et Institutis (Speyer, 1482)

Bankton, Andrew MacDowall, *Institute of the laws of Scotland in civil rights* (Edinburgh, 1751)

Bartolus of Saxoferrato, *Tractatus de insula*, in *Consilia quaestiones et tractatus Bartoli* (Lyon, 1535)

Bentham, Jeremy, *Rights, representation and reform: nonsense upon stilts and other writings upon the French Revolution*, ed. Philip Schofield, Catherine Pease-Watkin and Cyprian Blamires (Oxford, 2002)

Benton, Thomas, *Speech of Mr Benton of Missouri on the Oregon question*, delivered in the United States Senate, 22, 25 and 28 May 1846 (Washington DC, 1846)

Blackstone, William, *The commentaries on the laws of England*, 4 vols. (London, 1765–9)

Bland, Richard, *An inquiry into the rights of British colonies* (Williamsburg, 1766), reprinted in Merrill Jensen (ed.), *Tracts of the American Revolution 1763–1776* (Indianapolis, 1967)

Bluntschli, Johann Caspar, *Le droit international codifié*, 4th edn (Paris, 1886)

The theory of the state (Oxford, 1895)

Bonfils, Henry, *Manuel de droit international public*, 3rd edn, revised by Paul Fauchille (Paris, 1901)

Bowyer, George, *Commentaries on the modern civil law* (London, 1851)

Introduction to the study and use of the civil law (London, 1874)

Readings delivered before the Honourable Society of the Middle Temple in the year 1850 (London, 1851)

Bracton, Henry de, *De legibus et consuetudinibus Angliæ* (London, 1569)

De legibus et consuetudinibus Angliæ (London, 1640)

De legibus et consuetudinibus angliae, ed. George Woodbine with an English translation and notes by Samuel E. Thorne, 4 vols. (Cambridge, MA, 1968 and 1977)

Bulkley, John, 'Preface', in Roger Wolcott, *Poetical meditations* (London, 1725)

Carmichael, Gershom, *Natural rights on the threshold of the Scottish Enlightenment: the writings of Gershom Carmichael*, eds. James Moore and Michael Silverthorne (Indianapolis, 2002)

Chandler, Thomas, *A friendly address to all reasonable Americans* (New York, 1774)

Cicero, *On duties*, ed. M. T. Griffin and E. M. Atkins (Cambridge, 1991)

On ends, trans. H. Rackham (Cambridge, MA, 1914)

Cocceji, Samuel von, *The Frederician Code*, 2 vols. (Edinburgh 1761)

Introductio ad Henrici L. B. Cocceii Grotium Illustratum (Lausanne, 1751)

Introductio ad Henrici L. B. de Cocceii Grotium Illustratum (Lausanne, 1759)

Crashaw, William, *Fiscus papalis* (London, 1617)

A sermon preached before right honourable the Lord Lawarre (London, 1609),

Creasy, Edward, *First platform of international law* (London, 1876)

Cumberland, Richard, *A treatise of the laws of nature*, translated, with Introduction and Appendix, by John Maxwell (1727), edited and with a foreword by Jon Parkin (Indianapolis, 2005)

Davis, Garrett, 'On the Oregon question', speech delivered to the House of Representatives, 7 February (Washington DC, 1846)

Decisions of the Court of Sessions from November 1787 to August 1788, collected by William Steuart and Robert Craigie (Edinburgh, 1789)

Despagnet, Frantz, *Cours de droit international public*, 2nd edn (Paris, 1899)

La diplomatie de la Troisième République (Paris, 1904)

Essai sur les protectorats (Paris, 1896)

Dickens, Charles, *David Copperfield* (New York, 2000)

Dickinson, Daniel S., 'On the Oregon question', speech to senate, 24 February (Washington DC, 1846)

Digest of Justinian, ed. Theodor Mommsen (Philadelphia, 1985)

Diplomatic correspondence of the United States: Inter-American affairs, vol. XI, *Spain* (Washington DC, 1939)

ШПИЦБЕРГЕНЪ 1871–1912 [*Diplomatic correspondence Spitsbergen 1871–1912*] (St Petersburg, 1912)

Dix, John A., 'On the Oregon question', speech delivered in the Senate, 18 and 19 February (Washington DC, 1846)

Donne, John, *A sermon preached to the honourable company of the Virginian plantation* (London, 1622)

Dreghorn, John Maclaurin, *Observations on some points of law* (Edinburgh, 1759)

Engelhardt, Édouard, 'Conférence de Berlin', *Revue de droit international et de législation comparée*, 18 (1886), 96–8

'Étude sur la déclaration de la conférence de Berlin relative aux occupations', *Revue de droit international et de législation comparée*, 18 (1886), Part I, 433–41; and Part II, 573–86

Étude sur la déclaration de la conférence de Berlin relative aux occupations africaines suivie d'un projet de déclaration générale sur les occupations en pays sauvages (Brussels, 1887)

'Projet de déclaration internationale, proposé par M. Engelhardt, en vue de déterminer les règles à suivre dans les occupations de territoires', *Revue de droit international et de législation comparée*, 19 (1887), 175–9

Ferguson, Adam, *Essay on the history of civil society*, 6th edn (London, 1793)

Principles of moral and political science, 2 vols. (Edinburgh, 1792), vol. 2

Ferraris, Lucius, *Prompta bibliotheca, canonica, juridica, moralis, theological*, ed. Jacques-Paul Migne (Paris, 1863)

Ferry, Jules, *Discours et Opinions de Jules Ferry*, ed. Paul Robiquet, 7 vols. (Paris, 1897)

Gai Institutiones or institutes of Roman law by Gaius, with a translation and commentary by Edward Poste, 4th edn, revised and enlarged by E. A. Whittuck, with an historical introduction by A. H. J. Greenidge (Oxford, 1904)

Gallatin, Albert, *The Oregon question* (New York, 1846)

Galloway, Joseph, *Candid examination of the mutual claims of Great Britain and the colonies* (New York, 1775)

Gentili, Alberico, *De Legationibus libri tres*, vol. 1, a photographic reproduction of the edition of 1594 with an introduction by Ernest Nys (New York, 1924)

De jure belli libri tres, translation of 1612 edn, first published 1598, ed. John C. Rolfe, 2 vols. (Oxford, 1933)

Gray, Robert, *A good speed to Virginia* (London, 1610)

Grotius, Hugo, *Commentary on the law of prize and booty*, ed. Martine Julia van Ittersum (Indianapolis, 2006)

De jure belli ac pacis , 2 vols. (Washington DC, 1913, a reproduction of the 1646 edn)

De jure praedae commentarius, vol. 1, a translation by Gwladys L. Williams of the 1604 manuscript (Oxford, 1950)

De jure praedae commentarius, vol. 2, the collotype reproduction of the original 1604 manuscript in the handwriting of Grotius (Oxford, 1950)

The free sea, trans. Richard Hakluyt, with William Welwod's *Critique* and Grotius' *Reply*, ed. David Armitage (Indianapolis, 2004)

Hallifax, Samuel, *An analysis of the Roman civil law, compared with the laws of England* (London, 1774)

Heffter, Auguste-Guillaume, *Le droit international public de l'Europe* (Paris, 1873)

Hobbes, Thomas, *Leviathan*, ed. Richard Tuck (Cambridge, 1991)

On the citizen, eds. Richard Tuck and Michael Silverthorne (Cambridge, 1998)

Hoel, Adolf, 'Coal-mining in Svalbard', *Polar Record*, 2(16) (1938), 74–85

Holst, Hermann Eduard von, *The constitutional and political history of the United States*, trans. J. Lalor from the German edn of 1877–92, vol. 4 (Chicago, 1885)

Hooke, Luke Joseph, *Religionis naturalis et revelatae principia* (Paris, 1774)

Hume, David, *Essays moral, political, literary*, edited and with a foreword, notes and glossary by Eugene F. Miller, with an appendix of variant readings from the 1889 edn by T. H. Green and T. H. Grose, revised edn (Indianapolis, 1987)
A treatise of human nature (Oxford, 1958)
Hutcheson Francis, *On the natural sociability of mankind*, in *Logic, metaphysics, and the natural sociability of mankind*, ed. James Moore and Michael Silverthorne (Indianapolis, 2006)
Philosophiae Moralis Institution Compendiaria with a short introduction to moral philosophy, ed. Luigi Turco (Indianapolis, 2007)
A short introduction to moral philosophy in three books, 2nd edn (Glasgow, 1753)
A system of moral philosophy, 2 vols. (Glasgow, 1755)
Hyde, Charles Cheney, 'The case concerning the legal status of Eastern Greenland', *American Journal of International Law*, 27 (1933), 732–8
International law chiefly as interpreted and applied by the United States, 2 vols. (Boston, 1922)
Ickstatt, Johann Adam von, *Elementa juris gentium* (Wirceburgia, 1740)
The institutes of Justinian, ed. J. A. C. Thomas (Amsterdam, 1975)
Jefferson, Thomas, *Notes on the state of Virginia*, reprinted in Saul K. Padover (ed.), *The complete Jefferson* (New York, 1943)
Summary view of the rights of British America (Williamsburg, 1774), reprinted in Saul K. Padover (ed.), *The complete Jefferson* (New York, 1943)
Jessup, Philip C., *The United States and the world court* (Boston, 1929)
The use of international law (Ann Arbor, 1959)
Jessup, Philip C. and Taubenfeld, Howard J., *Controls for outer space and the Antarctic analogy* (New York, 1959)
Jèze, Gaston, *Étude théorique et pratique sur l'occupation* (Paris, 1896)
Kant, Immanuel, *Practical philosophy*, trans. and ed. Mary Gregor (Cambridge, 1996)
Keller, Arthur, Lissitzyn, Oliver and Mann, Frederick, *Creation of rights of sovereignty through symbolic acts 1400–1800* (Columbia, 1938)
Kingsbury, Susan Myra (ed.), *The records of the Virginia Company of London*, 4 vols. (Washington DC, 1906–35)
Kling, Melchior, *In quatuor Institutionum Iuris libros Enarrationes* (Lyon, 1550)
Klüber, Jean-Louis, *Droit des gens moderne de l'Europe*, 2 vols. (Paris, 1834)
Laet, Johannes de, *Nieuwe Wereldt ofte Beschrijvinghe van West Indien* (Leiden, 1625)
Lansing, Robert, 'A unique international problem', *American Journal of International Law*, 11(4) (1917), 763–71
Lemkin, Raphaël, *Axis rule in occupied Europe: laws of occupation, analysis of government, proposals for redress* (Washington DC, 1944)
Lieber, Francis, *Essays on property and labour as connected with natural law and the constitution of society* (New York, 1842)
Lindley, Mark Frank, *The acquisition and government of backward territory in international law* (London, 1926)

Locke, John, *Two treatises of government*, ed. Peter Laslett (Cambridge, 1960)
Lorimer, James, *The institutes of the law of nations*, 2 vols. (Edinburgh, 1884)
Magens, Nicholas, *An essay on insurances* (London, 1755)
Maine, Henry Sumner, *Ancient law* (Tucson, 1986)
International law (New York, 1888)
Manning, William Oke, *Commentaries on the law of nations* (London, 1839)
Martens, Georg Friedrich von, *Précis du droit des gens moderne de l'Europe*, 2 vols. (Paris, 1831)
Martitz, Ferdinand, 'Occupation des territoires: Rapport et projet de résolutions présentés a l'Institut de droit international', *Revue de Droit International et de Législation Comparée*, 19 (1887), 371–6
Michell, Abraham Louis, *Exposition of the motives founded upon the universally received law of nations, which have determined the King (of Prussia) upon the repeated instances of his subjects trading by sea, to lay an attachment upon the capital funds, which his majesty had promised to reimburse to the subjects of Great-Britain, in virtue of the peace-treaties of Breslau and Dresden* (London, 1752)
Mill, John Stuart, *Of property*, in *Collected works of John Stuart Mill. Volume II Principles of political economy* (Indianapolis, 2006; reprint of the Toronto University Press 1965 edn)
Three essays on religion, in *Collected works of John Stuart Mill. Volume X Essays on ethics, religion and society* (Indianapolis, 2006; reprint of the Toronto University Press 1969 edn)
Miller, David, 'Political rights in the polar regions', in *Problems of polar research* (New York, 1928)
Montmorency, J. E. G. de, 'The international position of Spitsbergen', *Journal of Comparative Legislation and International Law*, 18(1) (1918), 11–15
More, Thomas, *Utopia*, eds. George M. Logan and Robert M. Adams (Cambridge, 1989)
Moynier, Gustave, 'Lettre-circulaire de M. Moynier à messieurs les membres et associés de l'Institut de droit international', Geneva, 1 July 1883, *Annuaire de l'institut de droit international*, 7 (1885)
Norris, John, *The liberty and property of British subjects asserted* (London, 1726)
Nys, Ernest, *Droit international. Les principes, les théories, les faits*, 3 vols., 2nd edn (Brussels, 1904)
Etudes de droit international et de droit politique (Brussels, 1896)
Les origines du droit international (Brussels, 1894)
Ockham, William of, *Guillelmi de Ockham Opera politica*, ed. H. S. Offler, 2 vols. (Manchester, 1963)
Ortolan, Eugène, *Des moyens d'acquérir le domaine international* (Paris, 1849)
Otis, James, *The rights of the British colonies asserted and proved* (Boston, 1764)
Owen, Robert, 'Occupation of Oregon', speech delivered in the House of Representatives, 23 and 24 January 1844 (Washington DC, 1846)
Palmer, Roundell, Earl of Selborne, *Memorials: family and personal 1766–1865*, 2 vols. (London, 1896)

Phillimore, Robert Joseph, *Commentaries upon international law*, 4 vols. (Philadelphia, 1854–61)
Piccioni, Camille, 'L'organisation du Spitzberg', *Revue générale de droit international public*, XVI (1909), 117–34
Pradier-Fodéré, Paul, *Principes généraux de droit, de politique et de législation* (Paris, 1869)
Proudhon, Pierre-Joseph, *What is property?*, ed. and trans. Donald R. Kelley and Bonnie G. Smith (Cambridge, 1994)
Pufendorf, Samuel, *De jure naturae et gentium libri octo* vol. 2, translation of the 1688 edn by C. H. Oldfather and W. A. Oldfather (Oxford 1934)
Le droit de la nature et des gens, ou système général des principes les plus importans de la morale, de la jurisprudence, et de la politique, ed. Jean Barbeyrac (London [Paris?], 1740)
The law of nature and nations, trans. Basil Kennet, 5th edn (London, 1749)
The whole duty of man, according to the law of nature, edited and with an introduction by Ian Hunter and David Saunders (Indianapolis, 2003)
Purchas, Samuel, *Hakluytus posthumus or Purchas his pilgrimes*, 4 vols. (London, 1625)
Purchas his pilgrimage (London, 1613)
Purchas his pilgrimage (London, 1617)
Reddie, James, *Inquiries in international law, public and private*, 2nd edn (Edinburgh, 1851)
Reeves, Jesse Siddall, *The international beginnings of the Congo Free State* (Baltimore, 1894)
Report of the twenty-fourth meeting of the Australian and New Zealand Association for the Advancement of Science. Canberra meeting, January 1939 (Sydney, 1939)
Resolutions adopted by the General Assembly during its twenty-ninth session, www.un.org/en/ga/search/view_doc.asp?symbol=A/RES/3292%28XXIX%29&Lang=E&Area=RESOLUTION
Ritchie, David G., *Natural rights, a criticism of some political and ethical conceptions* (London, 1895)
Rivier, Alphonse, 'Nécrologie. M. Bluntschli', *Revue de droit international et de législation comparée*, 13 (1881), 612–30
Rolin-Jaequemyns, Gustave, 'Œuvre de l'exploration et de la civilisation de l'Afrique centrale', *Revue de droit international et de législation comparée*, 9 (1877), 318–21
Rousseau, Jean-Jacques, *The social contract and discourses*, trans. G. D. H. Cole (London, 1973)
Rudmose-Brown, Robert Neal, 'Spitsbergen: *terra nullius*', *Geographical Review*, 7(5) (1919), 311–21
Rutherford, Thomas, *Institutes of natural law* (Cambridge, 1754–6)
Salomon, Charles, *L'occupation des territoires sans maître* (Paris, 1887)
Sayre, Frances Bowes, *Experiments in international administration* (New York, 1919)
Schulte, Johann Friedrich, *Das katholische Kirchenrecht* (Giessen, 1856)

Scott, Ernest, 'Taking possession of Australia – the doctrine of *terra nullius* (no-man's land)', *Journal and Proceedings. Royal Australian Historical Society*, XXVI(1) (1940), 1–19
Scott, James Brown, 'Arctic exploration and international law', *American Journal of International Law*, 3(4) (1909), 928–41
Scruggs, William, *British aggressions in Venezuela: the Monroe Doctrine on trial* (Atlanta, 1895)
Seeley, John Robert, *The expansion of England* (London, 1883)
Shaftesbury, Anthony, Third Earl of, *Characteristicks of men, manners, opinions, times*, 3 vols. (Indianapolis, 2001)
Simsarian, James, 'The acquisition to legal title in *terra nullius*', *Political Science Quarterly*, 53(1) (1938), 111–28
'Sixième commission – Examen de la théorie de la conférence de Berlin sur l'occupation des territoires', *Annuaire de l'Institut de droit international*, 10 (1889), 173–204
Skeie, John, *Greenland: the dispute between Norway and Denmark* (London, 1932)
Smedel, Gustav, *Acquisition of sovereignty over polar areas* (Oslo, 1931)
Smith, Adam, *Lectures on jurisprudence*, ed. R. L. Meek, D. D. Raphael and P. G. Stein, vol. V of the Glasgow edn of the *Works and correspondence of Adam Smith* (Indianapolis, 1982)
Smith, John, *A map of Virginia* (Oxford, 1612)
A true relation (London, 1608)
Soto, Domingo de, *Releccion 'De Dominio'*, trans. and ed. Jaime Brufau Prats (Salamanca, 1964)
Staël-Holstein, Lage von, *Norway in arcticum* (Copenhagen, 1932)
Stanley, Henry, *The Congo*, 2 vols. (London, 1885)
Stiles, Ezra, *The United States elevated to glory and honour: a sermon* (New Haven, 1783)
Strachey, William, *The historie of travell into Virginia Britannia*, eds. Louis B. Wright and Virginia Freund (London, 1953)
Suárez, Francisco, *Selections from three works* (Oxford, 1944), 2 vols.
Symonds, William, *Virginia* (London, 1609)
Tartarin, Edouard, *Traité de l'occupation* (Paris, 1872)
Taylor, John, *Summary of the Roman law* (London, 1772)
'Treaty concerning the archipelago of Spitsbergen' on 9 February 1920, http://www.austlii.edu.au/au/other/dfat/treaties/1925/10.html
Twiss, Travers, 'Applicability of the European law of nations to African slave states', *Law Magazine and Review* (May 1876), 409–27
'Collisions at sea. A scheme of international tribunals', *Law Magazine and Review* (November 1878), 1–15
'Collisions on the high seas', *Albany Law Journal*, 12 October 1878, 287–8
'Le congrès de Vienne et la conférence de Berlin', *Revue de droit international et de législation comparée*, 17 (1885), 201–17
'The criminal jurisdiction of the Admiralty of England in the case of the *Franconia*', *Law Magazine and Review* (February 1877), 145–77

An epitome of Niebuhr's history of Rome (Oxford, 1836)
An international protectorate of the Congo River (London, 1883)
'An international protectorate of the Congo River', *Law Magazine and Review* (November 1883), 1–20
The law of nations considered as independent communities: on the right and duties of nations in time of peace (Oxford, 1861)
The law of nations considered as independent political communities: on the rights and duties of nations in time of war (London, 1863)
A letter to the Vice Chancellor of the University of Oxford (London, 1856)
'La libre navigation du Congo', *Revue de droit international et de législation comparée*, 15 (1883), 437–42
'La libre navigation du Congo', *Annuaire de l'institut de droit international*, 7 (1885), 242–9
'La libre navigation du Congo. Deuxième article', *Revue de droit international et de législation comparée*, 15 (1883), 547–63
'La libre navigation du Congo. Troisième article', *Revue de droit international et de législation comparée*, 16 (1884), 237–46
'On the international jurisdiction of the Admiralty Court in civil matters', *Law Magazine and Review* (May 1877)
The Oregon territory (London, 1846)
Two introductory lectures on the science of international law (London, 1856)
Vander Graef, Jacobus, *Syntagma Juris Publici* (1644)
Vattel, Emer de, *The law of nations*, edited and with an introduction by Bela Kapossy and Richard Whatmore (Indianapolis, 2008)
Vázquez de Menchaca, Fernando, *Controversarium illustrium* (Frankfurt, 1572)
Venezuela-British Guiana Boundary Arbitration, *The case of the United States of Venezuela before the tribunal of arbitration*, Venezuela, No. 1 (1899)
Counter-case presented on the part of the government of Her Britannic Majesty to the Tribunal of Arbitration, Boundary between British Guiana and Venezuela, Venezuela, No. 2 (1899)
The counter-case of the United States of Venezuela before the Tribunal of Arbitration, Venezuela, No. 5 (1899)
Further Documents relating to the question of the boundary between British Guiana and Venezuela. Dispatch from Her Majesty's Ambassador at Washington, inclosing the first part of the brief for Venezuela (London, August 1896)
Treaty between Great Britain and the United States of Venezuela respecting settlement of the boundary between the colony of British Guiana and the United States of Venezuela, London, 1987
'The Venezuela Arbitration', *The Times*, 28 August 1899, p. 5
'The Venezuela Arbitration', *The Times*, 21 September 1899, p. 4
Vitoria, Francisco de, *De indis et de jure belli relectiones*, ed. Ernest Nys (Washington DC, 1917)
Political writings, eds. Anthony Pagden and Jeremy Lawrence (Cambridge, 1991)

Wack, Henry Wellington, *The story of the Congo Free State* (New York, 1905)
Wallace, George, *A system of the principle of the law of Scotland* (Edinburgh, 1760)
Waultrin, René, 'La question de la souveraineté des terres arctiques', *Revue générale de droit international public*, XV (1908), 78–125
'Le problème de la souveraineté des pôles', *Revue générale de droit international public* vol. 16, 1909
Wharton, Samuel, *Plain facts: Being an examination into the rights of the Indian nations of America to their respective countries* (Philadelphia, 1781)
Wheaton, Henry, *Elements of international law*, 6th edn (Boston, 1855)
Whitaker, Alexander, *Good newes from Virginia* (London, 1613)
Winthrop, Robert Charles, 'Speech of Mr Winthrop of Massachusetts, on the Oregon question', delivered in the House of Representatives, 3 January (Washington DC, 1846)
Wolcott, Roger, *Poetical meditations* (London, 1725)
Wolff, Christian, *Jus gentium methodo scientificia pertractatum*, trans. Joseph H. Drake, 2 vols. (Oxford, 1934), vol. 2
Wollaston, William, *The religion of nature delineated*, ed. John Clarke (London, 1750)
Wood, Thomas, *A new institute of the imperial or civil law* (London, 1704)
A new institute of the imperial or civil law, 4th edn (London, 1730)
Zamboni, Giovanni Fortunato, *Collectio declarationum sacræ congregationis cardinalium sacri Concilii tridentini interpretum* (Rome, 1868)

SECONDARY SOURCES

Alexandrowicz, Charles Henry, *The European-African confrontation: a study in treaty making* (Leiden, 1973)
An introduction to the history of the law of nations in the East Indies (16th, 17th and 18th centuries) (Oxford, 1967)
Anaya, S. James, *Indigenous people in international law* (Oxford, 1996)
Anghie, Antony, 'Identifying regions in the history of international law', in Bardo Fassbender, Anne Peters and Simone Peter (eds.), *The Oxford handbook of the history of international law* (Oxford, 2012)
Imperialism, sovereignty and the making of international law (Cambridge, 2005)
Ansprenger, Franz, 'African perception of the new European policies in Africa during the 1880s', in Stig Forster, Wolfgang J. Mommsen and Ronald Robinson (eds.), *Bismarck, Europe and Africa: the Berlin Africa Conference 1884–1885 and the onset of partition* (Oxford, 1988)
Appleby, Joyce, *Liberalism and republicanism in the historical imagination* (Cambridge, MA, 1992)
Armitage, David, *Foundations of modern international thought* (Cambridge, 2013)
The ideological origins of the British Empire (Cambridge, 2000)
'John Locke, Carolina, and the two treatises of government', *Political Theory*, 32(5) (2004), 602–27

'Shakespeare's properties', in David Armitage, Conal Condren and Andrew Fitzmaurice (eds.), *Shakespeare and early modern political thought* (Cambridge, 2009)

'What's the big idea? Intellectual history and the longue durée', *History of European Ideas*, 38(4) (2012), 493–507

Arneil, Barbara, *John Locke and America: the defence of English colonialism* (Oxford, 1996)

Attwood, Bain, '*The law of the land* or the law of the land? History, law and narrative in a settler society', *History Compass*, 2 (2004), 1–30

Bailyn, Bernard, *The ideological origins of the American Revolution*, enlarged edition (Cambridge, MA, 1992)

(ed.), *Pamphlets of the American Revolution 1750–1776*, vol. 1 (Cambridge, MA, 1965)

Banner, Stuart, *How the Indians lost their land: law and power on the frontier* (Cambridge, MA, 2005)

Possessing the Pacific. Land settlers and indigenous people from Australia to Alaska (Cambridge, MA, 2007)

'Why terra nullius? Anthropology and property law in early Australia', *Law and History Review*, 23(1) (2005), 95–132

Barkan, Joshua, *Corporate sovereignty* (Minneapolis, 2013)

Beattie, James, 'Recent themes in the environmental history of the British Empire', *History Compass*, 10(2) (2012), 129–39

Beinart, William and Hughes, Lotte, *Environment and empire* (New York, 2007)

Bell, Duncan and Sylvest, Caspar, 'International society and Victorian political thought: Herbert Spencer, T. H. Green and Henry Sidgwick', *Modern Intellectual History*, 3(2) (2006), 207–38

Bell, Duncan, *The idea of Greater Britain: Empire and the future of world order, 1860–1900* (Princeton, 2007)

Belmessous, Saliha (ed.), *Empire by treaty: negotiating European expansion, 1600–1900* (Oxford, 2014)

Belmessous, Saliha, 'Greatness and decadence in French America', *Renaissance Studies*, 26(4) (2012), 559–79

Benton, Lauren, *Law and colonial cultures: legal regimes in world history* (Cambridge, 2002)

A search for sovereignty: law and geography in European empires, 1400–1900 (Cambridge, 2010)

Benton, Lauren and Straumann, Benjamin, 'Acquiring empire by law: from Roman doctrine to early modern European practice', *Law and History Review*, 8(1) (2010), 1–38

Berlin, Isaiah, 'Two concepts of liberty', in *Four essays on liberty* (Oxford, 1969)

Berman, Harold J., *Faith and order: the reconciliation of law and religion* (Cambridge, 2000)

Bertrand, Romain, *L'histoire à parts égales: Récits d'une rencontre Orient-Occident XVIe–XVIIe siècle* (Paris, 2011)

Blanc, Jan, 'Grotius, historiographe des Bataves au XVIIe siècle', in Chantal Grell (ed.), *Les historiographes en Europe de la fin du Moyen Age à la Révolution* (Paris, 2006)

Borch, Merete, 'Rethinking the origin of *terra nullius*', *Australian Historical Studies*, 32(117) (2001), 222–39

Borschberg, Peter, *Hugo Grotius' 'Comenarius in Theses XI': an early treatise on sovereignty, just war, and the legitimacy of the Dutch Revolt* (Bern, 1994)

'Hugo Grotius, East India trade and the King of Johor', *Journal of Southeast Asian Studies*, 30(2) (1999), 225–48

'The seizure of the Sta. Catarina revisited: the Portuguese Empire in Asia, VOC politics and the origins of the Dutch-Johor alliance (1602–c.1616)', *Journal of Southeast Asian Studies*, 33(1) (2002), 31–62

Boucher, David, 'The law of nations and the doctrine of *terra nullius*', in Olaf Asbach and Peter Schröder (eds.), *War, the state and international law in seventeenth-century Europe* (Farnham, 2010)

Bowden, Brett, 'The colonial origins of international law: European expansion and the classical standard of civilisation', *Journal of the History of International Law*, 7 (2005), 1–23

The empire of civilization: the evolution of an imperial idea (Chicago, 2009)

Brett, Annabel S., *Liberty, right and nature: individual rights in later scholastic thought* (Cambridge, 1997)

'Natural right and civil community: the civil philosophy of Hugo Grotius', *Historical Journal*, 45(1) (2002), 31–51

Changes of state: nature and the limits of the city in early modern natural law (Princeton, 2011)

Brooke, Christopher, *Philosophic pride: stoicism and political thought from Lipsius to Rousseau* (Princeton, 2012)

Buckland, William Warwick, *A text-book of Roman law from Augustus to Justinian* (Cambridge, 1921)

Buckle, Stephen, *Natural law and the theory of property: Grotius to Hume* (Oxford, 1991)

Burbank, Jane and Cooper, Frederick, *Empires in world history: power and the politics of difference* (Princeton, 2010)

Calloway, Colin G., *Pen and ink witchcraft: treaties and treaty making in American Indian history* (New York, 2013)

Canny, Nicholas P., *Making Ireland British 1580–1650* (Oxford, 2001)

Carey, Daniel, *Locke, Shaftesbury and Hutcheson: contesting diversity in the Enlightenment and beyond* (Cambridge, 2006)

Cavallar, Georg, *The rights of strangers: theories of international hospitality, the global community, and political justice since Vitoria* (Aldershot, 2002)

'Vitoria, Grotius, Pufendorf, Wolff and Vattel: accomplices of European colonialism and exploitation or true cosmopolitans?', *Journal of the History of International Law*, 10 (2008), 181–209

Cell, Gillian T. (ed.), *Newfoundland discovered: English attempts at colonisation, 1610–1630* (London, 1982)

Chakrabarty, Dipesh, *Provincializing Europe: postcolonial thought and historical difference* (Princeton, 2000)

Chandler, David, 'The revival of Carl Schmitt in international relations: the last refuge of critical theorists?', *Millennium: Journal of International Studies*, 37(1) (2008), 27–48

Chaplin, Joyce, *Subject matter: technology, the body, and science on the Anglo-American frontier, 1500–1676* (Cambridge, MA, 2001)

Claeys, Gregory, *Imperial sceptics: British critics of empire 1850–1920* (Cambridge, 2010)

'The "left" and the critique of empire c.1865–1900: three roots of humanitarian foreign policy', in Duncan Bell (ed.), *Victorian visions of global order: empire and international relations in nineteenth-century political thought* (Cambridge, 2007)

Conklin, Alice L., *A mission to civilize* (Stanford, 1997)

Connor, Michael, *The invention of terra nullius: historical and legal fictions on the foundation of Australia* (Sydney, 2005)

Conrad, Sebastian, 'Enlightenment in global history: a historiographical critique', *American Historical Review*, 117(4) (2012), 999–1027

Cooper, Frederick, 'Empire multiplied', *Comparative Studies in Society and History*, 46(2) (2004), 247–72

'Modernizing colonialism and the limits of empire', in Craig Calhoun, Frederick Cooper, and Kevin W. Moore (eds.), *Lessons of empire: imperial histories and American power* (New York, 2005)

'Postcolonial studies and the study of history', in Ania Loomba (ed.), *Postcolonial studies and beyond* (Durham, NC, 2005)

Corcoran, Paul, 'John Locke on the possession of land: native title vs. the "principle" of vacuum domicilium', *Proceedings, Australasian Political Studies Association Annual Conference* (2007)

Crowe, S. E., *The Berlin West Africa Conference, 1884–85* (London, 1942)

Deckers, Daniel, *Gerechtigkeit und Recht: Eine historisch-kritische Untersuchung der Gerechtigkeitslehre des Francisco de Vitoria (1483–1546)* (Freiburg, 1991)

Donahue, Charles, '*Ius* in the subjective sense' In D. Maffei (ed.), *A Ennio Cortese* (Rome, 2001), vol. 1, pp. 506–35

Dunn, John, 'The politics of John Locke in England and America in the eighteenth century', in John Yolton (ed.), *John Locke: problems and perspectives* (Cambridge, 1969)

Dworetz, Steven, *The unvarnished doctrine: Locke, liberalism and the American Revolution* (Durham, NC, 1990)

Elliott, John, *Empires of the Atlantic world: Britain and Spain in America, 1492–1830* (New Haven, 2006)

Fassbender, Bardo, 'Carl Schmitt (1888–1985)', in Bardo Fassbender, Anne Peters and Simone Peter (eds.), *The Oxford handbook of the history of international law* (Oxford, 2012)

Ferguson, Niall, *Empire: the rise and demise of the British world order and the lessons for global power* (New York, 2003)

Fincham, Gail and Hooper, Myrtle (eds.), *Under post-colonial eyes: Joseph Conrad after empire* (Rondebosch, 1996)
Fisch, Jörg, 'Africa as *terra nullius*: the Berlin Conference and international law', in Stig Forster, Wolfgang J. Mommsen and Ronald Robinson (eds.), *Bismarck, Europe and Africa: the Berlin Africa Conference 1884–1885 and the onset of partition* (Oxford, 1988)
Die europäische Expansion und das Völkerrecht (Stuttgart, 1984)
'Law as a means and an end: some remarks on the function of European and non-European law in the process of European expansion', in W. J. Mommsen and J. A. de Moor (eds.), *European expansion and law: the encounter of European and Indigenous law in 19th- and 20th-century Africa and Asia* (Oxford, 1992)
'Power or weakness? On the causes of the worldwide expansion of European international law', *Journal of the History of International Law*, 6 (2004), 21–6
Fisher, R. M., 'William Crashaw's library at the Temple', *The Library*, 30(2) (1975), 116–24
Fitzmaurice, Andrew, 'Anti-colonialism in Western political thought: the colonial origins of the concept of genocide', in A. Dirk Moses (ed.), *Empire, colony, genocide: conquest, occupation, and subaltern resistance in world history* (New York, 2008)
'The commercial ideology of colonisation in Jacobean England: Robert Johnson, Giovanni Botero and the pursuit of greatness.' *William and Mary Quarterly*, 64(4) (2007), 791–820
'A genealogy of terra nullius', *Australian Historical Studies*, 129(1) (2007), 1–15
Humanism and America: an intellectual history of early English colonisation, 1500–1625 (Cambridge, 2003)
'The justification of King Leopold II's Congo enterprise by Sir Travers Twiss', in Ian Hunter and Shaunnagh Dorsett (eds.), *Law and politics in British colonial thought* (New York, 2010)
'Liberalism and empire in nineteenth-century international law', *American Historical Review*, 117(1) (2012), 92–121
'Moral uncertainty in the dispossession of Native Americans', in Peter Mancall (ed.), *The Atlantic world and Virginia* (Chapel Hill, 2007)
'Neither neo-Roman nor liberal empire', *Renaissance Studies*, 26(4) (2012), 479–90
'Powhatan legal claims', in Saliha Belmessous (ed.), *Native claims* (Oxford, 2012)
'The resilience of natural law in the writings of Sir Travers Twiss', in Ian Hall and Lisa Hill (eds.), *British international thinkers from Hobbes to Namier* (New York, 2009)
Gallagher, John and Robinson, Ronald, 'The imperialism of free trade', *Economic History Review*, 6(1) (1953), 1–15
Garnsey, Peter, *Thinking about property* (Cambridge, 2007)
Gascoigne, John, *Cambridge in the age of the Enlightenment* (Cambridge, 1989)
Gibb, Paul, 'Unmasterly inactivity? Sir Julian Pauncefote, Lord Salisbury, and the Venezuela boundary dispute', *Diplomacy and Statecraft*, 16(1) (2005), 23–55

Goebel, Julius, *The struggle for the Falkland Islands: a study in legal and diplomatic history* (London, 1927)
Goldie, Mark and Wokler, Robert (eds.), *Cambridge history of eighteenth-century political thought* (Cambridge, 2006)
Gong, Gerrit, *The standard of 'civilization' in international society* (Oxford, 1984)
Gray, John, *Two faces of liberalism* (New York, 2000)
Grewe, Wilhelm G., *The epochs of international law*, trans. Michael Byers (Berlin, 2000)
Guldi, Jo, 'What is being occupied?', http://landscape.blogspot.com.au/2011/10/what-is-being-occupied.html
Haakonssen, Knud, 'German natural law', in Mark Goldie and Robert Wokler (eds.), *Cambridge history of eighteenth-century political thought* (Cambridge, 2006)
Natural law and moral philosophy: from Grotius to the Enlightenment (Cambridge, 1996)
Habermas, Jürgen, *Between facts and norms* (Cambridge, MA, 1998)
Haggenmacher, Peter, *Grotius et la doctrine de la guerre juste* (Paris, 1983)
Hamowy, Ronald, 'Scottish thought and the American Revolution: Adam Ferguson's response to Richard Price', in David Womersley (ed.), *Liberty and American experience in the eighteenth century* (Indianapolis, 2006)
Hebié, Mamadou, 'Les accords conclus entre les puissances coloniales et les entités politiques locales comme moyens d'acquisition de la souveraineté territoriale' (unpublished PhD thesis, Graduate Institute for International Studies and Development, Geneva, 2012)
Herring, George C., *From colony to superpower: U.S. foreign relations since 1776* (New York, 2008)
Hertslet, Edward, *The map of Africa by treaty*, 3 vols. (London, 1967, first printed in 1909)
Hill, Lisa, *The passionate society: the social, political and moral thought of Adam Ferguson* (New York, 2006)
Hill, Norman, *Claims to territory in international law and relations* (New York, 1945)
Hirschman, Albert O., *The passions and the interests: political arguments for capitalism before its triumph* (Princeton, 1997)
Hochschild, Adam, *King Leopold's ghost* (Boston, 1998)
Hochstrasser, T. J., *Natural law theories in the early Enlightenment* (Cambridge, 2000)
Hont, Istvan, *Jealousy of trade: international competition and the nation-state in historical perspective* (Cambridge, MA, 2005)
Hooker, William, *Carl Schmitt's international thought: order and orientation* (Cambridge, 2009)
Howe, Anthony, 'Free trade and global order: the rise and fall of a Victorian vision', in Duncan Bell (ed.), *Victorian visions of global order: empire and international relations in nineteenth-century political thought* (Cambridge, 2007)

Hsueh, Vicki, *Hybrid constitutions: challenging legacies of law, privilege and culture in colonial America* (Durham, NC, 2010)

Hunter, Ian, 'Natural law, historiography, and Aboriginal sovereignty', *Legal History*, 11 (2007), 137–67

Ignatieff, Michael, *Empire lite: nation building in Bosnia, Kosovo, Afghanistan* (London, 2003)

Ittersum, Martine van, *Profit and principle: Hugo Grotius, natural rights theories and the rise of Dutch power in the East Indies (1595–1615)* (Leiden, 2006)

Ivison, Duncan, 'The nature of rights and the history of empire', in David Armitage (ed.), *British political thought in history and literature, 1500–1800* (Cambridge, 2006)

Jèze, Gaston, *Étude théorique et pratique sur l'occupation* (Paris, 1896)

Jouannet, Emmanuelle, *Emer de Vattel et l'émergence doctrinale du droit international public* (Paris, 1998)

The liberal-welfarist law of nations (Cambridge, 2012)

'Universalism and imperialism: the true-false paradox of international law', *European Journal of International Law*, 18(7) (2003), 379–407

Keal, Paul, *European conquest and the rights of indigenous peoples* (Cambridge, 2003)

Keene, Edward, *Beyond the anarchical society. Grotius, colonialism and order in world politics* (Cambridge, 2002)

Kelley, Donald, *Foundations of modern historical scholarship: language, law and history in the French Renaissance* (New York, 1970)

Kercher, Bruce, 'Native title in the shadows: the origins of the myth of *terra nullius* in early New South Wales courts', in Gregory Blue, Martin Bunton and Ralph Crozier (eds.), *Colonialism and the modern world* (New York, 2002)

Kingsbury, Benedict and Straumann, Benjamin (eds.), *The Roman foundations of the law of nations: Alberico Gentili and the justice of empire* (Oxford, 2010)

Kley, Dale K. van, 'Piety and politics in the century of lights', in Mark Goldie and Robert Wokler (eds.), *The Cambridge history of eighteenth-century political thought* (Cambridge, 2006)

Koskenniemi, Martti, 'The advantages of treaties: international law in the Enlightenment', *Edinburgh Law Journal*, 13(1) (2009), 27–67

'Colonization of the "Indies": the origin of international law?', unpublished manuscript, 2009, available at: www.helsinki.fi/eci/Publications/Koskenniemi/Zaragoza-10final.pdf

'Empire and international law: the real Spanish contribution', *University of Toronto Law Journal*, 61(1) (2011), 1–36

The gentle civilizer of nations: the rise and fall of international law 1870–1960 (Cambridge, 2001)

'Histories of international law: dealing with Eurocentrism', *Rechtsgeschichte*, 19 (2011), 152–76

'International law and *raison d'état*: rethinking the prehistory of international law', in Benedict Kingsbury and Benjamin Straumann (eds.), *The Roman*

foundations of the law of nations: Alberico Gentili and the justice of empire (Oxford, 2010)
'International law as political theology: how to read nomos der erde?', *Constellations*, 11(4) (2004), 492–511
'International law in Europe: between tradition and renewal', *European Journal of International Law*, 16(1) (2005), 113–24
'Into positivism: Georg Friedrich Martens (1756–1821) and modern international law', *Constellations*, 15 (2008), 189–207
Lauterpacht, Hersch, *Private law sources and analogies in international law: with special reference to international arbitration* (London, 1927)
Lesaffer, Randall, 'Argument from Roman law in current international law: occupation and acquisitive prescription', *European Journal of International Law*, 16(1) (2005), 25–58
Lindqvist, Sven, *Terra nullius: a journey through no one's land*, trans. Sarah Death (London, 2007)
Lorca, Arnulf Becker, 'Eurocentrism in the history of international law', in Bardo Fassbender, Anne Peters and Simone Peter (eds.), *The Oxford handbook of the history of international law* (Oxford, 2012)
Mestizo international law: a global intellectual history 1850–1950 (Cambridge, 2012)
Louis, William Roger, *Ends of British imperialism: the scramble for empire, Suez and decolonization* (London, 2006)
Lower, Wendy, *Nazi empire-building and the Holocaust in Ukraine* (Chapel Hill, 2005)
Lupher, David A., *Romans in a new world: classical models in sixteenth-century Spanish America* (Ann Arbor, 2003)
MacDonagh, Oliver, 'The anti-imperialism of free trade', *Economic History Review*, 14 (1962), 489–501
MacMillan, Ken, *The Atlantic imperial constitution: center and periphery in the English Atlantic world* (New York, 2011)
Sovereignty and possession in the English new world: the legal foundations of empire, 1570–1640 (Cambridge, 2006)
Macpherson, C. B., *The political theory of possessive individualism* (Oxford, 1962)
Maier, Charles, *Among empires: American ascendancy and its predecessors* (Cambridge, MA, 2006)
Maitland, Frederic William, *State, trust and corporation*, eds. David Runciman and Magnus Ryan (Cambridge, 2003)
Malcolm, Noel, 'Hobbes, Sandys and the Virginia Company', *Historical Journal*, 24(2) (1981), 297–321
Reason of state, propaganda and the Thirty Years' War: an unknown translation by Thomas Hobbes (Oxford, 2007)
'A summary biography of Hobbes', in *Aspects of Hobbes* (Oxford, 2002)
Mancke, Elizabeth, 'Empire and state', in David Armitage and Michael Braddick (eds.), *The British Atlantic world, 1500–1800* (New York, 2002)
Manela, Erez, *The Wilsonian moment* (Oxford, 2007)

Mann, Kristin, 'African and European initiatives in the transformation of land tenure in colonial Lagos (West Africa), 1840–1920', in Saliha Belmessous (ed.), *Native claims: indigenous law against empire 1500–1920* (Oxford, 2012)

Mantena, Karuna, *Alibis of empire: Henry Maine and the end of liberal imperialism* (Princeton, 2010)

'The crisis of liberal imperialism', in Duncan Bell (ed.), *Victorian visions of global order: empire and international relations in nineteenth-century political thought* (Cambridge, 2007)

Marshall, P. J., 'Britain without America – a second empire?', in P. J. Marshall (ed.), *The Oxford history of the British Empire: the eighteenth century* (Oxford, 1998)

Marx, Leo, *The machine in the garden: technology and the pastoral ideal in America* (New York, 1964)

Mazower, Mark, *No enchanted palace: the end of empire and the ideological origins of the United Nations* (Princeton, 2009)

'The strange triumph of human rights, 1933–1950', *Historical Journal*, 47(2) (2004), 379–98

Mbembe, Achille, 'Necropolitics', trans. Libby Meintjes, *Public Culture*, 15(1) (2003), 11–40

McMillan, Alan Daniel and Yellowhorn, Eldon, *First peoples in Canada* (Vancouver, 2004)

Méchoulan, Henry, 'Vitoria, père du droit international?', in *Actualité de la pensée juridique de Francisco de Vitoria* (Brussels, 1988)

Mehta, Uday Singh, *Liberalism and empire: a study in nineteenth-century British liberal thought* (Chicago, 1999)

Merk, Frederick, *The Oregon question* (Cambridge, MA, 1967)

Miéville, China, *Between equal rights: a Marxist theory of international law* (Leiden, 2005)

Milet, Marc, *La Faculté de droit de Paris face à la vie politique, de l'Affaire Scelle à l'Affaire Jèze, 1925–1936* (Paris, 1996)

Miller, Jon, 'Stoics, Grotius and Spinoza on moral deliberation', in Jon Miller and Brad Inwood (eds.), *Hellenistic and early modern philosophy* (Cambridge, 2003)

Miller, Peter, *Defining the common good* (Cambridge, 1994)

Miller, Robert J., Ruru, Jacinta, Behrendt, Larissa and Lindberg, Tracey, *Discovering indigenous lands: the doctrine of discovery in the English colonies* (Oxford, 2010)

Moore, R. J., 'Imperialism and "free trade" policy in India, 1853–1854', *Economic History Review*, 17(1) (1964), 135–45

Morefield, Jeanne, *'Covenants without swords': idealist liberalism and the spirit of empire* (Princeton, 2005)

'Empire, tragedy, and the liberal state in the writings of Niall Ferguson and Michael Ignatieff', *Theory and Event*, 11(3) (2008)

Moretti, Marco, *International law and nomadic people* (Milton Keynes, 2012)

Moyn, Samuel, *The last utopia* (Cambridge, MA, 2010)

Moyn, Samuel and Sartori, Andrew, 'Approaches to global intellectual history', in Samuel Moyn and Andrew Sartori (eds.), *Global intellectual history* (New York, 2013)
Muthu, Sankar, *Enlightenment against empire* (Princeton, 2003)
Odysseos, Louiza and Petito, Fabio, *The international political thought of Carl Schmitt: terror, liberal war and the crisis of global order* (London, 2007)
Olivecrona, Karl, 'Appropriation in the state of nature: Locke on the origin of property', *Journal of the History of Ideas*, 35(2) (1974), 211–30
Otter, Sandra den, '"A legislating empire": Victorian political theorists, codes of law, and empire', in Duncan Bell (ed.), *Victorian visions of global order: empire and international relations in nineteenth-century political thought* (Cambridge, 2007)
Pagden, Anthony, 'Empire and its anxieties', *American Historical Review*, 117(1) (2012), 141–8
The Enlightenment and why it still matters (New York, 2013)
The fall of natural man, revised edn (Cambridge, 1986)
'Fellow citizens and imperial subjects: conquest and sovereignty in Europe's overseas empires', *History and Theory*, 44(4) (2005), 28–46
'Gentili, Vitoria, and the fabrication of a "natural law of nations"', in Benedict Kingsbury and Benjamin Straumann (eds.), *The Roman foundations of the law of nations: Alberico Gentili and the justice of empire* (Oxford, 2010)
'Human rights, natural rights, and Europe's imperial legacy', *Political Theory*, 31 (2) (2003), 171–99
'Law, colonization, legitimation, and the European background', in Michael Grossberg and Chistopher Tomlins (eds.), *The Cambridge history of law in America. Volume 1: Early America (1580–1815)* (Cambridge, 2008)
Lords of all the world: ideologies of empire in Spain, Britain and France (New Haven, 1995)
Pangle, Thomas, *The spirit of modern republicanism: the moral vision of the American founders and the philosophy of Locke* (Chicago, 1988)
Paquette, Gabriel, 'Colonies and empire in the political thought of Hegel and Marx', in Sankar Muthu (ed.), *Empire and modern political thought* (Cambridge, 2012)
Parekh, Bhikhu, 'Liberalism and colonialism: a critique of Locke and Mill', in Jan Nederveen Pieterse and Bhikhu Parekh (eds.), *The decolonization of imagination: culture, knowledge and power* (London, 1995)
Pateman, Carole, 'The settler contract', in Carole Pateman and Charles Mills, *Contract and domination* (Cambridge, 2007)
Patterson, Annabel, *Early modern liberalism* (Cambridge, 1998)
Péan, Pierre, *Une jeunesse française. François Mitterrand, 1934–1947* (Paris, 1994)
Pitts, Jennifer, 'Boundaries of Victorian international law', in Duncan Bell (ed.), *Victorian visions of global order: empire and international relations in nineteenth-century political thought* (Cambridge, 2007)
'Empire and legal universalisms in the eighteenth century', *American Historical Review*, 117(1) (2012), 92–121

'Liberalism and empire in a nineteenth-century Algerian mirror', *Modern Intellectual History*, 6(2) (2009), 287–313

'Political theory of empire and imperialism', *Annual Review of Political Science*, 13 (2010), 211–35

A turn to empire (Princeton, 2005)

Pocock, J. G. A., *Barbarism and religion. Volume two: narratives of civil government* (Cambridge, 1999)

Barbarism and religion. Volume three: the first decline and fall (Cambridge, 2003)

The Machiavellian moment: Florentine political thought and the Atlantic republican tradition, 2nd edn (Princeton, 1975)

Virtue, commerce, and history (Cambridge, 1985)

Pugliese, G., '"Res corporals", "res incorporales" e il problema del diritto soggetivo', *Studi in onore di Vincenzo Arangio-Ruiz*, 3 (1954), 223–60

Rabb, Theodore K., *Jacobean gentleman: Sir Edwin Sandys, 1561–1629* (Princeton, 1998)

Reynolds, Henry, *The law of the land* (Melbourne, 1987 and 2003)

Ritter, David, 'The "rejection of *terra nullius*" in *Mabo*. A critical analysis', *Sydney Law Review*, 18(1) (1996), 5–34

Rogin, Michael Paul, *Fathers and children: Andrew Jackson and the subjugation of the American Indian* (New York, 1975)

Rommen, Heinrich, *The natural law: a study in legal and social history and philosophy*, trans. Thomas R. Hanley and with an introduction by Russell Hittinger (Indianapolis, 1998 [1936])

Rothschild, Emma, 'Language and empire, c.1800', *Historical Research*, 78(200) (2005), 208–29

Rowse, Tim, 'Terra nullius', in Graeme Davison, John Hirst and Stuart Macintyre (eds.), *The Oxford companion to Australian history* (Melbourne, 2001)

Said, Edward, *Culture and imperialism* (New York, 1993)

Sartori, Andrew, 'The British Empire and its liberal mission', *Journal of Modern History*, 78 (2006), 623–42

Schmitt, Carl, *The nomos of the earth in the international law of the jus publicum Europaeum*, trans. G. L. Ulmen (New York, 2003 [1950])

Schneewind, J. B., *The invention of autonomy: a history of modern moral philosophy* (Cambridge, 1998)

Schoenrich, Otto, 'The Venezuela-British Guiana boundary dispute', *American Journal of International Law*, 43(3) (1949), 523–30

Schröder, Jan, 'The concept of (natural) law in the doctrine of law and natural law of the early modern era', in Lorraine Daston and Michael Stolleis (eds.), *Natural law and laws of nature in early modern Europe* (Farnham, 2008)

Seed, Patricia, *Ceremonies of possession in Europe's conquest of the New World 1492–1640* (Cambridge, 1995)

Shaver, Robert, 'Grotius on scepticism and self-interest', *Archiv für Geschichte der Philosophie*, 78(1) (1996), 27–47

Shaw, Malcolm (ed.), *Title to territory* (Aldershot, 2005)

Shimokawa, Kiyoshi, 'A brief history of post-Lockean unilateralism: Barbeyrac, Carmichael and Hutcheson on property', *Humanities: Christianity and Culture*, 43 (2012), 1–26

'The origin and development of property: Conventionalism, unilateralism, and colonialism', in Peter Anstey (ed.), *The Oxford handbook of British philosophy in the seventeenth century* (Oxford, 2013)

Sirantoine, Hélène, *Imperator Hispaniæ. Les idéologies impériales dans le royaume de León (IXe–XIIe siècles)* (Madrid, 2012)

Skarstein, Frode, '"A cursed affair": how a Norwegian expedition to Greenland became the USA's first maritime capture in World War II', *Polar Research*, 26 (2007), 181–94

'Erik the Red's land: the land that never was', *Polar Research*, 29(2) (2006), 173–9

Skinner, Quentin, *The foundations of modern political thought*, 2 vols. (Cambridge, 1978)

'A genealogy of the modern state', *Proceedings of the British Academy*, 162 (2009), 325–70

Liberty before liberalism (Cambridge, 1998)

'Political philosophy', in Charles B. Schmitt and Quentin Skinner, *Cambridge history of Renaissance philosophy* (Cambridge, 1988)

Visions of politics, 3 vols. (Cambridge, 2002)

Slattery, Brian, *French claims in North America 1500–1559* (Saskatchewan, 1980)

Sosin, Jack, *Whitehall and the wilderness: the Middle West in British colonial policy, 1760–1775* (Oklahoma, 1961)

Spector, Céline, 'Was Montesquieu liberal?', in Raf Geenans and Helena Rosenblatt (eds.), *French liberalism from Montesquieu to the present day* (Cambridge, 2012)

Squibb, G. D., *Doctors' Commons: a history of the College of Advocates and Doctors of Law* (Oxford, 1977)

Steinmetz, George, 'Imperialism or colonialism? From Windhoek to Washington, by way of Basra', in Craig Calhoun, Frederick Cooper and Kevin W. Moore (eds.), *Lessons of empire: imperial histories and American power* (New York, 2005)

Stern, Philip J., *The company-state: corporate sovereignty and the early modern foundations of the British Empire in India* (Oxford, 2011)

Straumann, Benjamin, 'The corpus iuris as a source of law between sovereigns', in Benedict Kingsbury and Benjamin Straumann (eds.), *The Roman foundations of the law of nations: Alberico Gentili and the justice of empire* (Oxford, 2010)

Hugo Grotius und die Antike (Baden-Baden, 2007)

'*Oikeiosis* and *appetitus societatis*: Hugo Grotius' Ciceronian argument for natural law and just war', *Grotiana*, 24–25 (2003–4), 41–66

Subramanyam, Sanjay, *Courtly encounters: translating courtliness and violence in early modern Eurasia* (Cambridge, MA, 2012)

Sylvest, Caspar, *British liberal internationalism, 1880–1930: making progress?* (Manchester, 2009)

'The foundations of Victorian international law', in Duncan Bell (ed.), *Victorian visions of global order: empire and international relations in nineteenth-century political thought* (Cambridge, 2007)
Taylor, Miles, 'Imperium et libertas? Rethinking the radical critique of imperialism during the nineteenth century', *Journal of Imperial and Commonwealth History*, XIX (1991) 1–23
Tierney, Brian, *The idea of natural rights* (Grand Rapids, 1997)
Tomlins, Christopher, *Freedom bound: law, labor and civic identity in colonizing English America, 1580–1865* (Cambridge, 2010)
Tuck, Richard, 'The "modern" theory of natural law', in Anthony Pagden (ed.), *The languages of political theory in early modern Europe* (Cambridge, 1987)
Natural rights theories: their origins and development (Cambridge, 1979)
Philosophy and government 1572–1651 (Cambridge, 1993)
The rights of war and peace: political thought and the international order from Grotius to Kant (Oxford, 1999)
Tucker, Herbert F., 'Introduction', *New Literary History*, 42(1) (2011), vii–xii
Tully, James, *An approach to political philosophy: Locke in contexts* (Cambridge, 1993)
A discourse on property: John Locke and his adversaries (New York, 1980)
Strange multiplicity: constitutionalism in the age of diversity (Cambridge, 1995)
Ulfstein, Geir, *The Svalbard Treaty: from terra nullius to Norwegian sovereignty* (Oslo, 1995)
Villey, Michel, *Critique de la pensée juridique moderne* (Paris, 1969)
Leçon d'histoire de la philosophie du droit (Paris, 1957)
Seize essais de philosophie du droit (Paris, 1969)
Waldron, Jeremy, 'The decline of natural right', in Allen W. Wood and Songsuk Susan Hahn (eds.), *The Cambridge history of philosophy in the nineteenth century* (Cambridge, 2012)
(ed.), *Nonsense upon stilts: Bentham, Burke and Marx on the rights of man* (London, 1987)
The right to private property (Oxford, 1988)
'Torture and positive law: jurisprudence for the White House', *Columbia Law Review*, 105 (2005), 1681–750
Wallis, P. J., 'The library of William Crashaw', *Transactions of the Cambridge Bibliographical Society*, 2(3) (1956), 213–28
William Crashaw. The Sheffield puritan (Transactions of the Hunter Archaeological Society, 1963)
Watson, Alan, *The law of property in the later Roman republic* (Oxford, 1968)
Westra, Laura, *Environmental justice and the rights of indigenous peoples* (London, 2008)
Weststeijn, Arthur, 'Republican empire: colonialism, commerce and corruption in the Dutch Golden Age', *Renaissance Studies*, 26(4) (2012), 491–509
White, Richard, *The middle ground: Indians, empires and republics in the Great Lakes region, 1650–1815* (Cambridge, 1991)
Williams, Robert A., *The American Indian in Western legal thought* (Oxford, 1990)

Linking arms together: American Indian treaty visions of law and peace, 1600–1800 (New York, 1999)

Wood, Allen W., *Kant's ethical thought* (Cambridge, 1999)

Yirush, Craig, *Settlers, liberty and empire: the roots of early American political theory* (Cambridge, 2011)

Young, Jeffrey T., 'The Humean foundations of Adam Smith's theory of property', *Journal of the History of Economic Thought*, 30(1) (2008), 49–64

Zandt, Cynthia van, *Brothers among nations: the pursuit of intercultural alliances in early America, 1580–1660* (New York, 2008)

Zapatero, Pablo, 'Legal imagination in Vitoria: the power of ideas', *Journal of the History of International Law*, 11 (2009), 221–71

Index

IDEAS IN CONTEXT

Edited by

DAVID ARMITAGE, RICHARD BOURKE, JENNIFER PITTS and JOHN ROBERTSON

1 RICHARD RORTY, J. B. SCHNEEWIND and QUENTIN SKINNER (eds.)
Philosophy in History
Essays in the historiography of philosophy
PB 978 0 521 27330 5

2 J. G. A. POCOCK
Virtue, Commerce and History
Essays on political thought and history, chiefly in the eighteenth century
PB 978 0 521 27660 3

3 M. M. GOLDSMITH
Private Vices, Public Benefits
Bernard Mandeville's social and political thought
HB 978 0 521 30036 0

4 ANTHONY PAGDEN (ed.)
The Languages of Political Theory in Early Modern Europe
PB 978 0 521 38666 1

5 DAVID SUMMERS
The Judgment of Sense
Renaissance naturalism and the rise of aesthetics
PB 978 0 521 38631 9

6 LAURENCE DICKEY
Hegel: Religion, Economics and the Politics of Spirit, 1770–1807
PB 978 0 521 38912 9

7 MARGO TODD
Christian Humanism and the Puritan Social Order
PB 978 0 521 89228 5

8 LYNN SUMIDA JOY
Gassendi the Atomist
Advocate of history in an age of science
PB 978 0 521 52239 7

9 EDMUND LEITES (ed.)
Conscience and Casuistry in Early Modern Europe
PB 978 0 521 52020 1

10 WOLF LEPENIES
Between Literature and Science: The Rise of Sociology
PB 978 0 521 33810 3

11 TERENCE BALL, JAMES FARR and RUSSELL L. HANSON (eds.)
Political Innovation and Conceptual Change
PB 978 0 521 35978 8

12 GERD GIGERENZER et al.
The Empire of Chance
How probability changed science and everyday life
PB 978 0 521 39838 1

13 PETER NOVICK
That Noble Dream
The 'objectivity question' and the American historical profession
HB 978 0 521 34328 2
PB 978 0 521 35745 6

14 DAVID LIEBERMAN
The Province of Legislation Determined
Legal theory in eighteenth-century Britain
PB 978 0 521 52854 2

15 DANIEL PICK
Faces of Degeneration
A European disorder, c.1848–c.1918
PB 978 0 521 45753 8

16 KEITH BAKER
Inventing the French Revolution
Essays on French political culture in the eighteenth century
PB 978 0 521 38578 7

17 IAN HACKING
The Taming of Chance
HB 978 0 521 38014 0
PB 978 0 521 38884 9

18 GISELA BOCK, QUENTIN SKINNER and MAURIZIO VIROLI (eds.)
Machiavelli and Republicanism
PB 978 0 521 43589 5

19 DOROTHY ROSS
The Origins of American Social Science
PB 978 0 521 42836 1

20 KLAUS CHRISTIAN KOHNKE
The Rise of Neo-Kantianism
German Academic Philosophy between Idealism and Positivism
HB 978 0 521 37336 4

21 IAN MACLEAN
Interpretation and Meaning in the Renaissance
The Case of Law
HB 978 0 521 41546 0
PB 978 0 521 02027 5

22 MAURIZIO VIROLI
From Politics to Reason of State
The Acquisition and Transformation of the Language of Politics 1250–1600
HB 978 0 521 41493 7
PB 978 0 521 67343 3

23 MARTIN VAN GELDEREN
The Political Thought of the Dutch Revolt 1555–1590
HB 978 0 521 39204 4
PB 978 0 521 89163 9

24 NICHOLAS PHILLIPSON and QUENTIN SKINNER (eds.)
Political Discourse in Early Modern Britain
HB 978 0 521 39242 6

25 JAMES TULLY
An Approach to Political Philosophy: Locke in Contexts
HB 978 0 521 43060 9
PB 978 0 521 43638 0

26 RICHARD TUCK
Philosophy and Government 1572–1651
PB 978 0 521 43885 8

27 RICHARD YEO
Defining Science
William Whewell, Natural Knowledge and Public Debate in Early Victorian Britain
HB 978 0 521 43182 8
PB 978 0 521 54116 9

28 MARTIN WARNKE
The Court Artist
On the Ancestry of the Modern Artist
HB 978 0 521 36375 4

29 PETER N. MILLER
Defining the Common Good
Empire, Religion and Philosophy in Eighteenth-Century Britain
HB 978 0 521 44259 6
PB 978 0 521 61712 3

30 CHRISTOPHER J. BERRY
The Idea of Luxury
A Conceptual and Historical Investigation
PB 978 0 521 46691 2

31 E. J. HUNDERT
The Enlightenment's 'Fable'
Bernard Mandeville and the Discovery of Society
HB 978 0 521 46082 8
PB 978 0 521 61942 4

32 JULIA STAPLETON
Englishness and the Study of Politics
The Social and Political Thought of Ernest Barker
HB 978 0 521 46125 2
PB 978 0 521 02444 0

33 KEITH TRIBE
Strategies of Economic Order
German Economic Discourse, 1750–1950
HB 978 0 521 46291 4
PB 978 0 521 61943 1

34 SACHIKO KUSUKAWA
The Transformation of Natural Philosophy
The Case of Philip Melanchthon
HB 978 0 521 47347 7
PB 978 0 521 03046 5

35 DAVID ARMITAGE, ARMAND HIMY and QUENTIN SKINNER (eds.)
Milton and Republicanism
HB 978 0 521 55178 6
PB 978 0 521 64648 2

36 MARKKU PELTONEN
Classical Humanism and Republicanism in English Political Thought 1570–1640
HB 978 0 521 49695 7
PB 978 0 521 61716 1

37 PHILIP IRONSIDE
The Social and Political Thought of Bertrand Russell
The Development of an Aristocratic Liberalism
HB 978 0 521 47383 5
PB 978 0 521 02476 1

38 NANCY CARTWRIGHT, JORDI CAT, LOLA FLECK and THOMAS E. UEBEL
Otto Neurath: Philosophy between Science and Politics
HB 978 0 521 45174 1

39 DONALD WINCH
Riches and Poverty
An Intellectual History of Political Economy in Britain, 1750–1834
PB 978 0 521 55920 1

40 JENNIFER PLATT
A History of Sociological Research Methods in America
HB 978 0 521 44173 5
PB 978 0 521 64649 9

41 KNUD HAAKONSSEN (ed.)
Enlightenment and Religion
Rational Dissent in Eighteenth-Century Britain
HB 978 0 521 56060 3
PB 978 0 521 02987 2

42 G. E. R. LLOYD
Adversaries and Authorities
Investigations into Ancient Greek and Chinese Science
HB 978 0 521 55331 5
PB 978 0 521 55695 8

43 ROLF LINDNER
The Reportage of Urban Culture
Robert Park and the Chicago School
HB 978 0 521 44052 3
PB 978 0 521 02653 6

44 ANNABEL BRETT
Liberty, Right and Nature
Individual Rights in Later Scholastic Thought
HB 978 0 521 56239 3
PB 978 0 521 54340 8

45 STEWART J. BROWN (ed.)
William Robertson and the Expansion of Empire
HB 978 0 521 57083 1

46 HELENA ROSENBLATT
Rousseau and Geneva
From the First Discourse to the Social Contract, 1749–1762
HB 978 0 521 57004 6
PB 978 0 521 03395 4

47 DAVID RUNCIMAN
Pluralism and the Personality of the State
HB 978 0 521 55191 5
PB 978 0 521 022263 7

48 ANNABEL PATTERSON
Early Modern Liberalism
HB 978 0 521 59260 4
PB 978 0 521 02631 4

49 DAVID WEINSTEIN
Equal Freedom and Utility
Herbert Spencer's Liberal Utilitarianism
HB 978 0 521 62264 6
PB 978 0 521 02686 4

50 YUN LEE TOO and NIALL LIVINGSTONE (eds.)
Pedagogy and Power
Rhetorics of Classical Learning
HB 978 0 521 59435 6
PB 978 0 521 03801 0

51 REVIEL NETZ
The Shaping of Deduction in Greek Mathematics
A Study in Cognitive History
HB 978 0 521 62279 0
PB 978 0 521 54120 6

52 MARY S. MORGAN and MARGARET MORRISON (eds.)
Models as Mediators
Perspectives in Natural and Social Science
HB 978 0 521 65097 7
PB 978 0 521 65571 2

53 JOEL MICHELL
Measurement in Psychology
A Critical History of a Methodological Concept
HB 978 0 521 62120 5
PB 978 0 521 02151 7

54 RICHARD A. PRIMUS
The American Language of Rights
HB 978 0 521 65250 6
PB 978 0 521 61621 8

55 ROBERT ALUN JONES
The Development of Durkheim's Social Realism
HB 978 0 521 65045 8
PB 978 0 521 02210 1

56 ANNE MCLAREN
Political Culture in the Reign of Elizabeth I
Queen and Commonwealth 1558–1585
HB 978 0 521 65144 8
PB 978 0 521 02483 9

57 JAMES HANKINS (ed.)
Renaissance Civic Humanism
Reappraisals and Reflections
HB 978 0 521 78090 2
PB 978 0 521 54807 6

58 T. J. HOCHSTRASSER
Natural Law Theories in the Early Enlightenment
HB 978 0 521 66193 5
PB 978 0 521 02787 8

59 DAVID ARMITAGE
The Ideological Origins of the British Empire
HB 978 0 521 59081 5
PB 978 0 521 78978 3

60 IAN HUNTER
Rival Enlightenments
Civil and Metaphysical Philosophy in Early Modern Germany
HB 978 0 521 79265 3
PB 978 0 521 02549 2

61 DARIO CASTIGLIONE and IAIN HAMPSHER-MONK (eds.)
The History of Political Thought in National Context
HB 978 0 521 78234 0

62 IAN MACLEAN
Logic, Signs and Nature in the Renaissance:
The Case of Learned Medicine
HB 978 0 521 80648 0

63 PETER MACK
Elizabethan Rhetoric:
Theory and Practice
HB 978 0 521 812924
PB 978 0 521 02099 2

64 GEOFFREY LLOYD
The Ambitions of Curiosity:
Understanding the World in Ancient Greece and China
HB 978 0 521 81542 0
PB 978 0 521 89461 6

65 MARKKU PELTONEN
The Duel in Early Modern England:
Civility, Politeness and Honour
HB 978 0 521 82062 2
PB 978 0 521 02520 1

66 ADAM SUTCLIFFE
Judaism and Enlightenment
HB 978 0 521 82015 8
PB 978 0 521 67232 0

67 ANDREW FITZMAURICE
Humanism and America:
An Intellectual History of English Colonisation, 1500–1625
HB 978 0 521 82225 1

68 PIERRE FORCE
Self-Interest before Adam Smith:
A Genealogy of Economic Science
HB 978 0 521 83060 7
PB 978 0 521 03619 1

69 ERIC NELSON
The Greek Tradition in Republican Thought
HB 978 0 521 83545 9
PB 978 0 521 02428 0

70 HARRO HOPFL
Jesuit Political Thought:
The Society of Jesus and the State, c. 1540–1640
HB 978 0 521 83779 8

71 MIKAEL HORNQVIST
Machiavelli and Empire
HB 978 0 521 83945 7

72 DAVID COLCLOUGH
Freedom of Speech in Early Stuart England
HB 978 0 521 84748 3

73 JOHN ROBERTSON
The Case for the Enlightenment
Scotland and Naples 1680–1760
HB 978 0 521 84787 2
PB 978 0 521 03572 9

74 DANIEL CAREY
Locke, Shaftesbury, and Hutcheson
Contesting Diversity in the Enlightenment and Beyond
HB 978 0 521 84502 1

75 ALAN CROMARTIE
The Constitutionalist Revolution
An Essay on the History of England, 1450–1642
HB 978 0 521 78269 2

76 HANNAH DAWSON
Locke, Language and Early-Modern Philosophy
HB 978 0 521 85271 5

77 CONAL CONDREN, STEPHEN GAUKROGER and IAN HUNTER (eds.)
The Philosopher in Early Modern Europe
The Nature of a Contested Identity
HB 978 0 521 86646 0

78 ANGUS GOWLAND
The Worlds of Renaissance Melancholy
Robert Burton in Context
HB 978 0 521 86768 9

79 PETER STACEY
Roman Monarchy and the Renaissance Prince
HB 978 0 521 86989 8

80 RHODRI LEWIS
Language, Mind and Nature
Artificial Languages in England from Bacon to Locke
HB 978 0 521 874750

81 DAVID LEOPOLD
The Young Karl Marx
German Philosophy, Modern Politics, and Human Flourishing
HB 978 0 521 87477 9

82 JON PARKIN
Taming the Leviathan
The Reception of the Political and Religious Ideas of Thomas Hobbes in England 1640–1700
HB 978 0 521 87735 0

83 D. WEINSTEIN
Utilitarianism and the New Liberalism
HB 978 0 521 87528 8

84 LUCY DELAP
The Feminist Avant-Garde
Transatlantic Encounters of the Early Twentieth Century
HB 978 0 521 87651 3

85 BORIS WISEMAN
Lévi-Strauss, Anthropology and Aesthetics
HB 978 0 521 87529 5

86 DUNCAN BELL (ed.)
Victorian Visions of Global Order
Empire and International Relations in Nineteenth-Century Political Thought
HB 978 0 521 88292 7

87 IAN HUNTER
The Secularisation of the Confessional State
The Political Thought of Christian Thomasius
HB 978 0 521 88055 8

88 CHRISTIAN J EMDEN
Friedrich Nietzsche and the Politics of History
HB 978 0 521 88056 5

89 ANNELIEN DE DIJN
French Political Thought from Montesquieu to Tocqueville
Liberty in a Levelled Society?
HB 978 0 521 87788 6

90 PETER GARNSEY
Thinking About Property
From Antiquity to the Age of Revolution
HB 978 0 521 87677 3
PB 978 0 521 70023 8

91 PENELOPE DEUTSCHER
The Philosophy of Simone de Beauvoir
Ambiguity, Conversion, Resistance
HB 978 0 521 88520 1

92 HELENA ROSENBLATT
Liberal Values
Benjamin Constant and the Politics of Religion
HB 978 0 521 89825 6

93 JAMES TULLY
Public Philosophy in a New Key
Volume 1: Democracy and Civic Freedom
HB 978 0 521 44961 8
PB 978 0 521 72879 9

94 JAMES TULLY
Public Philosophy in a New Key
Volume 2: Imperialism and Civic Freedom
HB 978 0 521 44966 3
PB 978 0 521 72880 5

95 DONALD WINCH
Wealth and Life
Essays on the Intellectual History of Political Economy in Britain, 1848–1914
HB 978 0 521 88753 3
PB 978 0 521 71539 3

96 FONNA FORMAN-BARZILAI
Adam Smith and the Circles of Sympathy
Cosmopolitanism and Moral Theory
HB 978 0 521 76112 3

97 GREGORY CLAEYS
Imperial Sceptics
British Critics of Empire 1850–1920
HB 978 0 521 19954 4

98 EDWARD BARING
The Young Derrida and French Philosophy, 1945–1968
HB 978 1 107 00967 7

99 CAROL PAL
Republic of Women
Rethinking the Republic of Letters in the Seventeenth Century
HB 978 1 107 01821 1

100 C. A. BAYLY
Recovering Liberties
Indian Thought in the Age of Liberalism and Empire
HB 978 1 107 01383 4
PB 978 1 107 60147 5

101 FELICITY GREEN
Montaigne and the Life of Freedom
HB 978 1 107 02439 7

102 JOSHUA DERMAN
Max Weber in Politics and Social Thought
From Charisma to Canonization
HB 978 1 107 02588 2

103 RAINER FORST
(translated by Ciaran Cronin)
Toleration in Conflict
Past and Present
HB 978 0 521 88577 5

104 SOPHIE READ
Eucharist and the Poetic Imagination in Early Modern England
HB 978 1 107 03273 6

105 MARTIN RUEHL
The Italian Renaissance in the German Historical Imagination 1860–1930
HB 978 1 107 03699 4

106 GEORGIOS VAROUXAKIS
Liberty Abroad
J. S. Mill on International Relations
HB 978 1 107 03914 8

107 ANDREW FITZMAURICE
Sovereignty, Property and Empire, 1500–2000
HB 978 1 107 07649 5

CPSIA information can be obtained
at www.ICGtesting.com
Printed in the USA
LVOW04*2319151216
517520LV00021B/389/P

9 781107 076495